Public Relations in Health Care

A Guide for Professionals

Kathleen Larey Lewton, M.H.A., A.P.R.
for the American Society for Health Care Marketing
and Public Relations of the American Hospital Association

D1414146

books are published by
American Hospital Publishing, Inc.,
an American Hospital Association company

The views expressed in this publication are strictly those of the author and do not necessarily represent official positions of the American Hospital Association.

Library of Congress Cataloging-in-Publication Data

Lewton, Kathleen Larey.
    Public relations in health care : a guide for professionals /
Kathleen Larey Lewton for the American Society for Health Care
Marketing and Public Relations of the American Hospital
Association.
        p.   cm.
    Includes bibliographical references.
    ISBN 1-55648-066-0 (paper)
    1. Public relations—Health facilities.   I. American Society for
Health Care Marketing and Public Relations.   II. Title.
    [DNLM: 1. Health Services—organization & administration.
2. Public Relations.   W 84.1 L678p]
RA965.5.L49   1991
659.2'83621'1-dc20
DNLM/DLC
for Library of Congress   90-14484
                                                                        CIP

Catalog no. 166122

©1991 by American Hospital Publishing, Inc.,
an American Hospital Association company

Printed in the USA

 is a service mark of the American Hospital Association used under license by American Hospital Publishing, Inc.

Text set in Trump
3M—01/91—0285
1.5M—4/93—0352

Audrey Kaufman, Project Editor
Sophie Yarborough, Manuscript Editor
Marcia Bottoms, Managing Editor
Peggy DuMais, Production Coordinator
Marcia Vecchione, Designer
Brian Schenk, Books Division Director

Dedication

This book is dedicated to the public relations professionals who give their personal best to help the health care industry meet the challenges of the 1990s. No matter what changes occur in the coming years, I believe that two things will always be true:

- As public relations professionals, we can best learn, grow, and develop our skills and professionalism by sharing with one another; we are indeed our own best teachers.
- Despite all the talk of profit margins and payers, contracts and cutting deals, the eventual long-term survival of hospitals and the health care system depends on the ability of our institutions to build and rebuild relationships with our constituents.

As public relations professionals, we must help our organizations not only to survive, but to thrive, by keeping sight of the mission for which society has always looked to us — caring for people.

Contents

List of Figures and Tables

About the Author

Kathleen Larey Lewton, M.H.A., A.P.R., has 20 years of experience as a communicator. Her achievements were recognized in 1984 when she was selected as one of *Glamour* magazine's Ten Outstanding Young Working Women and in 1989 when she was profiled in *Working Woman* as one of two "key people making news in hospital marketing."

Lewton began her communications career at age 18 as a reporter and editor for *The Daily Pantagraph,* a daily newspaper in her hometown of Bloomington, Illinois, where she worked while she was a student at Illinois Wesleyan University (B.A., English, 1970). From 1971 to 1976, she was assistant director of public relations at Bowling Green State University.

After earning a master's degree in journalism from Medill School of Journalism at Northwestern University in 1977, she was named director of public relations at Flower Hospital in Sylvania, a Toledo suburb. In 1982, she joined the staff of St. Vincent Medical Center, an 840-bed tertiary care hospital, as vice-president for marketing communications. She earned a master's degree in hospital administration from the University of Minnesota in 1988.

During 1989, Lewton's consulting firm, K. L. Lewton & Associates, worked with a variety of national and regional clients in health care, insurance, and professional association industries.

In 1990, Lewton became vice-president for marketing and corporate communications at University Hospitals of Cleveland, responsible for a staff of 28 in marketing, public affairs, physician relations, corporate sales, and communications. She is accredited by the Public Relations Society of America.

Lewton is past national president of Women in Communications, Inc. (WICI); past chair of the Health Academy of the Public Relations Society of America (PRSA); chair of the PRSA Task Force on the Status of Women in Public Relations; and has held committee positions with the Society of Hospital Planning and Marketing and the American Society for Health Care Marketing and Public Relations.

She has written and lectured extensively on health care market-ing and PR topics, including a 1989 cover story in *Public Relations Jour-nal.* She is a regular speaker at major national professional conferences and has been quoted in *Hospitals* and other trade journals. Work produced by Lewton and her staff has won more than 100 awards, including multiple American Society for Health Care Marketing and Public Relations (ASHCMPR) Touchstones, Academy for Hospital Pub-lic Relations MacEachern Awards, International Association of Busi-ness Communications (IABC) Gold Quills, and a district "Addy."

Personally, Lewton was named a Women in Communications, Inc., Headliner, the group's recognition of professional excellence, in 1989. She has been a MacEachern Fellow, won a Colby Award for professional achievement from Sigma Kappa sorority, and was one of Toledo's Ten Outstanding Young Women in 1984.

NOTE: *In early 1993, Ms. Lewton joined the public relations firm of Porter/Novelli in Chicago, where she is a vice-president respon-sible for the firm's health care practice.*

Preface

The process of writing a book—especially a book about the profession you've been a part of for nearly two decades—is exciting, challenging, and humbling.

The excitement comes from actually doing that which we all have on our list of "things to do when I have time"—reading all those journals and articles and publications that describe "the state of the art" in health care public relations. Equally enlightening and enjoyable was using my manuscript development as an excuse to bother peers and colleagues with incessant questions about where they see our profession heading—and how we're going to get there.

The dose of humility is frequently administered as you realize how complex and rapidly changing the health care PR field is—and as you compare your own professional efforts with the ideal strategies and tactics to which we all aspire.

And you constantly wonder: "Have I covered everything? What am I missing? Are there other techniques and theories that I haven't even heard of? Am I being too detailed—or not detailed enough?"

Finally, as the manuscript deadline approaches (and you get a two-week extension), you realize that no single textbook can ever fully exhaust the profession of health care public relations, because our industry and our craft continue to be in a state of almost constant change.

So you check for typos, tighten up some of the sentence structure, thank heaven that a great editor will pick up what you miss, add a few last-minute references—and send your manuscript off to become a book, a book that you hope will help newcomers to the profession gain an overview of the history, theories, and techniques of health care public relations . . . a book that you hope will also provide some new information, inspiration, or insights for even the most veteran among us . . . and a book that can also help those who are not PR professionals gain a clearer understanding of the value and role of public relations in the successful contemporary health care organization.

Acknowledgments

This book has only one author listed, but it is, indeed, the result of the contributions of many. To attempt to list all of those who provided ideas, inspiration, and support is risky, because inevitably someone will be overlooked. Nevertheless, this author wants to recognize some of the people who played a key role in making this book happen:

- Don Giller, Lauren Barnett, and the board of the American Society for Health Care Marketing and Public Relations (ASHCMPR), who realized the need for such a book and committed ASHCMPR's resources to fill the need.
- A core group of role models from the Health Academy of PRSA, who, I believe, are the "best and brightest" (and certainly the most fun) people in our field, whose comments and insights are reflected throughout this book: among them, Shirley Bonnem, Irving Rimer, Ken Trester, Frank Weaver, Steve Seekins, Frank Karel, Fran Driscoll, Nancy Hicks, John Deats, Harold Kranz, Ralph Frede, Aileen White, Al Bradshaw, David Richards, and Mike Killian. I'm proud to call these people colleagues, and even more thankful that they are also dear friends.
- The PR pros I worked with at St. Vincent Medical Center, who continually showed me how public relations ought to be practiced, with thanks for their special support to Judy Lang, Catharine Harned, Bob Mackowiak, Ellen Yunker, Toni Iannone, Diane Shemak, Mary Gregory, Nancy Light, and Steve Hanson; and with loving memories of Doris Jenkins, who taught us all more than we realized.
- My amazing support team of Jane McMeans, Tina Roth, Tina Dowling, and the incomparable Ron Reich, who kept me organized (they tried!) and did everything from getting my thesis manuscript prepared (on deadline) through creating a lovely memorial service for my mother. When rewards are given for the most genuine, caring, hardworking people in this life, these four will be at the top of the list.

- My Public Relations Society of America (PRSA) colleagues in Toledo (especially my coconspirators Mark Leutke and Jane Summerville) and across the country, including the all-time grace-under-pressure honoree Belle Sanders of the national PRSA staff.
- My Society for Hospital Planning and Marketing cohorts, who have educated and enlightened me for years: Judy Nieman, Marion Jennings, Dave Kantor, Karen Endresen, David Lincoln, and Bill Ferretti, gentlepersons and scholars all.
- The survivors: those dedicated peers who began together and actually made it all the way through the University of Minnesota's Independent Study Program (ISP) in Hospital Administration—Dick Brown, Laird Covey, Charisse Oland, Marquita George, Mary Mohni, Sandy McCormick, Deb Banik, and of course, even though they were "MHers," Ernie Carnevale and Chris Bliersbach.
- A remarkable group of women who came together from across the country to serve the national organization of Women in Communications, Inc., and will forever be both mentors and sisters: Nancy Peterson, Susan Chilcott, Pam Johnson, Karen Brown, Carolyn Johnson, Peg McKechnie, Linnea Lose, Jo-Ann Albers, Clara Harmon, Louise Ott, and Barbara Haas.

I also must specially recognize six individuals who have indelibly shaped my professional development, and also have provided unquestioning personal support:

- Harvey Beutner, Ph.D., journalist, scholar, and teacher, whose labors on behalf of his Illinois Wesleyan University students are today reflected in our achievements.
- Allen L. Johnson, who taught me more about running a hospital (through vision, inspiration, humor, and giving your staff support and praise) than any textbook ever could.
- Elizabeth Yamashita, Ph.D., who taught me that a woman doesn't have to be afraid of being tough and whose commitment to the professional development of her students at Northwestern University pushed us all to be better than we thought we could be.
- Vernon Weckwerth, Ph.D., the heart and soul and genius of Minnesota's ISP graduate program in health care administration, whose commitment to us "adult learners" made an M.H.A. an achievable goal and who actually made me (sort of) enjoy statistics.
- Pat Jackson, who gets my vote for the PR professional with the clearest vision of what public relations is, should be, and can be; whose commitment to professional excellence is unequaled; and who sets the example for all of us by unceasingly sharing his expertise and wisdom for the betterment of the profession and the world we serve.

- Chester Burger, truly a giant of our profession, whose insights have helped me create my own vision of excellence in public relations. Chet remains the role model for all of us who aspire to the highest standards of professional achievement and caring, civilized behavior. His friendship and support have helped me become the professional, and the person, I am today.

Six outstandingly successful professionals. Six supportive, caring people. Six good human beings.

Special thanks to my new colleagues at University Hospitals of Cleveland, especially Orry Jacobs, for their patience as I juggled completing this book with getting settled in at UHC.

And very special thanks to Brian Schenk and Audrey Kaufman of American Hospital Publishing, Inc., who have held my hand, via phone, and labored to help this manuscript become a book.

And finally, the people without whom I truly "wouldn't be where I am today":

- Good friends, like Becky and Jim Rohrs, and Dan and Karen Grafner, who've shared our lives and been there for us when we needed them.
- My siblings, Tom and Betsy Larey, who've put up with my lunacies longer than anyone and who remain two of the most interesting and fun people I know.
- My aunt, Mary White, a strong-willed, brave woman who helped unionize the telephone workers in Illinois and, as a top-ranking Democratic party official, took me out on the campaign trail to meet John and Robert Kennedy — and who showed me that women could, indeed, make it on their own.
- My dearest friend, Beth Kranz, whose faith in me has helped me discover who I am and who, by caring about me, helped me learn how to care about myself. She knows how special she is, and how empty my life would have been without her.
- And J. L., my patient and forgiving spouse, who has tolerated my craziness, shared and supported my dreams, picked me up when I crashed, been mad at the people who did me wrong, helped me remember to laugh, reminded me that I am not the center of the entire universe, and who never seems to 100 percent believe me when I say I'd never have made it without him (but maybe if I put it in a book, he'll finally believe it).
- And, finally, my mother, who coped with adversity in her own life so that she could focus all of her energy on taking care of her kids. By always believing in me and letting me know that whatever I did, she was on my side, she instilled in me the self-confidence that we all need if we're going to take risks, try to go beyond our limitations,

and, eventually, to succeed. I wish I'd told her all this, and more, while she was alive, but I think she knew.

And now that I've shared these thoughts, I realize that the best thing about writing a book is that it gives you the chance to recognize, in print, the people who have helped make your life so wonderful.

Introduction

Challenging. Fast-paced. Stressful. Rewarding. Above all—exciting. Those are just some of the words used by veteran health care public relations (PR) professionals in 1989 to describe their industry and their work.[1] The descriptions reflect the complexity of the field, a complexity that mirrors the state of the health care industry itself. They also reflect the dynamic and rapidly changing nature of health care public relations, changes that mirror the evolution of the role and public image of hospitals and health care providers in the United States.

These senior-level professionals candidly discussed the challenges (some hospitals call them problems), the work load, the crises, the demands, and the hectic pace that are routine for the health care PR manager. They also vividly described the rewards, the excitement, and the personal and professional satisfaction they derive from working in organizations that exist to prevent suffering, to heal the sick, to help the poor, and above all, to serve people. "It's not an easy profession," said one vice-president. "But overall, it's always very satisfying. It's never boring, and both the health care industry and the role of public relations in hospitals are changing, so there are always new challenges."

A brief look at the recent history of health care public relations shows just how significant the changes in the health care industry have been and how the role and responsibilities of health care PR managers have evolved and grown.

□ The 1950s and 1960s: A Kinder, Gentler Era

The 1960s and preceding decades were good times for health care organizations. Hospital beds were filled; in fact, the federal government continued to provide funding to build additional health care facilities. Insurance companies and the employers who funded their premiums paid hospital bills promptly and without complaint. Physicians were

1

satisfied with their autonomy and their standard of living. Patients generally followed orders, assuming that the care they received was appropriate and of high quality. Health care employees, for the most part, enjoyed their work and were satisfied to work in what was called a "recession-proof" industry.

In the 1950s, many health care organizations did not have a formal PR staff. Nurses handled patient education in person rather than via print or audiovisual methods. If the local press had any questions, they called the administrator. In institutions that did have a staff member responsible for public relations (often combined with other responsibilities such as directing volunteers or human resources), that person's role was sometimes fairly simplistic: producing brochures and information for patients, giving tours to Brownie and Cub Scout troops, and supervising special events such as open houses.

"Media relations" was generally limited to releasing patient information, although that practice varied widely from community to community. Some administrators refused to tell local reporters anything and in many towns, the media weren't very interested in what went on at local hospitals anyway. In some small (and not so small) towns, it was common practice to release each day's admissions and discharges to the local newspaper or radio stations. It was assumed that the patients' friends were interested in this information. Years passed before concerns for patient privacy put an end to this custom.

The health care PR person wasn't under pressure to promote feature story ideas to the media. Health care organizations felt little need to create awareness or preference because health care institutions had always received public support and favor. "We really didn't worry about what the public thought about hospitals, because the patients did what their doctors told them to do," recalled one retired hospital administrator.

By the mid-1960s, the practice of hospital public relations had become more sophisticated at some hospitals, as evidenced by the creation of the American Society for Hospital Public Relations Directors in 1964. Some 350 professionals joined the society in its first year, subscribing to its goals, as stated by Edwin L. Crosby, M.D., then president of the American Hospital Association:[2]

> We want the public to better understand hospitals and their services, because hospital care eventually touches every human life. The complexity of modern hospital care will increase with scientific advances. The public needs and wants to understand these changes. Hospitals must be ready to explain.

Those goals were laudable — and sensible — but generally did not reflect the mainstream thinking of most hospital administrators. In the

1960s, hospitals enjoyed a relatively unblemished reputation, and few could imagine that there would ever be a time when hospitals would be urgently trying to regain public confidence and support. Thus, there seemed little reason to launch proactive PR efforts to maintain and build on the public confidence that existed.

"We just took it for granted that hospitals—like schools and churches—would always have community support. We didn't have to tell people we were doing good work because they knew it. And frankly, we didn't see how public opinion could affect us." Hospitals were neither proactive in seeking public support nor reactive because there was essentially no public criticism. With regard to influencing public opinion, hospitals were generally inactive. The hospital administrators and PR staffers of that era could hardly have predicted the loss of public support that would occur in succeeding decades and how that shift in public opinion would affect the very survival of American hospitals.

□ The 1970s: The First Stirrings of Public Scrutiny and Criticism

The 1970s marked the beginning of what would become a radical shift in the public's attitudes toward health care institutions, as multiple forces converged to place the institutions under more scrutiny than at any time in their history. Among these forces were (1) payers' new-found concerns about what they were spending on health care and (2) the post-Watergate zeal of reporters flushed with investigative fervor. Although the full impact of these two forces would not be felt until the 1980s, health care executives began to experience the effects of payer and media scrutiny by the mid-1970s.

At first, it seemed that little had changed. Hospital growth continued unabated—new wings, new equipment, totally new facilities. Every hospital, it seemed, wanted to be all things to all people, offering the full spectrum of services from obstetrics to specialized surgery. Patients still followed physicians' orders—and when the physician recommended a stay in the hospital for "observation," that was fine with the patient and the administrator. The hospital's primary public—the physicians—were satisfied, and so were the patients.

But one health care public—albeit a public to which health care organizations had not paid much attention in the past—was beginning to experience the first pangs of dissatisfaction. Whereas hospitals were relatively unaffected by changing economic conditions, major corporations, which constituted the bulk of the hospitals' payer public, were being affected. And when corporations started to feel the effects of the economic downturn, they began to take a close look at their major expense items. What they discovered was that their employee benefits line item had been growing steadily and that the health care benefits they'd freely passed out during labor negotiations were becoming increasingly expensive.

The federal government was also starting to take a look at its budget line item for Medicare, the program that legislators had originally created to provide "free" health care for the nation's senior citizens. At a time when government expenditures were rising rapidly, Medicare costs were outpacing even the inflation rate. Analysts predicting the growth of the elderly population were beginning to issue warnings about what the program could eventually cost the country. State legislators had similar concerns about the costs of Medicaid programs.

In short, the people who paid the health care bills were beginning to ask questions. True, the questions from payers were at first only friendly probings; still, answering questions from "outsiders" was something health care administrators weren't used to doing. They were even less comfortable with being regulated by the government, but they soon had to learn how to cope with a national health planning system created by the government to put a rein on the hospital building boom.

Clearly, the times were indeed changing. The growing presence of the intrusive mass media was another unwelcome change. Reporters were beginning to ask questions about hospital plans, budgets, and occupancy rates; to demand information about public record cases; and to pursue any hint of a sensational story, be it employee unrest or a juicy malpractice case. When administrators tried to ignore the media, the reporters, enlivened with investigative fervor, became increasingly skeptical, and critical, of hospitals.

Coping with this media scrutiny and skepticism was only one of the challenges facing the health care PR staff. By the mid-1970s, most hospitals had created PR positions and the professionals in those positions were simultaneously attempting to define their role and to deal with these first stirrings of public criticism.

Media relations was a primary responsibility of the hospital PR office, many of which were one-person operations. As the days of perpetually friendly relations with reporters drew to a close, the PR people found themselves concerned with protecting patient privacy and explaining institutional actions that had previously been of little interest to the public.

At the same time, the PR staff was also coping with increased internal demands. Nursing departments asked for more printed materials to orient and educate patients. Chief executive officers (CEOs) and other managers asked for assistance in informing the public about new programs and services—the first stirrings of hospital promotion and marketing. Much of this promotion was focused on getting media coverage, which meant maintaining decent working relationships with those same reporters who were demanding answers to inquiries. In addition, the human resources staff needed support for employee communications programs. Development officers suggested doing external magazines to recognize donors and create public interest. Special events — from medical staff dinners to Auxiliary dances—were also placed on the PR managers' overflowing agendas.

Many PR directors found that their role was being defined for them and that it was often a reactive role—reacting to media inquiries and to the needs of the institution, rather than creating proactive communications and relationship-building programs to maintain the support of the general public that health care organizations had enjoyed throughout the 1960s. This absence of proactive, two-way communications programs with key publics reflected the perceptions and priorities of health care administrators at the time. Although health care organizations were being scrutinized and questioned by the media and some business and government leaders, many CEOs believed that this was a relatively insignificant or temporary phenomenon. Even those who took the scrutiny more seriously did not anticipate the effect the criticism would have on public opinion, and many other health care leaders were still unconcerned about public opinion. Finally, even those PR professionals who were concerned about shoring up relationships with key health care audiences were so busy reacting to an ever-growing load of daily responsibilities that they had very little time to plan proactive efforts.

Public relations professionals had very little incentive to take action because in the 1970s, even with reimbursement concerns growing, hospital occupancy remained high and revenues ample. Even the most astute industry analysts couldn't predict that only a decade later hospitals would be operating in the red, laying off employees, and closing down units in a fight for survival.

□ The 1980s: Keeping All the Customers Satisfied

By the early 1980s, even the most complacent health care CEOs clearly understood the need to pay more attention to the publics that were affecting health care organizations. Physicians—the organizations' most long-standing public—were increasingly dissatisfied. Payers—the public that started flexing its muscles in the 1970s—were launching full-scale attacks. And patients—a previously ignored public—were making demands. Health care leaders were coming to grips with the customer triad—physicians, payers, and patients—and discovering the difficulties in meeting the disparate and often conflicting needs and demands of these groups.

The payer rebellion was the critical issue for health care organizations in the 1980s. Both private payers—employers and their insurance intermediaries—and officials of federal, state, and local governments were taking drastic steps to reduce their health care expenditures. This ratcheting down took two forms: negotiating or imposing lower rates, and taking steps to actually reduce the amount of care provided. As payers and their intermediaries required preauthorization for and established limits on inpatient care, they also changed coverage policies to shift care to outpatient settings. This two-pronged approach had a doubly harsh impact on hospitals. First, inpatient admissions were reduced and lengths of stay shrunk, with the net result that occupancy rates dropped dramatically. Secondly, with the Medicare payment system of a standard price per case for specified diagnosis-related groups (DRGs) and other payers' discounted rates, many hospitals were not receiving enough income to cover the costs of the care they were providing. Budget cutbacks were routine, and employee layoffs became common.

The relationship between hospitals and payers continued to worsen as selective contracting plans became more popular and as lawsuits involving hospitals and insurers became almost routine in some parts of the country. In one two-year period in a middle-sized Midwestern city, three hospitals sued the Blue Cross plan because they had been eliminated from a managed care plan; then another hospital sued because it was eliminated from a second managed care plan; then Blue Cross sued several hospitals for actions taken during negotiations; then a major employer sued a major insurer for failing to pass along to the employer the discounts the insurer received from hospitals.

Hospitals responded to their shrinking revenue base by desperately trying to increase their market share by "getting into marketing," often operationally defined as creating new programs and services and taking patients away from the competition. Hospitals created new services at a dizzying pace—women's centers, alcoholism treatment programs, sports medicine clinics—and even ventured into some areas very new to hospitals, from operating ambulance services to buying and operating physician practices. Both selling new programs and attracting patients to existing programs involved new levels of promotional activities aimed at both physicians and patients. This was made more challenging because both of these publics were somewhat dissatisfied with hospitals.

The physicians' dissatisfaction was rooted in their concern over their own shrinking reimbursement and revenues, combined with a loss of autonomy as managed care plans, governmental agencies, and patients insisted on having more control over what physicians felt should be their own independent medical decisions. Although the hospitals weren't responsible for these occurrences, physicians often turned their anger on hospital CEOs and staff members. At the same time, physicians were realizing that hospitals needed them—needed their admissions and their support—and many became more demanding. "I can always take my patients to another hospital" became a common comment to the hospital CEO, and many hospitals responded by creating sophisticated medical staff relations programs aimed at marketing to and for physicians.

Simultaneously, hospitals were beginning to pay extra attention to the third component of the customer triad: patients. Following the public information and promotion programs of the 1970s and fueled by media coverage of health care issues, consumers began to take a more active role in making choices about their hospital care. Hospitals addressed the patient public in two ways: "guest relations" activities aimed at existing patients and marketing programs aimed at potential customers in the general public.

These direct marketing efforts were well received by consumers, but the side effects demonstrated the difficulties hospitals encountered in trying to meet the needs of each of the hospitals' three disparate publics. Consumers responded positively to hospital marketing efforts like patient amenities (gourmet meals, beautifully decorated rooms) and the acquisition of the latest technology [such as computed tomography (CT) and machine-readable identifier (MRI) scanners]. But payers reacted negatively, seeing these efforts as adding to the costs of health care. Patients responded positively to hospital communications and advertising that encouraged them to be informed and make choices about health care, whereas physicians viewed this as an invasion of their relationships with their patients. And though the consumers liked the marketing efforts, they were nevertheless an increasingly skeptical public, reacting to the business, government, and media outcries about costs and responding to media coverage of mortality data, malpractice suits, and other negative stories involving hospitals.

In the midst of this rapidly deteriorating environment, the hospital PR managers found their role continuing to evolve. As the responsibilities assigned to the PR department increased along with the outside pressures, many PR managers demanded and received increased budgets and staff.

Public relations staffs were dealing with media and public communication on a variety of new and potentially negative issues: layoffs, mergers and joint ventures, AIDS, quality of care, toxic waste, strikes, nursing dissatisfaction, and more. They were also developing increasingly sophisticated patient and employee communication programs and expanding such face-to-face community relations activities as speakers' bureaus, tours, special events, and health education programs.

In addition, many PR managers were either given full responsibility for or asked to assist in their institutional marketing programs. This responsibility usually began with the fourth *P* of marketing—promotion—but in some cases also included research and product development. Public relations staffs became involved in advertising—from pretesting to response measurement—and in developing comprehensive, multifaceted marketing communications programs. The American Society for Hospital Public Relations added *Marketing* to its name, becoming ASHMPR, reflecting the changing responsibilities of its members.[3] In March 1990 ASHMPR further modified its name, changing the word *hospital* to *health care*, becoming ASHCMPR, to embrace the many nontraditional settings in which health care services are delivered and the complexity of the organizations within which acute care hospitals were only a part.

Some of the more senior PR professionals became concerned that the emphasis on marketing was pushing traditional PR activities into the background, and there were CEOs who seemed to believe that the external pressures called for an either/or approach, questioning whether marketing or public relations was "better." Although these mass-market, mass-audience efforts were developed to generate big-dollar responses so vital to the health care organization's shrinking profit margin, many veteran PR professionals were also concerned about building, and rebuilding, relationships with key publics who could affect the health care organization's future.

In the late 1980s, the phrase "renaissance of public relations" surfaced in trade publication articles, with thoughtful PR executives pointing out that health care organizations needed to take immediate action to listen to and communicate with a number of important audiences. "Hospitals once enjoyed the total support of their communities," said one hospital PR veteran interviewed for the December 1989 issue of the *Public Relations Journal.* "While we cannot ever return to those simpler days, we can and must tell our story proactively, rather than simply reacting to criticism and complaints. We must reeducate and remind our publics of the vital work that we do and give them a context in which they can appreciate the contributions that hospitals are making to their communities, to the economy, and to the lives of millions of individuals and their families."[4]

Public relations professionals reasserted the validity of their traditional role of monitoring and building relationships with publics, and CEOs who were coping with the negative results of ignoring or taking public support for granted responded to public relations' message. And as the health care industry moved into the last decade of the century, skilled and dedicated PR professionals were preparing to meet the complex challenges facing their institutions.

☐ The 1990s and Beyond: New Opportunities for the Public Relations Professional

The challenges facing health care organizations in the 1990s demand the wisdom and expertise of public relations as never before. When an upscale consumer magazine like *New York* carries an article headlined "The New Bill of Health" describing health care as "what the fair-wage issue was to labor in the 1930s,"[5] it's obvious that the health care industry needs to salvage, strengthen, and recreate relationships with the publics that are essential to the industry's future.

An even stronger message came from a study of American consumers conducted by the *Los Angeles Times.*[6] Although more than 90 percent of the respondents indicated that they were satisfied with their personal health care, a solid majority said the entire system "needs many improvements" or "fundamental overhauling." From this type of public opinion swing comes legislation and regulation, which could fundamentally change the way health care organizations operate.

Clearly, the issues facing the industry are numerous and serious. Responding to an informal survey conducted in the fall of 1989 for a *Public Relations Journal* article, 20 experienced, senior-level health care PR executives described the health care industry in dramatic terms, for example:[7]

- "It's a white water revolution in health care."
- "We're witnessing the cataclysmic transformation of American medicine."
- "There are some incredible challenges and opportunities at the door of the public relations profession."

These PR professionals identified only two "rock-solid certainties" in their field. "One thing that's certain is change, change, change," said one respondent. "And the other thing that's certain is that public relations professionals have the opportunity to position themselves as key players in the efforts to cope with these changes."

The veteran practitioners noted that in health care organizations where PR executives are already seen as an integral part of the top management team, their roles are expanding to help their organizations cope with the changing external and internal environments. On the other hand, in the ever-decreasing number of organizations where public relations is not well established or valued, or is seen as a subset of marketing, one respondent predicted that: "when budgets get tight, as they are now and will be in the future, PR may be a target. Some CEOs still see it as an overhead department, and those departments can be vulnerable."

The conditions that the hospital industry is facing were summed up succinctly by Steve Seekins, vice-president for special projects of the American Medical Association, in a commentary in the national newsletter of the Health Academy of the Public Relations Society of America:[8]

> Competition in many areas is very tough. Physicians feel hassled. Hospitals are closing. Patients are worried. Business is concerned about paying the costs of health care. Government wants to control budgets, while regulation threatens to change forever the ways in which care is delivered.

The respondents also cited the relatively rapid decline in the public's image of hospitals. As recently as the mid-1970s, hospitals and physicians "wore white hats," as one veteran practitioner put it. "Doctors and hospitals were the good guys; nice, benign, serving people." In less than a decade, health care providers and intermediaries (insurers, HMOs, and so on) were handed "black hats" by the court of public opinion. And today, given the issues confronting the industry, it seems unlikely that "white hat" status will return soon, if ever. The image of the health care system seems to have been irrevocably changed.

That changing image is a reflection of a number of issues that the survey respondents identified as *critical:* funding, work-force shortages, quality maintenance, acquired immunodeficiency disease (AIDS), multiple audiences with divergent agendas, and competition among all segments of the health care industry.

Funding

Despite serious and consistent cost-cutting efforts, an image of free-spending, wasteful hospitals, physicians, and insurance plans prevails. Payers — employers, federal and state governments — rebelled by creating systems to force providers to cut costs. The result of all of these efforts has been a dramatic reduction in payments for hospital and physician services. And these revenue reductions will continue. "As the number of elderly patients on Medicare increases, hospitals are more dependent on the reduced, set payment rates of the DRG system. Similar revenue reductions come from managed care agreements with their corresponding discounts — hospitals can also lose revenue when insurance plans go out of business and can't meet any of their contractual agreements," noted one respondent. "The growing number of Americans with no health insurance — estimated at 30 to 35 million persons — is also contributing to the funding crisis, and when hospitals attempt to curb their free care in order to balance the budget, they risk public disapproval," said one PR consultant.

This ongoing reduction in funding from all sources has both short-term and long-term implications. In the short term, the push for cost cutting comes at a time when "the public's expectations for quality health care are higher than ever." For the long term, reduced revenues and profits mean difficulty in obtaining capital financing to purchase new, lifesaving technology and to refurbish the nation's aging hospital physical plants.

Another PR implication of the drive to cut costs involves a lack of public confidence. As health care providers and insurers have attempted to deal with the funding cuts through downsizing (laying off employees, cutting services, reducing capital and reserve funds), the negative free-spending image has begun to be replaced by one that's equally negative: that of a system that may be unable to provide the comprehensive, high-quality care that Americans have always expected. Although payers may applaud the cost-containment efforts, physicians, patients, and the general public are concerned that quality may be suffering.

Work-Force Shortages

The negative image of health care organizations has played a part in deterring young people from pursuing health care careers, and the women who have traditionally filled many health care jobs now have other career options. In addition, budget-cutting work-force reductions have meant increased work loads and higher stress for health care professionals. The result is a growing shortage not only in nursing, which the public is aware of, but also in a number of other fields, such as pharmacy, physical therapy, and medical technology. And media reporting on the shortages and resultant staffing problems at hospitals contributes to the erosion of public confidence in the system.

Quality Maintenance

"The quality of the American health care system is generally acknowledged to be the best in the world," said one PR vice-president, while his colleagues pointed to a number of factors which relate to that image of quality. "The development of lifesaving technology and drugs raises concomitant ethical issues. Who will get the drugs, transplants, treatments? How will we decide?" Concerns about liability and rising malpractice premiums are causing some physicians to limit or leave their practices and the hostile attitudes that physicians feel they are encountering ("the hassle factors") may be deterring some potential physicians from entering the profession.

The very act of measuring quality is a critical challenge for health care organizations. The industry has encountered difficulties in developing clinical indicators that can be standardized, and quantifying the quality of health service from the patient's perspective has been equally difficult. Maintaining quality in the midst of funding reductions and developing systems so that quality can be measured and evaluated will play an integral part in creating a sound, positive image of the health care system in the minds of the American public.

Acquired Immunodeficiency Syndrome

The impact of acquired immunodeficiency syndrome (AIDS) on the health care system had yet to be fully felt by the late 1980s. The director of public affairs at a major urban medical center said AIDS is the number-one issue facing academic medical centers and the issue is multifaceted. Health care PR professionals need to be involved in communicating with the public — both in terms of educating people who are at risk of contracting the disease and calming the hysteria about how the disease is and is not transmitted. Other issues PR practitioners will have to grapple with: patient confidentiality; the fears and risks of nurses, physicians, and staff who treat patients; access to and cost of care for AIDS patients; and how caring for AIDS patients will affect a health care organization's public image.

Multiple Audiences with Divergent Agendas

In the old "white hat" days, health care administrators could quickly list their key audiences: physicians and financial donors. Today, there are a growing number of increasingly vocal groups who believe they have a stake in American hospitals: employees, retirees, physicians, patients and their families, legislators, regulators, payers (employers and their intermediaries, insurers, HMOs, and so on), civic and business leaders, volunteers, vendors and suppliers, people who live near health care facilities ("neighbors"), media, and special interest groups ranging from abortion activists on both sides of the issue to the elderly, religious fundamentalists, and civil rights organizations. And the special interest groups like animal rights activists can have a profound impact on the health care system.

The health care organization's audiences are also becoming increasingly fragmented. Each of these stakeholder groups has subgroups with different concerns. The needs of young women patients may be very different from the concerns of elderly patients, for instance. The challenge for PR professionals, noted one respondent, is to communicate and build relationships with these smaller audiences, and to "forget this 'mass media' nonsense."

Competition among All Segments of the Health Care Industry

Each of the issues cited has an effect on each segment of the health care industry—hospitals, physicians, insurers and health plans, service/research associations like the American Cancer Society—and on the vendors, suppliers, and agencies that serve the industry. One of the effects has been to pit providers against each other, especially in terms of competition for funding and public support. One professional noted that hospitals and physician organizations have been on the verge of doing battle as congressional budget trimmers worked to limit federal outlays. And competition for public awareness and support affects all health-related organizations.

This competition comes at a time when the participants in the health care industry need to stand together, advised the senior PR practitioners. "It's the entire system that's under attack, and if any major segment is weakened—be it hospitals, physicians, or the insurers—eventually we all will suffer, including the general public and everyone in the industry. We have to stop letting the government and big business try to dominate us and pit us against each other to win cost concessions at the expense of quality," said one veteran.

☐ Purpose of This Book

The issues described in this introduction will shape the work of health care PR professionals well into the 1990s, and their responsibilities will expand to include more legislative and payer relations, greater participation in the development of more sophisticated employee recruitment and retention programs, and, above all, a renewal of the classical role of the PR counselor. Health care leaders in the 1990s, unlike those in earlier decades, now realize that the very survival of their institutions is dependent on forging mutually beneficial relationships with numerous stakeholder groups, and those leaders will turn to their PR executives for counsel and direction. The manager who is skilled in the modern practice of public relations will be well positioned to remain or become a key player in charting a path toward institutional survival and growth.

This book is designed to assist the PR manager in gaining a perspective on the function and performance of public relations in the health care setting, including:

- The role of public relations in the health care organization
- Integration of public relations with management functions

- Organization of the PR function, including staffing and using outside agencies
- Development of the institutional PR plan and product marketing communications plans
- Research and evaluation methods
- PR methods:
  - Stakeholder relations and issues management
  - Community relations
  - Media relations and crisis communications
  - Publications
  - Marketing communications and advertising
  - Audiovisual and other techniques
- Communication to special audiences:
  - Employees
  - Physicians
  - Payers
  - Legislators
- Ethical and legal considerations

The text provides a theoretical overview and practical advice on developing a health care PR program for professionals who are new to the health care industry; offers some new ideas and insights for the veteran health care PR manager; and provides CEOs and other executives with a view of how the PR function can contribute to the success of the contemporary health care organization.

References

1. Lewton, K. L. Health care: critical conditions. *Public Relations Journal* 46(12), Dec. 1989. Comments made during interviews conducted by the author during manuscript preparation. [Reprinted with the permission of *Public Relations Journal*, copyright 1989 by the Public Relations Society of America.]
2. Crosby, E. L., M.D. Verbal communication in June 1964 meeting of the American Hospital Association's Intradepartmental Committee on Public Information. [Quoted in *1989 Membership Directory of the American Society for Hospital Marketing and Public Relations*. Chicago: American Hospital Association, 1989.]
3. ASHMPR, *1989 Membership Directory.*
4. Lewton.
5. Byron, C. The new bill of health. *New York* 22(34):16, Aug. 28, 1989.
6. Most want health care overhauled. *Toledo Blade*, Feb. 4, 1990, p. 3-A.
7. Lewton.
8. *Newsletter of the Health Academy of the Public Relations Society of America.* Summer 1989.

Suggested Readings

Awad, J. *The Power of Public Relations.* New York City: Praeger, 1985.

Centre, A. H., and Walsh, F. E. *Public Relations Practices: Managerial Case Studies and Problems.* 3rd ed. Englewood Cliffs, NJ: Prentice-Hall, 1985.

Hicks, N. J., and McGee, D. T. Integrated strategies: a successful approach to hospital public relations. *Public Relations Journal,* Oct. 1981.

Lesly, P. The conflicting makeup of audiences. *Managing the Human Climate,* May–June 1989.

Olasky, M. N. A reappraisal of 19th century public relations. *Public Relations Review,* Spring 1985.

The Role of Public Relations in Health Care

The public relations manager plays a multifaceted role in the health care setting, but the two most essential roles are counseling senior management and creating communications and relationship-building programs to link the health care organization and its publics. Managing these roles requires not only professional expertise in communications and public relations, but also strong interpersonal skills, flexibility, a good sense of humor, and the ability to stay calm in crisis situations. Health care public relations is not a profession for persons who like fixed routines and unchanging order. It is ideal for those who enjoy responding to changing issues, coping with the unexpected, creating effective communications programs, and playing a key top management role in institutions that serve people and their communities.

□ Public Relations Counseling

"Success can only be conferred by outsiders," explained Pat Jackson, public relations counselor and past national president of the Public Relations Society of America. "You cannot proclaim your organization, product or policies to be successful. External publics must do that. This is why building relationships is the true bottom line."[1]

John Hill, the former CEO of the major international PR firm of Hill and Knowlton, put it more simply in his often-quoted statement that publics give organizations "the freedom to operate."

Hospitals are perhaps more dependent on that public permission, because hospitals "are born of the community and from the community they receive their sanction to provide health care," observed George Adams, publisher of *Health Care Weekly Review:*

> Hospitals in the United States operate at least in part as a public service. Most are blessed with the status of charitable enterprises, exempt from taxes and funded to a large extent through public finance. In this sense, they are debtors to society.
>
> Hospitals occupy a special place in society. The benefits of that niche are both tangible and intangible, but they are substantial. Hospitals do not receive this treatment as a consequence of divine edict. Rather, society allows hospitals to exist and operate.[2]

This theory is becoming reality for hospital CEOs, as noted in a cover story on service cuts in the October 5, 1989, issue of *Hospitals* magazine.[3] The story quotes one health care consultant who notes that "you start with financial issues because they are tangible and objective, . . . then the hard part comes—dealing with the political environment." This was echoed by another health care leader who noted that "the impact that a service cut has on relations with the community, hospital board, medical staff, and employees must all be considered." Failure to pay attention to this public impact—to ignore the impact of public relations—can derail the hospital's plans and actions.

Counseling Senior Management

It is because of the critical impact of the health care organization's publics that public relations must be positioned as one of the senior management functions, along with finance, human resources, operations, and legal concerns. The organization that will survive and prosper must make decisions and take actions that are operationally feasible, financially viable, legal, acceptable to employees—and that will either receive the support or avert the opposition of the organization's publics. The top management team must include experts in all of these disciplines, including a chief public relations officer who plays an integral role in decision making and operations analysis by counseling the management team on public actions and reactions.

Counseling is the core function of the PR profession, identified as the essential role for the senior PR manager within an organization. As counselor, the PR manager is responsible for scanning the external environment, directing the efforts to identify and monitor concerns of the institution's publics, and representing the interests of those publics to the management and leadership of the institution. The PR manager analyzes the institution's plans and advises management on potential public reaction, and then manages the process of engendering public support and managing negative reactions. In essence, the PR manager speaks for the external publics during management decision making, ensuring that their needs and concerns are considered and understood.

Moreover, in the contemporary practice of public relations, this traditional scanning of the external environment role has moved beyond just counseling on proposed decisions. Today's PR manager must also constantly assess the organization's operations and performance in light of the effect on its publics. Ralph Frede, A.P.R., one of the health care PR profession's most experienced and honored practitioners, described this role to a colloquium of PR and medical luminaries upon the occasion of his retirement in 1989.[4] "It has become apparent that communicating is not enough. It is important to be concerned with the organization's performance — policies, procedures, the way we do business. We want our organizations to be, not just seem to be. So we must counsel with management to put the house in order. Organizational performance assessment must be part of the public relations process." Frede also noted that health care executives are looking for "people who will help them address and interpret public response" — an apt description of the counseling role of the PR professional.

For the counseling role to be performed effectively, it is essential that the PR professional be an integral part of the top management team. The title and reporting relationship of the top-ranking PR staff member play an important part in determining the positioning of the *function* of public relations, as well as determining whether or not the person in that function will be perceived as one of the key players on the management team.

Most PR professionals, both in the investor-owned and nonprofit institutional sector, believe that reporting directly to the CEO of the institution is essential. This relationship is ideal from both a practical and a philosophical standpoint. On a practical level, the PR manager needs direct access to the CEO for several reasons. Direct access is essential in terms of clear, unfiltered communication between the institution's leader and its chief spokesperson. To be effective in presenting the institution's position to the public, the PR manager must be able to develop that position in concert with the CEO. And at times when public reactions or media inquiries require rapid responses, the ability to work directly with the CEO helps the PR manager meet these demands as quickly as possible.

An even more significant reason for the PR manager to report directly to the CEO is the nature of the counseling/advisory role. Because the effective PR manager is continually scanning the environment and monitoring the concerns of internal and external publics, he or she can often be the first person to become aware of developing problems. The sensitive nature of some of these problems, especially in terms of major decisions and the day-to-day operations that can cause negative reactions from various publics, means that often the CEO is the first person who needs to be advised about potential ramifications.

19

The PR person who has a confidential, trusting relationship with the CEO can be the "bearer of bad news" and can also provide the analytical and communications skills needed to address these problems.

From an image standpoint, of course, having the top-ranking PR officer report directly to the CEO is important because it sends a clear message to both internal and external audiences that the PR function is an integral part of administration. That message lends influence to the function and the individual, and provides the kind of "referred power" that can make it easier for the PR manager to do his or her job. But the most essential argument for advocating a direct report to the CEO is that the institution's communications and relationship-building functions work most effectively when the PR manager and the chief executive officer work together to anticipate, respond to, and develop programs to effectively work with the organization's publics.

There are, of course, many examples of effective PR managers who have reported to someone other than the CEO. In some health care organizations, the CEO position is an externally focused position, involving a great deal of work outside the institution, while the chief operating officer (COO) actually runs the institution. In this situation, it is argued that it is more sensible for the PR person to report to the COO, who is physically present in the institution more than the CEO. Although there is some logic in this argument (it's hard to report to someone whom you only see occasionally), it is somewhat flawed, given that the CEO's interactions with the external environment and critical publics would seem to require the involvement of, and advice from, the PR manager.

Another factor to be considered in terms of a COO reporting relationship is whether or not the other senior managers report to the CEO or the COO. If the other staff managers (finance, human resources, patient care, and so on) report to the CEO, then having the PR manager report to the COO sends the message that the position is not really a senior-level function. Alternatively, if these other staff managers report to the COO, it may be politically unwise for the PR manager to insist on a CEO reporting relationship because this insistence may be interpreted as a demand for special treatment. In such a case, the astute PR professional can request a joint reporting relationship. This can be tricky to manage, in terms of having two "bosses," but can work if the CEO and COO communicate well and have a strong, trusting relationship, and if they and the PR manager have a clear understanding of who's handling what. For example, one PR vice-president reported to and worked with the CEO on institutional image and external audience relations issues, but reported to and worked with the COO on employee communications and product/service marketing communications programs.

A second option is to establish consistent, clear lines of communication between the CEO and the PR manager. Public relations professionals who have successfully managed this type of relationship have generally done so by setting up frequent and routine meetings with the CEO; in addition, they have had instant and direct access to the CEO when a crisis arises, as well as when the PR manager needs to advise the CEO on potential problems and the methods of addressing and defusing those problems before they become crises.

There are, of course, a number of other reporting arrangements, including having the PR manager report to a senior-level planning, marketing, or even a development officer. There are two basic problems with these arrangements: (1) they generally preclude the kind of direct CEO access previously described, and (2) they position the PR role as a subset of planning, marketing, or development. Although there is some overlap in terms of the skills used by and work performed by planning, marketing, development, and PR staff members, each of these disciplines has a distinctive role and function within the organization. (A more detailed description of the relationships between these functions is included in chapter 3.) Public relations experts believe that the PR function is considerably different from the other three functions, and that the effectiveness of the PR role is enhanced when public relations is a separate, freestanding department or division within the organization. Of course, there are PR professionals who have been effective and successful while reporting to a planning, marketing, or development officer, but many of these people will candidly admit that this reporting relationship can be difficult to manage at times.

Persons entering the field of health care public relations who are offered positions that do not report to the CEO are often uncertain about whether to accept the situation and try to work around it or try to change it. This is clearly an individual decision. Many PR managers have been successful in presenting a strong case for the CEO reporting relationship and in negotiating that relationship before accepting the position.

In the final analysis, the PR professional must consider the responsibilities of the position and how the reporting relationship can enhance or diminish his or her ability to successfully handle those responsibilities. If the PR manager is to be held accountable for serving as the institution's spokesperson, communicating to and for internal and external publics, and building relationships for the health care organization, the PR manager must decide if he or she can meet those expectations within the reporting relationship that's offered. (A more detailed assessment of the special relationship between the CEO and the chief PR officer is included in chapter 4.)

Counseling Management Team Peers

The PR manager's role should also include counseling his or her peers—other staff and line operations administrators—and may also include serving as a counselor to the board of trustees and physicians on PR issues.

Development of effective working relationships among the PR manager and other administrative or management staff members is examined in detail in chapter 3. Special attention should be given to the PR manager's role as counselor to these peers.

The counseling process between the PR manager and other managers can take place on several levels, the most basic being when the PR manager is asked for professional advice on communications strategies and execution—for example, the radiology manager asking the PR manager for advice on promoting referrals to an MRI center. On a second and more significant level, the PR manager who is trusted and respected by fellow managers can become a valuable advisor and counselor on issues beyond promoting a service. Because of their communications expertise, PR managers are often asked by peers for advice on internal communications within the departments or divisions they supervise. And many operating administrators have also come to value the PR manager's analytical skills and sound judgment when the administrator needs help tackling a variety of operating problems and situations that have little to do with communications.

One support services administrator, for instance, recalled the valuable insights he received from his hospital's PR director while he was trying to reorganize a 60-person dietary department. "Our PR director didn't know anything about how to get food ready for trays and the cafeteria line," he said, "but she helped me figure out how to go about analyzing the alternatives and pointed out a number of small but important patient satisfaction side effects that I was missing because I was so focused on the departmental employees' needs." Another hospital operating vice-president noted that "whenever I am considering a major change in one of my departments, I sit down and hash it over with our PR vice-president. He has really good instincts about how people would react to things. I respect his judgment and the way he always could come up with several 'what if' scenarios that would help me make sure my final plan had a good chance of succeeding."

These types of relationships are essential if the PR manager is to be able to perform the counseling role in the most critical situations: when the PR manager has to initiate discussions about problems within a fellow manager's division or department. When the PR manager is performing the organizational performance assessment function that Ralph Frede described, he or she may discover problems that relate to

specific operating departments. For example, when the
following up on a complaint from a patient, or is anal
"front-line" employees meet and greet patients, problem:
ting department may become apparent. The PR manage.
responsibility of discussing these problems with the admitting
manager, representing the concerns of the patient public.

Obviously, discussions like this need to be handled effectively, so
that the primary objective—resolution of the problem—is achieved,
without offending the manager who "owns" the problem. And this
requires the same level of respect and trust that will help the PR
manager develop the kind of problem solver/advisor/confidant relationship that the operating vice-president previously described. This respect
and trust from fellow management team members make it much easier for the PR manager to effectively function as a counselor and
organizational performance evaluator.

A group of operating administrators who said they had very positive relationships with their institutions' PR managers were asked about
these relationships. They offered the following advice:

- Most important, be closed-mouthed. "If I talk with our PR director
  about a serious problem in one of my departments, I have to know
  that what I say won't be repeated to anyone else."
- If the PR manager learns of a problem in an operating department,
  "I want to hear about it first, directly from him. I don't want it
  brought up in some management staff meeting so I'm embarrassed.
  Don't go over my head—I'll return the favor."
- Be available and accessible. "When I need to consult with our PR
  director, it's usually because I'm in the middle of a problem or a major
  decision. I need to talk to her quickly—not in a week or two."
- Approach problem solving realistically. Understand the constraints
  on the operating manager. "I can only do so much—I've got to live
  within a budget, I've got supervisors who I can't change, my people
  are overworked. I need someone to help me work with what I've got—
  not tell me about theories and the ideal way to do it."

Pat Jackson adds this advice: "Don't give executives answers, give
them options. Line managers make decisions; staff managers are consultants. Letting the line manager off the hook by serving solutions
on a platter can be suicidal—because they are your answers, not his."[5]

Developing solid working relationships with staff and line operating managers not only enhances the PR manager's counseling role, but
also ensures that those peers will return the support by sharing information, alerting the PR manager to problems in the PR area, and working with the PR manager to address institutional performance problems.

Counseling the Board of Trustees

The relationship between the PR manager and the institution's board of trustees varies from institution to institution, and generally parallels the relationships between the board and other senior-level administrative staff. In some institutions, the CEO and the board choose to have the key staff administrators (finance, human resources, legal, public relations) participate in board meetings, sharing information and discussing plans and issues in their respective divisions. Alternatively, in other institutions only the CEO routinely interacts with the board, although other staff may occasionally be asked to present special reports.

Whatever the institution's method for access to and interaction with the board, it is important that the PR manager provide expert counsel to the board on issues and decisions that will have public impact, just as staff or outside attorneys are consulted when legal issues arise. The ideal situation is for the PR manager to interact routinely with the board on a variety of issues and to involve the board in the review of the institution's PR plans. Not only does this give the PR manager the benefit of the board members' input, it also helps engender their support of the PR function. If the usual pattern, however, is for the CEO to handle all board interactions, then it is up to him or her to make sure that the PR manager is involved when major issues or decisions are being considered.

If the PR manager is not routinely attending meetings of or making presentations to the board, one way of creating this important interaction is by working with a board of trustees PR committee. This committee can include board members as well as community PR and media representatives and should function in a consulting and advisory mode. (Avoid giving this kind of advisory committee final approval over PR or marketing plans by making it clear that only their expert advice and opinions are sought.) Generally, the chair of a committee like this is a board member who keeps the board apprised of PR activities and achievements and who may also seek counsel from the PR manager, on behalf of the board, when public impact issues and decisions are being considered. Although this isn't the ideal relationship, it is functional, and in many institutions is preferred by the board.

One very important and sensitive issue about which the PR manager may have to advise the board is the issue of conflict of interest. If there are board members who have financial interests in the organization, as suppliers or vendors, for instance, the PR manager needs to inform the board (through the CEO, if necessary) of the public opinion problems this may cause. It is assumed that legal counsel will also be addressing the legal ramifications; however, board members also need to be educated on the fact that health care organizations operate very much in the public eye, and that even if legal complications can be avoided, negative media and public reaction to conflict-of-interest situations can be equally damaging to the organization.

Counseling the Medical Staff

The role of providing PR counsel to members of a hospital's medical staff is nonexistent at some hospitals and a major responsibility at others. This role can include any or all of the following examples:

- Counseling a physician who is involved in a malpractice case and wants to know how to handle media inquiries
- Working with the chief of staff to develop programs to communicate with members of the medical staff
- Advising a new physician on how to communicate effectively with patients and office staff
- Talking with a physician about negative comments about him that have been included in patient surveys
- Justifying and engaging physician support for an advertising or marketing program

Most health care PR managers work in institutions where the physicians are independent practitioners, rather than being employed by the institution, and many of these physicians have skeptical or even negative impressions of public relations. Because the institutions are dependent on the support of these physicians in terms of admissions and referrals, it is essential that mutually positive relationships be established and maintained. The PR manager must therefore be very careful in interacting with physicians, in part because:

- Physicians are an integral part of any health care organization's relationships with its internal and external publics.
- Physicians have a tremendous impact on employee morale, especially the morale of nurses.
- In the minds of most consumers, as evidenced by comments on patient surveys, the physician and the institution are one entity.
- Physicians are ideal sources for media interviews and health education presentations.

Thus, it is important that the PR manager develop effective working relationships with the physicians who are primary admitters to the institution and with the elected and informal leadership of the medical staff. Physicians themselves offer some suggestions on how to effectively establish these relationships, and although physicians have very divergent opinions on public relations and marketing, these suggestions can serve as guidelines for the PR manager:

- *Be honest and accurate in all statements about the hospital and its programs.* Physicians are very sensitive to what they perceive to be "hype," and incorrect claims about an institution's being the first, only, or best in any given area can cause embarrassment to the physicians involved. For instance, in one Midwestern city, a TV news story about a physician being the first to perform a new type of surgery caused the physician to be questioned by the local medical society.
- *Be available and accessible to physicians — and that means on their turf and according to their schedules.* In many health care organizations, that means early morning meetings (before the 7 a.m. surgical cases begin), and it almost always means that the PR manager goes to where the physician is, rather than asking the physician to come to the PR office. That may mean conducting interviews standing in a corridor outside a surgical suite, or going to the physician's private practice office.
- *Respect the physician's point of view.* "I'm tired of hospital administrators telling me they know best," said one physician. "I'm tired of planners and marketers and reimbursement specialists telling me how to run my practice and what kind of patients should be admitted. I'm the one with M.D. after my name."
- *Use effective research to find out what physicians really want and need.* Chapter 7 describes the various research methods that can be used with the physician audience, and it is important that each health care organization survey its own medical staff rather than relying on hearsay or using national trend data. A medical staff, like any audience, has outspoken members at both ends of the spectrum of opinion on key issues. Responding only to those vocal minorities can cause a backlash from the rest of the medical staff. And assuming that physician concerns identified by national research are necessarily going to be similar to the concerns of a specific institution's medical staff can be a mistake.
- *Spend enough time with physicians to understand their values and motivation.* "Today, doctors are stereotyped as being obsessed with prestige and money," said one physician. "In fact, most of my colleagues are primarily concerned about having enough autonomy to take care of our patients the way we think is correct. When we complain about insurers or Medicare, it's because they're trying to take over patient care decisions that should be our decisions." Given most physicians' busy schedules, finding time with them can be difficult.

The senior PR manager should attend all medical staff functions that the institution's staff are invited to, and get around and talk to the physicians. "I found that the social hour before quarterly medical staff meetings was the greatest time to 'just talk' with our doctors," said one PR veteran. Setting up informal breakfast or lunch meetings with physicians is also helpful, as is another technique suggested by a physician relations director. "I call it 'being where they are,'" she said. "Every other week or so, I spend a morning in the medical staff lounge, where the doctors log in on the computer and leave their coats, and another morning in the coffee room in surgery. It's amazing how many things the doctors stop to talk to me about — things they probably wouldn't have taken the time to make a special call about, but things that are important."

- *Learn how to take criticism in stride, even if it's clearly unwarranted.* "There are doctors who tend to shout first and ask questions later," said one hospital administrator. "The PR people have to take heat about a media story that they had no control over or about a competing hospital's claims in an ad." In situations like this, the PR manager can explain and present the facts, but the physician may still be angry or blame the PR staff. Fortunately, that type of quick-to-anger physician is usually just as quick to cool off.

These suggestions can help the PR manager maintain what are clearly very important relationships with physicians. The PR manager who allows himself or herself to get caught up in confrontation situations with a physician — even when the PR staff is doing what it believes is right — can jeopardize his or her effectiveness with the CEO and with other physicians. Maintaining credibility and open lines of communication with physicians is integral to the PR manager's ability to fulfill the counseling role.

☐ Counseling: An Art and a Skill

"You can be the best practitioner in the world, but you fail if you don't know how to counsel," decreed PR expert Pat Jackson.[6]

Although the comparisons between legal counsel and PR counsel are common, in fact there are some major differences. First, the legal counselor has facts — laws, court cases, legal precedents — to rely on when advising a client. Public relations counselors can use audience research results and stakeholder analysis (see chapter 8) to bolster their contentions, but many times the experienced PR manager also relies on intuitive analyses and personal reactions to predict an audience's response to a health care organization's decision.

Second, the legal counselor can point to specific ramifications of a client's actions, in terms of civil liability or criminal charges, which are concepts that the client can clearly translate into "this is what could happen to me or my company." The PR counselor's warnings about negative public opinion, in contrast, sound more ephemeral, less concrete, and less critical to the company's survival. If the corporate counsel says "This decision could cause lawsuits," or the corporate finance officer notes that a proposed project carries tremendous financial risk, those predictions are given serious consideration by the CEO.

The challenge for PR professionals in all fields is to elicit the same level of serious consideration about the public opinion impact of institutional decisions. In the health care industry, fortunately, the majority of CEOs have come to understand the value of positive public opinion, and the consequences of negative public opinion.

In the short term, public opinion has an impact on admissions ("I don't want to go to that hospital," the patient tells the physician); on physician referrals ("We don't refer to that hospital," says a physician); on employee morale, on media coverage and scrutiny, and on donations. In the longer term, as explained by Robert J. Blendon, chairman of the Department of Health Policy and Management for Harvard University's School of Public Health, "shifts in public opinion lead to changes in political policy. Public confidence in health care has a direct impact on how tough the government gets with hospitals."[7]

One hospital CEO had this point brought home with stunning clarity when he met with a senior aide to his state's U.S. senator. "We laid out all the facts about how Medicare cuts were hurting hospitals, and the aide admitted that our data was unequivocal and that obviously hospitals were being hurt. But then she said she didn't think Congress would do anything to help the hospitals, 'because frankly, the public doesn't really care. We don't get any letters from our constituents praising hospitals, and when we talk with them, they complain about costs and poor service. And if the public doesn't care, sir, then you won't see any changes on Capitol Hill.'"

That CEO and most of his peers are now aware of the need for programs to build positive public opinion, although that need has to compete for rapidly shrinking revenues of health care organizations. That shrinking funding, combined with the less immediate and less tangible impact of negative public opinion, means that the PR manager must be credible, trustworthy, and persuasive in counseling management on the PR impact of organizational operations and decisions.

The *science* of counseling involves the PR manager in:

- Doing careful research, so that the audience's current concerns and opinions can be explained to decision makers

- Knowing, through stakeholder relations (see chapter 3), what the "hot button" issues are for the health care organization's key publics
- Continually scanning the external and internal environments for any signs of problems that could affect the organization

The *art* of counseling means that the PR manager must do the following:

- *Be trusted by the decision makers.* This trust results in part from perceived expertise (the belief that the PR manager is competent and knowledgeable because of training and experience) and in part from the PR manager's track record within the institution of having given accurate advice.
- *Know when and how to present advice.* This means learning whether the CEO wants sensitive issues initially discussed in private, or presented to the management group for input. It also requires that the PR manager learn the best method to present information to the CEO — does the CEO prefer to read a report and then discuss it, or does he or she want a verbal summary and then answers to his or her questions?
- *Understand the CEO's decision-making process and time frame, and work within it.* Pushing for a quick decision when the CEO prefers to take a slower, more deliberative pace can cause relationship problems with the CEO. On the other hand, some CEOs aren't interested in being backgrounded or discussing future issues and may resent the demands on their time. Similarly, management groups have their own "group style," and the PR manager needs to know how to work within that style.
- *Know when to back off.* There will always be institutional decisions or actions that the PR manager may not agree with, but the wise team member can tell when the consensus is building and his or her counsel is not going to change the decision. At that point, once the counsel has been offered and reiterated, the wise course may be to back off and do whatever possible to help implement the decision so it does not cause a negative public reaction.
- *Never, ever say "I told you so" when a predicted negative public reaction occurs.* If the PR manager effectively communicated his or her position during discussions that preceded the decision or action, the CEO and management team members will remember the advice all too well. An "I told you so" may result in defensiveness or anger from group members, whereas restraint — and leadership in developing plans to respond to the negative reaction — will earn positive regard from peers and superiors.

29

Providing PR counsel is never an easy task. Often the PR manager is bringing what the management team may see as "bad news," or is asking unwelcome questions that may derail a popular plan. By marshalling the facts and information needed and combining them with the effective interpersonal and group interaction skills outlined above, the PR manager can ensure that his or her professional counsel will be fully considered (and, it is hoped, appreciated) by the CEO and the management group.

☐ Communicating: Linking the Institution to Its Publics

The second major role of public relations in the health care organization is communicating, both from the organization to its publics and from the publics to the organization. Often this communications function is seen as the primary role of public relations, rather than the senior management counseling role. Although the importance of communications cannot be downplayed, it is essential that the PR manager not be seen only as a communicator. As one PR veteran explained, "If you're seen only as a communicator, they'll call you once the decision is made and tell you to explain it, rather than having you participate in the decision."

A thorough understanding of multistep communications process models (Rogers' source–message–channel–receiver–effect model, for example) is very helpful for the PR manager. Cutlip, Center, and Broom's *Effective Public Relations* provides an excellent and detailed discussion of the communications process.[8]

One-way communication—from the organization to its publics—has been a traditional role for the health care PR staff. In fact, that outward communication—magazines, newsletters, news releases, brochures, print and TV ads, direct mail, and more—was for years the sole focus of health care PR efforts. When ASHCMPR was founded, for example, the announcement noted, "We want the public to better understand hospitals and their services." This institutional orientation—"we want"—was the primary force behind PR activities in hospitals, and many other organizations, well into the 1970s.

Nowadays PR managers understand that listening to the organization's publics and representing the publics' concerns to management are equally as important, perhaps even more important, as sending out a continuous stream of messages.

Listening: The First Step in Two-Way Communication

Seeking, receiving, and responding to input and feedback from the health care organization's publics is an ongoing, multiphase process that is a primary responsibility of the PR staff. This process is described in detail in chapter 8 and is summarized here to demonstrate its role in the total communications program.

The incoming/receiving communications process begins with identification of all of the organization's publics—from the obvious, like employees and patients, to the occasional special interest groups, such as abortion activists, who infrequently interact with the organization. Once the publics have been identified, the PR manager directs a program of getting to know these audiences using a variety of research and interactive methods, including surveys and focus groups, informal meetings, and information flowing from specifically assigned liaisons. The publics' formal and informal leaders are identified, issues of concern are noted, and a process is established to continually monitor those issues.

For this inward communications process to be effective and useful, it must be comprehensive and continual. Doing a general community attitude survey, for instance, establishes baseline data about how the community as a whole feels about the institution at that particular time, but that is only a very preliminary step. Individual subgroups within that broad public must be identified, and because the subgroups' concerns and needs are evolving, they must be monitored on an ongoing basis. Another reason for continual monitoring is because the institution is continually active—making changes, announcing plans, creating programs and services—and all of this activity has an impact on multiple publics. These publics will then react in one way or another to the institution's activity, and those reactions should be anticipated, assessed, and responded to, if needed.

As noted in chapter 8, this process of building relationships and monitoring the opinions of the health care organization's publics is a major undertaking and one that can easily be overlooked, put off, or simply buried in the day-to-day activities of the PR department. However, this investment of time and energy in "preventive PR," which is designed to avoid negative backlash or damage to previously positive public relationships, is far preferable to the time and energy required to cope with a public opinion crisis. Once this audience monitoring process is in place, the PR manager can develop programs to communicate outward, from the institution to the publics.

Understanding the New Publics

Before considering communications methods and techniques, which are covered in detail in chapters 8 through 16, the PR manager should be aware of the characteristics of today's "new publics," which differ markedly from those of even a decade ago.

Cynthia Pharr, A.P.R., president and CEO of Tracy-Locke/Pharr Public Relations in Dallas, and past chairman of the Public Relations Society of America's Counselors Academy, describes the "good old days of mass marketing, . . . a time when a well-placed message on network television reached virtually every home in America, and when metropolitan newspapers were reliable marketing tools." Now, notes Pharr, "the good old days are gone forever," with the splintering of large, homogenous publics into dozens of distinct, smaller audiences.[9] This is a message of critical importance to PR professionals because it affects all of the communications methods and techniques involved in public relations.

In the health care setting, specific audiences that in the past were sent one message via one channel must now be analyzed to identify subgroups and their preferred messages and methods. The medical staff, for instance, is no longer a group of several hundred physicians who share common concerns and can be addressed via a single quarterly newsletter. Today's medical staff could be segmented in the following ways:

- *By degree of involvement with the institution:* major admitter, moderate admitter, infrequent admitter, nonadmitter. The major admitters are going to be far more concerned about nursing care and institutional operations than those physicians who never admit a patient. Conversely, the physician who rarely admits isn't going to be interested in learning the details about changes in medical records.
- *By attitudes about the institution:* supportive, neutral, antagonistic. The supportive physicians are more likely to attend a physician briefing about a new program, whereas the antagonistic staff members may become irritated by simply receiving the invitation to the briefing ("another PR ploy").
- *By demographics:* especially age and/or year of graduation from medical school. Recent medical school graduates are used to the "new routine" of medical practice: precertification, insurance company authorizations, peer review, and so on. When there's a change in charting requirements to satisfy Medicare or Medicaid, the younger physicians simply want to know what they're expected to do. Older physicians, who resent these "intrusions" in their autonomy, need to be communicated with more carefully, with explanations of why the changes are being made, how their compliance will help the institution receive more timely payments, and so on. Because of their attitudes, they need to know not only what, but "why should I."
- *By specialty:* family practice/obstetrics/pediatrics, medical specialties, surgical specialties. Research has shown that physicians in these three categories have very different characteristics, attitudes, and styles. Using the same communications channel with all three audiences would produce very different results.

Segmenting broad publics into smaller, more discrete audiences allows the PR manager to tailor a message and select a communications channel that works most effectively with each group. Using the medical staff model outlined above, for instance, the PR manager who is asked to communicate a major change in medical records charting might develop the following plan:

- For heavy and moderate admitters, use the basic channel of a detailed written communication, because they will be grappling with the new procedures every day and must understand exactly how they work.
- For older physicians, accompany the written communication with a personal letter from the CEO to provide a rationale and explain why this is so important to the institution.
- For physicians who tend to be antagonistic, follow up with a personal visit from a medical records staff member or PR staff member to help defuse any irritation.
- For infrequent or nonadmitters, refer to the change in their own newsletter (which is less detailed and more promotional than the heavy/moderate admitters' newsletter), and provide a phone number to call for more information. Don't bore them with details they don't need—focus their attention on persuasive messages that may lead them to admit more patients.

This process of audience segmentation is a necessity for the contemporary PR manager, especially in an institution like a hospital, which has relationships with so many diverse publics. Even an audience that was once perceived as totally homogenous—like volunteers—today is merely an identifying name for a collection of smaller groups of people with multiple and differing concerns and goals. Volunteers today can generally be segmented into a number of basic subaudiences: women/homemakers, women/employed full-time, women/physicians' spouses, men/retirees, men/employed full-time, adults/career changers or career experience, teens/career experience, teens/community service, teens/forced by their parents. The individuals in each of these subgroups became volunteers for very different reasons and have very different motivations. An appeal to action that works with one group will be ignored by another. Therefore, the effective PR program will target messages to each audience's concerns and will use channels that research has shown work best for each group.

If segmentation is effective in working with specifically identified publics like physicians, volunteers, and employees, it is even more effective in communicating with what is traditionally the most difficult audience: "the general public." The new microaudience PR approach calls for initial identification of two subgroups within the general public: those who care about the organization and its activities and those who are affected by the organization and its activities. People who fit into one or both of these categories are often called "stakeholders"– persons (who usually are in or can be categorized into smaller groups) who perceive that they have a stake in the institution. Once identified, these stakeholder groups can be monitored and analyzed in terms of their values, interests, and concerns.

Rather than appeal to a mass audience with broad-based messages that are so broad that they often end up appealing to no one, the PR program can send messages that touch on these groups' specific concerns, using channels that have been identified as effective for each stakeholder group. Mass messages to mass audiences (nonstakeholders) can then be abandoned, because there is little need for a health care organization to communicate with audiences who do not care about and/or will not be affected by the organization.

In addition to being aware of the need to divide audiences into smaller segments and identify stakeholders who are part of mass audiences, the successful PR manager in the coming decade will be aware that the values of individuals and groups are in a continual, slow process of evolution. Thus, the fact that members of a stakeholder group once held a specific value does not mean that this will continue in the future. Health care employees, for instance, have far different expectations of how they will be treated by a health care organization today than they did 10 years ago because their values have evolved from a primary concern with salary and job security to a primary concern with job satisfaction.

Writing in *The Futurist*, Joseph Plummer, managing director of PaineWebber/Young & Rubicam Ventures, identified a number of changing values that are emerging in the late 1980s (shown in table 2-1). The shift, Plummer points out, is from outer-directed values to more inner direction.[10]

Being aware of the values held by members of an audience or a stakeholder group is essential in terms of crafting a message to appeal to that group. When communicating to multiple publics about the creation of a freestanding outpatient surgery center, for instance, the PR manager would focus a message for a payer (business and insurer audience) on how outpatient surgery contains costs and is more efficient. An audience of parents would be offended by this bottom-line appeal, but would respond to knowing that the new surgery center setup allows parents to be with their children immediately before and after surgery.

Both values-orientation and audience-segmentation techniques are based on a key principle of contemporary public relations: effective communications programs focus on the needs and concerns of the

Table 2-1. Changing American Values

Traditional	New
Self-denial	Self-fulfillment
Higher standard of living	Better quality of life
Traditional sex roles	Blurring of sex roles
Accepted definition of success	Success is individualized
Traditional family life	Alternative families
Faith in industry, institutions	Self-reliance
Live to work	Work to live
Hero worship	Love of ideas
Expansionism	Pluralism
Patriotism	Less nationalism
Unparalleled growth	Growing sense of limits
Industrial growth	Information/service growth
Receptivity to technology	Technology orientation

Source: *The Futurist*, Jan.–Feb. 1989, pp. 8–13. Used with permission.

audience and link those concerns with the goals of the organization. Thus, modern health care public relations has evolved from the "we want the public to understand" approach of the 1960s, to a "this is how our institution is acting in concert with your needs" approach in the 1990s.

Outward-Bound Communications: Sending the Message

Once the audiences have been identified, segmented, and defined, and their values, needs, concerns, and expectations of the institution are understood by the institution's management, the PR manager can begin to develop communications programs that will send specific messages to these audiences.

More than half of this book is devoted to discussing the communications methods that are available to health care PR managers, including numerous techniques in community relations, media relations, publications, audiovisual communications, advertising and marketing communications, and so on. Indeed, one of the key challenges in developing communications campaigns today is selecting the right methods from such a wide array of options. Health care communications efforts today range from high-budget, mass-appeal advertising campaigns, complete with billboards and TV spots promoting a new women's center, to "quiet" little campaigns involving meetings of parents in someone's living room to listen to a speaker on teen drug use.

An overview of successful contemporary communications campaigns identifies a number of common characteristics:

1. *The campaign has clearly stated, measurable objectives.* For example, increase admissions to the pediatrics unit by 10 percent; generate 800 prospective nursing school applicants resulting in the acceptance of 50 students for admission; increase preference for hospital's heart services by 25 percent among consumers over age 65. Having clear objectives provides a target against which the campaign can be measured and evaluated and can help PR managers demonstrate the bottom-line impact of communications programs.

2. *The audience is clearly identified.* When a department head tells the PR manager that he or she wants to tell "everybody" about a new service, the manager helps the department head identify those consumers who are most likely to be interested in the service and crafts a message that will appeal to that audience's interests. A mobile mammography unit, for instance, would obviously appeal to women, but by using more audience research, the PR manager could discover that better-educated, younger working women are the most likely users of such a service. Then a message or messages appealing to those women's concerns would be developed. In this instance, several separate messages would be crafted:

   - For the college-educated professional woman, a message noting that mammography is a wise choice, using statistics on breast cancer recovery rates, and positioning mammography as a wise investment
   - For younger women, a high-tech, space-age gimmicky type of approach, positioning mammography as an "in" thing to do
   - For the blue-collar working mother, a convenience approach, stressing speed and the fact that the van comes to the work site, and positioning mammography as something important for mothers to do

3. *The campaign is multifaceted, using a number of methods and media, rather than relying on one single approach.* In today's very cluttered communications environment, a single method, such as direct-mail approach only, or a single exposure, like a one-time newspaper ad, is unlikely even to be noticed. Consumers are literally being bombarded with information, messages, and persuasive appeals. To get the consumer's attention, let alone make an impression or elicit a response, the PR program must send the message multiple times, in a variety of media.

4. *The campaign often involves at least one "personal" PR method to reinforce mass or impersonal media messages.* Whether it's a speaker at a PTA meeting or a professional women's group tour of a mammography unit, a business leader breakfast briefing or an open house, successful campaigns generally involve small audience, personal approaches in addition to or in place of the mass media.

5. *The campaign is long term, not short term.* Today's communicators understand that changing behavior (the bottom-line result) means first creating awareness (more difficult with crowded communications channels) and then creating preference, even more difficult with competing products and organizations fighting for their share of the consumer's mind and heart. This three-step process—awareness, preference, behavior—takes time, with the same message being sent consistently over months and years. The one-shot, generate-a-lot-of-calls campaign can produce a blip of immediate results, but consumers will revert to their habitual behavior. Actually changing behavior—whether it's hospital utilization, donations, or voting habits—takes a year or more.

6. *The campaign has a distinctive creative approach.* Health care PR efforts, like PR activities in many other industries, have tended in the past to fall into an "if it worked for hospital X" syndrome. Syndicated campaigns abounded, featuring a generic "insert your institution's name here" message. The "assets ad," which featured a few visuals and a litany of the hospital's selling points, were common. Today health care PR managers are looking for approaches that are audience-centered, focused on a single selling point, and relatively different from other approaches being used in their market.

7. *Individual purpose campaigns—to promote a service, recruit physicians, encourage donations, and so on—are related to and supported by an overall institutional image campaign that extends over a number of years and establishes the institution's differentiated position vis-à-vis the competing institutions.* Except for the few institutions that have already established clearly differentiated positions that are well known by the public (Mayo Clinic, Johns Hopkins), health care organizations need to develop and communicate a positioning message that creates an image in the public's mind.

Consumer research has shown that a poor image of the institution will often prevent a consumer from believing or responding to a specific communications campaign. Conversely, a positive image leads to a halo effect, with consumers ascribing positive attributes to a health care organization even in the absence of any information about that specific attribute. A positive image will lead to purchase behavior, whereas a negative image will deter that behavior, even if the consumer responds to the specific behavioral message.

Although the term *image communications* may convey the impression of some vague, touchy-feely messages, in fact, successful image campaigns send very clear messages to the institution's publics about what the organization is good at and what it stands for. Image positioning campaigns play a key part in developing reputation, along with actual customer experience and word-of-mouth endorsements. And in addition to enhancing the institution's single-purpose campaigns, a solid image and reputation will help the institution survive a crisis or negative event with the goodwill of its publics intact.

Using the principles outlined above, the PR manager can utilize the communications methods outlined in chapters 8 through 16 to develop effective, focused communications campaigns aimed at the institution's key audiences. As noted, these campaigns are one half of a two-way communications process that begins and ends with listening to the audiences, the individuals and groups that believe they have a stake in the institution and its activities. The goals of this communications process are to build relationships, engender and maintain public support, and minimize negative public reaction to the health care organization's decisions.

□ Summary

Since the inception of health care PR programs, the primary focus has been on the communications responsibilities, and that function is still an important role for the health care PR manager. However, as health care organizations grapple with the challenges facing them in the coming decades, the role of the PR manager must evolve into one that focuses on developing relationships with the health care organization's audiences to gain their support or counter their opposition.

In addition, there will be an increasing emphasis on the PR manager's counseling and analytical skills in terms of advising the health care organization's management team as it makes decisions about the organization's strategies and plans. To effectively fulfill this counseling/advisory role, the PR manager must be an integral part of the senior management team.

References

1. *pr reporter* 32(39):4, Sept. 25, 1989.
2. Adams, G. Communications as an ethical imperative. *Michigan Hospitals* 24(12):34, Dec. 1988.
3. Larkin, H. CEOs confront service cuts. *Hospitals* 63(19):38, Oct. 5, 1989.
4. PR opportunities of the future. *pr reporter* 32(38):2, Sept. 18, 1989.
5. Peters, R., and Lapierre, R. Conversations with four public relations gurus. Tips and tactics (supplement to *pr reporter* 32(4):2, Jan. 23, 1989).
6. Conversations with four public relations experts.
7. Blendon, R. J. When the public speaks, hospitals should listen. *AHA News* 25(35):8, Aug. 28, 1989.

8. Cutlip, S., Center, A. H., and Broom, G. M. *Effective Public Relations.* 6th ed. Englewood Cliffs, NJ: Prentice-Hall, 1985, p. 122.
9. Pharr, C. Capitalizing on splintering markets. *Public Relations Journal* 46(1):18, Jan. 1990.
10. Plummer, J. Changing values. *The Futurist*, Jan.–Feb. 1989, pp. 8–13. [Quoted in *Purview* (supplement to *pr reporter* 32(5):1, Jan. 30, 1989).]

Suggested Readings

Bernays, E. L. Defending public relations. *Public Relations Quarterly,* Spring 1978.

Brody, E. W. Changing roles and requirements of public relations. *Public Relations Review,* Winter 1985.

Chase, H. W. Public relations as a management function. *Public Relations Journal,* Mar. 1980.

Continuing PR embarrassments renew the mandate: practitioners' first responsibility is to monitor and be fully involved in daily operations — or else. *pr reporter,* July 24, 1989.

Jackson, P. The future of public relations and maybe the world. *pr reporter,* Jan. 4, 1982.

Lesly, P. Psychology and public relations counseling. *Public Relations Review,* Fall 1979.

Ristino, R. J. Public relations as a senior management function. *The ASHMPR Resource Collection.* Chicago: American Society for Health Care Marketing and Public Relations, 1989.

Integrating the Public Relations Function within the Institution

The public relations function does not exist independent of other staff and operating functions within any organization. There are staff positions that may have some responsibility overlap with public relations (human resources, planning, marketing, and development, for instance). All staff and operating managers are also part of the internal communications process and control decisions and actions that can have an impact on the organization's external publics.

Because of this functional overlap, defining the precise role of public relations in the context of other administrative functions is a challenge that exists in all industries. The areas of overlap must be identified and managed so that all managers are working together toward a common goal of institutional advancement.

This chapter discusses the PR role in relation to operating departments, employee relations, medical staff relations, development, planning, and marketing, with particular emphasis on the relationships between marketing and public relations. Because the administrative structures of health care organizations are so varied, it is impossible to cover every conceivable organizational chart. In this chapter, the discussion of the relationships among public relations and the other functions assumes that public relations, human resources, marketing, development, planning, and the operating departments are all separate functions reporting independently to a COO or CEO.

□ Public Relations and Operations

Public relations interacts with operating departments in two ways: meeting the departments' communications needs and monitoring the departments' decisions and actions in terms of their impact on stakeholders and the general public.

Serving the Operating Departments' Communications Needs

The PR manager needs to think of peers who manage operating functions as very special "clients" and should structure PR operations to meet the needs of these clients (see chapter 5 for details on structuring the PR function). A successful client relationship can result in positive outcomes for both the institution and the PR manager. By working with operating managers to develop effective internal and external communications programs for various services and products, the PR manager can ensure that the organization's total institutional communications program is coordinated and cohesive. In addition, by working with operating managers to meet their departmental communications needs, the PR manager builds strong working relationships with those operating managers, relationships that can help the PR manager be more effective on the job.

Some departments will need to communicate with internal audiences (employees, physicians), whereas others will need assistance in promoting their services to external audiences. Whatever the audience, the basic process for working with operating managers to meet their departmental needs is similar.

1. *The PR manager and the operating department head should analyze the department's communications needs and develop a communications plan.* (See chapter 6.) That plan should include a summary of what projects need to be completed, a timetable, a budget, and a clear delineation of who is responsible for each step of the plan. For example, if a patient information brochure is to be produced, the plan should note whether the operating department head or staff are responsible for gathering information and facts to be included, or whether that is to be done by the PR staff. If the department is one that markets its services to external audiences, staff members from the marketing department should also be involved in developing the plan.
2. *The PR manager should make sure the operating manager knows whom to go to for communications and PR services.* If the PR department is organized on a functional basis, with one staffer handling media relations, another handling publications, and so on, the PR department head needs to ensure that these PR staff members understand the operating department's total communications plan and coordinate their efforts to achieve consistency. If the PR department is organized as an in-house agency (see chapter 5), with staff members assigned as account executives for specific departments, the PR manager needs to ensure that the account executive is working effectively with the department head to implement the plan.

3. *The PR manager should establish a climate in which department managers feel comfortable consulting with the PR staff on all of their communications needs.* This is accomplished in two ways: telling and doing. That public relations exists to help meet departmental needs should be stated and restated by the PR manager. The PR manager should demonstrate that commitment by being accessible for consultation, by maintaining confidentiality (especially concerning employee matters), and by delivering the needed services on time and on budget.

4. *When all of the departmental needs add up to more than the existing PR staff can handle, the PR manager needs to negotiate with department managers to prioritize the projects, eliminate some (if necessary), or bring in outside help if funds are available.* This negotiation phase needs to happen at the beginning of the year or planning cycle so that department managers know what they can expect. Trying to meet everyone's needs by juggling an unrealistic work load can result in missed deadlines or budget overruns—which does not build positive relationships with operating managers.

Careful planning and attention to the needs of operating departments provides a sound foundation for the other facet of the PR manager's relationship with the operating managers: monitoring the impact of the departments' operations and plans on stakeholders.

Evaluating the Impact of Operations on Stakeholders

In chapters 2 and 8, the role of public relations is discussed in terms of communicating stakeholder needs when operating decisions are made. In addition, as noted in chapter 2, the PR professional needs to lead the efforts to proactively examine all facets of organizational operations. The PR manager needs to use all of the counseling skills described in chapter 2 to make sure that this process is a positive one and that operating managers don't feel that they are being critiqued.

Operating administrators believe that their main role is to deliver a service or perform a function cost-efficiently and cost-effectively. Compared with the PR manager, who must be concerned about all stakeholder groups, the focus of operating managers is far narrower— generally limited to their employees, their customers, and their budget. When the PR director, representing stakeholder concerns, points out potentially negative reactions, the response from the operating manager can range from "Thanks" to "Who asked you?"

This delicate situation is also faced by other staff managers. Human resource managers have to provide input to operating managers about their employee relations skills and problems. Finance managers have to monitor and critique operating managers' budgets and spending. At the same time, these staff managers have to provide support services to the operating managers.

This dual support/critique role is why persons in staff management functions need to maintain strong working relationships and credibility with the line managers and administrators. Because they are in a staff—not line—position, PR managers, even at the senior vice-president level, cannot compel operating managers to make decisions based on public impact. Instead, they must use counseling and persuasive skills and build effective working relationships with the operating managers.

The "how-tos" of developing those peer relationships are discussed in more detail in chapter 2 and the rationale to encourage line managers to consider stakeholder concerns is covered in chapter 8. The following advice can also be helpful:

- *Be supportive of and helpful to the line managers and administrators as they try to achieve their objectives.* This is probably the single best piece of advice because in the eyes of the line administrator, this support establishes the PR professional's credibility, commitment to the organization (versus commitment to personal gain or to external groups at the expense of the organization), and true value to the line administrator. This type of relationship then allows the PR director to influence, trade favors with, and receive support from the operating staff.
- *Whenever possible, deal one-on-one with the appropriate operating manager, in private.* For example, if the PR manager is receiving feedback from stakeholders about dirty or messy conditions in waiting rooms, this information should be passed along promptly, in person, directly to the facilities or housekeeping manager. Sending a memo means the information is known to secretaries and other employees who might see it. Sharing the information in a meeting can embarrass the other manager or make what should be a normal process of identifying problems to be solved seem like a confrontation.
- *Don't go over the manager's head unless there's no other alternative.* Because of the very nature of the PR function, the PR manager has access to a great deal of information, both positive and negative. This fact alone can make other managers somewhat nervous. When the PR manager has information about problems within a specific department or has concerns about the impact of a department's actions on a stakeholder group, going up the chain of command can result in a hardening of positions rather than solve the problems. A department manager who feels threatened may become defensive and

refuse to consider making changes for fear of appearing to have been wrong. The PR manager should work with the operating department manager unless or until it appears that the situation cannot be resolved and that very negative stakeholder reactions will ensue. Then the situation must be communicated to the operating manager's superior.

☐ Public Relations and Employee Relations

There are few stakeholder groups more important to the success of a health care organization than employees. "The employee public is number one everywhere . . . and health care is plagued by people problems," said *pr reporter.*[1] Employees are so important, in fact, that there are two administrative functions with overlapping responsibility for communicating with this important group: the human resources staff and the PR staff. Human resources has an obviously direct responsibility; public relations has a communications responsibility as part of its charge to maintain effective stakeholder relations. Developing an effective employee relations program is a joint effort between human resources and public relations. Without careful attention to cooperation, "a looming PR–HR fight could be to the 1990s what the marketing–PR war was in the 1980s," said counselor Stacey Smith at the 1989 national conference of the Public Relations Society of America.[2] (See chapter 15 for a complete discussion of employee communications.)

In most health care organizations, the human relations staff has the responsibility for staying in touch with employee concerns, needs, and issues, and it must be integrally involved in shaping the content of the messages given to employees. The PR staff, through its stakeholder relations responsibilities, also is responsible for monitoring employee concerns through different (yet complementary) channels, and these insights should be integrated into the message strategy. Ideally, the message strategy is developed jointly by the PR and human resources staffs.

Once the message content is determined, public relations can recommend the most appropriate communications methods to use and then seek human resources consensus. The PR staff members, because of their expert communications skills, are responsible for actually producing the communications vehicles — the newsletters, the magazines, the slide shows, the fliers, and so on.

In addition, when PR staff members, in their normal interaction with health care employees, learn about emerging or worsening employee concerns, they need to share this information immediately with their human resources staff peers and offer to help formulate plans to address the problem.

Employees are such a critical public for the health care organization that effective two-way communications are essential. That effective communication process can only be achieved when public relations and human resources work very closely together. This joint working relationship generally evolves naturally, with the human resources manager approaching the PR manager for involvement and input; however, if this has not or is not happening, the PR manager should take the initiative to offer his or her services to the human resources staff, by offering support and assistance similar to that offered to operating department managers.

☐ Public Relations and Medical Staff Relations

The relationship between the PR manager and the manager responsible for medical staff relations is very similar to that between the PR manager and the human resources manager. Message content should be a shared responsibility. Decisions about communications channels and vehicles should also be shared (perhaps more so than with public relations and human resources), because the medical staff relations professionals usually have some accurate insights into what channels are most effective with physicians and their office staff. Once those decisions are made, PR can implement the program—keeping the medical staff relations personnel very much involved in the process so they feel a strong sense of ownership in the final product.

It's important to note that physician relations is one of the emerging "stars" or growth areas in hospital management, and the PR professional who can work well with and support this area will enhance his or her standing within the organization. (Chapter 16 offers additional details about creating effective physician communications programs.)

☐ Planning, Marketing, Public Relations, and Development

Figure 3-1 shows a simple view of the relationships among these four functions. As illustrated in the figure, responsibilities in each of these functional areas bear a relationship to the responsibilities of the others and lead to a need for consistent communication. For example, planning bears primary responsibility for structuring the long-range plan, which in turn provides the context for product development in marketing, image development activities in public relations, and fund-raising targets for development. Although analytical and communications skills are important in all functional areas, planning and marketing share the primary

Figure 3-1. Relationships among Planning, Marketing, Public Relations, and Development

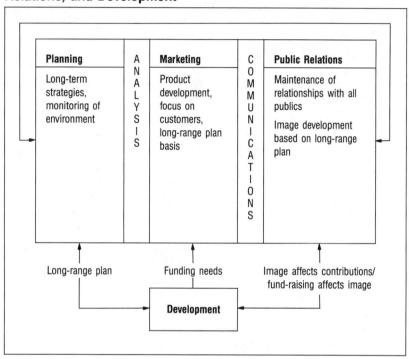

responsibility for the analysis that underlies the institution's long-range plan and specific health care services, and marketing and public relations share primary responsibility for communications efforts. The following sections describe the interrelationships in more detail.

Public Relations and Development

Public relations often serves as a support function for the development program, providing communications expertise and implementing specific projects for the fund-raisers. In addition, the development staff generally has a great interest in the efforts of the PR staff, because the public's image of the health care organization can have a major impact on donations and community support. The PR staff, conversely, is very concerned about the activities of the development staff because of the impact such activities can have on the institution's image. This should be a mutually supportive relationship, with the goal of maintaining a consistent approach in communicating with all of the institution's publics, including donors.

Public Relations and Planning

In most hospital settings, the planning staff is responsible for supervising the process of long-range planning. For that process to be effective, planners will want to involve all appropriate staff so that the plan is broad-based and reflects the needs and concerns of internal and external audiences.

As detailed in chapter 6, the integral involvement of public relations in the strategic planning process is essential for two reasons:

• If public relations has an effective stakeholder relations program in place (see chapter 8), the PR staff has access to information that's vital to the health care organization as long-term strategies are charted. The PR manager can identify the key concerns of stakeholder groups, so that those needs can be evaluated for inclusion in the plan.
• Public relations input on stakeholder responses to proposed strategies is critical while the management team considers all of the strategic options available to the organization.

Thus, when long-range planning sessions are held, the PR manager must be a key player so that the plans can accurately reflect the concerns of the external environment. Conversely, planners often have access to a wide range of information from stakeholder groups and can serve as liaisons to such groups as legislators, regulators, and community agencies. Planners can also help monitor stakeholders' concerns and share that information with the PR staff.

Along with marketing, public relations and planners are also involved in the analysis and research function. Ideally—and practically—the professionals involved in each of the three areas should coordinate their efforts so that research expenses aren't duplicated (and so that individual stakeholder groups aren't "overresearched").

Public Relations and Marketing

Because marketing is a relatively new health care management function, and because the same overlap between marketing and public relations exists in health care organizations as in every other industry, it is important to understand the relationship between the two functions.

Initially, it should be noted that the confusion that has resulted with the introduction of the marketing role in health care management is a normal response to change of any kind and mirrors similar confusion that has resulted when marketing was introduced in other industries (especially nonprofit industries). Health care organizations are going through the same type of assimilation process that has happened in other industries that have introduced new staff functions. When a hospital creates a formal training position, for instance, human resources and nursing education staff members can be confused about who's responsible for doing what, but the managers involved work together to sort out the confusion and develop a workable system. This same collaborative search for a workable system is taking place today with respect to marketing, public relations, and product line management.

There have been literally volumes of words written about the relationship between marketing and public relations in hospitals. The PR professional who wants to get an historical sense of the situation can do a literature search and come up with dozens of articles, but veteran PR consultant Nancy Hicks (Hill and Knowlton) sums it up as succinctly as anyone:[3]

> The battle is over who controls the communications function and whether the public relations officer reports to a marketing/planning director or to the CEO. Marketing directors view advertising *and by extension public relations* [emphasis added] as their rightful bailiwick. Public relations people want access to the CEO and wince at the thought of "planning types" editing their copy.

It's interesting to note that Hicks's comments underscore the existing confusion about the role and function of public relations, with many people defining it as an extension of advertising. In actuality, advertising is a technique or method, rather than a management function, and should not be used as a synonym for marketing or public relations. To sort out some of the confusion, it's helpful to look at the audiences and methods that are the domain of public relations and of marketing.

Audiences

Public relations is responsible for maintaining relationships with the health care organization's publics — employees, physicians, patients, legislators, payers, opinion leaders, activist groups, and so on. *Marketing* is responsible for developing and selling products and services to customers. This customer group can and does include a number of audiences — patients, physicians, and payers and bulk buyers.

Note the similarities. Both functions deal with publics. Note the differences. Marketing deals with one specific public — customers. Public relations also deals with customers but has the broader role of relating to all publics. In regard to the specific customer public, marketing is concerned with buying behavior (developing, placing, pricing, promoting, and selling products and services), whereas public relations' involvement centers on evaluating the customer group as a stakeholder public whose nonbuying behavior can have an impact on the health care organization's reputation.

Methods

Another overlap area occurs because the methods used by both disciplines are similar and, in some cases, duplicative. *Public relations methods* include research and analysis, media relations, publications (periodicals and special purpose), speakers' services, tours, special events, sponsorship of events, advertising, and stakeholder relations/ issues management. *Marketing methods* begin with market research and the four Ps (product, place, price, and promotion) and include direct sales. The list of promotional methods sounds remarkably like the PR methods list: special events, displays, direct mail, brochures, coupons, advertising, and so on.

The common ground is easily identifiable — both functions deal with customers (public relations views them as one of many publics; marketing views them as potential buyers), and both groups are extensively involved in communications. In addition, there is a mutuality of interest even in the areas where marketing and PR responsibilities differ. Public relations is not responsible for product development, pricing, and distribution, but can provide the marketing staff with valuable insights gleaned from their stakeholder relations programs. Marketing is not responsible for relations with many of the hospital's noncustomer publics, but can offer the PR staff expertise on research and analysis techniques that can be used with those publics.

The Impact of Public Relations on Customers and of Marketing on Publics

The institution's PR activities have a direct impact on the customers' image of the health care organization — and thus, their buying behavior — and marketing efforts are viewed by many noncustomer publics, thus having an impact on PR's stakeholder relations efforts.

Can negative public opinion really have an impact on customers and sales? Absolutely. Just as publics are aware of marketing efforts, so, too, are customers aware of PR efforts and PR problems.

- When the National Association for the Advancement of Colored People (NAACP) publicly attacks a hospital's hiring practices, it may make relations with black physicians and patients more difficult.

- When the local paper does an exposé on a hospital's nursing shortage, patients scheduled for surgery the next day may worry about the care they'll receive.
- When neighbors complain about hospital noise or hazardous wastes, environmentally conscious consumers form a negative opinion that may surface when their physician recommends a hospital stay.

Sophisticated marketers understand the impact of public relations on sales and value an effective PR program. And sophisticated PR professionals understand the impact that marketing activities can have on publics and their image of the institution.

Structuring the Marketing/Public Relations Relationship

There are a number of ways of placing public relations and marketing within the administrative structure. The most common seem to be: (1) merging them, with either a marketer or a PR manager in charge or (2) having separate departments with both managers reporting to the CEO, COO, or a vice-president. They may report to the same person or to different persons (such as public relations to the CEO, marketing to a planning vice-president). If the departments are separate, they can either function totally independently, or in an integrated way.

Obviously, when the issue is one of merging both functions, and either public relations being "under marketing," or marketing being "under public relations," some concerns are inevitable, just as there would be concerns if a hospital were going to have the human resources department report to finance, or medical staff relations report to the legal department. In a public relations–marketing merger, the PR professionals wonder why their discipline is seen as a subset of marketing (which it isn't), and wonder what marketing number-crunchers know about media and stakeholder relations. They're concerned that other noncustomer audiences will be ignored. If marketing is placed under public relations, marketers wonder how a PR vice-president can make decisions on pricing or set up an effective sales rep program. They're concerned that their customers—who are their universe—will get lost in the midst of "all those audiences."

Even in health care organizations in which the senior marketing officer and the senior PR officer are at equal levels, both reporting to the CEO and functioning independently, there is still the possibility of confusion over which function should control the communications process that's a part of both public relations and marketing. If both departments attempt to independently control "their" part of the communications process, with public relations handling institutional communications and marketing handling communications for specific products and services, the process can be duplicative and disfunctional, resulting in:

- Mixed messages — for example, with public relations positioning the health care organization as warm and caring, whereas marketing efforts send a high-tech message
- Hopelessly diffused messages, with each department using different looks and themes for the same products and services, some of which may be inconsistent with public relations' positioning strategy
- Marketing tactics that can upset stakeholder groups and create a negative public image for the institution (and result in people calling public relations to complain)
- Marketing issuing its own news releases ("well, the story's about a product"), leading the media to wonder who's in charge
- Public relations publicizing a new service in the hospital magazine, unaware that service start-up has been delayed
- Public relations and marketing both planning special events involving the same services, such as cardiologists and heart surgeons — public relations promoting the hospital's tertiary care image, marketing promoting referrals to the cardiac rehabilitation program

In addition to the public impact of this absence of cooperation, numerous internal issues can arise, from low staff morale to confused operating administrators who don't know who to turn to for communications projects.

Fortunately, there is an alternative to the organizational structures that have just been described. Regardless of reporting relationships and control issues, an *integrated* model can be developed that:

- Focuses on institutional objectives and results
- Matches the expertise of marketing and PR staffs to the tasks that need to be done
- Eliminates the waste of duplicating activity and expenses
- Helps alleviate frustration and anger, because everyone is involved, everyone's talents are used, and everyone shares in the achievements

In a detailed and thoughtful article in the July–August 1989 issue of *Hospital Marketing and Public Relations*, former ASHCMPR president Gary Buerstatte builds a powerful case for integration.[4] And Buerstatte takes that all-important first step of giving the process a name: *total institutional advancement.* Our colleagues in higher education selected this same term in the 1970s when the alumni, fund-raising, public relations, and publications associations merged to form the huge and powerful Council for the Advancement and Support of Education.

Several models of integration have been developed by PR professionals. Most share several key points:

- PR and marketing professionals respect each other's expertise.
- Both professionals have to be committed to the process to make it work—it can't be a one-way process.
- One person has to take the first step.

The latter point is critical. Rather than allowing confusion or competition to continue to the point at which the CEO or COO feels the need to mandate cooperative efforts, the PR or marketing manager can approach the other manager and suggest that they work together to present the CEO with a solution, rather than a problem. This proactive effort will enhance the credibility of both professionals.

Public relations and marketing professionals can be assured that integration does work and can have positive results for all involved, including the institution. The actual implementation will vary from institution to institution, depending on the size of the staffs, the availability of other resources, and so on. The following is one scenario of how integration can function:

1. A matrix team that crosses organizational lines is established, beginning with the PR and marketing staffs and possibly including representatives from planning, development, physician relations, patient relations, and related areas.
2. The team's first task, based on the hospital's long-range plans, is to develop an institutional positioning program (niche, theme, corporate look, and so on) that will be the base for all institutional advancement efforts. Examples range from "the hospital that gives you the best personal care," to "the medical center difference." The positioning program has to be effective with customers, stakeholder groups, physicians, potential donors, past patients, and so on. (That's why all those people are part of the team.) This overall positioning strategy is then integrated throughout all PR and marketing communications programs.
3. Research needs are identified by all group members and then the appropriate department (in some health care organizations it will be planning, in others marketing) develops a plan to accomplish that research using in-house staff (possibly from several departments) and external resources. For example, a major communitywide survey conducted by a professional research firm could be used to gather data on consumer needs for new health care services, as well as to measure awareness and impact of advertising and PR campaigns. In this way, multiple research needs can be accomplished as cost-

effectively as possible. Costs can be shared and prorated. Data and results are available to the entire team, so that everyone has a good understanding of what the customers and publics are thinking, needing, and wanting.

4. Institutional communications remain the responsibility of PR staff members, who take a proactive role in working with marketing staff to identify ways these vehicles can be used to promote specific products. They also work together on developing the messages. Examples would be using the health care organization's quarterly magazine, including feature stories about those products and services being marketed to the general consumer market, or making sure those services are included in story ideas that are pitched to the media.

5. Implementation of specific marketing communications projects should be assigned to the staff members who have the creative and communications skills — and more often than not, this means the PR staff. But they work directly with the marketers to interpret the message and to select channels and methods with which the marketer is comfortable. If marketing staff members have expertise or experience in communications and are thus viable candidates for implementing the communications efforts, a designated PR staffer is involved in reviewing and contributing to the process to ensure that the efforts are in synch with institutional positioning and won't set off hot buttons in any stakeholder groups.

6. When advertising agencies are used, they work with a marketing and PR team to ensure consistency of institutional and product messages and approaches.

The basics of this integrated approach are clear:

- Assign tasks based on talent and experience.
- Never duplicate.
- Share information freely.
- Remember that two creative minds are always better than one.
- Working together is more personally and professionally rewarding (and is much more pleasant for peers, subordinates, and CEOs).

Of course, the institution is the ultimate beneficiary of this integrated process. All publics — customer and noncustomer — receive a consistent, coordinated message. And the coordination of research, planning, and execution maximizes the impact of each communications effort.

The potential customers who receive the health care organization's magazine with a story on a new laser center will pay more attention to the ad they see the next day. The business leaders who hear your CFO talk about cost-containment successes at a Rotary meeting will remember when their companies select providers for a new preferred provider organization (PPO). Positive media coverage enhances the sales rep's ability to get in the door. And donors are more likely to give to an organization with a positioning theme that's used consistently to create a strong, positive image. As Buerstatte sums it up, "The examples are many. The principle is what matters."[5]

Implementing the Integrated Public Relations–Marketing Model

There are few who would debate the benefits of the integration philosophy, but implementation of the process too often gets hung up on organization charts and structure issues. In truth, there are no perfect models. The integrated-but-equal structure (with both public relations and marketing reporting to the CEO) seems to be preferred, but professionals who work in that structure can point out its flaws. And that's a key point: every structure can have flaws. There is no "perfect" model, and even if there were one, there will always be CEOs and COOs who have their own idea of what's perfect.

Instead of focusing on structure, or on who has the bigger budget, or similar issues, successful PR professionals have instead moved on to understand that the issues facing individual health care organizations, and the industry as a whole, are far too critical to waste time in turf battles. Instead, they are inviting or welcoming the expertise that marketers can bring to the institutional advancement process. It's not a "better" expertise—it's simply different. Some PR people may well believe that they are being forced to work with marketers who have little to offer, who don't understand health care, or who have some similar negative attribute—but even these PR people are finding that integrated efforts are far preferable to being perceived by the CEO as uncooperative. (They may also find that everyone has something to offer to the process.) Integration and total institutional advancement will typify the successful health care organization of the future, and the PR professionals who take the lead in implementing these concepts in their institutions will have taken proactive steps to enhance their own career success.

☐ Summary

For the PR manager to be successful in the health care setting, he or she must build integrated working relationships with the staff and operating managers, who can affect the PR manager's success in two ways:

- Staff and operating managers can contribute to or impede the success of the institutional PR plan because their actions can directly affect the institution's publics.
- Staff and operating managers who feel that their departments are being well served by the PR staff can become the biggest supporters of the PR function.

Additionally, because many of the PR manager's responsibilities overlap the responsibilities of other managers to at least some degree owing to shared audiences (public relations and human resources are both concerned with employee communications, for instance), the PR manager is dependent on cooperative efforts with these managers. Rather than fighting for control of any of these shared functions, the successful PR manager will work toward integration, involving the skills of all members of the management team to achieve the PR goals of the health care organization.

References

1. Will public relations and human resources clash in the 90s? *pr reporter* 32(35):1, Aug. 28, 1989.
2. Will public relations and human resources clash in the 90s?
3. Hicks, N. Patients and other publics. *Public Relations Journal* 46(3):28, Mar. 1986.
4. Buerstatte, G. End the debate with the total advancement concept. *Hospital Marketing and Public Relations*, July–Aug. 1989.
5. Buerstatte.

Suggested Readings

Being part of the management team. *pr reporter*, Nov. 21, 1988.

Novelli, W. D. Speaking out: marketing vs. PR—who's taking the prisoners. *Medical Marketing and Media*, July 1988.

The Senior Public Relations Officer and the Chief Executive Officer

James E. Burke, former chairman and CEO of Johnson and Johnson, the company that successfully weathered the Tylenol poisoning crisis with what is judged to be one of the most successful proactive public relations efforts in the history of American business, made a persuasive argument for a strong relationship between the CEO and the senior PR officer:

> The public is more deeply involved in those events that affect the corporation than ever before imaginable. The CEO will increasingly be challenged to act swiftly, decisively, and responsibly on all kinds of issues in a way that the public can easily comprehend. This means that the public relations executive should have easy and open access to the chairman's office, and the CEO must have an understanding of how essential it is for public relations to be an intimate part of the decision-making process.

Burke's comments were included in "The CEO Connection: Pivotal for the '90s" in the January 1990 issue of *Public Relations Journal*.[1] Author Lawrence Foster, who heads Johnson and Johnson's corporate PR division, asked CEOs who are known for their hands-on involvement in their companies' PR programs to share their views on the role of public relations. Their comments provide interesting insights into what CEOs expect and need from their senior PR officers:

> I need to know how the staff is working to optimize GM's public image. I need to know how those projects support GM's business goals. And, when it's appropriate, I need to be able to offer constructive input from the operating side.—*Roger Smith, General Motors*

Successful companies today have a communications strategy in place, and the CEO feels ownership of that plan and has been involved in its development.—*Kenneth A. Macke, Dayton Hudson Corporation*

Public relations . . . is a tool of corporate governance. It can be a unique and personal way for a CEO to communicate vision and leadership. At times it must be a reactive agent; . . . however, in its best form it should be viewed much like quality—as a strategic asset. That is, by balancing the interests of customers, shareowners, and employees, it must convert those interests into a coherent, long-term communications plan. That plan should produce a 'voice' that's heard above the clamor of competing claims, self-interest, and quick fixes. I need PR at my side, not in my wake. No public relations or plan can be successful in the long term unless the business execution is sound.—*Robert E. Allen, American Telephone & Telegraph Company*

PR must be an integral part of management to succeed. What seems to be missing from this basic "PR law" is the requirement for management to be an integral part of PR. If public relations makes a bottom-line contribution, then it is imperative that the CEO be involved in the major decisions of the PR department.—*Dr. Sheldon G. Gilgore, G.D. Searle & Company*

☐ The Chief Executive Officer's Expectations

The foregoing comments and those made during interviews between this author and hospital CEOs over a number of years identify a number of personal characteristics and traits as well as a number of professional skills that CEOs find valuable in their senior PR advisors. A description of the major expectations follows. The quotations in the following paragraphs are fictitious but are based on comments various CEOs have made to the author.

Information Source

The CEO expects the PR manager to be a source of information—to know what's going on in the hospital, in the city, in the marketplace, and nationally, and to be able to spot trends, identify opportunities, and anticipate problems that could develop into crises.

"My PR vice-president reads voraciously, and I get a steady stream of clips and articles from journals I don't have time to read and from publications I'd never normally see."

"Whenever I want some inside information—about local politics or what's going on at a competitor, my PR director either already knows or can find out. He has great contacts."

Shared Philosophy and Objectives

The CEO expects the PR manager to be able to think like the CEO does, to understand the CEO's values, philosophy, and objectives, so that the PR manager can anticipate what the CEO will want to know about, how the CEO may react to ideas or events, and actually be able to represent the CEO's views to external audiences when needed.

"My communications director makes sure that I hear about ideas that may have some sensitive implications, before people go off on their own and start implementing them."

"I'm very comfortable sending our PR vice-president to represent me at community meetings where decisions are going to be considered. She knows what I'd support, what I'd oppose, and what she needs to bring back for my consideration."

Loyalty

The CEO expects loyalty—and honesty. For many CEOs, loyalty doesn't mean blind obedience or being a "yes" person ("When my PR director thinks I'm wrong, I hear about it"), but it does mean that once a corporate decision has been made, the PR manager actively supports and works to implement that decision. And it means that if the PR manager has concerns or hears about problems, the information is shared with the CEO *first* and, generally, privately. The PR manager and the CEO need to agree on whether or not the PR manager can share concerns "publicly" in top management meetings, or whether the CEO prefers to hear about it in private.

"When we're in the process of making a decision, I expect all my staff—including the PR vice-president—to be honest about their ideas and opinions. But once that decision is made, I expect them to line up behind it—and because the PR staff has to communicate the decision to employees and outside groups, it is absolutely critical that they know how to close ranks."

Nonpartisan Viewpoint

The CEO expects the PR manager to take a broad view, representative of audience concerns and the health care organization's best interests. The PR manager cannot be seen as being an internal partisan, supporting fellow staff or operating administrators because of friendship or trade-offs, or even of representing the PR department's needs and interests at the expense of the overall organization. And when representing the concerns and issues of stakeholder groups, the CEO expects that the PR manager will be able to advise on a balanced approach to the often diverse and contradictory concerns of these audiences.

"I guess I count on my PR director to be above the infighting and be able to be a leader for the administrative team when it's time to make decisions about budgets and staffing. Yes, he's got to argue for his programs, but it has to be in the context that they're the hospital's communications programs, and when everybody has to make cuts, he needs to advise me on what we can give up if we have to."

"I don't need a PR director who comes running in a panic every time some external group is demanding action. I want an analysis, I want to know what happens if we acquiesce, and if we don't, I want to know what our alternatives are, and I need to know the implications of these alternatives on our other publics. I want reason—not a knee-jerk response."

Problem-Solving Orientation

The CEO expects solutions, not more problems tossed on the desk. If the PR manager is alerting the CEO about an emerging problem area, the alert should include preliminary recommendations about what could happen next, what actions the CEO could or should take, and how the PR manager can assist in addressing the problem.

"Every day I've got people telling me about problems and problems and problems. When our communications director tells me she needs to see me about a problem, I know it's something worth my time to consider, because she doesn't overreact, and I also know that when she comes in, she'll have some advice for me on where to go next."

Communications Skills

The CEO expects—even takes for granted—top-notch professional communications skills and the ability to acquire new skills when warranted.

"I don't have time to worry about the best way to sell our programs, or whether or not we should do a dinner meeting for some referring docs. I turn all that over to the PR director—that's what I hired him for."

"I've never heard my corporate communications VP say she doesn't know how to do something that we're thinking about—advertising or employee meetings, or whatever. I just assume that whatever I ask her to do, it will get done well. I guess if she hasn't done it before, she's smart enough to find out how to do it or get someone who can."

Commitment

Most CEOs expect their PR directors to have the same level of time and energy and single-focused commitment that they bring to their jobs. The PR manager may actually even spend more hours and more energy than the CEO — but he or she can't spend less, or appear to be less focused on the organization.

"I know my communications director is working on a graduate degree and has a lot of other things that are going on in his life — but he's here whenever I need him, and never drops the ball."

"When I've got what seems like a crisis — or even when I just need some help — I don't expect to have to fit into my PR director's busy schedule, or to hear that the PR staff doesn't have the time to get the work done."

Although this single-mindedness may seem unfair to the PR manager — or to any senior staff member — it's well to remember that the CEO is, after all, the boss.

Chief Executive Officer Involvement in the Public Relations Plan

Most CEOs want to have ownership of the organization's PR plan — to have it be "my" plan versus the PR manager's or the PR department's plan. And the PR manager should want and welcome this involvement, because the CEO who feels ownership is much more likely to support the plan and the PR staff.

"The PR director came in with 'his' plan — and acted like he owned it. No one ever asked for my opinion, my ideas, my thoughts — and I think I do have something to contribute. I'm the one out there in the community, hearing what people are concerned about. I assumed that I'd at least be consulted before the plan was developed. It was unfortunate — it took him several weeks to redo the plan so I thought it would work."

"I present the PR plan to the board — not to steal the show from our VP, but so that the board understands that this is the hospital's plan and I'm involved in it."

Articulation of Expectations

The foregoing expectations are, of course, reflective of the individuals who made the comments. Every CEO has his or her own preferences, idiosyncrasies, and expectations, and the PR manager needs to take the time to discuss these expectations with the CEO and also to observe the CEO's behavior to identify any unspoken expectations. The PR manager cannot just guess, or try to interpret, what the CEO expects—and if the CEO doesn't volunteer a definition of those expectations, then the PR manager needs to take the initiative and propose a list that the CEO can respond to and clarify. The PR manager who does not clearly understand the CEO's expectations risks learning, too late, that he or she has been going in the wrong direction, or behaving in a way that the CEO doesn't appreciate.

The PR manager also needs to identify the objectives and performance indicators that the CEO will use to evaluate the manager's performance as part of either a formal management evaluation system or an informal process. Ideally, this process of answering the question "How are you going to judge whether or not I've succeeded" should culminate in a written description of what the CEO and PR manager have agreed on.

Defining specific PR program objectives and measures of success (increased awareness of and preference for the hospital by stated audiences, media placements, responses to articles in publications, and so on) is relatively easy compared with coming up with performance indicators for the types of expectations outlined previously. If the CEO expects "loyalty," for instance, the PR manager needs to ask how the CEO defines loyalty and what kinds of behavior are seen as loyal or disloyal (getting specific examples that the PR manager can use to see how the CEO thinks). And the PR manager needs to get the CEO's commitment to provide feedback if the CEO believes the PR manager is doing something "disloyal."

□ The Public Relations Manager's Expectations

The PR manager brings his or her own expectations to the relationship with the CEO: access to the CEO, direct participation in decision making, CEO support for the PR function and role, and open communication with the CEO.

Access

Chapter 2 explains the reasons why the PR manager needs to report directly to the CEO—which is the primary expectation of most PR people in health care organizations and other industries and is described as the ideal model by PR educators and experts. The PR manager, who, for whatever reason, does not report directly to the CEO needs immediate access to the CEO on matters affecting the organization's public image. Depending on the PR manager's reporting relationship, this access may be direct (preferred) or through the PR manager's superior, although having to filter information through even one layer (PR manager to his superior, superior to CEO, and back) can be time-consuming at times when speed is important and can allow message entropy to occur (what the PR manager is told is not exactly what the CEO meant). For these reasons, PR managers who do not report directly to the CEO are advised to negotiate with their superiors to allow for direct access to the CEO when crises, media inquiries, or sensitive public reactions are involved. If the local paper is on deadline for a story about hospital CEO salaries (obtained from the hospital's form 990), the PR manager needs to be able to get the CEO on the phone to develop a response.

Direct Participation in Decision Making

Chapters 2 and 3 detail the critical role of public relations as a senior management function: representing the concerns of the health care organization's diverse publics, reviewing all decision alternatives in light of public reaction, and having firsthand an understanding of decisions to be able to effectively communicate them to the organization's internal and external audiences. A PR manager who is not part of top management may routinely encounter the following situations:

- Being asked to develop a communications message about a major decision without having all the background needed to fully explain the implications and ramifications
- Coping with negative public response to a hospital action—a response that the PR manager could have anticipated had he or she known about the action, or that could have been averted if the decision makers had had access to the PR manager's insight
- Getting media inquiries about a decision or action of which the PR manager hasn't even been notified

A prospective PR manager who is offered a position that is not part of the top management team needs to consider whether or not he or she can perform effectively and meet the institution's expectations. The PR manager in such a position has several options:

- Try to convince the CEO to make the position part of the team (which can be tricky if the PR manager reports to someone who is part of the team)
- Insist on being routinely and consistently briefed by the CEO on decisions that are being considered so that PR input can be provided
- Develop collegial relationships with members of the top management team, obtaining information on an informal basis and seizing opportunities for PR input

Support for the Public Relations Function and Role

Working with and for individuals who neither understand nor value the PR role can be a challenging—sometimes frustrating—experience. The PR manager can educate, persuade, and teach by example—but if public relations is tolerated as a "necessary evil," or described by the CEO as "fluffy stuff," then the PR manager has to question whether or not he or she can ever be successful.

One factor that should be considered is what the institution's definition of a successful PR program is. If the CEO and management are only interested in the *things* of PR—brochures, special events, and the like—then the PR manager who can produce those things may very well be considered highly successful. The rub comes when a trained and experienced PR manager, who understands the need for issues management, stakeholder relations, examination of every decision in terms of public relations, and so on, is not allowed to fully use his or her skills. This is, of course, a highly personal issue, and each PR professional must decide what situations he or she will tolerate.

Open Communication

The PR manager must be kept fully informed, well in advance, of even the most sensitive events, decisions, and plans. Just as CEOs request "no surprises" from their staffs, the PR manager must insist on no surprises. Additionally, the PR manager's advice and counsel should be accepted, considered, and respected. The successful health care CEO will not only accept input from the PR manager but will also encourage and demand it. Again, it's a personal decision as to what the individual PR manager will accept, but most PR professionals say they would find it frustrating to try to alert the CEO about potential problems only to have their input rejected or ignored.

☐ Summary

Superior–subordinate relationships, despite all the guidelines and models, remain highly personalized, especially at the CEO level. The PR manager who reports directly to the CEO needs to make a top priority of understanding and defining the relationship and seeking consistent feedback on performance. The PR manager who does not report to the CEO has a dual task—defining a successful working relationship with his or her superior and also establishing a method of two-way communication with the CEO.

Reference

1. Foster, L. G. The CEO connection: pivotal for the '90s. *Public Relations Journal* 46(1):24, Jan. 1990.

Suggested Reading

Nowlan, S. E., and Shavon, D. R. Reviewing your relationship with executive management. *Public Relations Quarterly,* Spring 1984.

Organizing the Public Relations Function

The basic responsibilities assigned to the health care public relations department are fairly standard from institution to institution—media relations, publications, community relations, patient communications, and audiovisual services. In addition, there are a number of other functions that are not traditionally part of a PR function outside the health care setting, but which are sometimes assigned to the health care PR manager, including mail and telephone systems or volunteer services. Finally, there are several newly emerging functions within health care organizations that fall under the purview of the PR manager, either as a direct responsibility or as an area of influence, such as guest relations or physician relations. So although the core responsibilities are usually similar, there is often a great deal of variation from one institution to another in terms of what functions the PR manager supervises. (Appendix A reports data from an ASHCMPR survey of hospital PR professionals and details the responsibilities handled by these individuals.)

There is also a great deal of variation in terms of size and organizational structure of the PR staff. The size of the PR staff can vary from the traditional operation of one person with a secretary to PR divisions of 20 or more members. In general, the larger the organization, the larger the PR staff.

As size varies, so do organizational structures. The most common types are the specialist model, with each staff member responsible for a specific function (publications, media relations, and so on), or the in-house agency or generalist model, in which staff members are responsible for all the communications needs of a specific hospital department or departments. There are also a number of hybrids of these two basic models.

Once the PR manager has selected an organizational model, a budget should be developed that reflects the institutional PR plan. Estimates of project costs, salaries and benefits, professional development expenses, and so on should be calculated to allow the PR function to carry out its plan.

Finally, the PR manager must manage his or her staff—from hiring to training, and from team building to incentives. Staff management can be a particular challenge, because the professionals with the "creative personality" required to excel at many of the communications functions of public relations do not always respond to traditional types of supervision and direction. One metaphor that's often used to describe the staff management responsibilities of a PR manager is that of coaching—picking the right team members, setting goals, helping them perfect their skills, observing their progress, creating strategies, and motivating them to excel.

□ Responsibilities Assigned to the Health Care Public Relations Department

In nearly every gathering of health care PR professionals from different cities, one question for discussion is "What areas are you responsible for?" The range of responsibilities is diverse and continually changing as health care organizations develop such new programs as senior citizen membership services and physician relations programs and assign these programs to the PR staff to manage. Additionally, ongoing restructuring of hospital staff and line functions, often a result of downsizing and elimination of some senior management positions, has also resulted in PR managers' being given new responsibilities.

Core Responsibilities

Despite the diversity, there is a core group of functions for which most health care PR departments are responsible (described in extensive detail in succeeding chapters). Those core functions generally include:

- *Publications*
    - Multiple publications for a variety of audiences, including patients, families, physicians, donors, and community leaders
    - Multiple formats, including magazines, newsletters, tabloids, brochures, annual reports, posters, and more
- *Media relations*
    - Responses to all media inquiries, 24 hours a day
    - Press releases and media kits
    - Placement of stories with local, regional, and national media outlets

- *Community relations*
  - Speakers' services and lecture series
  - Hospital tours
  - Open houses and special events
- *Employee communications*
  - Employee publications, ranging from daily information bulletins to bimonthly magazines to "video publications"
  - Special communications programs on topics such as AIDS, creating a smoke-free environment, and guest relations
  - Recruitment materials, ranging from brochures to multimedia productions
- *Marketing communications*
  - Comprehensive promotion programs, including media coverage, special events, advertising, and so forth, which are developed to promote both the health care organization's overall image and specific products or services (in some health care organizations with separate marketing departments, the responsibility for product/service promotion is assigned to that department)
  - Advertising, including print, radio, TV, outdoor, and direct mail
  - Collateral material, including letterhead, brochures, and posters

Related Responsibilities

In addition to these five functional areas, which are common to almost every health care PR department, there are a number of related functions that may report directly to the senior PR staff member, including:

- *Marketing.* In addition to the marketing communications functions that are generally assigned to the PR department, a number of health care organizations have assigned the responsibility for the total marketing program to the senior PR officer. This can include market research and analysis, new product development, development of business plans for products and services, as well as promotion plans and implementation.
- *Photography or audiovisual communications.* If seen primarily as a medical photography operation, this function may exist as a department separately from public relations. In teaching hospitals, medical photography and videography are very important to physicians, so the PR manager responsible for this function must be very sensitive to the physicians' concerns.
- *Fund-raising.* In small hospitals, this function may report to the PR manager, whereas larger health care organizations often have a separate development department or a foundation organized separately from the institution. Even when fund-raising is a separate

function, the PR department should have a clear line of communication with the development function.

- *Volunteer services.* This function is more likely to fall under public relations in a small hospital, and also more likely to be assigned to a female PR manager than to a male. Serving as liaison to a hospital's Auxiliary often goes along with responsibility for volunteer services. The key to successful management of the volunteer function is to hire or hang on to a volunteer director who is both extremely well organized and extremely good at making people feel needed and wanted.
- *Telephone and/or internal mail systems.* These functions are sometimes assigned to report to the PR manager because of "they're part of communications, aren't they?" reasoning. Although these functions fall more into the traditional support services area (laundry, dietary, and housekeeping, for example), there is some relationship to public relations in that both functions are very important to patient and physician satisfaction, and the telephone service is an integral part of the health care organization's overall image to the external audiences.
- *Health promotion.* If the health care organization's health promotion program is seen primarily as a communications effort—lectures, seminars, special events—it may be located within the PR department. In other institutions, the function involves providing health services such as screenings, testing, corporate wellness activities, and the like. If this function is assigned to the PR department, it is essential that a staff person with health/medical training and background (preferably a registered nurse) coordinate the service to ensure the credibility of the service among physicians and other health professionals.

Emerging Responsibilities

Finally, a number of functions are emerging to play a key role in today's health care organizations that may either report directly to the senior PR officer or require a great deal of PR staff involvement. These are areas that may begin as limited-scope programs assigned to community relations or marketing communications, but then grow to a point at which they should become separate functions with their own professional staff. These emerging functions include:

- *Physician relations.* Health care PR departments have traditionally been responsible for physician newsletters and other communications activities, as well as physician open houses and special events. As the importance of developing and maintaining positive relations with physicians has come to be recognized by health care executives, the creation of separate medical staff or physician relations departments has become more common. In some health care organizations, this function reports directly to the CEO (ideal from the physicians' point of view); in others, it reports to a vice-president for medical staff affairs or to the senior marketing officer. The physician relations function is described in more detail in chapter 16.

- *Legislative relations.* Because of the relationship between the health care organization's planning activities and local, state, and federal health facility regulations, the legislative relations function is often left to the organization's planning staff members. Too often, this means that the only time the organization has contact with government officials is when there's a problem with a regulatory or reimbursement agency, or when the organization needs approval for a certificate of need. Today, health care CEOs are realizing that legislators and government staff members are a critically important audience with whom the health care organization should be developing ongoing relationships. Developing these relationships requires skills and experience that are more typical of a PR manager than a health care planner, so this is another area in which PR managers are becoming more involved. The legislative relations function is covered in more detail in chapter 16.

- *Guest relations.* The term *guest* is used by many health care organizations to include patients, their family members, their visitors, and any other members of external publics who come to the institution. Guest relations programs run the gamut in terms of comprehensiveness, from one-time "let's all be friendly" training, to ongoing programs of research, to problem identification and consequent systems modifications to eliminate the problems. The guest relations function is sometimes assigned to the nursing or patient care department, where the focus tends to be solely on patients and families and their interaction with patient care departments. When the function is assigned to human resources, it generally is limited to employee training activities. The PR department is ideally suited to supervise the guest relations function, using research and analytical skills to examine the guests' interactions with the entire health care system and counseling skills to work with the operating department managers to eliminate problems. Another reason for assigning guest relations to the PR department is that, as discussed in chapters 2 and 8, the PR staff has traditionally been responsible for representing the needs and concerns of the health care organization's publics to management. Supervising the ongoing process of monitoring guests' interactions with the institution is a natural extension of this role, and because the problems identified may involve departments in a number of operating divisions, it is more appropriate to have a staff department supervise the problem resolution process than an operating department.

• *Special audience-specific products, such as senior citizen programs.* What have begun as communications programs aimed at specific audience groups, like senior citizens, are now growing into multi-faceted services or products that do not have a natural niche in the traditional organization chart. A senior citizens' membership program may be part of an existing geriatrics service, but in many health care organizations these types of audience-specific programs are being created and managed by PR departments. A women's information and resource center may be part of a comprehensive women's health product line, but if the institution only has an obstetrics department, it may be more appropriate to have the more broadly based women's health program under the supervision of public relations.

☐ The Staff Role of Public Relations: Establishing a Service-Motivated Department

Before discussing the alternative models, it is essential that the PR manager and staff have a complete understanding of the role of a staff function within an organization and a *commitment to functioning in a service mode.* The line-staff principle of management is used in nearly every type of organization. Line functions in manufacturing industries are those that produce and sell the product; in service industries, they are those functions that play a part in delivering the service to the customer. In the health care setting, the nursing, radiology, and dietary departments are examples of line functions. In both manufacturing and service industries, including hospitals, the staff functions are those that advise and assist the executive and support the work of the line or operating departments. These staff functions usually include finance, legal, human resources, and public relations; in most health care organizations, marketing is also a staff function.

Cutlip, Center, and Brown, in their landmark textbook *Effective Public Relations*, note that line management has final authority over decisions that affect the operations of the company, whereas staff management functions like public relations generally work in an advisory capacity.[1] This does not mean that staff managers do not have any involvement in nor impact on organizational decision making. In well-managed organizations where the expertise of the staff managers is acknowledged, the strong support of or opposition to a proposal by a respected staff manager can determine whether the proposal will be adopted or rejected.

Because it is vitally important to the organization's overall success that the PR manager's counsel be both sought and carefully considered by executive and line management, it is incumbent upon the PR manager to position himself or herself and the PR function as integral to the success of those line managers and executives. One important way of achieving this objective is to develop a service-oriented PR department.

The service model is based on the premise that the CEO and the executive staff are held responsible by the board for achieving organizational objectives, just as line managers are expected to achieve specific product/service and profit-producing objectives. If the executives and line managers see that the PR department is actively involved in achieving those objectives, then the PR manager and staff gain the credibility and trust that are essential if they are to perform the counseling role effectively.

On a more practical level, a service orientation can help ensure that the PR department is perceived as a vital and necessary part of the health care organization's operations. In the past decade and certainly in the decade to come, the financial situation facing hospitals has meant that all hospital departments have had to compete within the organization for a share of declining revenues. Although in most hospitals it is the CEO or COO who makes the final budget decisions, the opinions and ideas of all members of the top management team are usually taken into consideration.

Public relations professionals in health care organizations — and in many other industries — report that when these budget discussions take place, public relations and other staff functions are often described by operating managers as "overhead" departments that should be the first targets for budget cutting. "PR can be the first area to be scrutinized," noted one health care administrator, "because the operating people believe that they need the personnel department to help them manage their staff, and they need finance to help with budgets, and they need legal counsel to help them stay out of trouble — but unless the PR department has proven its value to them, the operating managers, it can be a target. Talking about how PR promotes the image of the hospital is fine, but the operating people need to see how PR helps them achieve their objectives." One way of ensuring that the operating managers believe that the PR function is valuable to them is by setting up the department as a service function, with a primary goal of meeting the needs of the operating units.

The key to achieving this service-orientation model is to think of the health care organization's executives, line operating managers, and even other staff departments as "clients" who need services from the PR department. When the PR manager considers the various models of organizational structures, it is important to evaluate them in terms of two questions:

- Will this organizational model be easy for our clients to use?
- Will this organizational model function effectively, so that my department can do high-quality work on a timely basis to meet our clients' needs?

□ Organizational Models for the Public Relations Functions

This section discusses alternative ways of organizing the basic PR functions. Other departments that may report to the PR manager (such as marketing, physician relations, volunteers) are assumed to function as separate units or departments.

There are two basic models for organizing a PR function involving more than one professional staff member (the one-person department is described in a subsection of this chapter): the functional/specialist model and the client-specific/generalist model. Most health care organizations have created their own "hybrids" of these models to meet the needs of their institution and to work within their staffing and budget limits.

Functional/Specialist Model

In the functional/specialist model, the most traditional of the models described in this chapter, the PR staff members each handle one specific functional responsibility such as publications, media relations, special events, or the like, and each staff member provides that category of service to all of the health care organization's departments and programs. A typical small staff might be organized as shown in figure 5-1.

Figure 5-1. A Public Relations Staff for a Small Organization

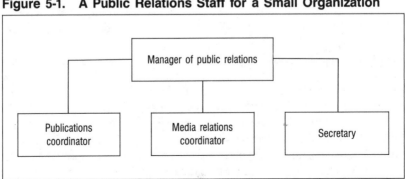

Tasks that do not fall into the publications or media relations area are handled by the manager, or they may be handled by the coordinators under the "other duties as assigned" item that is a part of a typical job description.

A larger staff could be organized as shown in figure 5-2. With additional staff, the functions can be broken down even further. The major strength of this type of organizational model is that the specialists become quite expert in their specific area. Staff members select the area in which they are particularly proficient and work in that area exclusively. The publications staff person, for instance, produces dozens of publications yearly—internal and external magazines, newsletters, brochures, posters, and special-purpose publications. This repetition and immersion in a specific function generally allows the staffer to develop a high level of expertise so that the department can provide the high-quality work that the internal clients expect.

This model is very comfortable for the staff members, who become very familiar with their "turf." And it can also be very functional for

Figure 5-2. Functional/Specialist Organizational Model

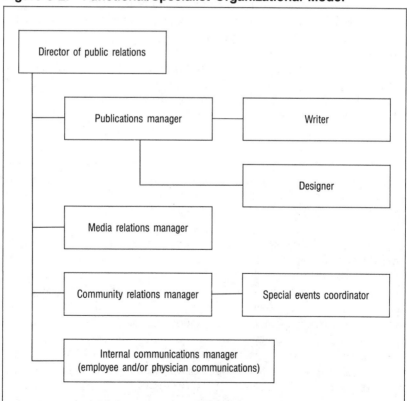

the PR manager, who knows instantly which staff member should be assigned to an incoming project—unless the project is something that doesn't fit within the normal definition of the specialist's responsibilities. This becomes more and more likely to occur as the work performed by health care PR departments broadens beyond the traditional functions.

The main drawback to this model is that it is less "user friendly" to clients who have multiple needs. For instance, the women's health center may need a brochure, assistance in planning an open house, and news releases sent to several newspapers. Working with a functionally organized PR department, the women's health coordinator may have to talk to two or three PR staffers in order to get the work that's needed. "I just educate one PR person so that he understands what we're doing, and then I have to talk to another one" is a common complaint from the operating managers. And the larger the department, the larger the number of specialists, which means more confusion for the clients. "I'm never sure who to call in PR—I always get referred to someone else," said one hospital obstetrics department manager. If the client doesn't make contact with the right PR staff specialist, some pieces may fall through the cracks. And if there are problems, the client isn't sure who should be held accountable.

Alternatively, all client work requests can be funneled through the PR manager, so that the client only has to make one contact. This adds to the work load of the PR manager, who has to interface with the PR staff on behalf of the clients, explaining what's needed and why. The PR manager also becomes the person the client holds accountable, and so is responsible for staying on top of all the pieces of numerous clients' PR programs. In larger health care organizations, as the number of requesting departments increases, and they request more and more services, the PR manager can become overloaded. Although some PR managers prefer this kind of centralized control, it definitely positions the staff as technicians, handling assignments that are handed out by the manager.

Another concern is the potential for lack of a consistent approach when a product or service communications program is produced in pieces, by different individuals, rather than as part of a comprehensive program. The PR manager can address this problem by bringing together all of the staff who are working on projects for a specific client so that everyone is working from a common understanding of the client's objectives and creative strategy.

The specialist model is also less flexible than other models. Rather than focusing on what techniques or methods would best meet the needs of the client department, the specialist model tends to make the client's needs fit within the capabilities of the department. There are problems when a client needs work done that doesn't fit into the purview of the PR department's specialists. When a technique like radio advertising is considered for a client, the PR manager has to figure out which of the specialists to assign it to, which can result in the nervous response "That's not my area." It can also result in poor-quality work being turned out by a staff person inexperienced in that technique. The alternative is to use outside help—either a free-lancer or an agency—to do the types of work that the in-house staff is not trained to handle, a solution that some PR managers prefer. "I know what my staff can do well, and that's what we do," said one manager. "When other types of work are needed, I hire it."

Another problem with specialization is that continued focus on and repetition of one task over and over, although it does lead to technical expertise in that area, can also lead to burnout and loss of creativity. The staff person can come to see his or her work as simply churning out one more brochure, or pitching one more story to the local TV stations, day after day after day.

On balance, the specialist model meets the service-oriented mandate of providing good-quality work to clients, as long as the work needed fits into the department's functional areas. But the model must be carefully managed to be user friendly to clients.

Client-Specific/Generalist or Account Rep Model

With the client-specific/generalist model, the PR department is set up somewhat like a PR or advertising agency, with each client department assigned to one PR staff member. The PR staff members, who are all generalists, are expected to meet all the communications needs of their clients—whether those needs include media publicity, brochures, special events, or advertising. (The exceptions are any technical positions, such as photographers or designers, who continue to fulfill those functions.) The PR staffer assumes the "account rep" role that is found in ad or PR agencies. Unlike most agencies, however, the PR staffer also functions as the "creative" staff for the client, actually developing the communications vehicles.

Generally, with this kind of model, related clients are grouped together. An example of this model is diagrammed in figure 5-3. As not all services fit into these categories, account managers will inevitably have some other clients.

Under a "pure" client-specific model, these account managers are responsible for producing literally everything the client departments need, from patient brochures to promotional videos. This requires the staff to have a great deal of expertise and skill, or to have access to external resources (free-lancers, agencies, or consultants) for those tasks the staffer isn't able to handle.

Figure 5-3. Client-Specific/Generalist Organizational Model

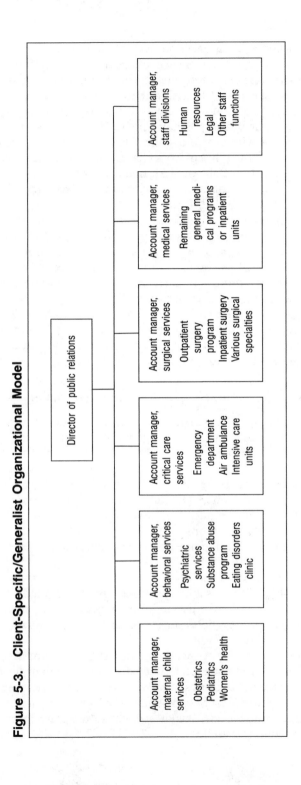

The PR department manager serves as consultant, creative director, and supervisor for the account representatives. He or she works with the account staff to develop communications plans, reviews and approves all work developed so that institutional quality and consistency standards are met, and monitors the account staff to make sure client deadlines are being met.

The main strength of this model is one-stop shopping for the client. Each client has a PR staff member who is completely familiar with that department. The account manager functions in an advisory capacity to the client, helping develop communications programs that support the client's operating objectives. The account manager sees that the programs are coordinated and that no pieces fall through the cracks, and is ultimately accountable to the client. When this model works effectively, the account manager works so closely with the client department that he becomes part of the client's "team." A behavioral services administrator at one hospital described her PR account rep as "one of the best members of my team. After she'd worked with us for about six months, she knew more about marketing substance abuse services than I did, and when she left the hospital, my staff gave her the same kind of going away party that they'd give to someone in our department."

Many PR staff members who work in an account rep structure say they find the system challenging and exciting. Rather than doing the same task over and over again for a variety of different clients, PR account reps get to try their hand at a number of communications techniques. This allows staff members to grow and develop professional skills, while the responsibility of coordinating the client's program develops managerial skills.

The other asset of this model is that it frees up the PR director from the day-to-day work of meeting with department heads on their projects, handing out assignments to staff members, and trying to make sure all of the staff members are doing their pieces of each client's overall communications plan. Under the generalist/agency model, the direct accountability for coordination rests with the account reps, with the PR director serving as a creative and strategic resource.

The major drawback of this model is that not all PR professionals are skilled in all the techniques needed by clients, nor do they enjoy or feel confident about doing "everything." The PR staffer who enjoys and excels in organizing special events may be very uncomfortable when it comes to writing advertising copy or supervising production of a brochure. This problem can be addressed by continuing education or training for the staff person (through professional development seminars or even enrollment in college courses), or by on-the-job training by the PR director or another staffer who is proficient in the skill in question. Nevertheless, forcing staff members to become generalists and expecting high-quality work in all the PR techniques can cause a great deal of stress for the staff.

In addition, while the internal clients benefit from and enjoy having their "own" account rep, there are a number of external audiences who prefer or need to have one source inside the organization. Some reporters, for instance, prefer to call the same PR person for all types of story ideas or interviews, rather than having to remember which account rep handles which type of client. It's also easier for a PR staffer to develop a collegial working relationship with the media if they are in constant communication, rather than working together only sporadically. Other external audiences, like groups seeking speakers, also find it more convenient to work with the same PR staff person month after month, rather than calling a different person each time the group needs a speaker.

On balance, the generalist, in-house agency model is very effective in terms of efficiency for the client, but may be less effective than the specialist model in terms of high-quality work, because the account managers may not be skilled in all PR techniques. Although these skills can be learned and perfected, the account rep model still causes problems for external audiences who prefer to relate to a specialist, such as a media relations manager or a speakers' service coordinator, rather than calling a number of different account managers.

Hybrid Models

A number of health care PR directors have created hybrid organizational structures that feature the best features of the specialist and generalist models.

Hybrid Model A: Combination Specialist/Account Manager

If the PR department has a number of staff members, a combination specialist/account rep structure can be established. Several staff members can specialize in the most commonly requested techniques— media relations, publications, community relations, for instance—to form an in-house creative team. Other staff members serve as account reps, working directly with the clients to determine strategies and develop communications plans. The account reps are responsible for coordinating implementation of those plans, whereas actual execution of specific elements of the plan are either done by the department specialists or by the account rep, depending on the account rep's level of expertise.

For example, the account rep for a hospital's heart center develops a multifaceted plan to promote awareness of the center on the part of referring physicians and the general public. Table 5-1 shows some of the items that could be included in that plan, along with which staff person would be responsible for implementing that item. This model offers the advantages of both organizational models—the specialists, with their expertise and skill, and the account reps who provide efficiency for the client and have a thorough knowledge of the client's products. It also meets the differing needs of staff members, allowing staff members who prefer to work in only one area to specialize, and those who are challenged by diversity to serve as account reps.

This hybrid arrangement also requires a great deal of teamwork from the specialists and the account reps to avoid the friction that can occur, especially if the account reps are going to actually implement some of the creative work ("I'm the publications expert"—"Well, it's my client"). Although account reps are held accountable for all client work under this system, they can't be effective unless the specialists (who are their peers) deliver on their responsibilities. And the specialist managers are also held accountable for their areas of expertise and need the cooperation of the client reps. The media relations manager, for instance, can't achieve story placement objectives if the client reps don't provide the needed information on time.

The PR director, of course, will work closely with the account reps and the specialists to ensure that clients' needs are being met, and can make it clear that teamwork is expected and will be rewarded—but it is up to the staff managers to develop good day-to-day working relationships with each other. It's also important that the team members agree, up front, on who is going to actually implement the various communications projects. In the above example, for instance, the account rep happened to be quite skilled in doing special events, so rather than turning this project over to the community relations manager, the

Table 5-1. Assignment of Heart Center Campaign Tasks with a Hybrid Public Relations Staff Organizational Model

Item	Implemented By
Special brochure to be sent to physicians	Publications manager
Anniversary party for heart surgery patients	Account rep, with advice from community relations manager
Media coverage of the party and a new laser angioplasty treatment that the cardiologists are using in Cath Lab	Account rep writes releases or gives info to media relations manager, who sends release and pitches story
Heart center physicians and nurses as speakers at local clubs and organizations	Community relations manager, as part of speakers' service

account rep chose to handle it. Because the community relations manager is held accountable for maintaining the quality level of special events, however, the account rep needs to interface with him or her and develop a plan on which they both agree.

Hybrid Model B: Dual Responsibility Structure

A second type of hybrid model — a dual responsibility model — gives each staff manager a dual responsibility for a specialized function and for client account management. This model requires fewer staff positions than the combined specialist/account rep model, but places far more demands on the staff in terms of expertise, managing a hectic work load, and teamwork.

With this model, each staff person is an "in-house expert" in one area — such as publications, media relations, special events, or advertising — and also has client account rep responsibilities. This model functions similarly to the combined model described above, but "stretches" each staff member to develop one area of expertise and also to coordinate several total programs for client accounts. As with the combined model, the availability of in-house specialists means that staff members don't have to handle anything in which they don't feel skilled, and all of the staff members share in the responsibility of direct client contact and accountability.

This model, although effective for meeting client needs for one-stop shopping via the account rep system, and effective for maintaining quality levels via the specialists, is probably the most difficult to manage. Each staff member has two major responsibilities to worry about — his or her specialty area and his or her clients. A typical day's to-do list for a publications specialist/maternal–child services account rep, outlined below, looks somewhat schizophrenic. The letter at the end of each item indicates whether this is one of the staff member's specialist (S) responsibilities or an account (A) management responsibility.

- Meet with OB manager about promoting new first-time mothers program (A)
- Finish patient brochure for teen psych unit (S)
- Work with designer on hospital annual report (S)
- Get details on pediatrics open house to media relations manager for release to TV stations (A)
- Talk to special events coordinator about open house plans — figure out who's going to handle details (A)
- Supervise photo shoot for next issue of hospital magazine (S)

It's important to note that while the media relations manager and special events coordinator are working with the maternal–child account rep on his client's projects, they are also coordinating their own clients' projects.

This type of system works best when the account reps implement as much of their clients' work as possible and the specialists function in a primarily advisory/in-house consultant capacity. If the account rep turns over implementation of the majority of his or her clients' projects, this can result in friction with other staff members.

Obviously, there can be as many different staff organizational models as there are sizes and types of institutions. The PR manager should create a structure that meets the three criteria for a successful client-service–oriented department: efficiency, convenience, and high-quality work. This structure should also take into consideration the size of the staff available to handle the work load and the strengths, capabilities, and preferences of those staff members.

The One-Person Department

The demands made on the solo PR manager are comparable to those made on departments with several staff members. Without priorities that are accepted by the CEO or whomever the PR manager reports to, the manager has two alternatives: try to do everything—and risk sacrificing quality; or personally decide which things will get done, which will not get done—and risk guessing wrong about which things aren't priorities to the CEO. In either case, the PR manager's sanity is at risk.

To negotiate work priorities, the PR director may need to do some research with colleagues to come up with estimates of how much time it takes to perform specific kinds of PR projects. Then he or she can put together a list of all of the tasks requested of or assigned to him or her, with time requirements, so that realistic priorities can be developed.

Generally, the items which are considered essential for a basic health care PR program are patient publications, handling media inquiries, and working with employee communications efforts—tasks that must be performed as part of daily operations. More externally oriented communications—the hospital magazine, promotional programs for products and services, placing media stories—are the next tier of priorities.

If there are in-house staff members who can assist with the basic priorities (nursing staff members who can do most of the writing for patient publications, for instance), then the PR manager's time is freed to work on the externally focused activities. A well-trained secretary can generally handle many routine media inquiries (patient conditions, for example). A volunteer can maintain clip files and answer routine phone calls, and in many health care organizations, dedicated and trained volunteers give tours, arrange speakers, and even help plan and implement special events.

The solo PR manager can also use outside talent for special projects or ongoing responsibilities. Although a full-service agency may be beyond the organization's budget, an experienced free-lance writer or designer, or a small, specialized agency can be effective and affordable. Finally, the solo PR manager should try to negotiate for all of the equipment and technological support possible, from computers to desktop publishing.

☐ Developing the Budget

Developing the health care organization's PR budget is comparable to developing any type of department or division budget in most companies, including line items for salaries, benefits, expenses, and so on. However, the PR budget has some specifics that should be considered.

Estimating Project Expenses

First, the budget must reflect, not drive, the PR plan. Once the organization's PR plan is completed (see chapter 6), the PR manager has a "shopping list" of items to be priced, such as:

• Magazine, four times yearly
• Media relations program, regional emphasis
• Six open houses
• Employee magpaper, monthly

The PR staff can then develop "specs"–details for each major item – so the items can be priced. For the publications items, for example, the staff must decide on size, number of pages, kind of stock, number of photos, ink color(s), quantity, and so forth, so printers can develop bids. Related costs – such as photography, design, mailing labels/service, and postage – must also be calculated. Some organizations develop budgets with functional line items (one line for postage for all types of publications, one line for all printing services, and so on), whereas others use project lines (one line for all costs relating to the magazine, one for the employee magpaper, and so on).

Estimating the costs for these projects can be done in several ways: seeking bids from vendors, looking back at what similar projects cost and adding an inflationary increase, or checking with colleagues or agencies to estimate the cost of a new project (such as a video). Few PR managers have the time to spec and get bids on every single project during the budgeting process. Most rely on general estimates to come up with a budget figure, and then adjust the project details to stay within that figure.

If the PR budget is to include the costs of all projects created for hospital departments or services (rather than having those items included in the budgets of the client departments, as described in chapter 3), the same process must be followed for these projects.

Estimating Salary and Benefits Expense

The second phase of budget development is the salary and benefits expense lines. If no new positions are being added, the manager can ask the human resources department for a projected average wage-and-benefits cost increase for the coming year and apply that number to the current year's salary budget. If new positions are to be added and job descriptions and salary ranges already exist for those positions, these dollars must also be included in the budget. If no job description exists, the PR manager needs to have the job evaluated through the standard procedure in human resources, so that a salary range can be established. It is usually wise to budget at least the midpoint of the salary range, or even higher, to give the manager some flexibility in salary negotiations when the time comes to hire the new staff member. Some health care organizations charge benefits costs (for example, health and life insurance) to the department budget; others carry it as one line item for the entire organization.

Estimating Professional Development Expense

The third type of budget item to be calculated is one that might be called "professional development"—dues to organizations, travel costs, registration fees for conferences, and subscriptions to professional journals. Typically, these expenses may be higher, per capita, in the PR department than in other hospital departments. Public relations professionals tend to be involved in at least one (if not several) of the national professional organizations. Attendance at one or two seminars or educational meetings each year is valuable for both the PR professional and the institution, allowing the professional to learn new techniques and get "revitalized" creatively. In addition, professional journals and magazines not only provide ideas on what is new in the field but also are great sources of inspired creativity.

Estimating Expenses for Consultants, Free-Lancers, Office Supplies, and Capital Items

Expenses for agencies, consultants, free-lance designers, and so forth must be available, although these costs may also be included in the total-project line item, if desired. As with any office, there must also be line items for office supplies, charges (if any) for photocopying, and so forth. The purchasing or material management department can assist with projections of cost increases for these items.

Finally, in most health care organizations, the PR manager will need to prepare a separate capital budget for capital items (such as furniture and computers) that either are relatively permanent (generally something that will still be around after three years, as compared to an item that will be used up) or cost above a certain dollar amount (ranges from $200 to $1,000 in most organizations). Many health care organizations require justification for all capital items: Is it new or replacement? How long will it last? Can it be depreciated? Why is it needed? What are the alternatives if it is not purchased?

Preparing the budget is probably one of the least-liked responsibilities of PR managers, or most managers, for that matter; however, it is one responsibility that has to be taken seriously. The PR manager has to live with — and live within — that budget for an entire year. In past years (or perhaps past eras), managers could get away with going over budget because health care organizations usually could absorb some expense overages in their comfortable profit margins. Today, no manager can risk going over budget, and PR budgets are watched more closely than other operating budgets, given the ongoing concern about the "value" of public relations in the health care setting.

Thus, the PR manager must budget carefully or risk not having enough funds to execute the PR plan. For that reason, many veteran PR managers include a line item for "opportunities"— things that may arise during the year (a chance to sponsor a special event that relates to hospital priorities, for example) that cannot be foreseen during budget preparation. The other alternative, should such a "golden opportunity" arise, is to take the funds out of existing budgeted projects.

"Budgeting is an enormous hassle," concluded one experienced PR vice-president. "But when I can accomplish all of our objectives in a quality way and stay on budget, then I've proved my professionalism and my managerial skills to my peers and my CEO. That's why I'm so careful when I develop that budget."

☐ Finding and Developing the Public Relations Staff

Hiring, training, supervising, motivating, rewarding, and retaining the kind of creative, flexible professionals needed to staff the PR function is a major responsibility for the PR manager.

Characteristics and Qualifications of Hospital Public Relations Staff Members

The traditional list of "essential skills" for most types of PR positions begins with writing, the core skill. Although contemporary PR people are involved in many different types of activities, writing in some form (reports, copy, plans, letters, speeches, and so on) remains the primary task, or is at least a major part of most PR projects. Verbal, graphic, and audiovisual communications skills are also important for most types of PR positions.

If a specific PR position is to be a part of the generalist model described in this chapter, it's preferable for the incumbent or applicant to have a broad background in communications work, with multifaceted hands-on experience in several areas. If the position is in the specialist model, it's almost essential that the applicant have either specialized training or related experience in the desired specialty. However, if the individual's background is limited to that one area, it may be difficult for him or her to take on new challenges or responsibilities if the demands of the position or the department change. Persons with a generalist background, or entry-level people, can be trained to fill a specialist role, but this requires more supervision by the PR manager.

The academic background of today's PR professionals varies. Many senior-level managers have degrees in the liberal arts or journalism; the younger professionals are more likely to have degrees in communications or public relations. Most PR managers agree that they make hiring decisions more on the individual's actual experience during and after college than on his or her major field of study.

The personal characteristics of successful PR professionals generally include being inquisitive and interested in the world around them, being analytical and able to think of new ways to attack old problems, being fairly detail-oriented and able to organize multifaceted projects, and being extremely flexible and able to juggle a number of different responsibilities at the same time.

There is a stereotype that the best PR people are gregarious extroverts; in fact, some of the most successful professionals are, by nature, fairly introverted people who can handle the public and personal interactions that are part of the job. Another stereotype says that PR people must be intuitive. In fact, what the layperson describes as an intuitive judgment by a PR person may be a reasoned judgment based on a quick mental review and analysis of past experience and facts uncovered by the research that is an ongoing part of PR management.

American Telephone & Telegraph's senior PR executives came up with this description of the qualities the corporation is looking for in a PR person:[2]

- Polished communications skills (verbal, interpersonal, written, and visual)
- Strategic thinking and results orientation
- Ability to counsel management
- Understanding of or experience in the mass media
- Skills in organizational or internal communications
- Knowledge of research and evaluation methods
- Externally focused, with broad interests
- **FLEXIBILITY!**

And Frances Friedman, chairman of GCI Group, Inc., writing in the January 1990 issue of *Public Relations Journal*, noted the need for "smart people, addicted to keeping up on the news," and people with "sound judgment, who can offer good advice to clients."[3]

Professionals come to health care public relations from all types of backgrounds, including journalism (still particularly helpful for media relations managers), PR work for nonprofit organizations, or staff positions at PR agencies. In recent years, as health care PR programs have become more comprehensive and salaries more competitive, professionals from corporate PR and marketing positions have also found health care a challenging and rewarding environment.

The PR manager who has a multiperson staff may want to look for diversity and balance when filling a staff position. If most of the staff have PR training and background, someone with media experience can be an asset. Or if the staff all come from a nonprofit orientation, a staffer who has worked in a corporate setting can add a new viewpoint. And a team of persons of different ages, races, genders, and ethnic backgrounds can be invaluable in creating PR plans that touch on the needs and interests of a health care organization's very diverse audiences.

Managing a Creative Staff

Although there are numerous excellent textbooks on staff management available to the PR manager, there are some specific techniques described by experienced PR managers that apply to the management of staff members whose primary responsibilities are to be *creative*.

1. Be open to new ideas—in fact, ask for new and different ways of doing things. Give the staff room to be creative.
2. If a staff member presents an idea or a copy draft or a design that you don't like or think will work, rather than saying that, first ask why he or she chose the technique or style. That may give you a clue to another way it could be done.

3. Get the whole team involved in brainstorming—the best ideas often result from one person coming up with a variation on someone else's idea, which was a response to another staff member's initial concept reinterpreted by yet another staff member. Remember the key rule of brainstorming—don't turn down or mock any ideas. Even the "laughers" are valuable—laughter is great for creativity.

4. Instead of saying "Do it this way," say "What if we tried . . . ." This approach is collegial rather than supervisory.

5. Try not to come up with your own vision of how a project should be done after you've assigned it to a staff member. Invariably, if your staff person has a different vision, you'll compare it with and probably prefer your own concept. There's nothing more frustrating for a staff person than to spend hours coming up with an approach only to be told, "I wanted it done this way" by the manager.

6. If you do have a concept already in mind that you feel strongly about, tell the staff person and let him or her run with it, perhaps suggesting some variations but basically implementing your plan.

7. Don't let your staff members guess about what they're supposed to be doing. Define your expectations, both in terms of work performance and style. If you want reports in writing, say so. If you care about things like standard working hours and signing out if they leave the office, make sure they know that. "Tell me what you expect of me" is the number-one request of staff members.

The PR manager who has a number of staff members also needs to focus on team building. Whether the staff is organized on the generalist or specialist model, or a hybrid of both, there needs to be close working relationships among the staff members.

One of the primary methods of building a team is involving the entire team in the development of the yearly PR plan for the institution, and in the development of plans for individual clients. A planning retreat—preferably off-site, in casual clothes—is an ideal setting for promoting informal interaction between staff members and for generating new ideas. Chapter 6 describes the process of developing the PR plan and notes that it is essential that the entire staff contribute to the plan. Staff participation is essential not only because participation builds a sense of "ownership" and responsibility for implementing the plan, but also because the more creative people who participate in the plan, the better the final outcome will be.

The planning retreat, while it has a defined, organizationally related objective, can also provide a great setting for social interaction and relationship building. One hospital PR vice-president, who had planned a midday "recreation break" for her staff planning retreat, found that the staff had such a good time playing "Pictionary" and "Win, Lose, or Draw" that they abandoned the agenda for the afternoon and played games the rest of the day. "When people work together in a very hectic and demanding environment, sometimes it's hard to remember how much we enjoy each other," she said. "The staff got more out of just enjoying each other's company than we would have had we stuck with our goal-setting agenda."

Another team-building essential is the weekly staff meeting, where the manager shares information from his or her participation in top management team meetings, and the PR staff members discuss what they're working on that week. This is an ideal time for discussions of client projects that involve several staff people, to make sure that everyone's on the same track, and for staff members to ask for advice, input, or brainstorming on creative challenges they're facing. The atmosphere should be informal, with time for sharing funny or awful things that have happened during the week. Participation in the meeting should be obligatory, although the manager should attempt to make the meetings so enjoyable and informative that the staff don't want to miss them. "One of my staff started bringing popcorn to the meetings," said one PR manager, "and then it blossomed into an organized 'snack responsibility' list and a competition as to who would bring the best treats."

One key to building a team spirit is for the staff to feel that the manager is honest and shares information with them. Just as all the staff members need to be involved in planning, they also need to be involved in seeing the health care organization's "big picture." As the organization's communicators, the PR staff members have to see where the organization is going and know what is planned to reach the organization's goals, rather than simply being focused on individual client projects.

The PR staff also needs to know what's going on within the institution. "I probably share more 'sensitive' information with my staff than do other VPs," said one hospital PR exec, "but by sharing it, I let my staff know that I trust them and know they'll keep confidential information to themselves." Because most PR staff people have at least rotating responsibility for media calls in which they may find themselves serving as the organization's spokesperson, they need to be as fully informed as possible. For example, if operating division managers are going to announce layoffs to their employees, the PR staff needs to know about the announcements in advance, in case it gets media inquiries. This also lets the staff members know they're trusted with sensitive information.

If the PR manager finds that differences of work styles or value systems are causing friction between staff members who have to work closely with each other, the institution's human resources or organization development staff can often assist by helping the staff members analyze their styles and attitudes. By understanding that there are differences, and understanding the characteristics of each individual's style, the staff members can gain insight into different ways to adapt their styles when working with each other.

Rewards and incentives are another important type of management tool for the PR manager. Among the preferred rewards or perks identified by one group of PR staff members were:

- The chance to participate in—and travel to—professional development seminars and professional association meetings ("especially if the meeting's in a neat location that I'd like to visit")
- A little unexpected relief time after a particularly hectic period ("My boss came in after we met a deadline on getting a major publication off to the printer and said 'Take the afternoon off—it's on me.' Was I grateful!")
- Not having to punch a time clock ("Everyone on our staff works long, hard hours—but some of us prefer to come in early and be home in time for dinner, whereas others hate to get up in the morning but will be here well into the evening. None of us are forced into a rigid schedule, and everybody appreciates that.")
- The opportunity to learn new skills—media buying, computer graphics or desktop publishing, video production, among others ("Our manager is always willing to let me try something new and to invest in the technology so we can stay current.")
- Support for the staff member who's taking courses, either in pursuit of a degree or to learn new skills ("I had a 4:45 p.m. class, and she always made sure I could get out of the office to make it to class. I made sure I stayed late on the days I didn't have class.")
- Getting credit for their work ("My boss always makes sure that people know who was responsible for doing a specific project. He never takes the credit himself—I know that even when we're not around, he makes sure the CEO and the other administrators know what we do. And when we enter awards competitions, he puts our names on the entry forms, not his.")
- The little things—the boss who brings in doughnuts when there's an early meeting, or orders in pizza when everyone's working late on a deadline, or sends flowers to a staffer who's had an exciting achievement, or takes the entire staff out to a movie one afternoon "because everyone was frazzled and we weren't getting anything done anyway"
- Personal attention—taking the time to get to know staff members' goals, interests, personal concerns ("My manager always takes the time to listen—really listen to what I'm saying. And when someone is going through a rough time personally, our boss is very supportive.")

- Being thanked—and appreciated—for their work ("I worked for a guy who always said that we should know he valued our work, and once a year he'd tell us that in a staff meeting. But my boss now seems to really make a point of thanking us for extra effort, right at the time, and letting us know when we've done good work.")

Most important, the PR manager needs to work consistently at team building and motivation. It's an ongoing responsibility, not a once-a-year occasion, because staff members need support and encouragement on a routine basis as they cope with hectic schedules, heavy work loads, and clients who can sometimes be frustrating. The PR manager who makes staff motivation and development a priority will be rewarded professionally, in terms of quality and quantity of staff members' work, and personally, by watching the staff develop and grow.

□ Outside Help: Using Consultants, Free-Lancers, and Agencies

Calling in outside help, in the form of free-lancers, consultants, or advertising or PR agencies, is an option when the PR manager needs:

- Supplemental staffing to handle the overload—either special projects or ongoing work that the in-house staff does not have time to handle
- Specialized expertise in areas in which the in-house staff isn't experienced, such as national media placements or speech writing
- An objective, outside viewpoint on sensitive issues like convincing employees of the need for a smoke-free environment, or on a major decision like developing an institutional positioning statement

Working with Free-Lancers

Most health care PR departments use free-lance graphic designers and photographers, even if there are designers and photographers on staff. And other institutions have found that free-lance writers, editors, or PR specialists can also be helpful.

A free-lancer is often the most cost-effective alternative for implementing specific one-time projects, like creating a special event or taking over an ongoing project such as an external audience newsletter. Public relations managers who routinely work with free-lancers offer the following advice:

- Look at samples of the free-lancer's work and make sure you see samples of the kind of work that you're hiring the person to do. Is the quality on a par with your own staff's work?
- Ask for references — and check them. Make sure you ask about dependability and reliability.
- When you find a free-lancer who handles an assignment well, try to work with that person again in the future. By developing a relationship, you can ensure that when you have a last-minute need, the free-lancer will give your work priority.
- Agree on compensation rates and methods up front. If it's an hourly rate, ask for an estimate of how many hours the job will take. If you're going to have the free-lancer handle an ongoing, routine project, you may prefer a retainer arrangement. Agree on who's going to pay for expenses like phone calls, mileage, and the like.
- Make sure the free-lancer has everything he or she needs to get the job done. That can include background information, a briefing on the objectives of the project, introductions to any staff members who will be working with the free-lancer, and even a name tag and parking pass if the free-lancer will repeatedly be working in the institution.
- Treat the free-lancers like professional peers — because they are. Many professionals choose to free-lance because they enjoy the freedom, and it can also be very lucrative. Public relations people who treat free-lancers like "second-class citizens" may find that they have trouble getting the free-lancer to take on a second assignment in the future. Good free-lancers don't have to hunt for work.

Asking for a Consultation

Public relations managers generally call in a consultant when they want "another brain to pick." Consultants are helpful in terms of developing PR and marketing strategies and plans and identifying effective institutional image-positioning statements. Consultants also specialize in disciplines such as market research or employee communications audits.

The consultant generally does not implement specific communications programs, but does provide an objective outside viewpoint. The consultant can pose new questions, spot trends that the staff may be missing, or identify new ways of approaching the same old problems. The consultant also brings a different perspective and ideas gained from working with health care organizations of similar size or scope in different parts of the United States. In the health care setting, the involvement of a consultant can also lend credibility to a plan or proposal. Health care CEOs and boards often use consultants, and knowing that the PR plan was developed with the advice of a consultant's "broad viewpoint" can help sell it to top management.

In selecting and working with a consultant, there are a number of things the PR manager should consider:

- Has the consultant worked with health care organizations of similar size, ownership, mission? There are differences among hospitals, and a consultant who has worked primarily with large, tertiary care hospitals, for instance, may not be familiar with the needs of small, rural hospitals.
- How long has the consultant worked in health care, and with how many clients has he or she worked? The field of health care consulting has been dubbed "the fastest-growing employment arena in the U.S." It's important that a consultant have a track record of experience—and the PR manager needs to verify the consultant's expertise by checking with a number of previous clients.
- What exactly does the PR manager want to get out of the consultation? Some PR managers bring in consultants simply to have another, outside view of the organization's positioning, PR, or marketing efforts—using the consultant as an evaluator. Others expect to receive more direction from the consultant, or expect the consultant to bring new ideas or strategies.
- What's the end product? A written report with recommendations? A verbal summary or comments about existing programs? A presentation to the board?
- What is the duration of the consulting arrangement and what is the payment method? The PR manager can contract with the consultant for a flat fee plus expenses for a specific assignment or put the consultant on retainer for a limited engagement. If the flat fee arrangement is used, does this allow the PR manager to contact the consultant for follow-up?

Public relations managers who are considering working with consultants are advised to do a great deal of homework before making a decision. Checking with a number of references and asking to see samples of completed assignments that are similar to the one in question help ensure that the consultant will be able to meet the health care organization's needs.

Working with the Public Relations or Advertising Agency

When a hospital PR manager has a major project or campaign to be undertaken that is beyond either the scope or the time and work-load limits of the in-house staff, he or she may turn to an advertising or PR agency. Many health care organizations use advertising agencies to develop ad campaigns, because this is one specialty that not all health care PR staff are experienced enough to handle. There are also PR agencies that develop advertising programs for health care organizations, although some exclude advertising from their scope of services. When a PR manager is considering bringing in an agency, there are three initial decisions that need to be made.

1. What type of agency—advertising, public relations, marketing, or specialty (direct mail, jingles/theme songs, and so on)? Although the lines of difference are becoming more and more blurred between the types of agencies, it is a mistake to assume that all agencies can handle public relations, advertising, and marketing with equal expertise. One guideline is to assume that how an agency describes itself is what it's best at doing; that is, if an agency says it's an ad agency, assume that its primary expertise is in advertising. To decide what type of agency is needed, the PR manager needs to define exactly what the agency is going to be expected to do. If the assignment is to develop an advertising campaign, then an agency that primarily does advertising is going to be preferred. There are PR agencies that do advertising, but the PR manager needs to determine if the PR agency's advertising capabilities are as comprehensive as those of an agency that does only advertising.

If the assignment is a comprehensive, multifaceted PR campaign, then a PR agency is probably the best choice, because the PR agency understands the art and science of public relations (which differs markedly from advertising). There are advertising agencies that have merged with PR agencies or created their own PR divisions, and thus offer both types of services, but the PR manager needs to assess if the PR capabilities are as strong as the advertising capabilities or if the agency will insist on including advertising as part of the PR campaign.

If the assignment is even broader—developing a total marketing strategy for a product or service—then an agency that specializes in marketing may be preferable, although often marketing agencies do not have the expertise in advertising or public relations that is found in PR and advertising agencies. The solution in this case may be to work with a marketing agency to develop strategies, and then to select an advertising or PR agency to execute the creative elements of the plan.

The key to selecting the right type of agency is to go beyond the agency account rep's assurances that it can handle "everything you need," and to talk to references and look at samples of the agency's work to make sure that its expertise matches the specific needs of the health care organization. Hiring an agency that's strong in public relations to do an ad campaign or a marketing strategy agency to develop PR materials can create a mismatch between capabilities and expectations.

2. What scope should the agency have—local, regional, national? Again, the task for the health care PR manager is to determine what the organization needs and what the organization's market area demands. There is no one "right" choice in terms of choosing between local or national agencies, but there are several factors that should be considered.

First, what's the scope of the campaign? If it's a national campaign targeted at national media or with ad placements in cities across the United States, then a national agency might be preferred for its contacts, knowledge of the national scene, and broad media-buying capabilities. There are also regional and local agencies in larger cities that have handled national campaigns. It's important to find out what the agency has actually done versus what the agency says it can do. If the campaign is regional in nature, aimed, for instance, at a multi-state service area, a regional agency with offices in key cities in the service area may be a good choice. For a campaign that's strictly local— one city—a local agency may have the best feel for the market and the local media.

Second, what's the market sophistication in terms of the campaign media? For TV advertising, for instance, there are metropolitan areas in which the production quality is highly sophisticated. In those cases, an agency that can turn out creative, highly polished, and well-produced spots is essential—even if the agency isn't located in the health care organization's home city.

Finally, what can the health care organization afford? If an organization's total budget for an ad campaign is $200,000 and the bill for creative and production work from a national agency is $150,000, then the organization doesn't have enough money left to get the ads placed. There is often a built-in bias toward a "big-name" national ad agency, because of the glamour factor, but because few health care organizations are launching national-scale ad or PR campaigns, in most cases and in most markets a regional or local agency can meet the organization's needs.

3. *What special focus should the agency have—hospital/health care, consumer, general?* There are strong arguments that are made for hiring agencies that specialize in health care, because they know the product, whereas a consumer-oriented or general agency will have to be educated about the nuances of health care products and purchase decisions. On the other hand, some professionals believe an agency that limits itself to one industry has too limited a view and may be too focused on consumer behavior in only one area, rather than understanding the totality of consumer behavior.

Both of these arguments have validity, and there are numerous examples of outstanding hospital ad and PR campaigns that have been developed by generalist and specialty agencies. In evaluating both types of agencies, the PR manager needs to consider two points:

- Can the general agency assign an account team with enough time and energy to learn the health care business, and can the institution's PR staff take the time and energy to educate them? Also, has the general agency had experience in direct consumer campaigns or does it do primarily business-to-business work?
- Does the health care specialty agency staff take a broad approach and seem to truly understand the consumer behavior process, or does the agency have a number of standard approaches that it tries to make fit the local market?

If neither type of agency seems to have an edge over the other in terms of ability to understand the market and the product, then the PR manager may want to base the final decision on the agency's creative strengths. (Details on how to find, hire, and work with an advertising agency are included in chapter 13.)

☐ Summary

The organization of the PR function depends on a variety of factors, including the size of the PR staff, the training and capabilities of the PR staff members, and the needs of the health care organization.

A key to the success of a small staff is negotiating priorities with the CEO and operating administrators. Unless agreement is reached on PR priorities, the staff members may find that they are asked to do far more than they can handle, without fully meeting the expectations of the health care organization's management.

For a larger staff, the generalist and specialist models both have strengths and weaknesses. The generalist/account executive model is more suited to effectively serving the needs of the internal client departments, but requires a crew of very talented and flexible staff members. The specialist model may be less efficient from the client point of view, but allows staff members to perfect their skills in a specific area.

The PR manager should assess the needs of the health care organization's client departments and the skills of the PR staff members and then select or adapt an organizational structure that is best suited to both. Then, whether the staff is small or large, and whichever organizational model is selected, the PR manager must develop a budget that reflects the institutional PR plan. Careful budgeting is imperative as the PR department will have to live within the constraints of that budget for one entire year.

References

1. Cutlip, S., Center, A. H., and Broom, G. M. *Effective Public Relations.* Englewood Cliffs, NJ: Prentice-Hall, 1985, p. 267.
2. Quoted in Wilcox, D. L., Ault, P. H., and Agee, W. K. *Public Relations: Strategies and Tactics.* 2nd ed. Cambridge, MA: Harper and Row, 1989, p. 85.
3. Friedman, F. Redefining ourselves to our clients. *Public Relations Journal* 46(1):31, Jan. 1990.

Suggested Readings

Bell, S. E., and Bell, E. C. Public relations: functional or functionary. *Public Relations Review,* Summer 1976.

Belzer, E. J. 12 ways to better team building. *Working Woman,* Aug. 1989.

Cochran, L. R. How to manage creative people. *Public Relations Quarterly,* Mar. 1985.

Donovan, H. Managing your intellectuals. *Fortune,* Oct. 23, 1989.

Grunig, J. E., and Hunt, T. Budgeting and decision making. In: *Managing Public Relations.* New York City: Longman, 1984.

Public Relations and Institutional Planning

The function of planning in today's health care organization involves two roles for the public relations manager: (1) being a key participant in development of the organization's strategic plan and (2) directing the development and implementation of the PR and communications plans for the organization and its products and services. Although there's a standard and tired old joke repeated by PR professionals—"I don't have time to plan because I'm in the middle of coping with crises"—experienced managers understand that the planning process is one of the most critically important functions they perform. They note that careful planning, among other things, can:

- Encourage systematic thinking, so that the PR activities are purposeful and coordinated, rather than a haphazard array of unrelated projects
- Force the PR staff to look ahead, to assess the external and internal environments so that roadblocks can be anticipated
- Let the PR staff take the offensive, functioning proactively to work toward specific goals, rather than simply reacting to events and audience demands
- Define roles and responsibilities, so that staff members can plan their own time and work load
- Help set performance standards for staff members and for the PR department or division
- Help maintain quality standards by avoiding mistakes (often expensive) caused by rushed, last-minute work

Taking the time out of often-hectic workdays to go through the planning process may seem difficult, but once a staff of PR professionals has completed a year of working with a fairly comprehensive plan, staff members will become firm believers in the value of the PR plan.

☐ The Role of the Public Relations Manager in Strategic Planning

As discussed in chapter 3, the integration of public relations in the planning process is essential for several reasons. The reason most often mentioned first is that PR managers need to be informed about and aware of all plans so that they can develop communications plans and anticipate public reaction. And that is certainly true. The PR manager who is not part of the process, who learns about the organization's decisions and plans second-hand or piecemeal, can hardly be effective in communicating with the organization's public.

However, there is a much more important reason that the PR manager needs to be integrally involved in strategic planning, a reason that affects both the validity of the plan itself and also the success of the decisions that are part of the plan. That reason is that the ranking PR officer is the senior management team member responsible for continually assessing and monitoring the health care organization's external publics. Put simply, the PR manager brings to the planning table some very critical information—what the publics want and need and how they will react to the organization's plans. The operating managers represent the needs of their divisions. The finance officer is concerned about the budget. The staff attorney examines legal ramifications. The CEO provides the vision. The planners gather data, analyze alternatives, and serve as facilitators for the planning process. All of this activity would essentially take place in a vacuum, with little attention to the organization's diverse and often contradictory publics, unless the senior PR officer plays a key role in development of the plan.

It can be argued that marketers and planners and even operating administrators, as part of their responsibilities for market assessment for their divisions' products and services, must all study and assess external audiences. Although that is true, each of these staff members looks only at segments of the organization's publics—very often, primarily at customer groups. The PR manager is responsible for monitoring and assessing the needs and concerns of all the organization's publics, including many key audiences who do not fall into the customer category (community opinion leaders, internal audiences like employees and volunteers, single-issue activist groups, people living near the institution, and others). Through the relationship-building process described in detail in chapter 8, the PR manager and staff are to be the organization's eyes and ears to these audiences, and conversely, to represent those audiences' viewpoints and predicted reactions to the organization.

This representation function is absolutely critical during the planning process. The health care organization that makes decisions about creating and cutting services and programs without careful attention to its internal and external audiences is doomed to failure. Developing the strategic plan ultimately involves making choices from a number of alternatives, alternatives that are typically evaluated on financial, operational, staffing, and legal criteria. Once the alternatives have been evaluated on these criteria, they must also be given a "reality check" by being examined on the basis of how the organization's publics will react. Given the impact that negative audience reaction can have on a health care organization, this public reaction analysis is one step that cannot be omitted from the planning process. For instance, the public's outcry over closing hospital services, as described in chapter 2, can actually force a hospital to reverse a financially sound decision to close a service. Only the PR manager can guide the management planning team through this analysis and evaluation process, fulfilling the counseling role that is the essential function of public relations in the institution.

☐ Development of the Institutional Image Plan

Developing a year-long PR plan for the health care organization actually involves the creation of multiple plans that are combined to provide a work plan for the PR staff. The first phase is to develop an overall plan for the health care organization as an institution. The second phase is to develop individual plans for specific products and services. The following pages describe the development of the institutional image plan; the development of plans for specific products will be discussed in a later section of this chapter.

The institutional PR plan has two primary goals:

- "Positioning" the health care organization with its key customers by creating a specific image of the organization, an image that will create awareness and result in these customers generally preferring the organization over its competitors and that will also serve as a context for specific product/service preference campaigns
- Developing relationships with key audiences to engender or maintain their support or to lessen or avert their active hostility

The second goal is addressed through the stakeholder relations/ issues management program detailed in chapter 8. This section will detail development of the institutional image-positioning plan, a plan designed to build customer awareness and preference for the health care organization in general.

101

Rationale for the Image Development Campaign

The issue of whether or not a health care organization needs to concentrate on developing a specific image in the minds of the consumer is often discussed by health care administrators, and there are those who question the value of image development. What PR professionals who have conducted audience research know, of course, is that every institution has an image in the minds of its publics. If research shows that the institution's existing image is positive, then the role of the image development campaign is to maintain and build on that positive image. If the institution's image is blurry or vague ("I don't know anything about the hospital") or is negative, then the image development campaign must attempt to build awareness and clarify the institution's attributes in the minds of the public, or to counter the negatives.

The health care organization that attempts to market specific products or services without maintaining or developing a positive and distinctive image in the market ignores the fact that in health care, image almost always leads product choice. Paul Keckley's research has shown that poor image is the chief barrier to the product purchase decision by consumers.[1] And a Hospital Advisory Board study shows that 41 percent of consumers select a hospital based on its "reputation," a figure that is much higher in some markets.[2] As James Foster observed: "The better known you are, the better regarded you will be. Awareness breeds familiarity breeds favorability."[3]

Research has also shown that there is a "halo" effect from having a positive image. If they have no information about which health care organizations offer specific services, or about the services themselves, consumers will assume that the organization with the most positive image not only has those services but is also the preferred choice for those services. A positive image can also increase the likelihood that the patient will accept a physician's recommendation to use a particular hospital, or that the patient in a managed care plan will select a physician who admits to the hospital with the positive image.

And although image alone can't create product/service preference or utilization, it can make the consumer more or less receptive to messages about a product or service. Rarely does any single health care organization have a product or service that is unique; usually competitors also offer similar services. In this case, a positive image can help the consumer differentiate between similar services.

In addition, even the best product campaign will rarely persuade consumers to override a negative image of a hospital (exceptions would be for services that are perceived as not really a part of the hospital, like fitness centers, wellness classes, and the like). A consumer who has a negative image of hospital A, a fuzzy or nonexistent image of hospital B, and a positive image of hospital C, is much more likely to choose or accept referral to hospital C's services. Thus, image development — beginning with developing awareness of the health care organization and its services, and then using persuasive communications to develop preference — is the cornerstone of the PR plan.

The development of the awareness/preference/image plan is coordinated by the PR staff and involves the CEO, the marketing staff, and the board of trustees PR committee, if one exists. Outside PR or advertising counsel may also be involved.

Development of Theme and Message Content

The image development team uses research, including competitive analysis and customer need/attitude/opinion surveys, to determine an overall communications theme for the health care organization. This theme in essence stakes the organization's claim to a unique position that differentiates the organization from its competing institutions. The theme says to the customers "This is what we are; this is how we are different from any other health care organization in this area" and reflects the market position that the health care organization occupies or is attempting to occupy.

The art of positioning is a relatively sophisticated marketing process that is covered in more detail in the sources referenced at the end of this chapter. This overview will provide a context for development of a communications theme.

There are many different positions that a health care organization can claim: least expensive/most affordable, most convenient, most luxurious, best or newest technology, most service-oriented, smallest, largest, busiest, most specialized — to name just a few. Determining the organization's unique position in a market requires consideration of these key questions:

1. *What is realistic?* Can a 200-bed community hospital realistically position itself as the tertiary care leader in a major metropolitan market? Or can a busy 700-bed tertiary care hospital truly position itself as "small and personalized?" Some positions can be factually verified — smallest or largest, for instance — but positions such as those need to be expressed in consumer benefit terms ("Being the largest means we can handle whatever type of care you may need"). Other positions (most service-oriented, most affordable) are going to require some type of evidence to support the claims, including comparative competitive data.

2. *What positions are the competing health care organizations already claiming or holding?* If a competing hospital has already identified

itself as the leading high-tech hospital, it will be more difficult for another hospital to try to also claim this position. Even if the second hospital is truly superior technologically, it is difficult to try to take over a position that is already held. Market research is essential to identify the public's perceptions of health care organizations in the market, because if the research shows that an institution is already clearly perceived by the public as the high-tech leader, for instance, it will be very difficult for another institution to challenge that position.

3. *What matters to the customers?* What attributes do they think are important? What makes a difference to them when they choose a hospital? Clearly, if the organization discovers through market research that the customers believe that experienced physicians, high-tech equipment, and modern facilities are their top-choice factors when it comes to preferring or using a hospital, then it makes little sense for the organization to claim the "friendly/service-oriented" position. Granted, there are instances in which the health care organization may discover that it seems to have none of the attributes that consumers say are essential. An organization in this situation can choose to revamp its strategic plan to develop attributes that more closely match customer needs and concerns. Or it can select a specialty niche that is unique in the market (either by focusing on a primary service, like diabetic patient services, or by focusing communications on a specific customer group, like senior citizens). Or it can go ahead and position itself for its strengths in an area that customers did not rate highly (the friendly/service-oriented niche, for instance) and use persuasive methods to try to convince the customers that this attribute really is important. The latter route is extremely difficult — trying to reorient customers' values is a long-term and correspondingly expensive proposition, with limited hope of success. It is far easier to develop services to meet existing needs, or cite attributes that match existing customer preferences.

Once a position is selected, as part of the strategic planning and marketing processes, the image development team then develops a communications theme and specific message points that present that position to the customers. For example, if a hospital's position is that of the area's leading tertiary care hospital, the communications theme could be "the regional medical center," emphasizing regional scope (versus local community hospital), critical care capabilities, high-tech equipment, and experienced physician specialists. This theme and the message points should be tested through focus group research to determine:

- Does the positioning theme matter to the customers? Or do they say "So what?"
- Do the customers understand what the theme means? Or does it have to be explained?
- Are the message points significant to the customers?

The message strategy can be refined after this research and, if needed, reviewed by additional focus groups.

Development of the Communications Plan for the General Audiences

The integration of the theme and message strategies into the existing general-audience PR programs — speakers' bureau, external publications, media placement, and so on — is part one of the institutional image development communications plan. This effort sends the message via broad channels to general audiences and also provides a consistent background for more targeted communications (which is part two of the plan).

The finalized theme and message strategies provide a proactive context for general communications activities, such as placing news stories, providing speakers for community groups, and selecting topics for external publications. Instead of reactive media relations — responding to media requests for interviews on topics the reporters have selected — the PR staff develops story ideas that relate to the theme and message strategies and proposes these stories to reporters. Instead of "filling orders" for speakers requested by community groups, the PR staff can suggest speakers on topics that relate to the message strategies. And instead of selecting a cover story for the health care organization's external magazine by thinking about which department head or physician would like some publicity, the editor plans the magazine's issues for an entire year, based on the theme and message strategies. Developing this part of the communications plan involves the following four steps:

Step One: Identify the methods that will be used to reach the general audiences. Chapters 8 through 16 detail a number of methods that can be considered (and it should be noted that many of these methods will also be used to communicate to specific target audiences and to promote products and services). A basic general-audience communications plan for a health care organization generally includes a proactive media relations program (story placement), several types of community relations activities (speakers' service, tours program, special events), some type of periodic publication aimed at the broad general audience (magazine, newsletter), one or more special publications (annual report, capabilities brochure), and possibly general institutional advertising (sometimes called "image" or "corporate" advertising). Availability of PR staff members and budgets should be considered when selecting an array of methods to use. And what methods the competition is using should also be considered. If, for instance, several hospitals are sending four-color, long-story, quarterly magazines to consumers, the PR manager might consider a newsier type of tabloid or a monthly health information newsletter.

Step Two: Develop preliminary budget plans for each of the selected methods. Although the budget items will differ for the various alternatives, the following is an example of items that should be included in the preliminary budget planning:

- Media relations — costs for media kits, print and video clipping services, printing and mailing releases, media days (when the media are invited for a day of briefing and tours), travel to visit reporters, development of video news releases or radio tapes, and so on
- Speakers/tours — costs for promotional materials (including mailing), giveaway items, fees or travel expenses for speakers, refreshments at meetings, gifts or apparel for volunteer tour guides, and so on
- Publications — costs for printing, typesetting, design, photography, free-lance writers, mailing lists, postage, and so on

Step Three: Develop preliminary targets and timetables. How often will the periodic publication be issued? How many media placements will be generated per month? How many speaker placement requests are expected per month? What annual or fixed-date special events (medical staff dinner, board annual dinner, hospital or major service anniversary observation, annual health fair, and so on) are scheduled and when? These dates and items are listed on a month-by-month calendar.

Step Four: Determine staffing needed to handle each of the on-going mass audience projects. At this point in the development of the total PR plan, the PR manager estimates what percentage of each staff person's time will be spent on these general-audience projects and makes note of this for reference when all of the components of the comprehensive plan are determined. Then, the manager can make adjustments, based on institutional marketing priorities, in the general-audience plan. For instance, if there are two major events and a kick-off of a heart service advertising campaign scheduled for the same month and involving all members of the PR staff, then the manager may eliminate or reschedule some lower-priority items.

Once the details of the general-audience plan are completed, the PR staff members move on to develop more specific communications plans aimed at target audiences.

Development of the Communications
Plan for Target Audiences

Part two of developing the institutional image plan involves targeted audiences. The image development team, in addition to creating a theme and specific message points, will also identify target audiences, based on the institution's strategic plan. These target audiences will differ from one institution to another, but may include:

- Physicians (medical staff members, potential staff members, referring physicians)
- Targeted potential patient groups (senior citizens, parents, and so on)
- Employees (so they're fully aware of the message and can be effective "sales reps" with their friends and associates)
- Volunteers and auxilians (considered by their friends to be "knowledgeable sources")
- Legislators and opinion leaders
- Other specific audiences who will be targets of specific product or service campaigns (the general-image messages will enhance the product campaign)

A specific plan is developed for each audience, beginning with a measurable objective, followed by a list of methods for reaching that audience. (Developing objectives is described in detail in the following section of this chapter.) For instance, the plan for the referring physician audience could have an objective of creating more awareness of the institution's specialized surgery and high-tech capabilities among family practitioners and internists in the secondary service area. Communications strategies could include a direct-mail brochure, a visit from a physician relations or outreach representative to describe the message strategies, stories in the existing physician newsletter, special open houses for new critical care units or high-tech equipment, and specific brochures or letters describing additions to the critical care/high-tech services.

Similar plans would be developed for each target audience, and then a grid like the one shown in table 6-1 can be developed. This is a simplified example, because there could be several dozen methods to reach each target audience. Laying each audience campaign out in a grid shows the total picture of the activities, ensuring that each audience is being reached through a variety of methods (following the M^4 rule, "multiple methods maximize the message," described in chapter 13) and is reached multiple times so that repeated impressions heighten awareness.

Then a preliminary timetable is established for each item — preliminary because it may have to be revised when all components

Table 6-1. Grid for Planning Elements of a Product Marketing Communications Plan for a New Outpatient Surgery Center

Audience	Method				
	Event	Speaker	Publication	Sales	External Magazine
Referring physicians	Open house	Surgeons at hospital physician meetings	Physician referral brochure	Physician liaison visits	
Senior citizens	Laser surgery tour	Dr. S. for senior centers	Direct-mail brochure on new technology		Profile of senior citizen who had laser surgery

of the PR plan are combined and it's discovered that the staff will have to produce 43 brochures in one month, for instance. Changes in timing can then be made to maintain a more even work load. Finally, a preliminary budget can be prepared — again, preliminary because once the total costs for all projects are added up, they may exceed the amount available and revisions will have to be made.

☐ Development of Product/Service Marketing Communications Plans

While the institutional image development plan is being developed, the PR staff is also involved in creating specific marketing communications plans for myriad health care services and products. These products and services include those identified in the organization's strategic plan as targets for direct promotion to audiences, as well as those indicated by operating departments and service areas as targets for communications projects or programs during the following year. Two initial questions that arise as part of this process are: who should create and control the marketing communications plan, and who should pay for implementation of the communications program?

Control of Product Marketing Communications Plans

The issue of control is often linked to budget — the thought being that whoever pays for the communications program should have total control. In fact, what works best is a "joint custody" arrangement. The service or department manager must be satisfied that the program meets his or her needs, is appropriate for the audience, meets his or her standards of quality, is acceptable to the physicians associated with the service or department, and so on. In short, the product's "owners" must feel satisfied and comfortable with the communications program, whether or not they are paying for it.

In addition, the senior PR executive must approve the program's objectives, methods, and execution, because the PR manager is responsible for maintaining quality and effectiveness of all communications activities and ensuring that the specific product plans are consistent with the health care organization's positioning and image development plans. Because of this role and responsibility, it is absolutely essential that *all* communications activities aimed at external or internal audiences be approved and supervised by the PR department.

Maintaining this level of control does not always mean that the PR department produces the work, especially if the department is understaffed and overworked with institutional priorities. In that case, there may be projects (such as patient brochures, for instance) that are created and written by the requesting department and simply edited and marked up for typesetting and simple layout by the organization's print shop. Or a department may work directly with a free-lancer or an agency on a campaign, with all work produced by the outside firm — but the PR manager must still have final approval on all phases of the project.

In larger health care organizations, maintaining this type of control can be difficult, because there are literally dozens of departments and programs that need brochures and other materials and may attempt to either develop them themselves or hire someone to get the work done without "going through PR." This can even be a problem in some smaller organizations with decentralized budgets. The result can be materials that are poorly done, inconsistent with the organization's image development campaign, in violation of design and graphics standards, or filled with grammatical or factual errors — the list is endless. And generally, regardless of the fact that the PR department may have had no involvement in the project, the PR manager is the person who receives the complaints from the CEO or external sources.

There are several ways to prevent this from occurring — developing policies requiring PR supervision of all communications projects, educating managers about these policies and why they're important, and instructing the purchasing department and finance departments not to authorize ordering or payment for any communications services that have not been approved by the PR department (setting up a dual-approval payment system is covered in the next section of this chapter). None of these methods is fail-safe; perhaps the two most important steps are for the CEO to make it clear to senior-level administrators

109

that "going around" PR is not to be tolerated, and for the PR manager to develop such positive relationships with his or her manager colleagues that they will be willing to cooperate. Certainly establishing the service-oriented PR department described in chapter 5 — the department that provides high-quality work and really helps the department and service managers meet their goals — is also important in making those product managers *want* to work with the PR department.

With this cooperative spirit in place, the PR manager can develop a team approach to creating the marketing communications plans for departments and services. The team will include the product/service manager and/or administrator and members of the PR staff. If the PR staff is organized on an in-house agency model (see chapter 5 for details on organizational structures), there will be a staff member assigned as an account manager for each product or service, and that account manager will work with the account planning team. (The PR manager may also want to participate in the planning process.) If the PR staff is organized on the functional model, then the PR manager will work with each product/service team and may choose to have the functional managers (publications manager, media relations manager, community relations manager) also participate in the planning so they understand their role and responsibilities in each service campaign. Additionally, if the health care organization has a separate marketing function, the marketing manager or a staff member may be involved in the team to address marketing research and other marketing-related facets of the business plan.

Financial Responsibility for Product Marketing and Communications Campaign Elements

Funds to pay for individual department or service marketing and communications campaigns' elements need to be included in the health care organization's budget. And the issue of "who pays" is closely related to the issues of responsibility for, control over, and satisfaction with the communications projects.

In some health care organizations, the budget is centralized in the PR department, which is expected to cover all of the organization's communications efforts, including staff time and expenses. In other health care organizations, the communications budget is totally decentralized, with costs allocated to the departments requesting the work. This includes both expenses (printing, ad time and space, typography, and so on) and a portion of the salaries of the PR staff members who produced the work. With the latter system, which is very similar to an ad or PR agency billing system, the PR staff members keep track of the hours they spend on each department's or service's work and their salary for those hours is charged to that department. For example, if a publications manager spent 20 hours one week developing a brochure for the maternity department, then 50 percent of his or her salary for that week (or 20 hours times his or her hourly rate) would be charged to the maternity department. There are positive and negative points for both of these systems.

With the communications budget centralized in public relations:

- The department and service managers can develop a free-spending, "We're not paying for it" mentality because the funds don't come out of their budgets.
- The requests for projects may exceed the funds that the PR department has budgeted and the PR manager then has to become a referee, trying to decide which department's work is more important than another's.
- The health care organization's total expenses for communications can be assessed easily because they are all in one budget.
- The PR staff members may not feel the necessity to gain the product manager's acceptance and support of the communications efforts for his or her department because the work can be authorized and paid for without the product manager's approval.
- The department and service managers may not feel a sense of ownership for the communications activities, even those which are prepared for their products, seeing the work, instead, as "PR stuff." This can lead to a lack of support from other managers when the PR manager seeks an expanded budget.

With communications expenditures decentralized in operating department budgets:

- The department manager is more likely to carefully consider the need for the project if the expenses for a brochure or an ad campaign come out of his or her department's budget.
- The product managers feel a real sense of ownership in their communications programs, because their authorization is needed for the budget for the programs.
- The PR staff members will pay more attention to making sure the product manager is happy with the work being produced because the product managers must approve the budget for the programs.
- A product manager whose budget is charged for the PR staff salaries to produce a project may feel he or she should have more authority over the PR staff person ("There's no way it could take that many hours to just write some copy") or that payment doesn't have to be made if he or she isn't satisfied with the work ("After all, I'm paying her salary").
- The time involved in keeping careful track of their hours in 15-minute increments can be an additional hassle for already busy PR staff members.

One approach that has worked well for a number of health care organizations is a modified system in which staff salaries and related staff costs (benefits, travel, and so on) are centralized in the PR department, whereas direct expenses for materials (printing, typography, media time, and so on) are charged to the departments. This avoids the problems involved with charging departments for PR staff time and achieves the positive results of ownership and prudent buying that come when the department or service has to budget for communications work, just as they budget for supplies and other expenses.

Initiating approval and payment for expenses can be handled in one of two ways. Public relations staff members can write the purchase orders (because they probably are more familiar with the vendors and specifications) and have the product manager cosign or authorize it. Alternatively, the PR staffer can give the product manager the purchase order information to write the purchase order, and then the PR manager can cosign it. Approval of bills is handled in a similar fashion. Whatever the method, the objective is for both the department paying for the expenses and the PR department to approve the expenditures and the plans they represent. In health care organizations where this system has been in practice for a number of years and where the department manager's trust and confidence level in the PR staff are high, the PR staff members may be authorized to write purchase orders without taking the time to get a cosignature from the department head. "My account manager knows what our budget limits are, and we work together on the plan, and I approve everything in advance, so it's fine with me if she does the POs. She knows I'll get the bills and I trust her," said one hospital product manager.

The main objectives in deciding on a budgeting and payment system should be:

- To develop a system that is functional, efficient, and satisfactory to the PR staff members and the department managers
- To ensure that the PR department has adequate control, via expenditure control, over all internal and external communications
- To ensure that the department/service/product manager has a feeling of ownership and satisfaction with the work produced by public relations on his or her department's behalf

Steps in Department or Product Communications Plan Development

Once the team of PR staff members and department/service manager is assembled, and the issues of joint custody and budgets and expenses are settled, then the process of developing the plan can begin. The departments' needs may be as simple as a series of patient education brochures for an inpatient nursing unit or as complex as a multifaceted PR and advertising campaign for a comprehensive heart and vascular service, but the process remains the same.

Step One: Defining Goals, Objectives, and Audiences

Before planning can begin, the PR manager must address a number of questions: Why is the plan being created? What is expected to happen as a result of the plan? Is there a problem that needs to be addressed, such as a lack of awareness or preference for the institution's cardiology services? Is there a need to move an audience to action, such as prompting potential patients to call the institution's physician referral service? Is there a need to maintain a strong awareness of one of the institution's preferred services and thus maintain market share?

Every program or service has an eventual goal on which the communications campaign is supposed to have an impact: more patients admitted, greater patient satisfaction, increased utilization of a service. Within that broad goal, specific objectives must be created for the communications efforts. If the goal is increased patient admissions to a specific inpatient service, how can the communications campaign specifically affect physicians, potential patients, or payers? For physicians, one objective might be to create greater awareness of the capabilities of that inpatient service. For potential patients, one objective could be to increase consumer preference for the service ("If I had a heart problem, I would prefer to go to hospital X") so that when the physician recommends hospital X, the patient agrees, or the patient actually asks the physician to admit him or her to hospital X. For payers, a campaign objective might be to inform the directors of managed care plans about the service's costs, lengths of stay, and complication rates, so that when the plan selects hospitals to contract with for this specific service, hospital X is given consideration.

One essential part of defining the objective is targeting the appropriate audiences. Which audience can affect the overall marketing goal? If the goal is increased admissions to an inpatient service, do the primary admitters to the unit also admit to other institutions? If yes, they are clearly a target audience. Are there physicians on the staff or in the community who are not now admitting patients to the unit, or admitting only a few patients? They would also be a good target audience for the campaign. If any of these physicians admit to other institutions and offer their patients a choice, then potential patients are also an important audience.

Once audiences are defined, specific objectives for each audience can be developed. The clearer the objective is, the easier it is to develop a specific action plan to achieve that objective. The more precise and quantifiable the objective, the easier it is to evaluate and measure how well the objective was reached. If the objective is to increase calls to the physician referral service, a target number needs to be set—for example, by 10 percent or by an additional 200 calls. And when the objectives are set, a method for measuring the results needs to be determined. For a direct-response goal, the results can be measured by counting the responses. For an awareness or preference goal, some sort of benchmark research needs to be done to measure the audience awareness and preference levels before the campaign and after the campaign.

It is important to select objectives that can actually be achieved by a communications campaign and that have results that can actually be attributed primarily to the communications campaign. When an objective such as "increase patient census in the pediatrics unit" is established for a physician or consumer communications campaign, it is difficult to isolate the precise impact of the campaign. Although the census may actually increase during the campaign, there are always other intervening variables that may have been primarily or partially responsible for achieving that result: for example, an outbreak of severe flu or upper respiratory infections in children might have occurred. It then becomes difficult to tie the communications campaign to the census increase or to determine if the campaign was even partially responsible for the increased admissions. For this reason, it's generally better to target communications efforts at something that they can actually achieve: greater awareness, increased preference, increased direct responses (calls, contributions, registration for seminars, and the like).

If the communications campaign objective is an outcome such as increasing admissions to the heart center inpatient units, an objective on which other variables can also have an impact, then a method for measuring the precise contribution of the campaign must be developed. In this example, if the admissions to the heart center inpatient units do increase, an analysis of other variables must be made along with the measurement of the impact of the communications activities. The broad impact of the campaign can be measured by precampaign and postcampaign research with the general audience, making the assumption that increased awareness and preference among this general audience would probably have contributed in some way to the increased admissions. This assumption can be challenged, however, and a better way to measure the actual contribution of the campaign to the increased admissions would be by interviewing patients admitted to the unit to determine their awareness of the advertising and to ask them if it had an impact on their decision to choose the hospital when their physicians asked them where they wanted to be hospitalized.

It should also be noted that, for what seem to be simple, routine, inexpensive projects, such as patient education brochures or external-audience newsletters that are part of a larger campaign, taking the time to set up elaborate measures of success may be counterproductive in terms of taking up staff time that could be better used. If the nurses using the education brochures report that the publications are helpful in teaching the patients, it's probably not necessary to survey the patients before and after their exposure to the brochures. If the overall goal of a communications campaign that includes a newsletter can be measured, it is probably not necessary to do a separate evaluation of the newsletter's impact. Granted, if there are concerns about whether or not the newsletter is needed, or if budget limits mean some methods may have to be excluded, it is helpful to have specific measurements on the impact of those methods (whether conclusions are drawn from measurement in the current campaign or at least made based on measurements taken in similar past campaigns).

Step Two: Situation Analysis

A situation analysis can be as simple as a 1-page report or as detailed as a 50-page document. The situation analysis is developed through primary and secondary research about the product, the competition, and the audience. (See chapter 7.) The situation analysis describes the product's strengths and weaknesses, the competition's strengths and weaknesses, the external environment, and any barriers that could affect the product, as well as the opinions, attitudes, concerns, and awareness/preference levels of the product's audiences.

Developing the situation analysis is a step that is easy to overlook or ignore in the press of time; however, it can be one of the most valuable steps in the planning process. First, it encourages (or forces) the product managers to realistically assess their products' strengths and weaknesses. This helps the product manager identify weaknesses that may have been overlooked and can probably be addressed, and it also helps the PR staff members that are developing the communications program to gain a better understanding of the product.

Second, it also requires that the product manager take a realistic look at the competition. Again, this can help the product manager discover modifications that may need to be made in the program or service. It can also help the manager or administrator who is considering creating a new service decide if there's really room in the market for this product. The manager may realize that creating the city's sixth mammography center may not be a wise move, unless a way can be found to differentiate the service or appeal to a specific target audience that hasn't already been captured by a competitor (that is, a special education/support program for younger women, a center with special hours for women who work outside the home, or a center that caters to the needs of older women).

Third, going through a situation analysis provides an opportunity for the product manager to identify any internal obstacles that might need to be addressed. For example, an outpatient surgery center manager may note that the main hospital information desk personnel are not helpful in directing early-arrival patients to the special outpatient surgery admitting area. The manager may have already been aware of these obstacles, but identifying them as part of a situation analysis can provide the opportunity for the product manager, supported by the PR staff, if needed, to approach the information desk manager or the administrator responsible for that function and ask for assistance in solving the problem.

The situation analysis is the vital process of looking inward and outward that can ensure that the product is as well defined, organized, and positioned as possible and that can also prepare a firm foundation for the communications campaign.

Step Three: Selecting Methods and Messages

Defining the messages that are to be sent as part of the communications campaign or project should be a group effort, with the product manager identifying specific strengths and audience concerns that have been discovered through the situation analysis research process and the PR staff members suggesting ways to turn these strengths into benefits that will appeal to the audience.

Once the messages have been defined, the following questions can help in the selection of what communications methods will be used:

- *Time frame* — How soon does the objective have to be achieved? Can a method that takes a longer time to achieve the objective be used (such as multiwave direct mailings), or is there a need for quick, heavy responses (via TV or radio ads or through calling on physicians personally)?
- *Budget* — What methods can be done well within the set budget? With a limited budget, selecting a method like TV or outdoor advertising means the production will have to be done so cheaply that quality will be compromised, or that the purchase of air time or billboards will be so limited that market coverage and frequency goals cannot be achieved.
- *Message* — What methods work best for sending the type of message that has been defined? If the message is detailed and factual, a print medium is probably best. If the message must have emotional impact, visuals — photos or video — are going to be important.

- *Audience*—What methods are preferred or used by the target audience? Customer research can identify how various audiences are currently receiving their health care and other information, and how they'd like to receive that information. Some physicians say they won't read newsletters or brochures but will take five minutes to listen to a presentation by a hospital representative (or physicians may prefer to have the information filtered through their office staff). Younger consumers are radio and TV oriented, whereas senior citizens may say they like to receive printed information mailed to their homes. Matching the method to the audience is very important.

Once these questions are answered, the PR staff members can review the array of methods available (covered in detail in chapters 8 through 16) and come up with alternatives. The PR manager or client account representative then reviews these alternatives with the client, recommending those that seem to be the best, and a final decision is made after costs have been detailed. The key question to ask when selecting communications methods is: What can we afford to execute in a high-quality way that will deliver our message as quickly as our timetable requires and is appropriate for the type of message we want to send and the audience that we've targeted?

Step Four: Developing the Work Plan

A work plan should include a timetable—what events are already tied into a specific date (the heart center's fifth anniversary, the opening of a new pediatric wing), when do we want to begin a TV campaign, and so on. The first timetable is a projection of what is desired—it may have to be revised when the comprehensive plan is developed and over-load situations are noted.

The work plan must also include responsibilities—who's doing what and when, broken down step by step. If the objective is to mail an announcement of an open house by May 15, when does the product manager have to provide information on details of the event so the PR staff members can develop the invitation and get it to the printer? It is very important that the work planning process specify very clearly what the PR staff is expected to do and what the product manager must do so that the PR staff members can meet these expectations. This helps the product manager realize that he or she has a vital part in this process and must do his or her part for the communications work to proceed on schedule. It also prevents problems with "culprit identification" when projects get off track. An estimation of the PR staff time to produce these communications projects should also be included.

117

The work plan should be approved by the product manager and the PR manager, and once this is completed, a finalized budget can be developed. Finally, the work plan should include details on measurement and evaluation, so that these important activities are not overlooked by the product or PR managers.

☐ Finalizing the Comprehensive Public Relations Plan

Once the institutional image communications plan, with its general-audience components and the target-audience components, and the department/service communications plans are prepared, the PR manager needs to lay out these plans together, month by month, with the projections on needed staff time included. This will allow the manager to assess the feasibility of the combined plans in terms of staffing and to answer the critical question: "Can we get all of this done?" If the initial answer seems to be "no," the PR manager has several options that can be considered.

The problem may be *timing*— 82 projects scheduled for completion in March; 23 in August. The PR manager, consulting with the staff and the clients, can attempt some schedule changes to balance the work over the 12-month period. It's often easier to shift ongoing general-audience projects (the quarterly magazine, for instance) to ensure that client projects that are tied to specific dates can be met. Or the PR manager may choose to bring in outside help during the heavy work-load months.

The problem may be *function imbalance*— the plans call for so many publications that the editors would have to work round-the-clock, whereas the media relations people will have time on their hands. The PR manager can decide to reduce the number of publications, use freelance or agency help, assign the overload to other PR staffers who have the skills, or take on some of the work himself or herself.

The problem may be *responsibility imbalance*— the account manager for maternal–child health services has several dozen multifaceted campaigns to produce, whereas the behavioral services account manager's clients have requested only minimal work. The PR manager can tap other staff members (function specialists or other account managers or the PR manager himself or herself) to assist the maternal–child health account manager, but the preferable solution is to segment the client's needs into more manageable work loads. If the imbalance in responsibility is projected to be a long-term situation, it may be necessary to restructure account manager assignments; perhaps the pediatric services and women's health services both need a full-time account manager.

Once these modifications have been made, if the work load is still far beyond the staffing available to handle it, the PR manager either needs to bring in more staff (adding positions or using free-lancers or agencies, if budgets permit) or needs to scale down the plans, based on the institution's strategic plan. If the health care organization needs to concentrate on building general-audience awareness, the first target for cutbacks would be the low-priority product campaigns. If general awareness is high but several key products need major campaigns, some of the general awareness activities can be reduced or eliminated. It is also important that the PR manager allow time for the staff members to handle the requests for unexpected and unplanned, but essential, projects that come up during the year and also to handle the crises that inevitably arise.

Finally, the PR staff members need time to think, to plan, to react, to relax, to evaluate, if they are to be effectively creative. Developing a PR plan that begins with staff members committed for 45–50 hours of work a week dooms that plan to failure. When the crises arise (and they always do), the planned projects get pushed aside and the staff gets behind. And even if they can catch up, working flat out, always racing to meet deadlines, eventually they'll burn out. Taking these things into consideration, the PR manager can make alterations, negotiate changes with product managers, review the combined plans with the PR staff members for their input and ideas (or cries of horror), and finalize the plan.

The next step — critical but sometimes overlooked — is to present the plan to the senior management team, not for their approval but for their review, comments, and input. They may also need time to review it with their managers and report their feedback. The goal of this process — which some PR managers may balk at ("After all, I'm in charge") — is to have everyone buy into the plan. This goal is achieved by having the senior management team members understand the plan, feel comfortable with it, and believe that it is the organization's plan, not the PR manager's or department's plan. If they buy into the plan and its goals, they will have a stake in helping to see that it is implemented (and their support can be critical in terms of making things happen operationally). And if they understand and accept the goals and the evaluation methods, then they will believe in the results at the conclusion of the campaigns.

Once senior management buy-in is accomplished (which should happen one or two months prior to the beginning of the organization's operational year, indicating that the planning process should probably begin three to four months earlier), then the plan can be implemented. Monitoring and evaluation efforts should be ongoing and are detailed in chapter 18.

☐ **Summary**

The word *plan* has two implications for the PR manager: (1) participation in developing the institutional strategic plan, and (2) development of the PR plan for the institution. Given the unique role of the PR manager in representing the concerns and needs of external publics, this senior-level staff member must play an integral part in development of the strategic plan. A plan developed without input as to the external publics' needs is essentially developed in a vacuum. Although marketing staff members may provide insights into the customer publics, the PR manager must also provide comparable insights into the organization's noncustomer publics. The PR manager also has to work with in-house clients and the PR and management staff members to develop a comprehensive PR and communications plan that includes general institutional image positioning and campaigns to promote awareness and utilization of specific services.

References

1. Keckley, P. *The Keckley Report.* Oct. 16, 1989, p. 11.
2. Hospital Advisory Board. Expert criticism of health care advertising and strategies. Washington, DC: Hospital Advisory Board, 1987, p. 17.
3. Reisman, J. Corporate advertising: PR in disguise. *Public Relations Journal* 46(9):27, Sept. 1989.

Suggested Readings

Peters, J. P., and Webber, J. B. *Strategic Thinking: New Frontier for Hospital Management.* Chicago: American Hospital Publishing, 1983 [out of print].

Peters, J. P. *A Strategic Planning Process for Hospitals.* Chicago: American Hospital Publishing, 1985 [out of print].

The Role of Research in Health Care Public Relations

Three out of four public relations professionals say that research is widely accepted in the field as a necessary and integral part of the PR process, according to a 1988 benchmark survey conducted by Ketchum Public Relations.[1] Why are more and more PR professionals using research as a basic tool? "To get inside the minds of the people in our key audiences," said one hospital PR vice-president. "To find out what consumers want and need, to target communications campaigns and to measure how well our campaigns have done."

A number of reasons underlie the growth of PR research, including:

- The increasing fragmentation and diversification of audiences, which makes it difficult to perceive the audiences' needs and even more difficult to target a message accurately
- The increasing isolation of publics (customers, employees, and so on) from institutions, which can result in problems turning into crises before institutional management is even aware of them
- Budgetary constraints that make it essential that PR managers avoid doing unnecessary campaigns (preaching to the converted) or doing campaigns that miss the mark

The list of what research can do for the health care organization is nearly endless, but among the key benefits of and uses for research are:

1. To probe the attitudes of specific audiences or publics
2. To measure true opinions of entire publics, rather than responding to vocal majorities
3. To identify opinion leaders who can influence audiences
4. To assess the attitudes and perceptions of the institution or of specific programs

5. To compare local statistics with national trends
6. To evaluate the results of PR and communications campaigns in terms of changes in awareness and preference
7. To identify community or other audience needs in terms of product and service development
8. To provide data for strategic planning efforts
9. To assist in the product development phase of marketing by testing pricing, location, product design, and promotional strategies
10. To measure customer satisfaction
11. To develop data that can be used in advertising or communications programs (such as consumer attitudes on smoking, which could be released as part of a promotional campaign to increase awareness of a cancer program)
12. To avoid the "we know best" syndrome, which can affect health care administrators or physicians and lead to development of services that are not marketable
13. To achieve credibility with top management by presenting a fact-based rationale, rather than taking an intuitive approach.

"Research can tell us what our publics and customers think, want, need, care about, and think about us," said one hospital PR director. "Research gives us direction and a starting point for our communications campaigns, because if you don't know how the publics think and feel, you can't know what or how to communicate with them.

"And research helps us develop benchmark measures so that we can determine if our campaigns succeed and achieve their objectives. After all, how can you tell if you're finished if you don't know where you started? And how can you say you've succeeded if you don't have an objective measurement tool?"

Although research is not yet a universal part of every health care PR program, its use has increased markedly in the past five years. In fact, in comparison to PR functions in other industries, it appears that health care PR professionals are in the forefront of the movement.

☐ Basic Research Applications for Health Care Public Relations

Health care organizations have been doing the most primary kind of research—customer research—for many years, well ahead of many other consumer service industries. The patient survey is a staple of health care management, although its methodologies and uses vary greatly from institution to institution. In addition to the standard telephone or mail patient survey, there are a number of other fairly common uses for research as part of the health care organization's PR and marketing programs:

- Situation analyses, noting competition and industry trends on a yearly basis
- Community or regional consumer attitude/opinion surveys— tracking consumer behavior and hospital use history, information sources, hospital awareness and preferences, health care choice and selection factors, physician utilization and dependency, insurance information, unmet health care service needs, and other areas
- Crisis impact-assessment "flash" surveys, conducted after events that may damage the institution's reputation, to determine public reaction to the event and help the institution plan how to deal with the damage
- Consumer focus groups, probing for reasons behind preferences and behaviors and testing responses to communications messages and media
- Surveys of specific patient subgroups, such as emergency department patients, substance abuse program families, and so on
- Surveys of referring agencies or individuals, including hospitals, emergency service personnel, and social welfare agencies
- Surveys of audiences for which the institution has or plans to have special services, such as seniors, women, or business leaders
- Physician surveys, including current medical staff members, physicians in the area who are not on the medical staff, and, if appropriate, referring physicians from the secondary service area
- Employee attitude and opinion surveys and focus groups on general employee satisfaction, plus special surveys on major compensation program changes
- Publication readership surveys (recipients of the institution's magazine, newsletter, or direct-mail literature)

There are many other applications for research by health care PR managers, but this list should be considered as "the basics" for the PR manager who wants to have a reality-based understanding of the health care organization's key publics.

☐ Research Methodologies

There are a number of textbooks that describe research methodologies in detail. This chapter will provide an overview for the PR manager, who should consult with in-house or external research professionals before making decisions about methodologies.

There are two basic types of research methodologies—primary research, which involves working directly with the research subjects (the patients, consumers, and so on), and secondary research, which involves using a secondary source for information about the primary research subjects (for example, asking parents what their teenagers are concerned about or reading a magazine article about teens' concerns).

Primary research is usually preferred because of its validity, but primary research is more costly and time-consuming to conduct than secondary research. Secondary research, on the other hand, is preferable to doing no research at all and can help identify subjects that should be pursued via primary research.

Secondary Research

Research from secondary sources is used to develop plans and rationales for primary audience research. It is also useful in making preliminary decisions about communications programs and projects. Among the most common types of secondary research are anecdotal research, literature review, peer research, existing surveys or poll data, trade group research, advisory panels, and mail and telephone call analysis.

- *Anecdotal research.* "What have you heard about . . . ?" Anecdotes can provide initial indicators of responses to an ad or PR campaign (for instance "everyone is talking about it") but cannot take the place of primary research to statistically determine how significant the campaign has been.
- *Literature review.* The PR manager can read and review articles from the popular press, trade publications, and other media to get an idea of what's happening in other markets, what the national trends are, and so on. This can help a PR manager identify issues that should be included in primary audience research and can also help narrow the list of possible PR methods, based on those that have been tried and proven workable in other areas.
- *Peer research.* The trendy word today is *networking.* Whatever the term, the process involves talking with colleagues about issues and trends in their markets, results of PR techniques they've used, ways they've handled crises, and so on.
- *Existing surveys or poll data.* There are times when surveys that have been conducted by other organizations may provide data that are useful. One pitfall to avoid in relying on other survey data is using the response statistics without knowing exactly how the survey was conducted and what questions were asked. The results of poorly designed and implemented research are of questionable validity.
- *Trade group research.* Trade groups like the American Hospital Association or local or regional hospital councils, or professional

associations like the American Society for Health Care Marketing and Public Relations, often conduct research projects. Again, although these data may be useful in terms of identifying national trends or suggesting areas that should be pursued at the local level, they should not be used for an individual institution's decision making. One exception is general consumer research on health care issues conducted by a hospital council; this research can be useful to hospitals in terms of identifying consumer concerns that the hospital needs to take into account in its own planning efforts.

- *Advisory panels.* Some health care organizations establish consumer advisory panels to provide input on specific topics, such as women's health concerns, senior citizen membership programs, and so on. This advice can guide the PR manager but cannot substitute for survey data from a random sample of the larger population.
- *Mail and telephone call analysis.* Health care organizations — and most businesses — already possess some valuable data that can be analyzed to identify trends and issues. Letters that are sent to the institution's CEO or departments and telephone calls from patients or other publics provide a wealth of data which, if carefully monitored, can provide "early warning signs" of emerging problems that need to be addressed.

Primary Research

Primary research involves directly surveying the members of the audience in question, usually a sample (smaller portion) of individual members of the entire audience. There are two types of primary research:

- *Quantitative research,* obtained by surveying a sample of a population, which provides what is called "hard data" (for example, 45 percent of the respondents prefer hospital A, 35 percent prefer hospital B, and 20 percent don't know), results that can be reliably extrapolated to the entire population
- *Qualitative research,* conducted in small group meetings or personal interviews, which provides "soft" information on the feelings and concerns of a small number of individuals, but which can't be extrapolated to an entire population

Quantitative/Survey Research

The two types of quantitative research most often used are telephone and written surveys of samples of a larger population. Mail surveys can often be conducted by the institution's staff, whereas telephone surveys generally need to be conducted by research firms that employ experienced and trained telephone interviewers.

Written surveys work best with audiences who have some sort of connection to the health care organization—employees, physicians, patients—and are thus more likely to take the time to complete the questionnaire. The advantages of a written survey, which is either distributed in person or mailed to respondents, are that it is less costly to administer and that it allows greater opportunities for the respondents to add personal comments. However, written surveys generally have a lower initial response rate and thus more surveys must be distributed or mailed to obtain the number of responses needed to ensure validity. This process can add months to the time it takes to complete the survey.

There are ways to eliminate some of the drawbacks of written surveys. One is to keep the questionnaire short enough that the recipients don't put it aside or throw it away because they think it will take too long to complete; 20 to 40 questions is adequate. Additionally, a survey sent through first-class mail will appear more important than one that is sent bulk mail or distributed with paychecks or as part of a hospital publication. Also, a personally addressed envelope is preferable to a computer label.

Another method for improving mail survey response is to include a return postcard with the survey. The respondent completes the questionnaire anonymously and returns the postcard separately. In this way, staff members can keep track of surveys that have not been returned and can follow up with those individuals.

Personal distribution of the survey has good and bad points. If a nurse hands the survey to the patient with a personal request that it be filled out when the patient returns home, this can stress the importance of the process. However, the patient can easily lose or forget about the questionnaire. Asking the patient to complete the questionnaire while he or she is still in the hospital is not advised because the patient's emotional and physical status may preclude concentration, or he or she may be concerned about confidentiality. One situation in which personal distribution works well is when employees are invited to meetings and asked to fill out an employee opinion questionnaire—but only if an outside researcher conducts the meetings and collects the surveys so that employees have no fear that their answers will be read by someone in the health care organization.

Telephone surveys are often used with consumer audiences. One advantage of a telephone survey is that the interviewers can continue to make telephone calls until the desired number of responses is completed. Telephone surveys can also be conducted more quickly, as compared with waiting for mail responses. However, a telephone survey is more costly to administer and is a more intrusive method than a mail questionnaire.

Sample Selection
With either written or telephone surveys, the general practice is to survey a sample, or portion, of the audience in question, rather than surveying the entire audience. This is done because it is more economical and takes less time to survey a sample and because modern sampling and survey methods guarantee an accuracy level that allows the sample to "speak for the population." What that means is that the results of the survey can be assumed to apply to the entire population.

In order to have confidence in the accuracy of a survey's predictive factor (its ability to predict the responses of the total population), it is essential that the sample be unbiased. To ensure an absence of bias, the sample must be selected randomly so that every member of the population has the same chance of being included in the sample. There are a number of methods of random selection, including selecting every 19th name on each page of the city phone book (which does exclude those persons without telephones or with unlisted numbers). Another increasingly used method is using a computer to generate lists of potential telephone numbers using all of the prefixes in the survey area and then randomly selecting phone numbers from that list. Two other sample selection methods include quota sampling (random selection within specifically selected and defined subgroups to ensure that all subgroups are represented in the survey) and purposive sampling (selecting a specific subgroup, such as opinion leaders).

Sample Size
Sample size is also a concern in terms of using the survey results to predict the behavior of the population. In general, for a telephone survey, a sample size of 400 to 500 persons is adequate for a metropolitan area of 250,000 persons; 600 to 800 persons for a larger metropolitan area; and 1,200 to 2,000 persons for a national survey. For a mail survey, a sample size of 200 completed questionnaires is the minimum acceptable, so depending on the response rate, the health care organization may have to mail several thousand questionnaires. Once the sample size has been established, the surveying process continues (mailing questionnaires or conducting telephone interviews) until the desired number of surveys is completed.

Questionnaire Design
Designing questionnaires is a very complex process that requires a great deal of expertise. Here are some general guidelines that the PR

manager can use, but it is usually wise to have a professional researcher either design or at least review the questionnaire.

1. Avoid leading or loaded questions. ("Don't you agree that only ignorant women would want to use a freestanding birthing center?")
2. Avoid double-barreled questions. ("Do you favor abortion and euthanasia?")
3. Pretest questions by having 10 or 15 people read the questionnaire and tell you what they think the words and questions mean.
4. Use cross-check questions for areas that are really important. Ask two questions that request the same information, but in two different ways ("Do you agree that hospital costs are too high? Do you disagree that hospital costs are more affordable today?").
5. Keep the questionnaire as short as possible—20 to 40 items on a written survey; a completion time of no more than 15 minutes on a phone survey is recommended.
6. Be careful about answer categories. Yes/no questions don't indicate how strongly the person feels about an issue. A four-point or five-point scale (a scale on which 1 is high and 5 is low or a continuum of possible choices ranging from *strongly agree* to *agree, neutral, disagree, strongly disagree*) gives you better data and gives the respondent more choices.
7. Don't skew the answer categories. ("How much confidence do you have in the hospital?" Answer categories of *a great deal, only some, not much, none at all* would skew responses toward the negative.)

People find it easier to complete a survey with what are called "closed-ended questions"—questions that give them a set of responses to circle, check off, or verbally choose. Open-ended questions ("What do you think about hospital costs") are intimidating to some people ("Uh . . . I don't know") and are very difficult to summarize when coding the data.

Qualitative Research

Qualitative research involves personally asking questions of individuals or a small number of people (called a focus group). This provides the opportunity to probe, to ask "why," and to observe group interactions. This kind of feedback is very helpful in pretesting advertising, PR, or marketing strategies or messages; in testing new program or service concepts; in pretesting a telephone or mail survey questionnaire; and in gathering more personalized, detailed responses to closed-ended survey questions. However, responses given in interviews or focus groups cannot be assumed to reflect the beliefs or attitudes of an entire population.

Because of that, qualitative research cannot be used in place of quantitative methods, but is often used in conjunction with, either prior to or following, a random sample survey.

Focus groups bring together 8 to 12 individuals who are part of a larger population. Focus groups can be composed of employees, physicians, patients, community leaders, and general consumers. When possible, it is recommended that each group be composed of persons who are somewhat similar — that is, persons employed in white-collar occupations and those in blue-collar occupations in separate groups, to see if there are any differences in their responses. Focus groups can also be selected by age or gender or other specific criteria that relate to the purpose of the research. For example, a health care organization doing research on locating an emergency care center in a suburban location would want to limit the focus group participants to persons who live in that suburb.

In most cases, focus group participants will provide more honest and candid responses if they do not know that the health care organization is sponsoring the focus group. To accomplish this, the organization hires a research firm that handles inviting and screening the participants and that provides a location away from the health care institution to conduct the group. In many communities, it is common for the research company to offer to pay the consumer participants $25 to ensure that they actually show up and form a group of sufficient size.

Focus groups should always be moderated by a trained professional. A representative of the client organization can often find it hard to remain unbiased (or anonymous), and keeping a group moving along with all members participating and no one dominating requires fairly sophisticated interpersonal skills.

The typical focus group will last from 90 minutes to two hours and focus group deliberations are often audio and video recorded, so that the PR manager can review the comments in their entirety. In addition, the PR staff often observes the focus groups from behind a two-way mirror. The moderator or the research company will also provide a written summary.

Personal interviews, conducted by a trained interviewer either anonymously (representing the research company) or on behalf of the health care organization, are often conducted in the offices of community leaders or key physicians. They are more expensive than focus groups, owing to the amount of time it takes to complete them one by one, but are sometimes one of the few ways to get input from busy physicians or businesspeople.

☐ Responsibility for Conducting the Research

Two of the reasons many health care managers give for not doing research are the expense and the lack of expertise; however, these barriers should not be allowed to compromise the value of doing audience research and should not overshadow the risks of making decisions without it.

There is often research expertise available within the health care organization. Planners, marketers, and medical research and education staff members often have experience in conducting survey research and designing questionnaires. (Generally anyone on the staff with a doctorate degree has training and experience in doing original research.) The health care organization's data processing department can handle tabulation and coding. And, with proper training, staff members or even volunteers can handle simple telephone surveys (although a trained interviewer is always preferable). In-house staff members can also handle arranging for and prescreening focus group participants.

If no resources are available in-house, or if the research needs are more sophisticated, there are alternatives to hiring major national research firms. Local colleges and universities today often have business research centers to work with local companies and can affordably handle the entire survey process. At the very least, most colleges have faculty members who are skilled and experienced in statistics and research methods and can advise the health care organization's staff. In many communities, there are small market research firms that can handle a total research program or will be happy to do components, whereas the health care organization does what it can in-house. Another alternative is to hire a research consultant who will advise on research methodology, survey design and administration, and data analysis, with the actual hands-on work being done by the health care organization's staff.

For a major, multifaceted research program (several phone surveys, focus groups, personal interviews, and so on) that's an integral part of a strategic planning or major communications campaign development, it makes sense to hire a comprehensive research firm if budget allows. This ensures that the work will be done professionally, comprehensively, and with the kind of methodological and statistical accuracy to give the PR manager complete confidence in the results.

☐ Summary

One of the hallmarks of the successful PR program of the coming decades will be the use of research for planning, assessment, and evaluation. Audience research will become increasingly essential as previously homogeneous audiences become segmented and fragmented. Audience research will help the PR manager understand the needs, concerns, and attitudes of the health care organization's key audiences.

Marketing research, from pretesting of communications campaigns to competition analysis, is an integral part of PR and promotion efforts. And evaluation research—to determine the results of PR efforts—will eventually be required as PR managers are asked to justify their budgets and, in some health care organizations, their very existence.

Reference

1. *Ketchum Nationwide Survey on Public Relations Research: Measurement and Evaluation.* New York City: Ketchum Public Relations, 1989, p. 2.

Suggested Readings

Baer, D. H. Selling management on public relations research. *Public Relations Quarterly,* Fall 1983.

Broom, G. M., and Dozier, D. M. *Using Research in Public Relations: Applications to Program Management.* Englewood Cliffs, NJ: Prentice-Hall, 1988.

Dillman, D. A. *Mail and Telephone Surveys: The Total Design Method.* New York City: John W. Wiley and Sons, 1978.

Duboff, R. S., and Baytos, F. J. Use of focus group technique in public relations research. Paper available from Public Relations Society of America, Counselors Academy, New York City, 1982.

Keckley, P. *Market Research Handbook for Health Care Professionals.* Chicago: American Hospital Publishing, 1988.

Lindenmann, W. K. Dealing with the major obstacles in implementing public relations research. *Public Relations Quarterly,* Fall 1983.

Smith, D. L. How to buy research services. *Public Relations Journal,* June 1980.

Developing Stakeholder Relationships as the Foundation for Proactive Issues Management

In their noted textbook on public relations, Cutlip, Center, and Broom identify the critical role of public relations in an organizational setting: "Maintaining mutually beneficial relationships between an organization and the various publics on whom it depends for success or failure."[1] Today, those publics that all types of organizations "depend on for success or failure" are often referred to as stakeholders, groups of individuals who can affect and/or be affected by the organization. When a stakeholder group proposes an action that can affect the organization or has a reaction to an organizational policy or decision, an issue is created. Management of these issues—these stakeholder actions and reactions—is an integral function of contemporary public relations. Issues management expert Lloyd N. Newman, president of the Newman Partnership, Ltd., advised PR professionals to be "the manager of issues management," the "secretariat" of issues that top the CEO's agenda. Newman defines this as one of the newest and most important roles for PR practitioners in the 1990s.[2]

The first challenge for the PR manager is to help the organization's management team understand that stakeholder actions and reactions can have the most profound impact on the organization, in terms of:

- Creating an external environment in which the organization can either flourish or perish
- Raising issues to which the organization must respond
- Reacting negatively to the organization's actions or issues and attempting to block the organization's attempts to achieve its objectives

- Reacting positively to the organization's actions or issues and supporting the organization's attempts to achieve its objectives

When the management team understands the profound nature of the impact that stakeholders and issues can have on the organization, there may be an initial tendency toward something close to panic or despair, a feeling of "we're completely at the mercy of the external environment." The PR manager's role at this point is to help the management team learn that issues can, in fact, be anticipated and predicted, controlled to varying degrees, and handled in a way that minimizes negative stakeholder actions and reactions and maximizes positive stakeholder actions and reactions—through a process called *issues management*. The two-phase process of educating management and gaining support for issues management begins with identifying the impact of stakeholders and issues on the health care organization.

☐ The Impact of Stakeholder Issues on Health Care Organizations

Few organizations have a greater need for effective stakeholder relations programs than today's health care organizations. As discussed in detail in chapter 2, health care organizations exist and operate with the permission and support of their communities and their publics. And today, as noted in chapter 1, health care organizations have an ever-growing audience of special interest groups and concerned publics—stakeholders who are influenced by or want to influence the organization. These stakeholders can have a profoundly positive or a critically negative effect on the organization, either helping the organization achieve its key goals or stopping the organization in its tracks.

On a macro scale, federal legislators have admitted that they feel safe in continuing to cut funding for health care reimbursement because as one senator's aide explained it, "We don't hear anyone complaining or defending the hospitals. You're not very popular right now."

On a micro scale, health care organizations across the country have found their often well-intentioned institutional plans becoming the center of local controversies. One major Midwestern medical center was forced to revise a previously approved, already-in-motion, multimillion-dollar master campus site plan when neighbors, surprised at the proposed closing of one block of a neighborhood street, organized and got the city planners to rescind their approval of the plan. The result: a "campus" divided by a busy city street, and thousands of dollars in architectural fees wasted. In another example, a small community hospital was amazed to find itself in the *National Enquirer* and on syndicated TV shows when the hospital's firing of a staff physician who prayed with and preached to patients was protested by an unexpected audience: fundamentalist religious groups.

For the health care PR professional, identifying and building relationships with these publics and identifying their key issues of concern is a pivotal role and responsibility. It's a role that, when done well, can not only benefit the health care organization but can also enhance the PR professional's standing within the organization. As health care organizations' ability to survive becomes even more dependent on gaining public support and avoiding public controversy, health care CEOs and boards are going to want, need, and demand a PR staff that can manage stakeholder relations and issues that affect the organization.

☐ The Goal of Issues Management

The emerging art and science of issues management has a broad goal of effectively dealing with those issues that can affect the health care organization's survival. This includes issues that are created by stakeholders (such as senior citizens asking the hospital to waive the Medicare deductible) and issues that are created when stakeholders react to the health care organization's actions (closing a service or asking for support in passing a bond issue, for instance).

The ultimate goal of stakeholder relations and issues management is to help the health care organization avoid making decisions or taking actions that will result in confrontations with stakeholders (especially confrontations that might damage the organization). For that to happen, stakeholders' concerns have to be considered by management when decisions are made. As described in chapters 2 and 6, the PR manager must "represent" those stakeholders' issues by describing predicted responses to actions proposed by the health care organization. Ideally, every action—especially changes—should be viewed through the eyes of each stakeholder group, with a resulting analysis that segments those groups' probable response to each option that's being considered as *actively support, support, be neutral, oppose,* and *actively oppose.* It's especially important to note which groups will change positions (from support to opposition) depending on which option is selected and to chart those groups that have clearly contradictory interests. This will help management in situations in which, no matter what decision is made, some stakeholders are going to be upset; management can then clearly weigh the pros and cons of upsetting one group rather than another.

As an example, consider St. Eligius Hospital, which is considering closing its high-risk prenatal clinic. The clinic loses money, there are other hospitals providing the same service, and the small number of patients are strictly poor women who aren't perceived as having much "clout." On the surface, this seems to be a fairly simple issue to manage. The small group of patients may get upset, but they can go to another clinic, and the hospital saves money, which pleases payers. A preliminary stakeholder analysis, however, reveals the following:

- Sending patients to another hospital won't pacify them; they want to stay with the physicians they have, and the other clinics are too far away geographically to be accessible.
- The patients are mostly black and might appeal to the NAACP to support them; the patients and/or the NAACP would probably go to the media.
- The media can either play the issue positively, as a hospital taking steps to contain costs, or negatively, as a hospital "dumping" poor patients.
- Some physicians would support the closing because it frees up funds for their programs or services; physicians who refer patients to the service would be very concerned.
- Payers (insurers, employers) would support the closing because it eliminates duplication of services and reduces costs. If the patients or NAACP made it a public issue via media, this payer support could weaken or evaporate.
- Employees would be split into three groups. The clinic staff would be concerned about job security. Some other employees would feel the closing is antithetical to the hospital's mission of caring for the poor. Still other employees would support the closing because it might preclude cuts in their departments.
- Negative media coverage and stakeholder reaction could have an impact on donations, legislative support, and so on.

Performing this kind of predictive analysis allows hospital management to understand the ramifications of the decision, prepare strategies to proactively communicate with and shore up support from key stakeholders, and have response strategies for those groups who will react negatively.

But how does the PR manager lay the groundwork so that this type of predictive analysis and resulting issues management can be performed accurately? The process begins with, and is dependent on, establishing an effective stakeholder relations program — an ongoing, continual program of identifying, analyzing, communicating with, and monitoring the concerns of the health care organization's key publics, the stakeholder groups.

☐ The Basics of Stakeholder Relations

An understanding of the basics of public opinion development and the persuasion process provides helpful background for consideration of the issues management/stakeholder relations functions.

An Overview of Public Opinion Formation

The term *public opinion* generally refers to a mass phenomenon and is defined as the sum of the opinions of individuals on an issue that affects them, or as a collection of views held by persons interested in the subject. The greatest impact of public opinion is on legislation and governmental activity, although changes in public opinion can have an equally profound effect on corporations and nonprofit organizations. The process of developing or changing public opinion is cyclical and ongoing.

As shown in figure 8-1, on any given issue of public concern, such as public funding for organ transplants, a social value or mass sentiment exists. This sentiment will continue to exist until something intervenes to create a public issue. In the case of funding for organ transplants, the intervention can be an event (such as a state legislature

Figure 8-1. The Cyclical Nature of Public Opinion Formation

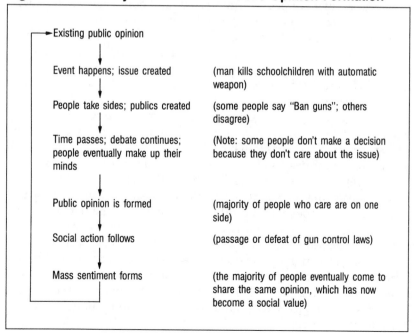

deciding to end Medicaid funding for transplants) that leads a public figure or vocal special interest group (physicians) to bring the issue to the forefront. The larger or more dramatic the intervention, the greater the resulting swing in public opinion. The intervention creates or reinforces publics—people who have a self-interest in the issue—and public debate ensues. After the passage of time (the length of time depends on how forcefully the intervening event or campaign catches the public's attention), the public makes up its collective mind, and measurable general public opinion can be identified. This formation of public opinion generally leads to social action (such as a law requiring Medicaid funding for transplants), and a new or reconfirmed social value is formed—until another event or change attempt intervenes. The process is, indeed, cyclical and ongoing, and only the shortsighted ever pronounce an issue as "settled, once and for all."

Public relations professionals should be aware of two things that can have a major impact on how quickly public opinion can shift. Those two factors are the dramatic/tragic/horrifying nature of the event and the amount of media coverage it receives. Passage of gun control legislation in California in the spring of 1989 happened far more quickly than anyone could have predicted, given the strength of the progun forces and previous apathy on the part of many citizens. However, an event—the slaughter of schoolchildren by a man with an automatic weapon—was so horrifying that it affected even those who had previously been uninterested, and continual media coverage focused attention on the issue for weeks after the actual event. Citizens may ignore broad, societal issues, but when an event happens that they can relate to personally, the issue becomes of concern to them. And although the media cannot dictate social policy, they can help frame the public's agenda by focusing on specific events and ignoring others.

Among the types of galvanizing events that can have a major impact on public opinion about health care institutions are incidents of patient dumping, cases where hospital staff members have been implicated in the deaths of patients (leading to concern about the quality of care) or, on a longer-term scale, continuous media and opinion leader commentaries about the costs of health care. In the first two examples, if the incident is limited to one hospital, the public is more likely to see this as just an isolated incident rather than a problem affecting the entire health care system. Thus it is less likely that a major shift in public opinion would occur. With the ongoing coverage of health care costs, highlighted by stories about specific incidents such as the apocryphal $5.00 aspirin, there is an incessant impact on the public's awareness that is gradually leading to a shift in public opinion and calls for reform or change.

Persuasion: Influencing and Changing Public Opinion

The process of attempting to change or influence public opinion, and resultant behavior, is called persuasion. The basic steps in the persuasion process are:

- Identifying all existing and potential stakeholder groups
- Identifying formal and informal opinion leaders
- Analyzing the groups' current and emerging issues that relate to the health care organization
- Developing a well-planned communications campaign that relates to the stakeholders' values and concerns and uses effective personal and mass communications techniques (as described in chapters 9 through 16)
- Continually monitoring the stakeholders' issues and reactions to organizational behavior

The characteristics of a successful persuasion campaign are:

- The message is tailored to the current climate
- The message is built on the audience's beliefs
- Formal and informal opinion leaders are targeted
- Sincere and expert sources are used
- Events and actions — convincing by doing — are used, rather than words — convincing by telling
- The campaign is based on integrity and truth, to avoid becoming propagandistic

Persuasive methods are generally used in three types of situations:

- To change or neutralize hostile opinion (reactive)
- To crystallize latent positive attitudes and move these latent supporters to action (proactive)
- To reinforce favorable opinions and maintain a reservoir of goodwill (proactive)

Most PR leaders, researchers, educators, and authors will agree that the proactive functions are the most important to the future of their organizations (if for no other reason than to avoid public opinion crises). However, many PR managers find that they spend much of their time on reactive functions — coping with negative stakeholder reactions — rather than crystallizing latent positive attitudes and reinforcing favorable opinions. A well-planned program of stakeholder relations and issues management can reverse this priority, enabling the PR professional to focus on developing effective stakeholder relationships that will maintain existing goodwill and build communications channels that can avert public opinion crises.

☐ Development of the Stakeholder Relations Program

As it was noted earlier, in the hectic day-to-day world of health care public relations, the PR manager may find that he or she spends more time grappling with problems that present themselves than with taking a proactive approach to stakeholders. When the nurses are talking union, when the physicians are talking about the perks they've been offered by a competing hospital, when the local media are asking about an ugly malpractice suit, when the state legislature is voting to cut outpatient funding effective immediately—it may seem hard for the PR professional to carve out time even to think about stakeholder relations or issues management. Although this may have been the short-term reality for many health care PR managers, today they are taking the long-term view, developing stakeholder relations programs that will reduce the problems, surprises, and public image crises that take so much time to handle. Although conflicts of opinion and controversies with key publics can never be completely eliminated, an effective stakeholder relations program can put the PR manager and the health care organization in a better position to address these issues quickly and effectively as they arise. "Crisis management," said Lloyd Newman, "is failed issues management. The key is to find the critical issues before they find you."[3]

There are four steps involved in stakeholder relations, each of which will be described in the following pages:

1. Identifying all of the stakeholder groups
2. Analyzing stakeholder groups' structures, leaders, and issues
3. Developing communications strategies to build relationships
4. Continually monitoring stakeholder groups' actions and reactions to predict and manage the issues that affect health care organizations (issues management)

Step One: Identifying the Stakeholders

Whether the term used is *audience, public,* or *stakeholder,* the meaning is simple: identify all those groups that believe they have some sort of an interest or stake in your organization. As respected PR pro Ron Rhody (senior vice-president, Bank of America) advises, "stop thinking of mass public opinion, and concentrate on micro-opinion—reaching those who care or will be impacted."[4]

This process can be initiated and even independently completed by the PR staff members, who can usually do a very good job of identifying most or all of the health care organization's stakeholders. There are, however, two compelling reasons for broadening the process:

- First, if the identification process is completed by the PR staff alone, the process becomes "a PR function," rather than an essential institutional function. Key people—especially the organization's senior management—can easily ignore, forget, or refuse to acknowledge the validity of the process and its findings. If senior management is involved in stakeholder relations from the very beginning, there's a much greater chance that the stakeholders' issues will be considered during institutional decision making.
- Second, involving as many people as possible in the stakeholder identification process ensures that small but important audiences aren't overlooked. The old adage about too many cooks spoiling the broth does not apply here. Because the goal of the identification phase is to develop a comprehensive list of stakeholder groups, it is helpful to have input from a group of people with diverse viewpoints and experiences. Newman noted that issues management is a process involving not only the CEO, "but virtually every other executive with decision-making power."[5]

One of the most effective stakeholder identification methods begins with the PR staff developing a master working list of stakeholders. Then senior management staff members are brought into the process. To help them understand the concept of "who has a stake," a fictional case study can be used in which participants read about a case involving an issue at a fictional hospital and try to identify all the groups that believe they have a stake in the issue. This "practice run" helps senior managers realize how many different groups can have a stake in the hospital's policies and actions.

The process can then be expanded to managers and department heads to derive a dual benefit. The managers can help identify stakeholder groups that might be overlooked, and through their participation in the process become more aware of the PR ramifications of the health care organization's actions. Involvement of the organization's board of trustees, advisory boards, and even medical staff leadership can also provide an additional "accuracy screen" to ensure that all stakeholders are identified.

Each organization's stakeholder groups will differ and it's essential that every organization conduct its own analysis. Using a "standard list" of stakeholders from a textbook or magazine article assumes that all health care organizations are like some generic model in some generic community. However, as an example, most hospitals have the following types of stakeholder groups:

- Employees, a group that can and should be divided into more specific groups based on demographics, job class, and attitudes (such as high-seniority women nurses who are angry with hospital management)
- Board of trustees, committees, advisory boards
- Customers:
  - Physicians (active admitting staff, inactive or rarely admitting staff, referrers, splitters, potential recruits) and their office staffs
  - Patients (past, current, potential)
  - Payers (actual payers, including officials in federal and state agencies, benefits administrators for businesses and employers, as well as insurance companies, managed care plans, and their third-party intermediaries)
  - Related groups such as patient families and visitors
- Donors (past, current, and potential, including foundations and grant sources)
- Volunteers, auxilians, and similar groups affiliated with the institution (each should be considered as a separate audience)
- Regulators (federal, state, and local governments; certificate-of-need authorities; and so on)
- Media (separated into owners, editors/news directors, reporters)
- Community opinion leaders — business, civic, religious, and so on (formal and informal)
- Community organizations, ranging from the NAACP to the prolife and prochoice groups
- Competing health care organizations
- Vendors and suppliers

Depending on the institution, other stakeholder groups range from labor unions to investors, religious orders to animal rights groups, and so on. *Special attention* should also be paid to identifying special interest groups that may not have evidenced any interest in the institution to date, but have interacted with other health care organizations or whose goals relate in some way to health and human services.

The key objective of the identification phase is to be all-inclusive, rather than limiting. Some audiences may eventually be placed low on a communications priority list, but all should be acknowledged by the health care organization's management and the PR staff so that at least minimal awareness of the group's concerns can be maintained.

The final combined list may seem daunting in its size and complexity—"too many on the seesaw," as John Blair noted in the summer 1988 issue of *Hospital and Health Services Administration*[6]—but if the list is comprehensive, then the health care organization can begin to implement a "no surprises" stakeholder analysis and relations program.

Step Two: Analyzing Stakeholder Groups

Once the stakeholder groups have been identified, they must be analyzed so that they can be prioritized in terms of the group's potential impact on the health care organization. This phase will include a great deal of secondary research (already-existing materials about the group, interviews with people who know about the group, anecdotes, and so on) and possibly some primary research (interviews with group leaders and members, telephone or written surveys, and so on). (See chapter 7.) For those obviously critical audiences (employees, physicians, and patients, at the minimum), it is expected that formal research is already being conducted regularly in the form of employee and physician attitude surveys and patient surveys.

The goal of the research phase is to find out the following information about each stakeholder group:

- Who are the formal and informal leaders and what are their backgrounds, leadership styles, and personal concerns relating to the health care organization and the community?
- What are the group's purposes, goals, and activities?
- What are the group's concerns, issues, and "hot buttons" relating to health care and hospitals?
- What is the group's strength/power (reputation in the community, evidence of clout with direct decision makers, and so on)?
- Is the group prone to action, and if so, what type (legislation, letters to the editor, boycotts, pickets, and so on)?
- Is the group involved or likely to be involved in any coalitions (formally or informally)?
- What are the group's internal and external communications channels? How does the group communicate with its own members? How does it receive information from and disseminate information to external sources?
- What is the group's current involvement with the health care organization or persons or programs that are part of or related to the organization?
- What is the group's current position on or opinion of the health care organization?

Doing this research must, by necessity, be a group effort. Although the PR staff can coordinate the process and do a great deal of the research, it is always more effective to involve the health care organization's managers or staff members (also board members and physicians) who are either members of or have some personal knowledge of the stakeholder group. These individuals can either perform the research or can advise the PR staff. For example, a cardiologist who is on the board of the American Heart Association can advise the PR manager about that group's leaders and how they feel about the hospital, whether or not the group is likely to complain about the hospital's planned public education campaign, and how the group may react to TV ads promoting the hospital's heart center.

In order that this phase doesn't get lost in the shuffle of day-to-day responsibilities, it's important that a timetable be established so that some realistic deadline pressure keeps the process moving. Generally, six to eight weeks should be sufficient for at least the basic information to be gathered on any individual stakeholder group, provided that the research work is being handled by a number of staff members.

What is discovered as part of the analysis process? *First, the PR manager learns facts about the concerns of each group*, rather than guesses or intuition. These facts can form the basis for sound decision making and resources allocation. One hospital CEO had spent literally thousands of dollars on designing a luxurious medical staff lounge and dining room because he believed that this was the number-one issue with the physicians, based on his conversations with a few of them. Personal interview research with the hospital's physicians revealed that their real issues were high-quality nursing care, availability of high-tech equipment, the hospital's aging surgical suites, and maintaining the hospital's residency programs. And although many companies, including hospitals, are devoting energy and dollars to developing on-site day-care centers, a 1989 survey of employees from U.S. companies conducted by Sirota, Alper and Pfau showed that day care was one of their least important concerns, whereas a safe environment, good benefits, open and honest communications, and respect were most important.[7]

Research with each stakeholder group may reveal equally surprising results. And even if the concerns turn out to be totally predictable, the PR professional will nevertheless be able to proceed with relationship building on a sound footing, sure of his or her information.

Second, the research phase will help the PR professional more accurately classify the larger stakeholder groups (employees, physicians, patients) into smaller segments based on shared concerns and attitudes. This makes effective communications more achievable. As Philip Lesly noted, "to approach any sizable audience on the assumption that it is cohesive will lead to communication mistakes."[8] Lesly noted that any large audience will include people who:

- Have differing levels of sophistication and knowledge
- Think in concrete terms or abstract terms
- Respect facts, as well as others who lean toward a more mystical approach
- Are receptive to communications, whereas others are indifferent
- Have opposing interests on many subjects
- Are picture-minded or word-minded

Research will help separate the larger audience into smaller, more homogenous segments. Research will also help identify those individual stakeholders who may actually have multiple roles and relationships with the health care organization and need to be classified in several stakeholder groups. State legislators, for instance, can be classified both as payers and regulators. Neighbors can also be patients, physicians, and civic opinion leaders. Careful identification of these dual relationships is important in terms of message determination. Using an "anti–city government" strategy to help persuade neighbors to support a zoning code change would backfire if one of the neighbors is also a city councilman.

Once the research has been completed, the stakeholder list can be arranged in priority order according to how critical an impact the group can have on the health care organization and how prone that group is to actually taking action. In categorizing stakeholder groups, the PR staff (preferably working with the CEO and selected board members) should identify those groups that have the greatest threat potential and cooperation potential using the following criteria, identified by professor John D. Blair:[9]

- Does this group control key resources we need?
- Is this group more powerful than the health care organization?
- Is this group likely to take action (based on analysis of past activity)?
- Is this group currently positive, neutral, or negative about the health care organization?
- Is this group involved in or could it become involved in any coalitions?

By answering these questions, stakeholder groups can be classified into primary/secondary, critical/essential/insignificant, or other classifications that will give the staff some direction as to which groups must be communicated with and how often.

A second analysis, which is often overlooked in this process, should be performed to identify issues on which key/primary stakeholders have concerns and needs that are directly contradictory. For example, upscale patients may have a strong desire for facility and service amenities or longer lengths of stay for rest and recuperation, whereas payers feel exactly the opposite. The identification of these conflicting needs/concerns is an essential step that must be completed before the health care organization moves on to institutional decision making (discussed in more detail in the issues management section of this chapter).

Step Three: Developing Communications Strategies to Build Relationships

Once the PR professional has a clear picture of each stakeholder group and priorities about which groups are most critical to the health care organization's survival, the next phase involves examining existing relationships with these stakeholders. The stakeholder groups will generally fall into one of four categories:

- *Primary:* stakeholder groups that are well known (employees, physicians). These groups are generally assumed to be supportive of the health care organization, and formal liaisons and communications channels exist and are maintained.
- *Secondary:* stakeholder groups that are somewhat known (volunteers, vendors, neighbors). These groups can be latently supportive of or opposed to the health care organization's actions; formal liaisons may exist; communications channels are generally sporadic, focused only on that group's specific relationship to the health care organization (that is, a newsletter about volunteer news), or exist only when a problem arises with that group.
- *Overlooked:* stakeholder groups that may have been ignored in the past (employers of patients, special interest groups) or communicated with only when the health care organization had a specific issue relating to that group. These groups can be latently supportive of or opposed to the health care organization's actions, and routine communications channels are often nonexistent.
- *One-Issue:* groups of individuals, generally interested in a specific cause, who are not typically identified as ongoing stakeholders, but who can assume a stakeholder role when an issue that relates to their cause and the health care organization arises. These cause-related groups tend to respond to issues that will have a negative impact on their cause and thus can be categorized as being latently negative. Routine communications channels with these groups are almost always nonexistent.

There are obvious differences among the stakeholder groups in each of these categories and in the ways the health care organization communicates with and relates to them. And there is a wide range of communications methods that can be used, ranging from the impersonal (newsletters, mailings, and so on) to the personal (advisory boards, liaisons, small group meetings and briefings, and so on). Although each health care organization's relationships with its stakeholders will vary, the following section provides an overview of some typical situations.

Maintaining Relationships with Primary Stakeholders

Most health care organizations do a fairly good job of maintaining relationships with their primary stakeholders (physicians, employees, board members, and so on). Formal lines of communication obviously exist with primary stakeholders, including health care administrators who have responsibility for communicating to these audiences. However, it is during the process of developing or evaluating a stakeholder relations program that those relationships should be carefully examined in light of the research findings, either to validate the effectiveness of the existing efforts or to identify changes that need to be made.

For example, the physician research may reveal that there are very clear-cut differences (of concerns, hot buttons, and communications channels) between different segments of the physician group. If the health care organization's existing physician relations program communicates with all physicians using the same methods and messages, the stakeholder research phase can be the ideal time to restructure that program based on the real differences among segments of that audience. The result could be a physician relations effort that would use slightly different versions of a common message, disseminated through multiple channels, based on the issues of concern to the various physician segments. (See the "Understanding the New Publics" section of chapter 2 for a detailed example of how a "homogenous" audience, like physicians, is actually composed of a number of very different subaudiences who will respond to very different communications techniques.) The PR manager should identify areas where public relations can support, supplement, or contribute to improved communications and relationship building.

Improving Relationships with Secondary Stakeholders

Generally, communications between the health care organization and its secondary stakeholders (volunteers, auxilians, vendors, people who live nearby, and so on) may not be as consistent and comprehensive as the relationships with the primary stakeholders. Secondary stakeholders fall into two basic categories, latent positives and latent negatives.

Latent positives are groups of individuals who have a voluntary relationship with the health care organization (volunteers, donors, members of seniors programs) and are assumed to be supportive because of their ties to the organization. Generally, there are staff members who have responsibility for some kind of communications and relationships with these types of groups, although the staff members' focus may be simply limited to the group's role (that is, a volunteer director communicates with the volunteers primarily about their schedules, working assignments, and so on, rather than discussed any broader organizational issues). Groups that are latently positive can be moved into the active support category through effective communications and relationship building.

These latently positive secondary stakeholder groups may receive only the predictable communications from the health care organization (newsletters of information about "their" news rather than broader organizational concerns) and may rarely be asked to become active supporters. For example, there are health care organizations that overlook board committee members as active support sources when the organization is grappling with city or state legislators or negotiating with companies for preferred provider organization (PPO) participation. And volunteers and auxilians are not always tapped for participation in legislative relations programs.

In order to be able to ask for and receive this type of active support, the health care organization's management and PR staff members must treat these groups as stakeholders, educating and informing them about the broad range of the organization's activities and concerns. The PR manager can work with the staff person who is responsible for relations with that group (the volunteer director, for instance) to make sure that the messages and channels used to reach that group include information about organizational issues and strategies, clearly communicating what that group can do to support the health care organization. Additionally, when the PR staff members are developing a broad-based communications campaign on an important issue, the PR manager should make sure that the staff member who works with these audiences is effectively communicating the message, rather than simply assuming that, for instance, the volunteer director will make sure the volunteers understand about the organization's new building program.

Latent negatives include groups of individuals who have an involuntary relationship with the health care organization (neighbors, vendors, emergency rescue personnel) and who may tend to feel somewhat negative about the organization because of the nature of the organization's impact on them and because they may feel the organization acts without considering the impact on their group. Building relationships with these groups is essential to prevent them from becoming full-fledged antagonists.

Groups that may be latently negative require careful attention to address their concerns and issues. Unlike latent positives, these are groups for which the health care organization probably has not identified a formal liaison person. There may be individuals with whom the group members generally interact (for example, the neighbors may interact with a planner or facilities staff person, emergency medical service (EMS) squads probably interact with the emergency department supervisor, and vendors will routinely see the purchasing staff). Those staff members, however, do not see their role as a liaison, nor do they feel a sense of responsibility for developing positive relationships with those groups.

Thus, the first step is for the PR professional to identify an appropriate liaison person. This may be the person with whom the group members routinely interact, if that person has a relatively positive existing relationship with them and has the appropriate communications and monitoring skills. Or it may be another staff member who has a related linkage (rather than the emergency department supervisor, the liaison to EMS squads might be a designated emergency department nurse or staff physician) or who has a linkage to the stakeholder group (a manager who actually lives near the institution could be an ideal liaison to the neighborhood groups). The key factors in selecting a liaison are (1) that the person does not have an existing negative relationship or image with the group (too often the staff person with whom group members interact may also be the person they like the least) and (2) that the person is skilled at the receiving part of two-way communications. If a choice has to be made, a good listener is more valuable as a liaison than a skilled public speaker.

The key role of the liaison is to monitor the stakeholders' concerns and share them with the PR staff. Although the liaison will be responsible for informally communicating with the stakeholder group personally, the PR staff can provide coaching and message strategies, can handle the more formal communications with the group, and can also meet directly with the group (or identify additional spokespersons to meet with the group) when the situation warrants. The liaison is the health care organization's eyes and ears and also fills the critical role of face-to-face relationship building. It's important to note that the liaison should not only be interacting with formally organized groups and elected leaders, but also with informal leaders, members, and individuals who are not part of a formal group.

The liaison becomes someone the stakeholders can count on for information and who will represent their concerns to the health care organization. If problems arise, the liaison is also the person who closes the communications loop by returning to the stakeholder group with a response from the health care organization. Even if the response is not what the group wanted, experience has shown that a problem is less likely to escalate into a confrontation if the group actually receives a response and the response comes from someone whom the group members know and trust.

It is important to note that in most cases creation of formal, impersonal communications channels (like newsletters) for these stakeholders is not recommended. A personal liaison is far more effective and less expensive, and if a formal channel exists, the PR staff (and the liaison) may be more inclined to "just put it in the newsletter" than to make face-to-face contact. Finally, formal communications methods tend to be outbound — talking to the stakeholders — rather than inbound — listening to their concerns.

Developing Relationships with Unknown or Overlooked Stakeholders

The third category of stakeholders are groups who do not automatically come to mind when one identifies the health care organization's audiences, or groups that move into a stakeholder role only when a specific issue arises as a response to the organization's actions. In this category are groups such as employers and legislators. For example, employers (owners or CEOs of area businesses) were historically ignored as a health care audience, even when they (not the insurers) paid the bills. The effectiveness of current efforts to communicate with this group can be hindered because the group feels it has been ignored in the past. Another example is legislators, who are often considered only when the health care organization wants something or when the legislators' actions threaten the organization. Communicating only when an issue arises is far less effective than maintaining an ongoing relationship.

Identifying groups such as these as legitimate stakeholders is the first step in ensuring that their concerns are taken into consideration by the health care organization's management, and that they are regularly communicated with by the organization. Because of the broad nature of these groups, they may need to be classified into smaller segments (employers of past inpatients, employers who control a large volume of the organization's current inpatient volume, legislators who represent the organization's district, legislators who serve on health-related committees, and so on) so that relationships can first be built with those who can have the most impact on the health care organization. As with other secondary stakeholders, a liaison needs to be identified and charged with the responsibility for maintaining contacts with audiences that will have an ongoing stakeholder relationship with the health care organization and monitoring concerns that can be addressed before they escalate into crises. These liaisons do not have to be PR staff members and, in fact, may be more effective if they are not. The health care organization's CFO, senior administrators, planner, and even CEO may fill the liaison role.

With very large groups (employers, for instance), the liaison role may take a two-pronged approach. The first step would be for the liaison to personally identify himself or herself to all members of the stakeholder group by letter or appearance at a meeting, so that they are aware that this communications channel with the health care organization exists. Formal, ongoing communications programs such as a newsletter or yearly briefing meeting can also be established to reach the larger group.

The liaison may then select a smaller sample of the larger stakeholder group to interact with personally and more frequently, whether through personal interviews, small group meetings, an advisory board, or other methods. It is unrealistic to expect that the staff member liaison to employers could build a relationship with 500 or 600 people (in major metropolitan areas), but a sample of 25–30 employers who are representative of the total group can provide accurate and timely information.

Maintaining Information on One-Issue Stakeholder Groups

This is a very broad category, ranging from civil rights groups that become stakeholders only if they feel the health care organization is violating the rights of employees or patients, to special interest groups (animal rights activists, prolife, prochoice groups, and so on) that don't want to hear from the health care organization as long as the organization's actions and policies are acceptable to the group, because they need to concentrate their attention on organizations that don't conform to the group's standards. Because these groups are only sporadically concerned about their stake in the health care organization, or only get involved with the organization in response to specific issues, building formal, ongoing relationships is difficult.

Dealing with these groups is a very individualized matter for each health care organization, depending on the relationships the organization has had with the groups in the past. Ideally, the PR staff needs to have a data base with accurate and timely information about each of these groups — goals, formal and informal leaders, communications channels, past activities, and so on — so that if a problem does arise, a plan can be drafted quickly. At the very minimum, a data base with names and phone numbers of contact people needs to be updated regularly. When a reporter calls and asks for a response to NAACP charges against the health care organization, the PR manager can't waste precious time trying to find out who the local chapter president is and how to get in touch with him or her. Updating this data base can be handled by a secretary or a trained volunteer or can be a joint project of a local hospital association or PR society, with all members pooling information and sharing access to the data.

If there are specific groups with whom the health care organization has had problems in the past, then more intensive efforts need to be maintained — ranging from careful monitoring of the group's activities and public communications (media and newsletter analysis, for instance) to ongoing informal communications with key group leaders or members. If the group's leaders are openly antagonistic, it is better to try to find a member who is willing to communicate with the health care organization. Involving leaders from these types of groups in an existing advisory board, or inviting them to periodic small group meetings, is also a more time-efficient way of staying in touch than designating a liaison for each individual group. The decision on what tactics to use should be made on the basis of the group's power and stature within the community (whether they are viewed as legitimate or simply as gadflies) and on how frequent and neutral or negative the interactions with the health care organization have been in the past. There may be some special interest groups that are so powerful and are so tied into the health care organization that they may actually need an individual liaison (for example, animal rights groups and major teaching/research hospitals). Once these three steps — identification, analysis, and establishment of communications strategies and relationships with the health care organization's stakeholder groups — have been completed, the PR manager and staff have laid the groundwork for an ongoing issues management program.

Step Four: Identifying and Managing the Issues

There are three phases of issues management: monitoring stakeholders' issues; representing these issues during the health care organization's decision making; and managing relationships and communications when the health care organization and a stakeholder group collide.

Phase One: Monitoring Stakeholders' Issues

One pitfall to avoid is going through the stakeholder identification process, determining the issues and concerns for each group — and then assuming that these concerns and issues will stay the same over a period of months and years. Each group needs to be monitored continually so that any emerging issues can be identified and taken into consideration by the health care organization's management. Potential coalitions also need to be monitored, because many stakeholder groups are becoming more sophisticated at advancing their causes by getting other (sometimes loosely related) groups to stand with them. When a group concerned about the health care organization's equal opportunity hiring forms a coalition with a group of disgruntled employees trying to unionize, the power of that coalition is far greater than either group individually.

Obviously, the liaisons are the first and primary source for monitoring. They know the turf, they know the players, and they should be in contact frequently enough that they can even spot emerging issues before the group actually takes a stand on those issues. The goal is anticipation, rather than reaction. For example, a liaison to a neighborhood community action group can alert the health care organization's management when informal conversation includes more and more comments and concerns about noisy helicopters, employee cars exceeding the speed limit on neighborhood streets, and so on. The health care organization can then take action to handle the issue of concern, and through the liaison can address the concerns before the neighbors issue a statement to the press or complain to the city council.

Other methods for monitoring include:

- *Following media coverage of the group's activities on a national and regional, as well as local, level.* Liaisons can report on what's a hot issue in the local employer community; national business magazines give insights into the trade associations and major national employers' hot issues (which will often become a local issue at some point in the future).
- *Reviewing all external communications issued by the stakeholder group*—newsletters, mailings, media statements, and so on.
- *Being part of hospital and health care trade associations and professional societies that provide "insider information" on key health care stakeholders.* For example, the American Hospital Association and state associations provide information on federal legislators and officials. The American Association of Medical Colleges extensively monitors the animal rights activists.
- *Reading what the stakeholders themselves read.* Subscribe to the publications that physicians receive, for instance, to become familiar with what their sources are telling them (American Medical Association information is especially important).
- *Being where the stakeholders congregate for business and social purposes.* The hospital should pay for staff members to be involved in Rotary, Kiwanis, the Chamber of Commerce, country and golf clubs,

and so on, because often more accurate information can be gained from a casual social conversation with a physician or business leader than from a formal interview.

Phase Two: Representing Stakeholder Concerns to Management

As explained in the first section of this chapter—with the "closing the clinic" example—it is essential that stakeholders' concerns and potential reactions be considered in terms of the health care organization's decisions and operations. The PR manager, who develops and manages the stakeholder relations program, should be responsible for representing those stakeholder concerns for management consideration, and for predicting the stakeholders' reactions to the health care organization's actions.

As noted, the ideal situation is when stakeholder concerns and responses are routinely considered as part of day-to-day operating decisions. Unfortunately, the reality in most health care organizations is that some stakeholders' concerns are considered all of the time (physicians); most stakeholders' concerns are considered some of the time (if the decision is perceived as earthshaking or the project is one that the organization really wants to do); but rarely are all stakeholders' concerns routinely reviewed every time a decision is made. Except in the most progressively managed health care organizations, stakeholder concerns are considered informally, sporadically, or after the decision has been made—and often the stakeholders' concerns are simply dismissed.

How can stakeholder response analysis become a routine part of decision making? The PR manager must first persuade management that the risks of ignoring stakeholders will cost more time and money (in responding to crises) than the time involved in performing the analysis. This may sound like a simple proposition, but many health care PR managers report that even after the health care organization has had to cope time after time with crises it has generated, some top management staff members are still reluctant to make stakeholder response analysis a part of standard operating procedures.

If stakeholder response analysis is being omitted from the decision-making process, the PR manager has an alternative. He or she can simply perform the response prediction analysis independently, and during the decision-making discussions present only the concerns of those stakeholders who may react negatively. The most common scenario is the "If we do A, group X will do B" analysis, as outlined earlier in the chapter. The primary goal is to ensure that top management is aware—in advance—of the possible negative consequences of changes in policy or programs, so that it can be prepared for unfavorable stakeholder response.

Public relations managers need to avoid making the mistake of thinking that stakeholder response must govern the health care organization's actions ("If group A is going to publicly oppose us, we shouldn't do this"). In fact, there will always be times when a stakeholder group reacts negatively to a health care organization's action. Stakeholder analysis can help minimize the negative response by identifying which stakeholders are going to have problems with the decision, so that proactive communications programs can be planned before the decision is even announced. Stakeholder analysis can also identify the groups that will agree (actively or latently) with the decision, and can be called on for support.

For the PR director to direct an ongoing program of stakeholder analysis and present the concerns of key stakeholders means that the PR director is part of the top management decision-making team, as described in chapter 2, rather than someone who is called in after the decision has been made and is then told to "do a press release on this." As Harold Burson, one of the giants of the PR field, noted, in the 1940s through the 1960s, management asked public relations, "How do I say it?" In the late 1960s, it was "What do I say?" Now, said Burson, the goal should be a quantum step: having management ask PR "What do I do?"

This means routine involvement in all facets of daily operations, because every operating decision has a potential impact on a stakeholder group. No one put it more succinctly than Pat Jackson in the *pr reporter* (July 24, 1989): "Proactive public relations begins in continually investigating the daily routine of the organization—even if it means getting in the way of line execs. Instead of waiting for gaffes to occur—damaging reputations and bottom lines—PR can monitor operations for impact on reputation and relationships."[10]

In health care organizations, these operating decisions range from those that are obviously significant—closing, expanding, or creating new services, decisions that have an impact on patients, physicians, payers, neighbors, legislators, and so on—to those that may seem less significant but can still cause negative responses from some stakeholder groups. Even something that seems as simple as raising parking garage rates, or closing the cashier's window on Saturdays, can result in a negative response from affected groups. *pr reporter* calls these "little goofs that lose customers." The PR manager has a dual role in the decision-making process: first, guiding the decision-making process so that stakeholders' concerns are considered, and second, developing the communications strategies to present decisions to the affected groups in the most positive way.

In many health care organizations, the PR manager is involved when "major decisions" are contemplated. What is even more important is that the senior PR professional is involved in decisions at all levels of the health care organization—especially in what may seem to operating administrators as "mundane things" like raising fees for parking garages, moving vending machines, or sending out letters to patients with past-due accounts. It's these mundane actions that often cause stakeholder revolts, which end up as hot stories in the local paper—and which could have been predicted and either prevented or at least minimized by a skilled PR professional and a good proactive communications effort. As noted in earlier chapters, the PR manager has to be continually involved in assessing the health care organization's operations, from the point of view of the organization's publics. This "involvement" means being present at all administrative meetings when these decisions are considered or discussed and building positive counseling relationships with other members of the management team so that the PR manager's input will be received positively.

Finally, it's important to note that continually bringing up potentially negative stakeholder concerns to the top management team can result in the PR person being viewed as the harbinger of bad news, because there are rarely decisions that are going to be greeted positively by all stakeholders. One PR director, viewed by his peers as quite skilled in stakeholder relations, was told by frustrated administrators, "We don't care what they think—quit trying to get in our way by predicting gloom and doom." That phenomenon, the loneliness of the issues manager, is of concern to senior PR professionals in health care and in any industry that comes under great public scrutiny and has a number of stakeholder groups that oppose or are angry with the company. Public relations practitioners in health care organizations, public utilities, and the oil industry, for instance, all share common concern over having to point out time and time again that the decisions and actions of the organization's management may be greeted with an outcry from one of their stakeholder groups. Unfortunately, predicting stakeholder response is one of the most critical functions of a senior PR professional. Some CEOs value the function and welcome the input; others may not recognize the value of the input.

In an organization where prediction of stakeholder reaction is not yet valued, the PR manager may experiment with a variety of techniques either to make the "bad news" more acceptable, or to cope with possible resentment from CEOs, board members, and fellow administrators. Among those techniques:

- *Enlist allies from among the PR professional's peer group who are sensitive to public opinion and are willing to speak up.* They can either jump in and support the PR director's comments, actually represent the stakeholder's concerns, or provide the opening for the

PR director by asking the right question during management discussion of the proposed decision. If a change in the traffic pattern around the institution is being considered and the PR manager wants to point out that neighborhood groups may react negatively, a supportive peer can ask, "What will the neighbors think of this plan?" giving the PR manager the opening to present the analysis of the neighbors' concerns without appearing to be opposing the plan.

- *Involve as many members of top management as possible as liaisons to stakeholder groups with which they're comfortable.* Once they've filled that role, they are much more sensitive to the need for the health care organization to consider stakeholder concerns. And if they want their stakeholders' concerns taken seriously, they have a vested interest in ensuring that a stakeholder response analysis process exists.

- *Use humor and honesty to defuse resentment.* One veteran PR vice-president says she often prefaces her comments about negative stakeholder responses by noting that she doesn't enjoy being the bearer of bad news, but that being aware of stakeholder concerns will benefit the health care organization in the long run.

- *If a public opinion crisis occurs because stakeholder concerns weren't identified or were ignored, carefully use the opportunity to reeducate the group about how stakeholder response analysis could have helped prevent or defuse the crisis.* The key word is *carefully*— whining "I told you so" in the midst of the crisis is not a way to win peer support. The reeducation may best be accomplished informally, rather than in a formal group meeting where it may seem like an attack or power play.

- *Ask the resisters what could be done to get them to feel comfortable with stakeholder analysis.* Some veteran health care CEOs and senior administrators come out of a tradition of "We'll do what we want to—we don't need to consider those outsiders." As with any public, the PR director needs to present the process in terms of the individual's self-interests, explaining that the process is not a way to take away the CEO or administrator's power, but rather a way to enable him or her to be able to get things done without problems and opposition from stakeholder groups, which could end up derailing his or her efforts.

- *Use peers and professional associations as personal support groups.* The discussions at meetings of health care PR groups and national associations or groups like the Public Relations Society of America often center around the common concerns members share in trying to make stakeholder relations a reality within their organizations. This kind of sharing will help the PR manager broaden his or her perspective and realize that he or she is not the only professional dealing with this concern. Additionally, peers can offer advice and suggestions based on their own experience in implementing stakeholder analysis programs.

Phase Three: Managing Issues When Organizational and Stakeholder Interests Collide

There are few issues on which the health care organization can manage to please all of its stakeholders. And as discussed earlier, health care organizations have key stakeholder groups whose basic concerns and needs are in total opposition almost all of the time.

By instituting a program of stakeholder relations and issues management, the PR professional will have all the tools at hand to preempt active opposition on many issues, by knowing in advance what the stakeholder's hot buttons are, who the key leaders are, how to communicate with them—and by having liaisons in place who have established trusting relationships with these stakeholder groups. Although the groups may still oppose certain actions, often an effective stakeholder relations program can mute the intensity or minimize the impact of the opposition, while simultaneously highlighting and strengthening the support of positive stakeholder groups.

Nevertheless, stakeholder interests and actions of the health care organization are going to collide at some point. The issue can originate with the health care organization—the organization seeks stakeholder support for a certificate of need for a new computed tomography (CT) scanner or OB unit and payers react negatively. The issue can originate with a stakeholder group—senior citizens ask the health care organization to waive the Medicare deductible. Or the issue can arise when a stakeholder group reacts negatively to a decision by the health care organization—as simple as when the Auxiliary members become upset when their office is moved to another building, or as serious as when a hospital creates a new program to notify patients when their hospitalization benefits have ceased and families accuse the hospital of dumping because the letter is poorly written. The third situation is the most difficult to manage: when a number of stakeholder groups have strong and conflicting responses to an action by the health care organization (as described in the example at the beginning of this chapter of a hospital closing a high-risk prenatal clinic).

There are a number of essential steps that should be taken when an issues crisis arises:

1. *Make sure that the health care organization has a defensible position.* The best defense for an action that may offend some stakeholders is that it is the right and ethical thing to do. This sounds

very basic — but many public opinion crises result when institutions are "caught" doing something that is clearly unethical or deliberately damaging to a public. This will prevent the health care organization from being caught in a damaging public exposé (see chapter 10 on media relations) and having to "admit guilt." Being able to say, "We made the decision with the best interests of our most important public — our patients — at heart" is a stand that is difficult for an opposing stakeholder group to attack.

2. *Communicate effectively and in advance with supportive stake-holder groups and with key internal publics.* Max Fisher, director of corporate communications at Purina Mills and a veteran of managing public opinion crises, notes that Exxon might have avoided some PR problems if it had immediately communicated with its credit card customers about the oil spill situation in Alaska and the clean-up efforts.[11] If the PR professional predicts a negative public response from a stakeholder group, it's critical that the health care organization's other publics hear the organization's side of the controversy from the organization before they read about it in the paper and form their own negative opinions.

3. *Immediately communicate with the angry stakeholder group(s).* Use existing liaisons, involve other supportive stakeholders who have ties to the opposing group, and involve appropriate top management of the health care organization. Use personal, private channels rather than communicating through the media.

4. *Remember that the stakeholder group may choose to go public, via the media.* Variations on a health care organization's response can be drafted in anticipation of media calls, based on predicted stakeholder comments that are identified by the PR staff. Avoid a "no comment" response if at all possible, because to the public it implies arrogance, unconcern, or uncertainty. If the other group goes public first and the media ask for a response from the health care organization, the PR manager should first share that response with the stakeholder group so that they hear it from the health care organization before they read it in the paper.

5. *Work from a premise of identifying common ground, when possible.* Make win/win the goal and enter into the communications process with the knowledge that some sort of compromise may be needed. In fact, when decisions are made, a range of compromise options should be established at that time. Be sensitive to the stakeholder leaders' need to save face if they appear to be giving in to the health care organization, and identify things the health care organization can to do help them look like winners.

6. *If the issue involves conflicting stakeholder concerns, share the nature of these conflicting priorities with the involved stakeholder*

groups and with the media, if the issue has been made public. Often the situation appears to the media and the general public to be two-sided: the health care organization versus a stakeholder group, with scant attention paid to the concerns of other stakeholders. For example, in a service closing scenario, the focus may be limited to the health care organization and the affected patients. The health care organization's private and public communications should note that the organization's decision is also a response to concerns of other involved stakeholders (insurers, employers, other health care organizations, and so on).

7. *When being confronted by a one-issue stakeholder group, proactively lay out all sides of the issue.* Teaching hospitals have done an outstanding job of presenting the benefits of animal research for patients when the hospitals have been attacked by animal rights activists.

8. *Always take the highest possible ground.* Whether the health care organization has initiated the issue and is seeking stakeholder support, or the organization is defending itself from criticism from a stakeholder group, it is most effective if the organization presents its decision or action in the context of better patient care, saving lives, and so on, rather than in terms of market share or budget constraints. Pointing out that closing one underutilized service (arthritis rehab) will provide funds for strengthening or continuing to provide a vital service (neonatal intensive care) can frame the issue in a way that will engender stakeholder and general public support.

9. *If the situation cannot be resolved and one party has to lose, continue to maintain the relationship.* If the health care organization wins, careful attention must be paid to salvaging a relationship with the stakeholder group. If the health care organization loses, the PR manager must help administrators resist the natural tendency to allow the antagonism to color future decisions.

Special Situation: Working with Activist Groups

Activist groups present a special challenge for the health care PR manager, because many of the most vocal and well-organized groups have a special interest in health care organizations (animal rights groups, right-to-life activists, and so on). There are a number of excellent articles listed in the references at the end of this chapter that describe this process in detail, but here are some of the basic tips, excerpted from *pr reporter*[12] and Philip Lesly's *Managing the Human Climate:*[13]

- Treat activist groups as equals, not as irritants.
- Let them know you've done your homework and understand their point of view.

- Don't communicate *at* them — communicate *with* them.
- As much as possible, let adversaries participate in discussions of proposed changes or decisions.
- Watch your reactions carefully; many groups take action just to force you into an overreaction.

Chapter 11, on crisis communications, provides an excellent example of how New York University dealt with an animal rights group in a way that avoided overreaction.

☐ Summary

Health care organizations exist in a macroenvironment, perceived as public institutions (even if privately owned) and allowed to exist and operate with the consent of "the public." That public is composed of numerous stakeholder groups — internal and external, primary and secondary, latently positive and latently negative. All have their own specific view of the world — and of the health care organization — and need to be communicated with in a way that will maximize their support.

A positive issues management and stakeholder relations program can help health care organizations survive and prosper by generating stakeholder support, making decisions with stakeholder concerns in mind and understanding the ramifications of those decisions, and avoiding or effectively responding to issues that arise when stakeholders do not support an action or decision of the health care organization. Without an issues management program that is grounded in identifying and building relationships with stakeholders, a health care organization is in a sense operating blind, unaware of the potential reaction to its actions and unable to marshal stakeholder support when needed.

It is a major responsibility of the PR manager, as Lloyd Newman pointed out, to make issues management a basic part of doing business.[14] This may require education, persuasion, and gentle coercion (by pointing out incidences of what has happened to health care organizations that have not anticipated stakeholder response) — but the alternative is to repeatedly have to deal with problems and crises that arise when stakeholders are ignored.

References

1. Cutlip, S., Center, A. H., and Broom, G. M. *Effective Public Relations.* Englewood Cliffs, NJ: Prentice-Hall, 1985, p. 212.
2. Managing issues management. *Public Relations Journal* 46(1):14, Jan. 1990.

3. Managing issues management.
4. Rhody, R. One on one interviews best way to handle media during crisis – and anytime. *pr reporter* 32(29):2, July 17, 1989.
5. Managing issues management.
6. Blair, J. D. Too many on the seesaw: stakeholder diagnosis and management for hospitals. *Hospital and Health Services Administration* 33(2):153, Summer 1988.
7. What do employees want most today? *pr reporter* 32(24):3, June 12, 1989
8. Lesly, P. The conflicting makeup of audiences. *Managing the Human Climate* [supplement to *pr reporter* 32(18):1, May–June 1989].
9. Blair, Too many on the seesaw.
10. *pr reporter* 32(30):1, July 24, 1989.
11. Stanton, A. On the home front. *Public Relations Journal* 46(9):15, Sept. 1989.
12. Letting adversaries participate dispels their feelings of abuse, creates singleness of purpose. *pr reporter* 32(11):1, Mar. 13, 1989.
13. Lesly, P. Major trends lose touch with people. *Managing the Human Climate* [supplement to *pr reporter* 32(10):3, Mar.–Apr. 1989].
14. Managing issues management.

Suggested Readings

Bernays, E. L. *The Engineering of Public Consent.* Norman, OK: University of Oklahoma Press, 1985.

Crabbe, R. E. Managing issues and influencing public policy. *Public Relations Review*, Summer 1985.

Ehling, W. P. Use of "issues management" in public relations. *Public Relations Review*, Summer 1983.

Grunig, J. E., and Hunt, T. Identifying organizational linkages to publics. In: *Managing Public Relations.* New York City: Holt, Rinehart and Winston, 1984.

Petty, R. E., and Cacioppo, J. T. *Communication and Persuasion.* New York City: Springer-Verlag, 1987.

Pires, M. A. Working with activist groups. *Public Relations Journal*, Apr. 1989.

Six building blocks of good relationships. *Purview*, Feb. 5, 1990.

Community Relations

Community relations techniques, which once formed the core of health care public relations but were eclipsed by media relations and marketing communications in the 1980s, have reemerged to play an integral role in what *pr reporter* calls "the new decade of personalized relationships." As *pr reporter* predicts, PR professionals will find the 1990s shaped by two occurrences:[1]

- The decline of mass markets and mass media, which had dominated since World War II, into a continuing fractionation of publics, which means targeting smaller and narrower groups
- A sense of empowerment felt by more and more individuals, or at least a firm desire to have a voice in decisions that affect them, which means appealing to them personally, not just to some socioeconomic grouping of which they are *assumed* to be a part

Public relations professionals in all industries—but particularly in the human service industries that need community support, "the consensus needed to operate" described in chapter 2—are reexamining and updating the old "tried and true" community relations techniques and drawing on an array of new methods for building these personalized relationships.

What's defined as "community relations" varies from institution to institution—and throughout the PR industry—but can generally be divided into the following two categories:

- Ongoing relationship-building strategies, which are described in detail in chapter 8
- Specific techniques, ranging from speakers' bureaus to opinion leader briefings, which are used as part of the health care organization's image-building efforts directed at general and target audiences and can also be used as part of specific marketing communications campaigns

A number of these techniques will be highlighted in this chapter, although there are as many variations of each technique as there are PR professionals, and the range of effective methods is limited only by the imagination. These person-to-person, face-to-face, "up-close-and-personal" tactics are increasingly forming the heart of multifaceted PR campaigns, with mass audience methods used for message support and enhancement.

☐ Bringing the Audience to Your Turf

For many health care organizations, using community relations methods that bring the public into the health care facility is an essential strategy for creating awareness and reducing barriers. "If people have been in a hospital, they're less afraid of it," said one community relations manager. Another noted that "we've spent thousands to upgrade our inner-city buildings, which used to be pretty awful, but we have to get people down here to see how nice it is now."

Although there are a number of obstacles that may serve as barriers to getting the public into the health care facility (ranging from location to convenient parking to people's nervousness about even visiting a hospital), hospitals in particular also have assets to offer: "dramatic" sights and scenes, experts who can personally talk about medical developments, free meeting space, health screenings in which everyone's interested, and more. The two key determinants of the success of "bring 'em in" community relations programs are:

* Finding the right hook—the topic, the event, the speaker—that's interesting and exciting to the audience (consumer research is very helpful in finding these hooks)
* Making it easy for them to get to you—timing of events, access (parking and signage), maps and directions, and so on

Conducting Tours

Medical shows have always been popular on television because people are fascinated by getting a glimpse inside a hospital. What may eventually become routine to hospital employees is dramatic and intriguing to the layperson: operating rooms, nurseries full of newborn babies, emergency department trauma suites, CT scanners and lasers, even "behind the scenes" in laundry and dietary.

Every health care organization should have a regularly scheduled tour program, if for no other reason than to accommodate the groups that call: generally groups of kids—school classes, Brownies and Cub

Scouts, and so on. The institution's image is not enhanced when a second-grade teacher is told "We don't do tours" (because the PR staff doesn't have the time), especially when it's possible to create a simple program that takes up very little staff time. Although the initial motivation behind setting up such a program may be simply to avoid criticism for not having a program, the health care organization will find that building positive relationships with teachers, school systems, and parents is an important way to enhance the organization's image.

The simplest of tour programs can be set up by:

1. *Creating a "basic tour" that includes departments that can fairly easily accommodate tours and that are exciting and interesting to the school groups.* The managers and staff members of those departments have to be willing to participate, including having a staff member who can be available to conduct the tour group through the department. This does not have to be the department manager — in fact, getting to be the department tour leader is an enjoyable break from the routine for extroverted employees. The tours should include some departments where there can be some hands-on activities (donning masks and mini-sized gowns to walk through the obstetrics unit to see the nursery, or having a nurse or technician demonstrate putting a cast on one of the children).

2. *Recruiting a group of volunteers, with the cooperation of the volunteer services director, to serve as guides to welcome, orient, and take the tour groups from department to department.* Being a tour guide should be positioned as a highly selective and preferential role and potential volunteers should actually be recruited through personalized invitations and a special luncheon. Giving the volunteers a special name ("VIP Guides," "Ambassadors," and so on) and special badges or outfits (blazers or sweaters with the health care organization's logo) helps reinforce the elite status of these positions. A special training and orientation program, with presentations by department heads and a review of the tour guide manual, should be conducted quarterly so that new guides can be recruited on an ongoing basis.

3. *Establishing specific days and times for tours that work with school schedules, the health care facility's department work loads, and with the volunteer tour guides' preferences.* Limiting tours to three or four standard times (Tuesdays and Thursdays from 1 to 3 p.m., Mondays from 3 to 5 p.m., and Wednesdays from 10 a.m. to noon, for instance) means that volunteers can make commitments to being available for a specific time, rather than having to be on call. It also makes it easier on the institution's departments that are involved in the tours.

165

4. *Setting up standard protocols with security, parking, and other ancillary departments so that special arrangements don't have to be made every time there's a tour.* Instead, a monthly schedule of tours can be sent out and all departments will know what their role is.
5. *Assigning tour coordination to a PR staff member or a well-trained clerical staff member.* The coordinator's responsibility is to handle tour requests, schedule the tour, assign a tour guide (or contact the volunteer director or a volunteer assistant to schedule a tour guide), and confirm the tour in writing to the school group and all appropriate departments of the institution. Some health care organizations have had success in having a volunteer coordinate the program, but this can cause problems in terms of having someone available during normal working hours to handle phone calls (few volunteers want to be at the hospital 40 hours a week).
6. *Developing special "take-home" materials, making sure the parents are aware of their child's visit and allowing the kids to serve as conduits to get information to the parents.*

Once this basic program is in place, the health care organization can either simply leave it in place so that it's available when requests are received, or it can choose to promote the program as a way of building relationships primarily with schools and teachers and secondarily with parents.

This basic program can also serve as a starting point for a more sophisticated effort toward bringing in specific, target audiences. "Targeted tours" are created to appeal to specific groups, which are proactively approached by the health care organization and invited to use the institution's meeting space, with the tour (and a speaker or presentation) as the "hook." For instance, a hospital seeking to build awareness of its women's services would create several tour options with hand-picked tour leaders—the mammography center, conducted by a radiologist; new birthing facilities, conducted by a maternity nurse; surgical suites, followed by a presentation by a plastic surgeon; and so on. These options would be packaged into a promotional brochure or mailing that would be sent to targeted women's groups (mothers' clubs, professional women's networks, and so on) with follow-up phone calls, and the tours and programs would be supervised by a PR staff member, to ensure that everything goes smoothly.

What the health care organization offers these groups is an "instant meeting"—a place with free meeting space, a ready-made program, and, if desired, very reasonably priced catering services. What the health care organization gets in return: access to members of these target audiences on a personal basis; the ability to educate, inform, and build awareness of specific programs and services; and the chance to erase any preconceived ideas about the organization's physical facilities. One woman who participated in her professional women's network tour of a hospital's mammography center said, "I'd never even been at this hospital before, but now I feel like I know the doctor and the mammography technicians. This is where I'll come when I need an exam." And because people who join associations or become part of groups are more likely to be informal opinion leaders, their personal exposure to the health care organization can have a concentric information flow effect.

Note: Health care organizations that do not choose to create or promote these kinds of special tours can still make meeting space available to targeted outside groups to at least get them inside the institution. A PR staff person should be involved in these arrangements to ensure that all the details are handled smoothly. Invitations should only be extended when the PR person is sure that internal systems are in place to make the group's visit a pleasant one.

Conducting On-Site Special Events

Open houses—once the basic hospital special event—have evolved into myriad interesting opportunities to bring publics to the facility. Once the publics' concerns about access and parking are handled (include maps and free parking information in all event invitations and announcements) and audience research indicates the times and days that are preferred by the public (it varies from community to community), the PR staff can develop numerous on-site special events to appeal to various publics. The possibilities are limitless, but following are some examples of the various types:

- *For senior citizens,* weekly screenings and/or health presentations by physicians or health care staff members. Senior citizens have the time, enjoy the events, and when a coffee and pie (or other dessert) hour is added, it adds socialization and a warm, positive "bonding" between senior citizens and the staff who are there to talk with them.
- *For kids,* special tours or "hands-on" open houses, including a doll and teddy bear clinic, getting mock casts applied, listening to their own heartbeats, and so on, with presentations and time for parents to talk with pediatric and emergency department staff members about safety and prevention.
- *For families living near the institution,* quarterly neighborhood socials, including free movies in the institution's auditorium for the kids, displays or screenings for parents, and a reduced-price menu in the cafeteria.
- *For grade schools,* art competitions with all the entries displayed in the health care institution and parents and kids invited to a special reception and awards ceremony.

- *For the general public,* open houses with drama. At the opening of a new surgery center, have a neurosurgeon peeling grapes with a laser; at an emergency department open house, have a trauma team stage a mock disaster drill. If the public is going to be invited in, don't declare places off limits. They expect to be able to go inside cath labs and CT scan rooms – and to meet and talk with physicians. If the health care organization has in-house live video capabilities, participants in the institution's auditorium can observe a surgical procedure via closed-circuit television (but make sure it's not too gory).
- *For the general public,* healthy heart recipe contests, with the final cook-off in the institution's auditorium, presided over by dietitians with cardiologists as taste testers.

Among the keys to successful on-site special events are the following:

- Remember that people don't naturally want to come to a health care facility (even for a fun event, the facility still feels scary), so the event has to be special.
- If the health care organization is located in a metropolitan or inner-city area, provide easy-to-follow information on how to get to the facility, safe and free parking, and so on.
- Match day and time with the target audience – late morning, lunch, or early afternoon times may be good with mothers of toddlers, whereas working women may prefer right after work or a weekend day. Do research to find what works for your audience.
- Make sure you get names, addresses, and other data on participants, to add them to the marketing data base.
- Make sure the event has a health or health-related focus to avoid criticism about wasting the organization's funds or being frivolous.
- Consider giving away door prizes because although there is some debate about the "appropriateness" of door prizes and incentives (drawings for scrub suits, and so on), they do help achieve the objective of bringing the public into the health care facility. (Registering for a health-related door prize is a good way to capture attendees' names for the marketing data base.)
- Use take-homes – printed materials, calculator wheels to determine the percentage of fat in foods, even the ubiquitous refrigerator magnets – as a method to prolong the contact and keep the health care organization's name in the participants' consciousness.
- Be imaginative. If every other health care organization is doing cholesterol screenings, try something different.
- Above all, remember that the point of special events is building relationships – and that means people meeting people. Audiences

want to meet "medical people"—physicians, nurses, technologists—not PR people. If the only people from the health care organization who will be at a heart center open house are going to be volunteer tour guides and the PR staff, rethink it.

Building Linkages with Key Audiences

Two techniques for creating awareness and beginning to build relationships with target audiences include events such as briefings for opinion leaders and creation of advisory boards.

Opinion Leader Briefings

At opinion leader briefings, targeted opinion leaders hear a presentation on a special topic (selected either for its appeal to that audience, such as cost-containment efforts presented to a business leader group, or for its dramatic appeal, such as laser surgery) and then hear an "insiders' overview" presented by the CEO or chief of staff. For successful implementation of such briefings:

- *Use research to identify true community opinion leaders*—a group that generally includes but is not limited to business executives. Leaders from churches, the minority community, professional women's networks, social service agencies, civic groups, and government should also be included.
- *Don't "typecast"; that is, invite all the same type of people (all minorities, senior citizens, ministers, and so on), or pick a topic aimed at a specific group,* such as a women's health update for a briefing of professional women. That isolation technique can backfire and seem patronizing or perfunctory. When a group of black church leaders find themselves in a briefing on sickle cell disease, they may respond by thinking, "Oh—this week they're talking to the minority community." It may be more difficult to accomplish, but it's better to mix groups and select topics that are of interest to a broad audience. Those topics do exist—most opinion leaders are concerned about community-related topics like access and cost containment, and most adults are intrigued by the dramatic new medical techniques.
- *Make the program topic and the presenter the "hook" that will get them in the door so the CEO can do the broader pitch.* Just offering a broad "update on our hospital's progress" isn't enough of an attraction.
- *Make sure the timing is right.* This is critical. In some communities, business breakfasts are de rigueur, whereas in other areas, the after-work cocktail reception works best. Whatever the time of day, keep the event reasonably short (1½ hours maximum) and do not,

169

not, not run overtime. Business execs seem to get particularly irritated by meetings that run late (especially when it's on their personal time) and going overtime projects an image of the undisciplined nonprofit mentality of which health care organizations are accused.

- *Keep the group small enough to be personal.* From 12 to 15 (20 maximum) is a workable size. If the group gets larger, the event goes from being a briefing to being a lecture.
- *Leave time for questions for the presenter and the CEO.* And make sure both are very comfortable with dialogue and can think quickly on their feet. When opinion leaders are invited to hear about heart surgery, they may very well raise questions about whether or not too many inappropriate procedures are being performed. And no matter what the CEO talks about, he or she will get questions about costs. Both have to be well rehearsed and able to field hostile questions without getting defensive.
- *Don't limit the health care organization's representation to the presenter, the CEO, a PR staff member, and the dietary staff members who serve the food.* If one objective of the event is to build relationships, it's important that the guests meet and talk with the organization's staff members—not sit and talk with other guests. These events are a good opportunity for senior management staff members and physicians (those who are good minglers) to meet the community as part of the health care organization's team.
- *Make the food appealing, but not overly elaborate.* Tasty and healthy foods are required (one business exec reported that he attended a breakfast briefing on heart disease and was served bacon, eggs, and cinnamon rolls with icing).
- *Follow up on an ongoing basis.* Bringing in opinion leaders for a once-a-year briefing is not a way to build relationships and seems insincere to participants. Follow-up contacts are essential and can range from periodic newsletters with "inside" information about the health care organization's plans to personal contacts with the senior managers who participated in the briefings. (These liaison arrangements are discussed in chapter 8.)

Most community opinion leaders are concerned about health care and hospitals, to varying degrees. Health care organizations can take advantage of this interest to bring opinion leaders "onto the property" so they can see, firsthand, what the health care organization is accomplishing.

Advisory Boards

Advisory boards take the opinion leader contacts to a more formal, ongoing level. Generic advisory councils can seem meaningless to participants because they do not have the responsibilities of a board of trustees; however, advisory boards formed to work with specific programs can provide helpful input to the health care organization and also give participants a specific role.

For instance, a women's health center advisory board can provide input on consumer research, serve as a mini focus group/sounding board for product development ideas, host programs, or invite friends to learn more about the center and advise on promotion efforts. Members of this type of focused advisory board, if enthusiastic about the program, also somewhat naturally become ambassadors for the program among their constituent groups and are seen as more credible spokespersons than a representative from the health care organization.

Creation of a successful advisory board entails:

- *Defining a specific role for the board members as advisors who provide advice and counsel and may also take on more specific participatory roles when requested by the staff.* It needs to be clearly stressed that the advisory board members do not have approval rights for the program, nor do they have any authority over day-to-day operations.
- *Selecting advisory board members who are truly representative of the program's audience.* An advisory board for a parent health and safety education program should include parents from all the demographic groups that the health care organization serves or wants to serve, along with educators and others who work with children.
- *Assigning one staff member to work with the advisory board who is clearly responsible for keeping the board members informed and ensuring that they feel involved.*
- *Determining in advance a number of activities in which the board members can be involved so they feel that they are being helpful.* "Not feeling useful" is one of the main complaints of advisory board members.
- *Actually seeking and using advisory board input.* Meetings should be more than just a show-and-tell by the health care organization's staff members. Although it's important that the board members be informed, it's equally important for them to inform and educate the health care organization about the concerns of the public and how the organization is being perceived by the public.
- *Establishing specific terms of appointment for advisory board members — usually a year — so that new community representatives can become involved and that advisory board members don't get burned out or bored.*

If these criteria can't be met, it's probably better to avoid creating an advisory board. The absence of an advisory board isn't a problem for the health care organization, but creating one and then not involving the members appropriately can create poor relationships between the health care organization and community leaders.

☐ Taking the Health Care Organization Out into the Community

Taking the health care organization out into the community—via events, speakers, sponsorships, and personal liaisons—avoids the barriers that prevent publics from coming to a health care facility, but can also require even more careful planning and attention to detail from the PR staff, along with the cooperation and commitment of the health care organization's physicians, nurses, and managers, who are going to be the organization's representatives. The benefits of "out of the suites, into the streets" include:

- *Reach and access*—the ability to get out to audiences who might never come to the health care facility
- *Impact*—the positive impression made by the health care organization's personnel who "came to our school (church, office)," which is heightened by the fact that the health care organization's staff members took the time to be at the meeting, health fair, and so on
- *The element of surprise and the humanizing effect* that occurs when a physician or a nurse is met in an unexpected setting like a church or a shopping mall, rather than a medical setting
- *The satisfaction of staff members who are involved in the outreach effort* that gives them a fun break from their day-to-day routine (and many staff people really enjoy the chance to show off their expertise to outside audiences)

The Speakers' Bureau Updated

As with a tours program, one of the primary reasons that health care organizations should consider creating speakers' programs is to avoid the negative impression created by saying, "Sorry—we don't provide speakers" to a community group. The more important reason is that a targeted, effectively managed speakers' program can be a key to building relationships and creating awareness as part of a general image-building program, and can also be an asset to a product marketing communications campaign.

Whether the speakers' service is designed generically, to respond to community requests, or proactively to place speakers as part of marketing communications efforts, the following steps ensure that the service functions effectively:

1. *Select topics first* based on existing requests and research with community audiences. Generally, topics that help people learn how to stay healthy or topics that are dramatic or exciting work best.
2. *Carefully select speakers*—don't ask for volunteers. Speakers can include physicians, nurses, pharmacists, health educators, credit counselors (who can explain billing and reimbursement to senior citizens), dietitians, and a number of other types of staff members who can speak on topics that are of interest to the health care organization's target publics. Once potential speakers are identified, the PR staff person assigned to coordinate the speakers' program should attempt to listen to the speaker—at a continuing education conference, at an in-service program, or even just when he or she is speaking as part of a staff or department meeting. If there's a question about an individual's ability to be an effective presenter, the person could be invited to brief the PR staff on the topic.
3. *Position participation in the speakers' service as an honor,* with invitations and special recognition and rewards (a dinner, gifts like tote bags or portfolios, and so on). It should also be made clear that being part of the speakers' service includes participating in training (which may be just a brushup for the experienced presenters) and having a schedule that is flexible enough to handle at least one presentation a month. (The physician relations or medical staff marketing manager can be helpful in identifying physicians who are trying to "grow" their practices and would be interested in exposure and in recruiting those physicians to participate.)
4. *Train speakers.* Rather than having a PR person do this training (which can get somewhat sensitive in terms of critiquing style), use a local trainer or perhaps a speech professor from a nearby university.
5. *Set up systems for efficiently booking speakers.* Three-part forms that include all of the details—group name; information on expected audience size and composition; date, time, and location with directions; audiovisual equipment needed; group's expectations of topic, length, nature, and style of presentation; and (very important) names and phone numbers for the contact person and for the speaker, including a phone number that can be used the day or night of the presentation in case there are any last-minute problems. The PR staff person fills in all the information and sends one copy each to the speaker and the group.
6. *Develop appropriate support materials for speakers*—at the very least, a general promotional brochure (you have the audience's attention—don't miss a chance to communicate) and a matching slide show that can be used with a portable slide projector (like a CaraMate). Specialized brochures and handouts, displays, videos, and multiprojector slide shows can also be developed, depending

on the budget available and number of times the program will be presented.

7. *Promote the speakers' service* via mailings to community groups, announcements in the media, and follow-up phone calls. When calls are received, respond promptly and efficiently—nothing's worse than saying, "Call us for speakers," and then not delivering.

8. *Develop follow-up and evaluation systems*, including providing the group contact person with a confidential evaluation form that is to be returned to the speakers' service coordinator. Good evaluations should be shared routinely with speakers. If negative or mixed evaluations are received, the coordinator should arrange to accompany the speaker on an upcoming booking ("We try to go out with all of our speakers at least once during the year") to assess. If there is definitely a problem, the coordinator needs to determine whether it's better to try to address the problem or just let requests for that topic magically "dry up."

Again, as with tours, the PR staff can move into a proactive mode, selecting target audiences that are important to the health care organization's overall image goals or to specific products or services, and approaching those groups about placing a speaker on a topic that relates to the group.

Special Events: From Mega to Mini

The shopping mall health fair has become almost a tradition in many communities, but the focus of community special events is shifting from participation in mega-events to smaller, more targeted events. In fact, many PR managers now question the value of committing budgetary and staff resources to staffing displays or exhibits as part of large health fairs where they will be one of dozens of hospitals and health care providers. "It's hard to make a real impact on consumers when they're going from booth to booth," said one PR director, whose research showed that participants in multihospital community health fairs had very little recall of which hospital had which booth or display. In addition, the mass audience approach doesn't easily facilitate personal interaction between the hospital staff and the public.

A more effective alternative is the *solo health fair*, in which one health care organization sponsors the entire event, so that the organization's name and logo are predominant and so that every person who comes to the health fair meets many staff members of the health care organization. "If everything the consumer sees—every display, every demonstration, every handout, and every name tag on every nurse and doctor—says hospital X, then you're making an impact," advised a PR manager. With effective promotion, this kind of health event can draw thousands of participants.

Another relatively new type of community-based event goes to the other extreme – the small-scale 1990s version of the *Tupperware party*, with a health focus. These small group sessions, hosted by an individual who invites 10–15 of his or her friends to his or her home, allow for more personal interaction and relationship building than do large-scale events. A woman obstetrician-gynecologist can discuss some very specific women's health concerns and issues with a dozen 25-year-old women who are good friends. A group of parents who live in the same neighborhood are more comfortable talking about problems with their teenagers to a substance abuse therapist while sitting around a family room drinking coffee than asking a personal question while sitting in an auditorium with several hundred strangers. Another benefit of the small-scale "party" is that it allows participation by physicians or other staff members who may not be comfortable doing formal presentations before large audiences.

These events can be organized by using the mass media to announce the program, or by targeting specific individuals (parents of former teen alcoholism center patients, mothers who've had babies in the past six months, and so on) who would be willing to invite some of their friends and host a party. The PR staff can provide preprinted invitations or develop letter formats, or the host can handle this task. The host provides simple refreshments and the health care organization furnishes an effective, personable speaker or speakers, along with any audiovisual, display, or handout material.

The key to a successful small group event is to provide a comfortable, warm atmosphere that makes participants feel at home. The goal is dialogue between the speaker and participants, rather than a formal presentation. And follow-up mechanisms (a parents' hot line, a women's resource center phone number, and so on) should be in place.

Once the event is over, the PR staff should coordinate follow-up thank-you letters (preferably personal letters from the presenter, even if the PR staff has to write them for the presenter to sign) and make sure that participants are added to the health care organization's data base to receive ongoing mailings. Clearly, small events like these must be repeated consistently to reach a larger number of people, whereas the big health fair type of event provides access to greater numbers, but with less intimacy.

A *hybrid event* – a cross between the large shopping mall health fair and the small home discussion – is the church or school event. This type of event is more personalized (and usually easier to organize) than a large health fair, because rather than a mass, multifaceted audience, the focus is on a more homogenous audience (such as members of a church, or families with children in the same school).

Examples of school events are the whole-school, day-long health event involving a multidisciplinary team from the health care organization. One hospital's school health day program involves setting up a mobile "operating room" in the gymnasium, having presentations going on in classrooms on a variety of topics, and closing the day with a whole-school health rally. A "healthy decisions day" for junior high school students includes an afternoon of interactive demonstrations and small group teaching sessions, with prizes for students who participate in every activity. Parents are involved in determining what topics will be included (choosing from a list including drugs, alcohol, AIDS, teenage pregnancy, obesity and anorexia, and so on). The teens are given materials to take home, and parents are notified in advance so they can follow up with discussions at home.

Churches often welcome mini–health fairs held on Saturdays or after services on Sunday. Other smaller-than-a-mall events can be held at country and athletic clubs, colleges, and neighborhood and senior citizen centers.

Sponsorships and Underwriting of Community Events

Another community relations approach is the sponsorship or underwriting of everything from 10-kilometer marathon runs to jazz concerts during summer festivals. Health care organizations are increasingly being asked to "demonstrate your community spirit" by paying sponsorship fees that can cost several thousand dollars.

There are a number of questions that need to be answered before making a decision about sponsorship or underwriting:

- Will sponsorship of this event help achieve one of the health care organization's public image or program marketing goals? And how will the health care organization measure the impact? Often, "visibility" is the immediate answer, but a way to measure this visibility and the relationship between any increased visibility and the health care organization's objectives must be developed.
- Does the event "fit" with the health care organization's image and mission? Sponsoring a 10-kilometer run fits with a hospital that's positioned as a wellness advocate or has a strong sports medicine program. Underwriting a jazz concert as part of a summer arts festival would seem to have little relationship to an acute care hospital.
- What specifically does the health care organization get for its money? A sponsorship line in a printed program booklet? The organization's name on 2,000 T-shirts that participants will wear around the community for months to come? Banners at the festival? "Goodwill"–

the chance to build better relationships with leaders of the event's sponsoring group?

- What are the true costs of involvement, beyond the cash donation? One hospital, as part of being a sponsor of a summer arts festival, was "allowed" to have a staffed display that eventually involved more than 300 hours of staff time to develop and staff.
- Is this a one-time opportunity, or are there chances to follow up with participants?
- If the organization is only putting its name on the event, is it worth the cash contribution?

The last question is often not easily answered. On the surface, it would seem obvious that just getting the health care organization's name in a program, on a banner, or on a T-shirt is hardly the best way to spend several thousands of dollars out of the PR budget. Wouldn't an ad campaign or a direct-mail brochure be a better use of the money? The answer to that question depends on the sponsoring group and the event's audience. Sponsoring an event at an inner-city recreation center festival is a way of demonstrating a commitment to the minority community. Being a principal underwriter of an ongoing symphony concert series puts the health care organization's name in front of a very selective audience several times a year.

Because the bottom-line value of these sponsorships cannot be precisely measured, some health care administrators believe that they should be avoided. The PR manager, however, should rely on his or her knowledge of the community, the importance of the sponsoring group's relationships to the health care organization, and the nature of the participants or audience before determining how the sponsorship will fit with the institution's general PR or product marketing communications plans.

Personal Involvement: The Emissary Method

Another low-key, long-term community relations strategy is to use the health care organization's managers and staff members as "emissaries" to key community groups or publics. One hospital PR director developed a list of all the key civic organizations in the community — from Rotary to Junior League — and then asked managers to indicate which, if any, groups they were active in. Then administrators and managers were asked to volunteer to join or get involved with the remaining organizations (when possible). These "emissaries" were not expected to hype the hospital or continually talk about the hospital to other members, but rather to simply make sure other members knew about their hospital affiliation and to share with the PR staff any negative comments or concerns about the hospital.

The PR staff can also coordinate a concerted effort to have the health care organization's administrators and managers appointed to important civic boards so that they can both represent the health care organization and gather information from the civic organizations. (These types of liaison arrangements are discussed in greater detail in chapter 8.)

In an even more proactive, large-scale way, some health care organizations have sent teams of their employees into the community to knock on doors and talk with the home owners about the organization's capabilities and plans, recruit volunteers, and provide information about a new service or program. This employee corps is not only a way to promote the health care organization, but also a way to give employees a role to play in the PR and marketing activities. This type of up-close-and-personal effort can also be an important research tool, because the employees can ask the residents for input and can also answer any questions the residents may have (noting any that need future follow-up). Clearly, employees would need to be carefully selected and trained, but the value of a personal visit, even if the employees aren't all perfectly articulate salespeople, is hard to match.

The health care organization's employees can also participate in high-visibility community service projects, such as cleaning up a park area near the health care facility, helping inner-city residents install donated smoke alarms, sponsoring a paint up–fix up day to help neighboring home owners, and so on. Again, these types of activities bring the health care organization's employees into personal contact with the public and promote a positive image for the organization.

□ Using Health Education as a Public Relations Tool

Providing more formalized health education programming, either at the health care facility or at community sites, is a community relations strategy that many health care organizations use for general public relations and for specific marketing communications campaigns. The range of health education activities is enormous — from single-session baby-sitting clinics to ongoing diabetes education programs, from simple screenings in the health care setting to mobile vans equipped to provide multiple screenings at major public events like fairs or at churches, and so on, on a repetitive basis. Support groups can be the "ties that bind" special groups to your health care organization — persons suffering from chronic diseases, Alcoholics Anonymous and other recovery groups (including head trauma, burn, and other types of accident victims), family support groups, and so on. These are often people who have been and may continue to be users of the health care organization's services, so providing them with the opportunity to meet staff members and to obtain professional staff support for their groups (if requested) is a good way of ensuring their goodwill.

In developing health education programs, the PR manager needs to consider the following factors:

- To maintain quality and participant satisfaction, these programs should be developed by a nurse educator or health professional.
- Physicians should be involved in planning and/or approving the programs to ensure that they support the program and understand that the health care organization is not trying to take business away from them.
- Program topics and subjects should be selected based on audience interest (measured through community research), community need (what programs aren't already being offered), and relationship to the health care organization's PR and marketing goals.
- Location should be carefully considered. If the health care facility is accessible to the target audience, this facility can be used. If the health care facility is not perceived as convenient (or safe) by the public, then a popular and accessible community site should be used.
- The issue of whether to charge should be analyzed. Charging even small fees for participation may help offset the costs of the program, but will deter some persons from participating.
- Participation goals should be realistic. Several health educators participating in an American Hospital Association seminar on ambulatory care noted that community residents surveyed would voice interest in and support for these programs, but actual participation was lower than the stated interest would seem to indicate. Planners need to take the natural, human, "I don't have the time/energy" factor into consideration.
- On-the-spot assessment and education should be provided for screenings, as well as a follow-up mechanism to encourage persons whose results are outside the normal ranges to see their physician. Support funding may be available through pharmaceutical companies — and make sure you investigate all the liability angles.

The PR manager who is considering launching or preparing to launch health education programming should realistically assess the purpose, objectives, potential results, and staff costs of doing this programming in relation to other methods that could be used to achieve PR objectives. Secondary research, via computerized literature search and discussions with peers, will help the PR manager maximize the effectiveness of the programs.

□ Summary

The four keys to successful community relations programming are:

1. A specific objective should be developed for each program, even if it's one that's hard to isolate and measure, such as "build visibility." The program's role in the PR or marketing communications plan must be clearly defined.
2. The smaller the event, the more personalized it should be. With larger events, personalized attention is sacrificed to gain access to larger numbers.
3. Community relations efforts should be ongoing, with a long-term focus, rather than short-term, scattershot projects.
4. The goal should be to introduce the health care organization's people to representatives of the organization's publics—to begin the process of relationship building.

Public relations experts predict that the 1990s will mark the end of the mass media era and the beginning of the personalized relationship era. Health care organizations are uniquely positioned to capitalize on this trend because they have people, facilities, and products that are interesting (even fascinating) to most of the general public.

Reference

1. In new decade of personalized relationships and communication, changes in techniques, strategies and practitioner attitudes are predictable. *pr reporter* 32(1):1, Jan. 1, 1990.

Suggested Reading

Bates, B. *Community Relations Handbook.* New York City: Random House, 1979.

Media Relations

Contemporary health care organizations exist as part of an external environment and are dependent on the support of the communities they serve. Thus, health care organizations have both a need and a responsibility to communicate with the audiences that comprise their external environments, including legislators, regulators, donors, past and potential patients, and the members of the "general public" who are part of their communities.

One significant way in which health care organizations communicate with their communities is through the mass media— newspapers, magazines, radio, and television—and today media interest in health care organizations is greater than in any previous decade, for several reasons:

- Health care organizations in the aggregate are major employers and major consumers of resources.
- Because of the perception of even private hospitals as "public" institutions, reporters feel they have a right to know what's going on inside health care organizations.
- Hospitals care for persons involved in newsworthy events, from car accidents to children in need of transplants, and thus have information the news media need.
- Health care organizations generate exciting and "heartwarming" stories.
- The public is avidly interested in health and medical stories, and the media respond to that interest (nearly every major paper in the country has a medical or health reporter, and "TV doctors" are becoming routine).

Health care PR managers understand the need to use the media as a communications channel to reach their audiences and the need to respond to media inquiries so that their side of controversial issues can be presented. And many health care CEOs say they understand the need to deal with the media because it's "good PR." Additionally, a strong case can be made that health care organizations have an ethical imperative to communicate openly and freely with the media, as the advocates of the public's right to know.

Yet despite the fact that this need and responsibility to work with the press is commonly acknowledged, hospital executive Christine Fones noted, "I sometimes sense a general reluctance within our ranks to speak to the press."[1] Fones identified the primary reason why hospital executives, and even PR staff members, are sometimes reluctant to answer the phone when they know the press is calling: "basic human fear."

Commented Fones, "There are plenty of solid reasons to feel apprehensive about being interviewed by a person who has a significant measure of control over the way we, our organizations, and our programs will be presented to the public. We all go through the anxiety of wondering if we will be understood. We ask ourselves if the words we choose will do justice to the idea or program we are promoting. Will our arguments be accepted, or at least fairly and accurately portrayed? What will our competitors say when asked the same questions? And what will our peers and superiors say when they see our answers?"

This reluctance is not limited to health care executives — national studies show that most business leaders are very mistrustful of the media — nor is it totally unjustified, given the examples of the damage that media coverage can do (as illustrated in the 1981 film *Absence of Malice*). However, advised Fones, "we have to move beyond our fears, rational as they may be, so we can deal clearly with the central question: Will the interests and values of this organization be better served by our comments or by our silence?" Except in rare circumstances, the answer is that silence does not serve the health care organization's best interests, and that, to the contrary, "a policy of sincere and accurate public comment projects an image of leadership, a responsiveness to the needs and concerns of the community, and a message of strength to competitors and naysayers."

Public relations managers who understand the value of working with the media are also aware of the power of the press and the limitations of using the media as a communications channel. The mass media have the power to:

- Reach a mass audience, generally larger than the combined audiences reached by other PR methods (advertising, of course, can reach equally broad audiences — but at a far greater cost than media coverage, which is essentially free)
- Reach a broad audience, getting the message to general public groups that may not be reached through the hospital's targeted methods

- Add credibility ("I know it's true — I saw it in the paper") to enhance the impact of messages that are also being sent through other PR methods
- Conversely, undercut the credibility and effectiveness of PR campaigns by presenting contradictory information or creating a negative image of the health care organization

There are corresponding limitations to relying on mass media as part of a PR campaign. With mass media, the PR manager lacks:

- Control over *accuracy* or completeness of message because the reporter and editor/news director are in charge
- Control over *timing* of when the message will be communicated
- Control over the *reach* of the message because it is nearly impossible to measure what percentage of the audience actually read, saw, or heard the story
- The ability to achieve *frequency* of message transmission because generally the story is only covered once

With this perspective in mind, the PR manager can develop a media relations program that balances the needs of the media, the ways the health care organization can use the media, and the fact that health care organizations, although they are looked on as public service institutions, are not institutions of totally open public record. Health care organizations — even those that are publicly owned and/or operated — provide services that are private and personal, and there are significant legal and liability limits on what information can be released.

Because of this, the role of the health care PR manager in working with the media is more challenging than that of PR professionals in other industries. Public agencies or organizations are required by law to maintain open records. Private businesses or organizations can keep nearly all information confidential. Health care institutions are somewhere in the middle — for the most part, they are privately owned organizations that are not required to release information, and, in fact, are required by law to keep some information confidential, but they are perceived by the press and the public to be "public service" organizations, with resulting expectations about openness. Meeting those expectations while adhering to legal restrictions is a critical task of the PR manager when undertaking a media relations program.

□ Understanding the Mass Media

When compared with other communications methods, mass media offer the pluses of speed and reach, but are less personalized and more difficult to control in terms of content. Print media can be retained and reread and are better for communicating facts and details. Newspapers have the broadest impact and the greatest speed of getting the message out, whereas magazines are slower, but reach more targeted audiences. Books are a much slower medium, reach a more limited audience, but can be more influential than newspapers or magazines.

The broadcast media can convey broad messages, but cannot be retained and reviewed (few people tape and review TV news). Television is a powerful medium because it appeals to two senses — hearing and sight — and can elicit highly emotional responses. Radio offers the greatest speed of message delivery, can be used to reach target audiences, and can be more flexible than television or print media.

America's nearly 10,000 newspapers provide a number of opportunities to tell the health care organization's story, including straight news stories, features, columns, local angles for national stories, trend wrap-up stories, letters to the editor and op-ed columns, news and feature photos, and special-focus supplements. Although the main focus of PR activity is generally news or feature coverage, the other types of newspaper stories listed provide other effective ways to convey a message. For instance, in some papers, local feature columnists may be read more widely than the news reporters, and the op-ed page is a must read for opinion leaders. The PR or media relations manager should analyze the content of every paper in the health care organization's primary and secondary service area to identify all of the opportunities for story placement, and also analyze the needs of the local wire service reporters or stringers, who can facilitate national coverage.

The trend among America's 11,000 magazines is specialization. Although the large news weeklies and business publications may be better known to the general public, there are literally thousands of smaller magazines that are read by very specific audiences — from senior citizens to working mothers to residents of a specific city. And special-purpose magazines — from trade and hobby publications to airline magazines — offer opportunities to reach other specialized populations.

Local TV news programs tend to reach broader audiences, although some audience targeting is available via interview and public service programming, public service announcements (PSAs), sponsorship of syndicated programs, and local access cable programs.

Radio news used to be the primary method of communicating via the airwaves, but today call-in interview and talk shows are having a very powerful impact in many communities. Informal announcements or "plugs" by disc jockeys, plus PSAs and "community bulletin board" announcements, are also available.

In addition to understanding the capabilities and opportunities provided by the mass media, the PR manager also needs to have some insights into the concerns and needs of news reporters and editors, with whom they'll be dealing on a routine basis. At a 1988 conference on relationships among the media, physicians, and ethicists, TV reporters noted that they need pictures, faces, and people who can talk in tiny bites of information. And a focus on an individual — the child who needs an organ transplant — is preferred to a general story — statistics on transplantation, for instance.

Reporters also need prompt answers and information, the confidence they're being told the truth, and for the PR manager to help them get the whole story, rather than trying to hinder them. The fact that what the reporter terms "hindrance" may seem to the PR person as "just doing my job" is one example of the differences between the two professions, differences that must be acknowledged and addressed.

A 1988 study of PR professionals and reporters found that there were other differences between the two groups:[2]

- Public relations professionals report that they have more autonomy in their work, whereas journalists report that their greatest source of dissatisfaction is lack of autonomy.
- Journalists perceive that there are more opportunities for advancement in public relations than in journalism.
- Public relations has more women at all levels, whereas a greater proportion of women journalists are at the reporter level.
- Public relations people feel much more valuable at their organizations than do journalists.
- Journalists (especially at non-Guild newspapers) say they consider leaving the field primarily because of low salaries, whereas PR pros report a high level of salary satisfaction. Salary is more important to PR professionals, whereas journalists stress status, defined as working for a prestige paper or winning recognition for their writing.

Dennis Wilcox, Ph.D., who conducted the study, noted that there are also definite differences in personalities of journalists versus PR people. "Journalists tend to be loners, and they have a reputation of being negative, cynical, whereas PR people are optimistic and happy." This glimpse into the personality differences between journalists and PR professionals can help the PR manager in approaching and dealing with reporters on a day-to-day basis.

☐ Working with the Media

There are generally six ways in which the PR staff interacts with reporters, editors, and news directors:

1. Developing ongoing relationships with media representatives
2. Responding to media inquiries and requests for interviews
3. "Pitching" or attempting to place stories
4. Conducting press conferences, tours, or events
5. Fighting battles—during and after the story
6. Communicating during crises (covered in chapter 11)

The prerequisite to any of these interactions is the development of a detailed media relations policy that guides the PR professionals and hospital staff members in all contacts with the press.

The Media Relations Policy

The media relations policy sets forth guidelines and limits and outlines the health care organization's approach to dealing with the press. Every employee in the health care organization should be familiar with the basic points of the policy, especially those specific items that might affect the individual employee, and all administrators and managers should be educated and continually reeducated about the policies. This is essential because of the impact that an inaccurate or negative story can have on the health care organization's image and standing in the community (as well as the patient confidentiality issues that can result). Although individual policies will vary, the following sections are examples of what should be included (or at least considered for inclusion) in the health care organization's policies, with suggestions on specific policies and procedures.

I. Statement of Philosophy

An opening statement of philosophy should include recognition of the media's legitimate interest in the health care organization's activities, the health care organization's interest in disseminating newsworthy information to the public via the media, and the health care organization's commitment to positive working relationships with the press. This statement must also state clearly that the health care organization's primary ethical and legal obligation is to the care, safety, and confidentiality of its patients and their families. It is also a good idea to note that when there is a conflict between protecting a patient's rights of privacy and a commitment to providing information to news media, the patient's rights will always prevail. Finally, this opening statement should detail the health care organization's ownership status, relating that to the actual legal requirements and limitations on release of information in that state and by federal agencies.

II. Protocol for Media Contacts

Protocols must clearly state, in detail, to whom, when, and how media contacts are to be made and handled. In many health care organizations, the PR staff is the sole initial contact for all information, including patient conditions. In other institutions, the admitting department is authorized (with specific limits) to release patient conditions and birth and death information, as designees of the PR department. Some institutions allow administrative assistants or another designated administrative staff person to release patient information at night.

Names, titles, and phone numbers of spokespersons, PR staff members, and the CEO should be included. (If names of other administrators are included, even if just for information purposes, this means media may call them directly.) It's generally a good idea to include PR staff members' home phone numbers, too, as well as direct-dial pagers or beepers.

Protocols describe specific procedures for reporters—what number to call, day and night; how to reach an on-call PR staffer; what back-up method to use if they can't reach that staffer; and so on. Try to anticipate what could go wrong with the system and what the reporter should do. Also include a statement on why the media must contact a spokesperson (that person has quickest access to information, can facilitate setting up interviews or filming, and so on) so that the media understand the *why* of the procedure. And note what will happen if they try to bypass public relations and go directly to a source (they'll just be referred back to public relations and will have wasted their time).

The policy should also include a statement for employees and managers in the health care organization, noting that any information to be released (with the exceptions noted above) should be forwarded to the PR department, and any media queries should be referred to public relations. However, although the policy can prohibit any nondesignated employee from serving as a spokesperson for the health care organization and releasing health care information, it cannot prohibit employees from talking with the media about their personal opinions.

Among the other areas that may need to be covered, depending on the health care organization's preferences, are designating a spokesperson for medical staff affairs (in some hospitals it's the chief of staff) and clarifying the role of the PR department in coordinating requests for interviews with medical staff members. These procedures will vary from institution to institution—in some institutions, public relations coordinates all such requests, whereas in other institutions, the physicians who are not employees of the health care organization prefer to be contacted directly by the press and serve as independent medical sources rather than as representatives of the health care organization. This is an area that needs to be negotiated with the medical staff leadership.

III. Policies on Release of Information

The section of the media relations policy dealing with the release of information should include a philosophical and legal statement about the patients' and families' right to privacy during a very stressful time in their lives. This approach is different from stating the *health care organization's* concerns — it asks reporters to consider the personal rights, sensitivities, and concerns of the *patient* and family. It should also reference legal restrictions and any other principles which shall be used to determine what patient and hospital information shall be released.

For example, the Toledo Hospital's media policy states:[3]

Spokespersons will use the following guidelines when releasing information:
1. The laws of the State of Ohio governing release of confidential information and the rights of individuals;
2. Respect toward the patient's health, well-being, and privacy;
3. The ethics of the medical profession;
4. The concept that factual information about the hospital and its departments, corporate entities, and subsidiaries may be released to the public unless there is reason to withhold it.

The laws about what kind of patient information can — or must — be released vary from state to state. Patients are generally divided into two categories — private and "public record" patients, the latter being those who have been involved in situations that are by law reportable to public authorities such as the police, coroner, or public health officer. In some states, and according to the policies of some health care organizations, no information can be released about private patients without their express written consent (stated consent). In other states and health care organizations, certain basic information will routinely be released unless the patient specifically instructs that it be kept confidential (implied consent). If laws or regulations don't mandate a method, the health care organization's legal counsel should determine whether stated consent or implied consent should be the policy.

Additionally, some states require hospitals to release basic information on public record cases, whereas other states make no separate provision and require that all patients be treated in the same way (which means that the hospital must get permission to release any information). It is *critically important* that the PR manager regularly consult with legal counsel for updates on state laws and any new developments in interpretation reflected in court decisions and not automatically use a national guideline or assume that information about public record cases can be released without consent.

The section of the media relations policy dealing with the release of information should also include a description of what kind of information will be released about patients. The American Society for Health Care Marketing and Public Relations' "General Guide for the Release of Patient Information by the Hospital" (reproduced as appendix B) is a useful set of guidelines for this section, as it includes:

- *What biographical information can be released about the patient.* The guide recommends name, address, occupation, gender, age, and marital status, although some states and hospitals limit this to name, address, and age, and some states require patient permission to release even this information.
- *Definitions of the standard descriptions of the condition of a patient — good, fair, serious, and critical.* Note that descriptions such as "guarded" or "stable" are not recommended. It's also important to make sure that nurses and other staff members know the definitions of each term so that when they say "serious," the PR manager knows what it means.
- *Guidelines on the release of information about accidents or injuries* (which vary depending on the nature and cause of the injury). The policy should definitely note those instances in which the health care organization will not provide any information or by law cannot provide information, which can include cases of psychiatric or substance abuse patients, sexual assault victims, or patients with sexually transmitted or communicable diseases.

The release-of-information section of the media relations policy should also note that the health care organization is not responsible for releasing information about accidents, assaults, crimes, and so on — the police or involved law enforcement or emergency personnel should be contacted for information about the circumstances that resulted in the patient's injury. Additionally, the policy should note that information on coroner's cases should be released by the coroner. Finally, it should explain the guidelines on release of information about transplant recipients and organ donors (prior consent of patient or next of kin required).

The best guideline about release of patient information is "if in doubt, don't." It's easier to cope with a reporter who's irate than a patient who's suing.

IV. Requests for Interviews, Photos, or Filming

Because of the media and public interest in what goes on in health care organizations, the PR manager must be prepared to handle requests for interviews, photos, and filming, involving not only the organization's staff members and physicians, but also patients and their families.

A. Patient Interviews, Photos, or Filming

It is preferable that the PR staff members field all requests for interviews with patients (including shooting photos, video, or film) for two reasons: (1) it protects the privacy of the patient, and (2) it ensures that the PR department knows when media are going to be in the health care institution. However, reporters often try to contact the patient or family directly by calling the patient's room or the family's home. Many people do not know that they have the right to refuse to talk with the media and end up giving telephone interviews (or even consenting to in-person interviews, with photos or filming) because they think they have to (or a reporter implies that a patient who was in an accident is a public figure and has to consent).

To prevent this kind of situation, PR staff members in health care organizations that tend to handle a lot of public interest cases should be proactive—approaching and counseling the patient and/or family as soon as possible, advising them of their rights, and helping them understand the alternatives. (One hospital even provides wallet-sized cards that nurses in the emergency department and intensive care unit can immediately give to families when they arrive at the hospital if they can't immediately meet with the PR staff.) Some patients prefer to have all media calls referred to the PR department, which can shield them or screen requests and help the family decide if they want to do the interview. Others do not want any media contact and authorize the PR department to refuse all calls. They need to be educated on how to handle media calls if they receive any (yes, it's OK to hang up if needed). Still other patients and families are willing (some are even eager) to do interviews and may want to work directly with the media. In this case, the PR manager cannot deny them that opportunity but can advise them of the risks and pitfalls and can insist that the PR department be notified whenever a reporter is going to be interviewing the patient in the health care facility.

Whatever the situation, if the patient *does* consent to an interview, photos, or filming, a consent form must be signed and kept on file in the PR department as well as in the patient's medical record. Any refusal of media contact should also be brought to the attention of appropriate personnel, including the nursing supervisor on the patient's unit and, if warranted, the organization's legal counsel.

B. Interviews, Photos, or Filming with the Health Care Staff
The section of the media relations policy dealing with interviews, photos, or filming should indicate, again, that all requests for information — including interviews, photos, or video — must be made to the PR department. If a patient will be involved, even if peripherally (in photo of a new piece of equipment, for instance), it should be noted that the patient and patient's physician must give permission.

Additionally, the section should note that patient care takes precedence over any media activities, so that scheduled interviews and photo or video shoots may have to be canceled or unexpectedly interrupted with no notice if patient care is involved (for example, the physician has to perform an emergency procedure, the patient's condition worsens, the equipment or facility is needed for treatment, and so on). The media need to understand that media requests are worked in around patient care activity, and are not allowed to disrupt that activity.

Finally, the section should note in the strongest terms that any news media reporters, photographers, videographers, and so on will be escorted by a PR staff member or designee at all times when in the health care facility, and that any media representative who violates or attempts to violate this policy will be subject to being escorted immediately from the property and possibly denied admission in the future. It is essential that this policy be clearly stated, emphasized, and strictly enforced.

Veteran health care PR managers can cite example after example of reporters getting to the patient's bedside — even in intensive care units — and upsetting the patient, risking the patient's health, and also putting the health care institution at risk for a lawsuit. In one urban hospital, a reporter walked into a private conference room when an emergency department physician was briefing a family about the condition of their father, who had been injured in a car accident. The physician assumed that the reporter was a family member; the family members, who were in shock, thought the reporter was a hospital employee. The result was a painfully detailed description of the man's injuries and of his family's grief — an intrusion on their privacy for which the family held the hospital responsible.

Once this policy is established, the health care organization must take all possible steps to enforce it. Information desk and security personnel need to be particularly vigilant, and all employees need to know that if reporters, photographers, or videographers show up in their department unescorted, they should detain them (and notify security if necessary) and call public relations. It is legally and ethically incumbent on the health care organization to protect patients' privacy.

V. The VIP Patient

Although case law in invasion of privacy cases tends to support the concept that VIPs, by becoming public figures, give up some of their rights to privacy, most state laws concerning release of patient information do not differentiate between the "common citizen" and the VIP. Thus, the health care organization should follow the same policy in regard to VIPs (government officials, entertainment and sports figures, and so on) that is used for other private patients. However, even in states where basic information can be released on all patients unless they specifically refuse, it is a sound idea to ask for a release from the VIP patient. The policy should also note that it is the responsibility of the admitting or emergency departments to immediately notify the PR department when a VIP is admitted, so that the staff can meet with the patient and/or family to discuss handling media inquiries.

Building Relationships with the Media

Successfully handling media inquiries and placing stories depend in large part on the relationships that the PR manager and/or media relations manager establish with primary media sources. These sources should include local health/medical reporters; newspaper city, feature, editorial page, and assignment editors; TV and radio news directors and assignment editors; as well as similar personnel in regional and national media outlets (depending on the size and scope of the health care organization).

At the very least, the PR manager should meet these individuals personally (on visits to the papers or stations, or by inviting them to lunch individually or as a group from each outlet). Use these meetings to get specifics on what the paper or station is looking for—ask them to tell you in as much detail as possible what kind of stories they prefer. This can vary from station to station, paper to paper—some are big on features, others want a hometown angle on a national story, and so on. And monitor this periodically—emphases can change. Preferably, the PR manager stays in touch with these individuals on a routine basis either by working on a story together or just calling to "touch base."

The primary relationships the PR/media relations manager has are with the health and medical or general-assignment reporters who routinely cover the health care organization. To build these relationships, the PR manager should:

- *Be accessible—routinely, consistently, with a designated second-in-command or contact person if the PR manager isn't available. "I'll* even put the CEO on hold when one of our reporters calls," said a PR director.

- *Be honest—every time, all the time.* It's better to simply say "I can't tell you that now" or "I don't know" than to risk lying to or covering up with the reporter you have to continue to work with. It truly takes only one incident of a reporter feeling that he or she has been "burned" by a PR person to destroy any hope of developing a productive relationship.

- *Be helpful—even if it doesn't result in a story.* If you don't have a physician who can do an interview on cystic fibrosis, tell the reporter what health care organization does or might. Give the reporter tips about health stories—and about any other kind of stories. Reporters earn points with their editors by suggesting ideas for other beats, too. Be available to do a lot of backgrounding—explaining how national events will affect local hospitals, and so on—that doesn't result in a story, but does help the reporter.

- *Understand the reporter's needs, frustrations, and restrictions.* The study cited earlier in this chapter provides some insight into the state of mind of reporters today, and talking informally with the reporter can elicit other clues as to the kind of situation the reporter is facing. A PR director once asked a reporter, "Why are you screaming at me—you know I can't give you this patient information until the child's family has been notified," and the reporter replied, "I know that—but my editor just screamed at me to get the kid's name or get fired." Reporters' approaches, insistence, urgency, and even some of the questions they ask may be determined by their editor or news director—and their final stories can be severely altered by an editor long after the reporter has gone home.

- *Deliver a strong pitch for a story—but don't whine, threaten, or beg.* Telling a reporter "My job is on the line if you don't do this story" puts the reporter in an uncomfortable position and doesn't build a strong image for the PR manager.

- *If there's a problem, go to the reporter first.* Reporters say that going over their heads is the most common "sin" of PR people. "When they want stories, they're all over me—but if there's a problem, they call my editor. It doesn't make me want to work with them in the future."

- *Understand what "off the record" means—and the risk you take when using it.* There are reporters who will go off the record; whether they can be trusted is a test of time. If you aren't absolutely sure the reporter can be trusted, don't risk it. And remember that there's no such thing as retroactive off the record. Once it's said, if not prequalified, it's news.

- *Don't try to buy, bribe, or coerce reporters.* It makes them feel sleazy, and you look sleazy. Many papers even have rules prohibiting reporters from letting sources pay for their lunches—respect the limits the reporter works under. *Do not* give reporters gifts of any kind.

- *Be careful with "exclusives."* If a reporter comes up with the story idea, don't share it with other reporters. If others get wind of it and call, you can't deny them, but then you can warn the original reporter to give him or her the edge. And when pitching a story, don't use an exclusivity promise to make the story seem more exciting—the story either works for the reporter and the editor or it doesn't, and offering exclusives irritates the other reporters you have to work with every day.
- *Give the reporter as much information as you can* on why you have to say no—to a question, interview, and so on. Let the reporter see the constraints under which you work.
- *Say thanks if it's warranted.* Don't gush or give the impression of being patronizing or manipulative—just let the reporter know if you thought a story was well done. They rarely get compliments from sources or their own editors. If the reporter did an unusually good job—explaining a highly technical subject, coping with difficult sources or interview conditions, and so on, let the reporter's superiors know about it—but don't do this routinely, or it will seem insincere.
- *Respect the reporter's professionalism, and expect yours to be respected in return.* Let the reporter know that you are in control of the process—because that's your job—but go out of your way to let the reporter know that you want to be helpful.

Handling Media Inquiries and Interviews

"Channel 5 is on the phone." The PR manager knows that the reporter will probably need one of two things—an answer to a question or an interview (possibly with photos or videos). The following pages provide some guidelines in responding to each of these types of request.

Inquiries and Requests for Information

If a reporter requests information, the PR manager needs to know:

- Are you on deadline? If yes, when's the latest we can get you the information?
- Tell me all the questions you have so I can get them all answered at once.
- What's the subject and context of the story (where do these questions fit in)?
- Can you take the answers from me, can you accept information from a source via me, or do you need to talk to a source directly? And if I can't get a source by your deadline, what's your alternative?

The PR manager is then obligated to respond to the reporter, by the deadline indicated, from the source requested (if possible) — even if the answers are not available by deadline. That may mean having to say "I can't get the information yet" or explaining why the health care organization cannot provide an answer or a comment.

Note: In nearly all cases, an unadorned "no comment" is a bad answer. It sends a message of arrogance or unconcern to the public that reads it — or implies that the health care organization has something to hide. If there are legal, patient confidentiality, or ethical reasons that the health care organization cannot provide answers, then the PR manager should explain this. Commenting on the specifics of a lawsuit is generally inadvisable, according to lawyers — although the PR manager could provide an answer like, "The hospital is firmly convinced that the care provided to the patient was in accord with accepted standards of medical practice, but we cannot comment on the specifics of the lawsuit." Refusal to violate patient confidentiality can be directly stated, and comments about competitors' actions can be answered: "The hospital believes that hospital X is acting in its best interests, which is its responsibility. We would not presume to comment on its actions."

Media Interviews

The key facts the PR manager needs to know when organizing a media interview are: *who* does the reporter prefer to interview, *when* (get a range of times and days), *where* (generally on your turf), and *what* (details on the reason for the story, the approach or slant, what kinds of subjects the reporter wants to cover, who else is being interviewed, and when the story is slated for publication/airing, and so on). The PR manager needs as much information as possible to share with the source.

Almost without exception, reporters don't like to interview PR people as primary sources. They may be willing to do a background interview with the PR manager, but they want sources — the CEO, a physician, the infection control manager, and so on — to quote in the story.

To set up the interview, the PR manager needs to:

1. Select a source. The source must meet two criteria — he or she should be extremely knowledgeable on the subject and should also be comfortable being interviewed. If it's a TV or radio interview, the source should also be very articulate with a good voice, able to synthesize ideas into brief "bites" of information, and, for television, must present an appropriate appearance.

   At health care organizations that routinely receive a lot of requests for interviews, it is recommended that the most commonly used sources—including the CEO, physicians who specialize in "hot" topics, and often-quoted staff members (infection control, finance, and other specialists)—go through a formal media training program. This training can be conducted by in-house PR staff members, if they have the experience or skills, or by outside consultants. There are agencies, media training firms, and consultants who provide this service.

2. Make sure the source is prepared. Let him or her know all the information you found out from the reporter. Identify the key points that should be made during the interview. Develop a list of all the possible questions that the PR staff thinks the source might be asked. Help him or her practice answering them, making sure that the key points are worked into the answers and that medical or administrative jargon is avoided. If the interview is for television or radio, help the source get the answers down to short, pithy comments—and for television, consult with the source on wardrobe. If the source wants to rehearse a radio or TV interview, set this up using in-house staff members. Arrange some signals that you might use during the interview to alert the source about how he or she is handling a sensitive topic, so that on seeing the signal, he or she draws the PR manager into the conversation to clarify.

   There are a number of books that provide more-specific details on handling interviews (see references), but some of the key points to share with sources include:

   • Don't answer hypothetical questions. If the question is edited out of the interview, you're quoted saying, for example, "If the legislature cuts Medicaid funds by 40 percent, we'd probably have to refuse to admit patients" as if it's a given.

   • Don't speak for someone else when asked "Why is hospital X doing this?"

   • Don't answer only yes or no for a TV or radio interview. If the interviewer asks a question that calls for a yes/no answer, give that answer and go right on to make one of the key points. ("Yes, that's an important issue, Kevin, and equally as important is the hospital's concern for . . .").

   • Don't accept unfamiliar facts or statistics, or assumptions with which you don't agree. Don't even repeat them—you could end up on television with just those words used.

   • Don't argue or get angry with the reporter, especially on camera. The viewers don't see the reporter's sneer—they do see your anger.

   • Unless it's a live TV or radio interview—when you have to keep going no matter what—you can always ask for a pause to think and regroup. If you're being filmed or taped, and you trust the reporter, ask for a pause. If you fear that the reporter might use the film of you saying "Could I have a break, please," just have a coughing fit and ask for a drink of water.

3. Set a time and place for the interview. Pick a place that will make the source feel comfortable. Make sure the reporter knows that the PR or media relations manager will be present.
4. During the interview, take notes about what is said (questions and answers) or, if you feel it's necessary and you ask the reporter in advance, tape the interview. If you believe the source is incorrect, off-base, or introducing a sensitive subject that the reporter didn't even ask about, intervene—with a clarification or a personal observation, to give the source time to regroup.
5. After the interview, thank the reporter and the source. Most sources find interviews to be from somewhat to very stressful and they need reinforcement and encouragement to do it again in the future.
6. Once the story is printed or aired, if there is a problem with it, talk about it with the source and determine whether or not to request a clarification (see the last section of this chapter).

Setting up successful media interviews is an art and a science, requiring careful attention from the PR manager.

Handling the Negative Story

Media relations policies and procedures work fairly smoothly when the requests for interviews or information are about positive topics. And when there's an actual crisis, the crisis management plan goes into effect (see chapter 11). When the story isn't a crisis, but has negative overtones—layoffs, financial problems, closing a service, and so on—there is often a tendency for media relations philosophies of open and honest communication to be questioned by CEOs and other administrators.

However, that's just the time when those principles must be adhered to, because the more the health care organization appears to be stonewalling, the greater the damage to its public image. The negative event has occurred; it can't be denied. Internal sources will eventually confirm it to the media, even if only anonymously. Once the media call about a negative story, it's because they already have the story. If the health care organization's executives deny it or attempt to downplay it, they risk being publicly identified as liars. If they say "no comment," they appear to be either arrogant or insensitive and the public assumes that they have even worse things to hide. And a "no comment" response denies the health care organization the opportunity to have its side of the story presented.

The guidelines for dealing with a negative story include:

- Consult with legal counsel, the CEO, and appropriate administrative staff members — but don't get bogged down in arguments about whether or not to respond. Be clear and firm — we're not discussing whether to respond; we're discussing how to best frame our message.
- Respond promptly and fully — it's better to have only one long, negative story than a series of follow-ups as the reporters learn more and more details. Remember Watergate. And the sooner the story appears, the sooner the incident is over and forgotten. (The public has other new, exciting stories to think about.)
- Cooperate with the reporter. Getting angry or defensive only puts the reporter on the attack; being cooperative and professional, and explaining the health care organization's position, gains credibility for the PR manager with the media. Total candor has also occasionally resulted in a story being treated in a more routine fashion than the "investigative exposé" that would have resulted if the PR manager had evaded, avoided, and tried to deny the story or withhold details. The PR manager's style (which is, of course, determined by the constraints imposed by the CEO) can actually contribute to the way the reporters perceive the importance of the story.
- Frame the health care organization's message in terms of the public's interests. One hospital PR vice-president, when handling questions about top management layoffs (including the elimination of her own position), made a compelling case that the management layoffs would allow the hospital to hire more nurses and respiratory therapists, thus benefiting patient care.
- Make sure that while the PR manager is serving as spokesperson and handling the media, other PR staff members are communicating to key internal audiences — employees, physicians, board members. They will be asked about the story by their friends and colleagues and can either add credibility to the health care organization's message or undercut its credibility.

Pitching Stories

The health care organization should routinely be looking for story ideas to share with the media, along with seeking media coverage for major events and activities. "Pitching" a story involves the same kind of marketing approach described in chapter 13. The product — the story idea — has to be newsworthy. It can be about something new, different, bigger (avoid better — the media hate coping with that kind of value judgment) or it can be a happy or sad feature story, for example. For television, the story has to have some kind of visuals — BOPSAs (bunch of people sitting around) are a news director's nightmare.

The approach used to pitch the story must also be appropriate. Reporters, editors, and news directors almost universally agree — put it in written form, either as a formal release, a query, or a "story idea" format. Many health care organizations have preprinted news release mastheads and story idea sheets for use when requesting that a reporter be assigned to the story (versus having the release rewritten for a newspaper). These request-for-coverage releases should be brief, include the five *W*s (who, what, when, where, why), have a strong lead and descriptive headline, include a contact name and phone number, and be double-spaced and stapled.

Unless the story is late breaking — an unplanned event that's happening on the spot (a surprise birthday bike for a little boy who's been in the hospital for 18 weeks after a notorious car accident, an unusual surgery or procedure, and so on) — do not try to pitch the story by calling the media that day. The average editor receives several hundred bits of information every day — your call can get lost in the shuffle, or can simply irritate the editor, who has to write down all the information himself or herself. However, if you believe that a story is really a good one, it's OK to make a follow-up call to editors to see if it's been assigned, or what needs to be done with it to make it more attractive.

Pitching stories with "go sees" (visiting the news editor in person) or gimmicks are inappropriate for health care. But sending a media kit of background information on the topic, with pictures, satisfied patient stories and statistics, and so on, is an effective technique.

Pitching stories to national media is a very specialized process that not every health care PR manager is experienced in; most rely on pickups by the wire services to bring their stories to the attention of national press. If the health care organization believes that it will consistently have stories that are of interest to national media (groundbreaking research, trendsetting transplantation, and so on), the media relations manager needs to become familiar with the national media health/medical reporters and the bureau chiefs in the health care organization's region (sending a specialized media kit with a letter, followed up by an introductory phone call or visit). Unless a story is truly of national magnitude (the Jarvik 7 heart, for instance) and is going to be covered by all media, the better method for a national placement is to target the story to a specific program or reporter's particular interest (the network's morning news shows, for instance, have reporters who specialize in people triumphing over adversity, quirky/funny stories, and so on) and pitch it carefully, consistently, and exclusively to that reporter or managing editor.

If the health care organization only occasionally has a story that might have some national appeal, it's probably more cost-effective to hire a PR firm with experience in and contacts already established with the national media. Additionally, health care organizations need to consider what the real value of a national story is in terms of their primary service area. If the health care organization is one of the few that attract patients from across the country or a broad region, then national stories are helpful. Otherwise, the primary value is egocentric—"Look, we made the national news"— with some residual image boosting with the local audience (although only a fraction of the local audience will even see the story).

Press Conferences and Media Events

Many PR textbooks spend several pages describing how to do a press conference. The truth is that, for most companies, including hospitals, there's rarely any reason to do a press conference because of two things. First, calling a press conference implies a solid news story to reporters. Unless it's something big—a major expansion initiative, the closing of a service (you might as well initiate the press contact, because they'll hear about it anyway), the purchase of a piece of equipment unique to the area—the reporters will just be irritated at having to attend. Or worse, they'll think the PR staff members are foolish—not the way to develop an equitable relationship. Second, there are other methods that work as well or better, particularly individual media interviews that are less stressful to the participants (media and health care organization sources), appear to be less staged, and allow each media outlet to have its "own" type of story.

Press tours to show off facilities, to see demonstrations of new techniques or technologies, or to update regional media can be very effective. These tours, or media days, generally last for a few hours, with several things going on (CEO briefing, tour of several new facilities, demonstrations by physicians of new techniques like laser surgery, briefing by specialists on the hot new treatments in their specialty, and so on, plus breakfast or lunch). These events provide regional reporters, often from weekly papers, with material for an immediate story, and ideas and sources for follow-up and related stories—"I came away with enough material for a whole series," said one participant. They also allow the PR staff members and the reporters to get acquainted or reacquainted.

If a press conference is deemed essential—because of time constraints or because the CEO insists—it should be held at a time and location that are preferred by the media. The "star" should be prepared to make a statement and to answer questions. It's not a conference if the spokesperson reads the statement and refuses to answer questions. The spokesperson should be someone who meets the expert and articulate criteria for interviews, plus someone who can handle a larger audience and can stay calm with questions being shouted.

There are a number of tried-and-true press conference rules. These include using schoolroom-style tables and chairs, having visuals and handouts available, sending kits and/or tapes to reporters who did not attend, having the conference somewhere easy for media to get to, and limiting the conference to 30 minutes.

Fighting Battles

Although most PR managers report fairly positive relationships with the media with whom they deal, there will always be problems that need to be addressed. For example:

1. *The setup.* The reporter asks for an interview about family therapy in chemical dependency treatment and concentrates all of his or her questions on why the health care organization substance abuse unit doesn't provide free care to anyone who needs it. The PR manager later discovers that the whole focus of the story is and always was why health care organizations are shirking their responsibility to care for the poor.
2. *The violation of media policy and/or patient privacy rights.* The reporter bullies a patient's wife into granting an interview when she initially said no.
3. *The downright rude reporter who offends a source during an interview.*
4. *Placement and treatment of a negative story in such a way as to make it seem like a "big" story.*
5. *Inaccuracies.*

Rude reporters can be difficult to deal with, but rarely will a complaint make a difference other than to irritate the reporter. "You take what you get" is the basic philosophy most PR managers espouse. However, if there are consistent problems with the reporter (repeatedly contacting and harassing the health care organization's staff members directly and/or at their homes, rudeness to patients or guests, and so on), the PR manager should consult with colleagues at other health care organizations to see if this behavior is consistent. If so, the PR managers of these organizations may want to talk to the editor or news director as a group—but with the awareness that some papers and stations encourage their reporters to be "aggressive" and that complaints from sources are, in fact, an indication that the reporter is doing his or her job. Additionally, if the reporter finds out about the complaints, he or she may simply become more difficult to deal with. The PR manager has to assess how serious the reporter's behavior really is—if it's simply irritating (even very irritating), it's probably best to tolerate it.

On the other hand, the repeated violation of media policy (sneaking into the health care facility to pressure a patient for an interview, for instance) or repeated setups (misrepresenting the focus of the story to ambush a source during an interview) should be discussed first with the reporter, and then, if needed, with an editor or news director. The health care organization has few alternatives—the reporter can be banned from the property, but that can create a sense of war that is counterproductive. Appealing to reason, patient privacy, and the need to maintain good working relationships is the best approach to take with the editor or news director.

The inaccurate or slanted story or treatment (a story about layoffs of 10 employees is headlined "Hospital slashes work force; employees devastated and patient safety threatened," and placed on page one) presents a situation that has to be handled very cautiously. The first response of the CEO, physicians, and employees may be: "Demand a retraction! Write a letter to the editor! Sue!" However, the following questions should be considered before a course of action is chosen:

1. Where and when was the story printed or aired? Front page Sunday paper? Eleven p.m. Friday news? How many people might have seen it?
2. Is it really bad, or are we overreacting? Taking the time to ask a few outside sources to review the story (a video clipping service can generally deliver a postairing tape within 10 to 24 hours) provides an objective perspective that even the PR manager can't match. One PR manager asked several corporate PR people to assist; another said she finds that her neighbors are good "common man" barometers: "When I say, 'What did you think of that story on Channel 1 about the hospital's layoffs,' and they say, 'What story,' then I have at least an indication about whether or not we're overreacting."

   If there is serious concern about an extremely damaging story, in many cities the PR manager can hire a research firm to do some quick surveying to measure awareness of the story and consumer reaction to it.
3. How long will the public recall this story? The old thesis used to be that a newspaper story was worse than a TV story because people could reread the newspaper story. But today, fewer people read newspapers and television can create powerful images that people don't easily forget.
4. Will the correction story solve the problem—or make it worse? If the inaccuracy is something simple and factual—the story said the hospital did 1,500 births in a year and the number is actually 5,000—that's a fairly simple correction. If the inaccuracy was contained in an otherwise positive story, the PR manager needs to ask

if it is really necessary that it be corrected—if yes, ask for the correction.

If, on the other hand, the problem is with an inaccuracy in a story about a negative issue (layoffs, a malpractice suit, patient safety, and so on), then the key question is: will asking for, and getting, a printed or broadcast correction, or submitting a letter to the editor, only prolong the publicity or make it worse? Most PR managers believe that the best thing to do with a negative issue is to get it over and done with as soon as possible. Getting some type of clarification often only serves to get the story back in the paper or on the air, usually just as people are starting to forget about it or when it's losing its sense of urgency. Additionally, asking for a correction allows the reporter to rehash the entire issue, so it appears to the public, because of the repeated coverage, to be an even more serious problem. Finally, even if you get a correction, is there any way of knowing that it will be read or seen by the same people who saw the original story—or will the message also be sent to people who missed the original story so that you've now increased the number of people who are aware of the negative story?

If a correction or clarification is deemed to be necessary, there are several methods that can be used:

- With newspapers, you can request an item in the "corrections" column. These are generally restricted to correcting factual inaccuracies— wrong numbers, names of individuals, and so on. A letter to the editor can be prepared—but this letter may not be read by many of the people who read the original story, and may make it an issue of interest for people who missed the original story but will ask friends, "What's this all about." If a letter is written, it should be absolutely factual and unemotional—no accusations or criticism about the paper or the reporter. And limit the letter to the length the newspaper requests—it's better for you to edit your statement than to leave it to the editorial page editor.
- The health care organization has the option—although it's rarely done—to buy advertising space to state its case. One hospital used this method after a story about a cancer treatment being performed at the hospital included quotes from a local physician stating that the hospital wasn't qualified to be doing the process, and so on. The newspaper had no reason to correct or clarify the story because the physician was quoted accurately and comments from the hospital had been included in the story. And although the hospital had not been told of the physician's comments and given a chance to respond directly to them, the paper refused to do a follow-up story. The hospital, feeling

that its standards of quality and its ethical standards had been questioned, decided not to wait the standard three to four weeks for a letter to the editor to be printed, and elected to pay for ad space in order to get the reply in the paper quickly and without the space limitations of a letter.

- With a TV broadcast, if the PR manager hears an inaccuracy while the story is being broadcast, a quick call to the station can result in an on-air correction during that news program. Once the program is over, few stations will run a correction in a later broadcast unless the error would subject them to a potential lawsuit. Another alternative is to request a follow-up story, revisiting the issue from another angle, during which the health care organization's points can be made. Again, if it's a very negative story, this will merely cause it to become an issue again.

With rare exceptions, PR managers have found that the best general policy is to let negative stories die as quickly as possible. The public's attention is being drawn in a number of different ways every moment, and although a negative story may cause an immediate uproar, that uproar generally dies down fairly quickly as the public focuses on the newest hot stories and issues. The exceptions, of course, are those truly horrendous situations like a baby kidnapping or an orderly murdering patients, which are covered in chapter 11 on crisis communications.

☐ Evaluating the Media Relations Program

Good print and video clipping services can help provide the most basic measure of a media relations program — counting how many papers and stations used a story. The newspaper and/or magazine clipping service is a good investment for the health care organization that has a specialized media relations program and has stories picked up by newspapers outside the local community. Although it sounds cost-effective to say, "Let's just subscribe to the papers and do the clipping ourselves," that can actually mean subscribing to dozens of papers — and *reading* them. (Or usually, letting them pile up in a corner.)

Video clipping services are helpful for health care organizations that routinely get TV coverage. Generally, the services charge a participation fee to have specific stations routinely monitored, and then a flat fee for each story that's requested. Yes, the PR staff members can try to tape stories themselves, with the risk of missing the story ("My VCR wouldn't record; I didn't get home from work in time"). Additionally, the PR staff members may not always know in advance when a story they may later want to review is going to air — national stories, trend stories, stories about competitors. Paying the monitoring fee means that stories can be requested after the fact, because the service tapes entire newscasts.

By counting clips and monitoring video, combined with staff-kept records about radio stories, the PR manager can come up with a batting average — number of placements times potential audience. As noted in chapter 18 on evaluation, this is only the grossest measure of a media relations program, because it measures only the behavior of the media — the editors and news directors who chose to use the story. It's an effective way to measure how well the program is functioning — which should be a major concern of the PR manager — but does not measure the changes in consumer awareness, preference, and behavior that contribute to bottom-line objectives.

Specific tracking research can be commissioned before and after a major media blitz to check changes in consumer awareness and preference. The research attempts to detect changes in awareness and preference among those persons who saw the media coverage compared with those who did not.

Finally, when general consumer research is conducted, questions about where the consumers get their information about health care should be included to measure the impact of news coverage and identify the consumer's media usage habits. A media relations program should not be judged solely on its own merits but rather in relation to its contribution to the health care organization's broad communications program, which is aimed at increasing audience awareness of specific information about the organization, enhancing the organization's positive image, and increasing consumer top-of-mind preference for the organization and specific services.

☐ Summary

Media relations has always been a primary function of the health care PR program. In the coming decades, the emphasis will shift away from general, news release-oriented media efforts to more focused, specialized placements in targeted publications and outlets. As the mass media decline in importance and utilization by consumers, PR managers will look for smaller, more specialized media to reach key audiences.

Equally important will be the PR manager's ability to handle media scrutiny that may be increasingly skeptical or even hostile. Health care is one of today's major stories, and as the public's preoccupation with health and medical stories continues, so will media attention. The successful PR manager will concentrate on developing effective working relationships with local media that can have an impact on the health care organization's future in the community, rather than looking for more glamorous "national media placements."

References

1. Fones, C. No comment: an ethical decision. *Health Progress* 68(6):23, July–Aug. 1987.
2. New study comparing job satisfaction, other differences between practitioners and journalists will help understand media personnel, manage public relations staff. *pr reporter* 32(3):1, Jan. 16, 1989.
3. The Toledo Hospital, Toledo, Ohio. Media policy. Used with the permission of J. S. Summerville, vice-president, corporate communications.

Suggested Readings

Altschull, J. H. *Agents of Power: The Role of the News Media in Public Affairs.* New York City: Longman, 1984.

Aronoff, C. Credibility of public relations for journalists. *Public Relations Review,* Fall 1975.

Howard, C. M. How to say "no" without alienating reporters. *Public Relations Quarterly,* Winter 1986–1987.

Newsom, D., and Scott, A. *This Is PR: The Realities of Public Relations.* Belmont, CA: Wadsworth, 1985.

Stocking, H. S. Effect of public relations efforts on media visibility of organization. *Journalism Quarterly,* Summer 1985.

Crisis Communications

Health care organizations, when compared with other types of businesses and organizations, are more likely to be involved in crisis situations, particularly of the following three types:

- Situations of caring for the victims of natural or man-made disasters, from tornadoes to multiple-vehicle crashes
- A crisis that directly involves the health care organization—a baby kidnapped from the nursery, an orderly murdering patients, a visitor attacked in the parking garage, the crash of a medical helicopter, a surgeon becoming infected with AIDS
- A major controversy, often involving special-interest activist groups from right-to-lifers to animal rights activists

Each of these three categories of crisis is discussed in separate sections of this chapter. All crises can be difficult to handle—but they can be handled and weathered. And when a crisis occurs, the PR manager is expected to be able not only to handle the crisis but also to protect the health care organization's image and reputation. Careful advance planning can play an important role in achieving those objectives.

☐ Action Planning for Crises from External Causes

When the crisis is external—for example, an airplane crash, a major fire, a gas leak at an elementary school—the health care facilities that receive the victims of the disaster become the center of attention for the media. Handling this responsibility efficiently and effectively can enhance the health care organization's relationships with reporters and editors. If there are problems, not only do media relationships suffer, but the health care organization's image, as projected by the media, can also suffer.

Before a tornado strikes or a school bus crashes, the PR manager should develop a step-by-step plan of how the media and the release of information will be handled. This plan should be part of the health care organization's disaster plan, and all members of the PR staff and administrative and management staff should be familiar with the PR guidelines.

Creating a Disaster Communications Plan

The following items should be included in the health care organization's disaster communications plan:

- *How public relations will be notified about the external disaster.* Preferably public relations will be one of the first departments to be notified, once the CEO and patient care areas have been alerted. Most health care organizations use a multicall or chain calling method of notification (as well as using the health care facility's paging system to sound the general alert), so it is feasible for PR to be notified at the same time as the patient care departments.
- *What PR staff members will do what — and where they will be stationed.* There are three primary functions that must be fulfilled by PR staff members or PR designees: gathering information to be released to the media, answering media phone calls, and working with the on-site media. If the health care organization has a one-person PR department, that PR person must handle the spokesperson role, both with reporters who are on-site and those who call on the phone. The information-gathering role can be performed by a designee — often a senior staff manager who is not needed for patient care and can be trusted to secure and relay accurate information.

  The best place to gather information is in the emergency department, where the PR person or designated information gatherer can physically count the number of victims received, refer to patient charts or victim tags for identification, and get answers from the emergency department physicians and staff. The person stationed here must be able to get information without getting in the way of patient care.

  This information, as it is gathered, should be relayed to the on-site location where the media are being held and to the staff person handling media phone calls. If two staffers are splitting up the media duties (one on-site, one on phone), they may be in two different locations, but both must receive exactly the same information.

  It is not advisable to have the same person in the emergency department gathering information and also releasing it, for three reasons. First, while taking a media call, the PR person is not able to be busily gathering information. Second, if the PR manager is in the emergency department, that's where the media will want to be. Third, if there's only one PR person, he or she must be with the media, because they get very frustrated if they're confronted by a secretary or someone who has no idea how to handle them and merely acts as a "guard."

Note: It is important to set up two separate processes for releasing information to the media and to victims' families. The PR staff can't handle both responsibilities; patient reps, a nursing administrator, or a human resources administrator should handle the families. However, there's no need to duplicate functions—the PR information gatherer can serve a dual function and get information, including names of patients received, to the area where families are being held. The person coordinating the notification of families should notify the PR staff as this is accomplished, so that the victims' names can be released to the media.

- *Where on-site media should be sent and located.* An on-campus media center is essential. The place should be identified in advance and should be well away from the emergency department or areas where patients or family members will be held. The media center must have plenty of electrical outlets and a copy machine nearby, be large enough to accommodate a number of reporters and TV cameras, and have the capability to have a number of telephones hooked up. Some type of area where TV reporters can do stand-ups and interviews is also essential, as are chairs and tables. All reporters should be brought to this media center (they'll show up in the emergency department, at the main desk, and at other entrances), where a spokesperson will be available to them at all times, releasing information as soon as it becomes available. Coffee and soft drinks should be provided, along with some basic food if the reporters are going to be on-site for a long period of time. The plan should indicate the reasons why reporters are confined to the media center (patient privacy and immediate access to information).

- *What information will be released and how.* Given the need for notification of next of kin—a process that can take hours during a large-scale disaster—the initial information that the health care organization will release is the number of victims brought to the health care facility, a summary of gender and ages (if known), a brief description of their injuries (if available), and a summary of conditions (6 admitted in critical condition, 14 in serious condition, 11 in surgery, 10 treated and released). It should also note that the health care organization's personnel may be available for interviews *if* this does not interfere with patient care, and describe procedures for setting up a media pool if the demands for interviews exceeds the staff's ability to handle them.

209

- *How reporters can get answers via the phone.* It is recommended that a special, dedicated phone line be created to be used only by media in the case of a disaster (at other times, the phone is not connected). If the PR manager is going to handle on-site and phone-in media inquiries, this phone should be located in the media center. If there are other PR staff members available, the phone can be located in the PR office, the main switchboard room, and so on. There must be phone communication between this location and the media center, to ensure coordination of information release.

Once the disaster communications plan is developed, both the internal audiences (administrators as well as managers and employees in affected departments, such as security, switchboard, and main information desk) and the external audiences (media, public safety officials, and so on) should receive copies.

Putting the Plan into Action

The first step in putting the plan into action is rehearsal—mock disaster drills that the health care organization conducts, and community-wide disaster drills in which all health care organizations participate. These drills can identify any snags in the system.

When a disaster is announced, the PR staff members and their designees should immediately move from their offices (or be called in from home) to go to their assigned places. A previously prepared disaster box with pencils, pads, phone lists, a general description of the health care facility, media name tags, a copy of the hospital and communications disaster plans, gum and candy, and so on should be taken to the media center.

The designated information gatherer goes to the emergency department and begins to count the number of victims received. This is recommended because once patients start arriving and being triaged and sent off to X ray, surgery, and other departments (and their charts sent off along with them), it is usually difficult for the emergency department staff members, who are still taking care of patients, to maintain an accurate count. As information is gathered and verified, it can be released through the media center and via phone.

The PR staff members may need to talk with their colleagues at other health care organizations to get a feel for their organization's involvement and to coordinate notification of families who have victims at several health care facilities. The media center and PR disaster plan should be in operation until the media have received all the information they need and have moved on, checking back only for condition updates.

□ Action Planning for Internal Crises

Just as any health care facility may be notified to expect incoming victims from a natural disaster, so, too, may any health care organization have a crisis that occurs within the health care facility—when the organization is not just a source of information about the story but actually *is* the story. A fire or explosion, a staff member inadvertently or deliberately injuring patients, a visitor kidnapping a baby or holding patients hostage, a patient committing suicide, a visitor being murdered in the garage, a Life Flight helicopter crashing—the possibilities are endless. The only thing that's sure is that these types of situations could happen in any health care organization. Every health care organization should consider these possibilities in advance, and the PR manager should take the lead in developing guidelines for handling the organization's crises.

The philosophy of this plan must be open and honest communications, within the limitations of the law and responsibilities for patient privacy. "Within the constraints of the law and marketplace (for hospitals, that means patient privacy regulations), we should tell the whole story honestly and candidly, even if news is bad. The public's right to know is greater than whatever embarrassment we might face as a result of admitting a mistake," advised Ian Rolland, CEO of Lincoln National Corporation.[1]

A number of points should be covered in the plan, including who's in charge during a crisis, who's notified first, what the first steps are, what key media questions management must have answers to, how the media will be handled, and how other important audiences (patients, employees, physicians, and other "customers") will be handled.

Establishing the Crisis Management Team

A working team of key administrators should be designated to manage a crisis, to monitor the crisis, and to make decisions and communicate to internal and external audiences. This team must include the CEO, COO or top patient care and other administrative officer, legal counsel, and PR counsel. The CFO may be part of the team or must be available to the team. The team should be kept as small as possible to facilitate quick decision making.

That the PR manager must be part of this team seems clear—the most negative results of a crisis are often the organization's damaged reputation and image (witness Exxon)—but this message has not yet been fully accepted by CEOs. A national Golin Harris survey of CEOs revealed that most of them would consult a COO and CFO first, legal counsel second, and the "top communications officer" third.[2] This may be more reflective of corporate priorities (the CFO can help determine bottom-line impact on profits), but it also reflects an interesting view of PR managers. If the CEOs do, indeed, think of them as "communications officers," rather than as part of the decision-making team, then obviously the PR staff would be called to communicate the message after the decisions are made. Informal, anecdotal research with health care PR managers indicates that the situation is much better in health care organizations, where the PR manager is almost always part of the crisis team, at least in an advisory role to the CEO.

Planning a Course of Action

Because crises are so varied, it's impossible to list all initial actions that might have to be taken in every situation (if it involves a law being broken, contact the police; if it's a fire or explosion, decide when or whether to evacuate, and so on). However, it's wise for the team to discuss potential crisis situations in advance and talk through possible courses of action, so that when the crisis happens, the team feels some degree of familiarity with it. One ideal way of making sure this happens is to convene the crisis team whenever another health care organization—locally or nationally—has a crisis, and ponder, "What would we do if that happened here?"

When a crisis occurs, the crisis management team members need to be notified (which, of course, requires that the staff person in charge of the house on nights and weekends know when to contact the CEO) and brought together, preferably in person but via phone if needed. All departments then need to be informed of the basic details of the crisis and notified of the chain of command (for example, "President Nelson is handling the situation and all questions or information should be referred to him at extension 4156").

While operating staff members handle the details of the crisis— seeing that the fire is extinguished, that security personnel are brought into the nursery and OB unit after the kidnapping, and so on—the crisis management team must address the issues of legal, financial, and public image implications, including release of information to the media and other internal and external publics.

Communicating during Crisis

The first step in determining a communications plan may be to fight the "no comment" mentality of other crisis management team members, including CEOs and legal counsel. Jan Michelsen of Indiana

University Medical Center identified reasons for this high-level resistance in a 1988 article quoted in *Purview.*[3] Among the reasons:

- Some believe that if they withhold information today, the situation will disappear tomorrow.
- Some are paranoid about the media or have been "burned" in the past.
- Some believe that the risk of speaking up may be too great to bear personally or politically.

In addition, some health care administrators believe that "if we don't say anything, they don't have a story," which is hardly the case.

It is preferable to have addressed the need to be open and honest with the press during crisis team planning sessions before the crisis happens. If that battle needs to be fought, it should be fought then, not in the middle of the crisis. There are a number of arguments that can be advanced, but perhaps the most convincing is to simply review current cases in which negative public opinion has been as damaging to the organization as the crisis (Exxon's Alaskan oil spill, R. J. Reynolds's Uptown cigarette fiasco, and so on).

Once the "no comment" mentality has been overcome, the next step is to review the potential crises that might occur and to identify the key questions that might be asked during each of the potential crises. The PR staff can be invaluable in playing the role of reporters. Generally there will be one key question—the first thing that reporters will ask—that will need to be the focus of the crisis team during the initial moments of a crisis. For example, when considering what would happen if a medical helicopter crashed, the team could predict that the key question would be "Is the helicopter program going to continue?" The team can then role-play and come up with alternative answers.

When the crisis actually occurs, as basic operating decisions are being made, the PR manager may have a window of time before the media begin calling—but that can be a very brief period. If the crisis involves law enforcement or public safety personnel (fire, explosion, person with a gun in the emergency department, and so on), the media will be on the phone and on the scene in a matter of moments. The media plan detailed in the first section of this chapter should be put into place, with an emphasis on ensuring that the spokesperson in the media center has information and answers to questions. It's also important to take the time to identify the key audiences and stakeholders who will be most concerned about and affected by the crisis, so that messages can be developed with their concerns in mind and specific communications vehicles developed to reach them directly.

The crisis may be of a different nature—something that can be kept quiet at least initially, like an incident when patients' oxygen lines were being snipped in the hospital. The key decision that must be made in situations like this is whether to call the media *before* the story leaks out and they descend en masse. In the case of the snipped oxygen lines (no patients were injured or died), the hospital approached the media, knowing that eventually an employee or patient would notify them. The hospital gained two things from this: (1) the chance to present the facts in a calm, unhysterical atmosphere and (2) the admiration of the media for being so candid. The resulting stories were handled very tastefully by the media — as compared to the probable page-one story that would have resulted if the media had felt they were "exposing" the story.

During any kind of crisis communications, the patient's privacy must be protected, and the health care organization must also communicate quickly with its internal publics, including employees and physicians. Too often, the crisis management team's focus is on coping with the crisis and communicating with the media — and employees are left to depend on the grapevine or to watch the TV coverage. Given that crises are stressful for employees — they may be working in departments involved in the crisis or being asked questions by their family and friends — they should be a primary focus of communications. Unlike most other audiences, they are personally involved. At the very least, a cascading communications network should be activated, with information shared with administrators, who meet with managers, who then quickly meet with their employees. Written information — even if it has to be photocopied and hand-delivered — should be circulated as news and details become available. A call-in or prerecorded hot-line message system can also be helpful in quelling rumors.

If the crisis involves a death of an employee or patient, the magnitude of the situation should be recognized by having the CEO meet with groups of employees, and ongoing grief support systems should be immediately activated. The human resources, employee assistance, psychiatric, and pastoral care departments can assist in this process.

Medical staff members will also be very concerned about any crisis that occurs, and although they may be more difficult than employees to reach quickly, steps should be taken to inform as many of them as possible. Someone from the crisis team should meet with the medical staff officers, and written information can be posted in the medical staff lounge or electronic message system. One hospital that wanted to alert physicians to a highly negative story that was going to break in the paper the next day hired a delivery company at premium prices and sent a briefing letter to all medical staff members within a five-hour time period.

☐ Action Planning for Crises Arising from Controversy

The headlines in PR journals tell the story of the growth of controversies surrounding health care organizations:

- Experts predict 90s will be era of new activism, more vigorous than ever; some are adopting extreme methods to drive causes[4]
- Toxic trauma unites public opinion in push for new ethic[5]
- People with disabilities comprise burgeoning, valuable public which requires special consideration[6]
- Rising issue category: unwinnable because they're moral problems — like abortion[7]
- No longer dismissed as weirdos, animal rights groups are now threatening medical research[8]

pr reporter notes that the activism of the 1990s is not a resurgence but a continuation of social values that existed in the 1960s, 1970s, and 1980s. But today's activists are different in several ways.[9] The composition of the groups is becoming much more mainstream, and they are more likely to use:

- Terrorist methods, from spraying fur coats with paint to bombing abortion clinics
- Civil disobedience, a tactic used by groups as disparate as antinuclear activists and labor union members
- More sophisticated PR and persuasion techniques, methods as professional as those used by PR managers

Chapter 8 discussed identifying, monitoring, and attempting to build relationships with activist groups that believe they are stakeholders in the health care organization — and of course some of those are among the most vocal and active groups, including animal rights and abortion (pro and con) organizations.

There are times when all of the health care organization's efforts to work with these groups fail because the groups will be satisfied with nothing less than a total policy reversal, an action the health care organization is unwilling to take. At those times, the health care organization may become the target of what John Deats describes as "break-ins, unruly demonstrations, and acerbic press conferences."[10] Deats, director of the office of public affairs at New York University (NYU) Medical Center, successfully encountered an animal rights demonstration in 1986, and his experiences offer guidelines on how to deal with a confrontation with an activist group.

Deats noted that medical centers in the past had tried to ignore or minimize the issues, but that as the activists continued their efforts, they achieved successes with legislators. "Passivity in the face of this challenge leads to serious constraints on the conduct of biomedical research."

When the medical center learned that it was to be the target of a major animal rights demonstration, a team of "all the principles"—CEO, deans, committee chairs, scientists, and security personnel—was gathered to develop "an institutional consensus" from which to move forward. The first step was a study of the animal research facilities, with an eye to security *and* how the facilities would look "to a layman." Attention was also paid to employee morale.

Deats and staff then began focusing the medical center's positioning on the issue, choosing to create "human rights as a parallel issue to animal rights. Within the context of care and caring, we wanted to show the benefits humans had derived from animal experimentation." The best method for doing this, they concluded, was with a living example—a two-year-old girl whose life had been saved by surgical techniques perfected through animal experiments. The child and her parents were the focus of a news conference held one day before the animal rights group had planned a press conference. A wheelchair-bound patient and the husband of a woman with Parkinson's disease also participated, pleading for the continuation of scientific research, using animals when needed, to study their ailments. Finally, research scientists spoke, explaining the necessity for animal experimentation and providing facts about the humane treatment of laboratory animals. The media picked up on the story, and it was used before the animal rights story broke. "It established a pro-research agenda, instead of the usual formula of the institution responding defensively to extremist claims," noted Deats.

The demonstration took place, with NYU security personnel working with the city police. Security was not breached and nine demonstrators were cited for blocking an entrance. "The physical security aspects of the episode were managed with effectiveness and professionalism," which was important because of the presence of media. The discretion with which the demonstrators were handled "allowed the issue to remain the treatment of the laboratory animals, rather than the handling of the demonstrators." A medical center spokesperson was also at the site to refute the demonstrators' contentions. "While the activists' position was well reported in the daily press, the views and rationale of this institution were also represented," concluded Deats—and that, of course, is the best possible outcome of confrontations with activist groups. "The medical center concluded the risks of speaking out were significantly less than the problem to be faced by remaining silent, passive, and victimized."

New York University Medical Center's efforts represent excellence in strategy and execution and their model can be adapted by other health care organizations. For example:

- Planning a strategy should be a team effort involving all the key players. A philosophy and communications strategy can be formulated well in advance of any activity.
- Health care organizations that are likely to be targets of activist groups usually know it. Every health care organization should, as part of its issues management program, identify which, if any, groups might confront the organization and carefully monitor those groups.
- Activists usually announce their intentions well in advance so that they can get media coverage. This allows the health care organization plan to preempt.
- The health care organization's case must be framed in the best interests of the public—not the health care organization. Instead of "We need . . . we want," the message should be "In order to help our patients/community, and so on, we are doing. . . ."
- The health care organization's preemptive actions can actually capture and reframe the agenda.
- The health care organization loses if it appears to be harassing demonstrators or overreacting with anger or defensiveness. The more unruly the demonstrators are, the more professional and polite the health care organization's staff members should be. And don't attack the group's right to express its opinion.

The PR manager who believes that his or her health care organization may be a target for activist groups should not put off thinking about it, hope it won't happen, or assume that it can be handled at the last minute, using routine media relations techniques. Proactive planning can help an activist attack from becoming a crisis.

□ Beyond Crisis Planning

As PR "guru" Philip Lesly noted in the July–August 1989 issue of his *Managing the Human Climate* newsletter, "crises and emergencies are, by their nature, unpredictable. Few would occur if the victim could really plan for them."[11] Lesly notes that crisis planning can help executives think about what might happen and ponder alternatives, but that every crisis will be different—different circumstances, different needs, different sources, different internal conditions. "It's useful to plan for emergencies and crises, but it's dangerous to rely on those plans. As always, the most critical element is the intelligence, experience, judgment and skill of the people who will be calling the shots."

Mary Nowotny, a crisis communications specialist with Aaron D. Cushman & Associates, noted that crisis planning can even backfire by creating "dangerous overconfidence."[12] Nowotny observed that although there will be those circumstances that can be predicted in detail, there will also be occurrences that no one anticipates — ranging from unexpected ramifications to unexpected audiences to unanticipated media attention. (One relatively straightforward crisis that Nowotny was involved in was handled very well with the local media but ended up being covered by national press because a local paper reporter was a stringer for the *New York Times*.)

"The two most important lessons learned" from the crises Nowotny has managed are: "Even the most carefully laid plans must be constantly re-evaluated and refined. . . . Secondly, planning is just the beginning. Every crisis is different, and when one actually occurs, it's a mistake to assume that a plan will provide the best answers. In a crisis, the best defense is staying on your toes." It is also well to remember that PR's ability to deal with a crisis effectively means being part of the crisis management team — to advise on decisions and to develop effective communications programs to minimize the impact of the crisis.

☐ Summary

Health care PR managers generally have an edge on PR professionals in most other fields because health care organizations are more likely to anticipate and plan for some types of crises. Too often, however, the focus is on the health care organization's reaction to external crises, rather than on the development of plans to deal with a crisis that occurs *in* a health care facility.

The PR manager needs to take the lead in getting the CEO and top management team members to think about what kinds of crises could occur in which the health care organization would be the focus of attention — from the crash of an emergency medical helicopter to a baby kidnapping to the murder of patients by a nurse. And the PR manager should play a key role in developing a general plan of action for such crises and in implementing the plan if such crises occur.

References

1. CEO: corporate social responsibility is more than philanthropy. *pr reporter* 32(28):1, July 10, 1989.

2. Survey of CEOs' crisis-time behavior. *pr reporter* 32(47):3, Nov. 20, 1989.
3. Michelsen, J. At odds over openness. *Currents* 14(10):36–39, Oct. 1988.
4. The status of social movements. *pr reporter* 32(2):1, Jan. 8, 1990.
5. Toxic trauma unites public opinion. *pr reporter* 32(16):1, Apr. 17, 1989.
6. People with disabilities comprise burgeoning valuable public. *Tips and Tactics* [supplement to *pr reporter* 32(39):1, Sept. 25, 1989].
7. Rising issue category: unwinnable because they're moral problems. *pr reporter* 32(2):1, Jan. 9, 1989.
8. Barnes, F. Politics. *Vogue*, Sept. 1989, p. 542.
9. The status of social movements.
10. Deats, J. R. How to cope: a public affairs/security integrated approach to animal welfare demonstrations. *Journal of Healthcare Protection Management* 3(2):99, Feb. 1987.
11. Lesly, P. Why crisis plans are vulnerable. *Managing the Human Climate* [supplement to *pr reporter* 32(27):1, July–Aug. 1989].
12. Nowotny, M. R. Best laid plans vs. reality. *Public Relations Journal* 45(9):17, Sept. 1989.

Suggested Readings

Fink, S. *Crisis Management: Planning for the Inevitable.* New York City: AMACOM Books Division of the American Management Association, 1986.

Irvine, R. B. *When You Are the Headline: Managing a News Story.* Homewood, IL: Dow Jones-Irwin, 1987.

Meyers, G. *When It Hits the Fan.* New York City: New American Library, 1987.

Pinsdorf, M. *Communicating When Your Company Is under Siege.* Lexington, MA: Lexington Books, 1986.

Publications

Publications are one of the most traditional communications methods and have been a mainstay of health care public relations for decades. Creating the health care organization's magazines, newsletters, and brochures is often the most time- and budget-consuming function performed by the PR staff, and publications play an important part in the communications mix.

The primary value of publications is their tangibility. Publication readers have something to hold in their hands, something to keep as long as they want, that is unlike watching a TV commercial or participating in a tour or special event. The publication is a link between the health care organization and the reader. Publications can convey facts and emotion via words and pictures, and are (within reason) not subject to the limitations of advertising, media coverage, or community relations methods in terms of limits on time and space to send the message and limits on the amount of time the audience has to absorb the message.

A health care organization's publications can generally be divided into the following two categories:

- Periodicals—publications that are routinely issued to specific audiences, such as magazines that are sent to external audiences, employee newsletters, physician office staff briefing sheets, and so on
- Special-purpose publications—annual reports, patient handbooks and educational brochures, posters, fliers, promotional brochures, calendars, and so on

These publications often consume up to half of the PR budget owing to costs for design, typesetting, printing, and mailing, and can require the full-time attention of one or more staff members who are continually involved in getting out issues of the periodicals and updating or developing new special-purpose publications.

Despite their "tried-and-true" status as a basic PR technique, PR professionals today are seriously evaluating the use of publications in light of the growing rate of illiteracy in the United States. Although many promotional publications are targeted toward audiences that can reasonably be expected to be literate (such as community leaders and public officials), publications aimed at patients or potential patients ("general audience") may in fact be aiming at people who can't read them.

In addition, audience members who can read are often suffering from the dual problem of too many things to read and too little time to read them. Readership studies conducted by numerous organizations show that in nearly all cases only a small percentage of intended audiences actually read even the best publications, according to Pat Jackson's *pr reporter*. And even those stalwart readers "see only a small percentage of the issues or information presented. This double whammy," the article notes, "has made publication staffs the first choice of downsizers, with good reason: large sums spent for dubious impact."[1]

Because of these external audience changes and the internal scrutiny, the traditional reliance on publications —"when you want to communicate with an audience, give them a brochure"— is now giving way to a more careful analysis of why existing publications are being produced and why new publications should be created. Because health care organizations have been such heavy users of publications, this analysis process is of particular importance to the PR manager.

☐ The Communications Audit

This communications audit process begins with identifying *all* of the publications that the health care organization is producing or purchasing. The results can be surprising. "We discovered literally dozens of brochures that departments were producing on their own, or buying from outside sources," said one publications manager.

Once the identification phase is completed, the following types of questions are answered about each publication:

1. How often is this publication issued?
2. If this publication is not a periodical, when was it first published and when was the last time it was updated?
3. Who is responsible for producing this publication? (Specify role of department staff, PR staff, outside professionals, and so on.)
4. How long does it take to produce this publication? (Designate each function — conceive, write, edit, design, photograph, typeset, print, mail, and so on.)

5. What is the total budget for this publication (by function)?
6. How is this publication distributed?
7. What is (are) the primary audience(s) for this publication?
8. What is the purpose of this publication—what is it supposed to get its readers to do (such as give money, be more aware of services, understand a diagnostic procedure, and so on)?
9. How do we evaluate this publication? How do we decide if it is achieving its goals?
10. On a scale of 1 (low) to 10 (high), how important is this publication to (a) the objectives of the department or service that uses the publication and (b) the health care organization in general?
11. If we did not have this publication, what method would we use to communicate to the audience? (Be creative—what about videos, personal teaching, meetings, or advertising?)
12. What would we do with the money spent on this publication if we didn't do the publication? (Again, be creative.)

These questions allow the PR manager and the manager of the department using the publication to take a semiobjective look at the publication and determine its value. If the PR manager wants to take a rigorous look at publications—which often happens when major budgetary decisions are being made—an outside consultant can be brought in to perform a more detailed and objective audit.

After the audits are completed and decisions made about what publications are going to be retained, revamped, or rejected, the PR staff should then reexamine every step of the publications' development process to ensure that the publications are as effective as possible. This is also a good time to revisit the "form or function" debate that has raged among publications editors and PR people for years. The debate centers around the question: "Does a publication have to be well designed to be effective?" Those who say no generally frame their arguments around the waste of money on glossy paper, four-color photos, glitzy special effects, and so on. They also point out that it's the substance that counts—the words and the message—not the glitz. Those who say yes insist that a publication must be attractive to the readers or they won't pick it up, and that expensive paper and printing catch readers' attention.

The real answer probably lies somewhere in between. Effective design—readable type, easy-to-scan format, no visual distractions—does encourage and enhance readership, and poor design can deter the reader from even trying to read the substance. But effective design does not necessarily mean expensive. There are a number of examples of inexpensively produced but well-designed publications—no gloss or glitz, but effective typography and layout. Additionally, the true measure of a publication is whether or not it achieves its objectives—but generally, it's difficult to be successful if the design gets in the way of readership. A truly awful publication—cheap appearance, bad design, and so forth—may serve to convey specific information but may also have the effect of creating a negative, "cheap" image of the institution.

The final verdict: glitz and gloss aren't necessary; sound design and attractive (if inexpensive) printing are. The PR goal is to achieve the objective of the publication in a style consistent with the health care organization's overall image goal.

☐ The Health Care Organization's Periodicals

Nearly every health care organization publishes some type of internal publication (for employees, physicians, volunteers, and other audiences), and many publish external publications aimed at "the community." (Internal publications are covered in chapters 15 and 16 on employee communications and physician relations.)

External periodicals—magazines, newsletters, or tabloids—can fall into several categories, including:

* General-purpose periodicals aimed at a broad audience, ranging from community leaders (civic, business, opinion) to donors to past patients
* General-purpose periodicals aimed at one or more specific audiences (business leaders, elected officials, church leaders, and so on)
* Health information publications aimed at past patients and/or potential patients (consumers who can be targeted by demographic categories)

When developing a periodical, the more specific the objectives can be, the easier it is to create a graphic look and content for the publication. The question that needs to be answered is: What do we want the recipients of this publication to do as a result of receiving it?

Most general-purpose periodicals aimed at broad audiences are part of a comprehensive image development program and often have correspondingly broad awareness goals. "Keeping the public informed" is an often-stated goal, but that more specific goal of creating a high level of consumer awareness needs to be seen as part of a strategy to affect consumer behavior and to achieve a level of consumer preference for the health care organization. The magazine's contribution to awareness levels can be measured by including stories on one or two specific services that may not be promoted through other methods and then conducting a follow-up survey to determine reader familiarity with those services. Surveys can also be undertaken to determine whether readers translated that awareness into action and elected to make use of the services featured in the magazine.

The periodical aimed at a specific audience may have similar awareness goals, but the publication generally is limited to material of particular interest to the target audience. Achievement of these awareness goals can be evaluated by measuring awareness levels before and after topics have been covered in several issues of the publication.

Consumer health education publications are becoming a popular alternative to the broad-audience, general-information periodical. The reasoning is that consumers are more interested in reading information that they can use and that will benefit them than reading information about the health care organization's newest programs and services. There is some logic to this reasoning, although the publication that contains only health education stories ("Cholesterol and YOU") and does not at least reference or mention related services of the health care organization can hardly achieve an objective of increased awareness. The purely altruistic health education periodical, unsullied by any promotional objectives, can at best create a vague friendly feeling on the part of the recipient (and friendly feelings are hard to measure).

A more effective alternative may be to create a hybrid—a general-information/promotional magazine with a heavy emphasis on practical health maintenance information for the consumer, or a health education-oriented publication that weaves promotional messages into the stories ("How St. Luke's 'Healthy Living' program can help YOU control cholesterol").

There are several keys to developing effective periodicals:

1. Content must be tied to the health care organization's communications and marketing objectives. The periodical should be seen as a primary communications method to be used as part of the health care organization's image development campaign, with stories that relate to the organization's institutional positioning, and as an important channel for marketing communications campaigns, with stories focusing on services and products that are targeted for consumer promotion. The periodical can also include calls for action to elicit direct responses from consumers, although these responses are generally limited to requests for more information, rather than a direct consumer purchase. Nevertheless, these direct responses can be used to "qualify" consumers for further marketing communications efforts.
2. The approach should be "them" oriented. If "we" want to promote awareness of our heart center, what related topics are "they" interested in?

3. In the days of *USA Today,* shorter stories, more graphics, and quick readability are essential. (The section of this chapter entitled "Principles of Effective Writing and Design" details writing and design techniques that enhance publication readability.)
4. Although developing mailing lists is often the least thought about task involved in periodicals, but is one of the most significant, and thus should be given careful consideration. Sending a periodical to inappropriate audiences wastes money; not communicating to an important external audience wastes opportunity. Some of the issues relating to mailing list development are the following:
   - Who's on the list now? Who controls who goes on the list? If no one can identify who half of the people on the list are (and why they're important to the health care organization), how did they get into the computer?
   - Who ought to be on the list? Image development and marketing communications objectives identify target audiences that should be considered for addition to the mailing list.
   - Are all of the audiences with whom the health care organization already has relationships included on the mailing list—past patients, donors, people who respond to ads or call for information and use referral lines?
   - Who maintains the mailing list? Is there an in-house staff person who can handle the responsibility (or will mailing list corrections get done when all other work is completed—which may translate to once a year at best)? If the list is maintained by a mailing house, can the health care organization make sure it has easy access, total control, and complete confidentiality?
   - Who makes sure the list is updated? And how? Paying for return postage is an expensive but effective way of keeping the list current. Even with those ongoing updatings, the list needs to be periodically reviewed (and coded so that each name can be identified as part of an audience category).
   - If the health care organization is buying mailing lists, how precise can the organization be in specifying targets for the list company so that the organization is not spending money to send a periodical to someone who's not part of one of its target audiences?

In addition to these four guidelines, and the tips in the "Principles of Effective Writing and Design" section of this chapter, *pr reporter* offered a series of hard-hitting recommendations in the June 5, 1989, issue. "Publications now: how to develop effective publications in an over-communicated world" provided solid advice to the hospital PR manager or publications editor.[2]

1. Strategize each step in the usage cycle:
   - Receive
   - Scan or read headlines to decide whether to read further
   - Read
   - Understand
   - Believe
   - Act

   Most publication editors put all their energy into the reading step—which makes the giant, often fatal assumption that folks are going to, even want to, read.

2. Analyze the brevity factor:
   - How many subjects per issue are readers expected to handle?
   - How many pages?
   - How often issued?

   Are your answers dictated by the old idea that a schedule must be met . . . or by actual usage studies? Why must it be more than one page (a flier or a poster)? Why must it come out weekly, monthly, or whatever, instead of when there's something important to communicate? How many readers ever ask for a back issue or notice if one is missed?

3. Force editors to edit—and link everything they do to organizational goals—by limiting each issue to three or four key topics. The goal is communication, not giving readers more to read or providing entertainment. Editors must work closely with management to select topics, then edit them to reasonable length. Use charts, pictures, or other graphics to convey the message.

4. Analyze what kinds of stories people would read. What stories are they actually interested in that won't compete with other media they presently use? *pr reporter* suggests debates, arguments, discussions of sensitive topics, "things that really involve them instead of preaching at them."

5. Perform readership studies to determine which stories are actually read. If audiences indicate that they are reading only some articles or are reading the publication only occasionally, can the least-read material be dropped and still maintain the majority of the present readers who actually read? You're not pleasing readers by offering as much material as you can cram in.

6. Analyze who among the publication's recipients read the publication. If opinion leaders or influentials are reading and the rest aren't, why not target these key people with another medium, maybe a medium that is more personal than print?

7. Use research, both in pretests and in postpublication evaluations, to determine communication effectiveness. *pr reporter* suggests Fog and Flesch tests (methods of evaluating the reading level required

to understand the publication), as well as clocking the reading time required and asking panels if they clearly understand what the stories are saying. Set up advisory panels of non-PR people, nonwriters, and nonpublications people and ask them to be brutally honest, focusing on the stated objectives of the publication.

8. Evaluate whether the medium *is* the message. For glossy or design-conscious publications, is the value of the publication achieved merely by being seen by its target audience, whether they read it or not? If that's the point, is the cover really a "WOW," and can you be sure that it's actually being seen by the target (or being tossed away by a secretary or other gatekeeper)?

9. Assess the "family and reminder factor." Even if the recipients "never crack the cover," does the publication remind them that they're part of the family, that they have a link to the health care organization? Does it remind them that they're supposed to do something (make a donation, get an annual checkup, whatever)?

10. Evaluate cost-effectiveness. Could reputational/reminder value be attained with a smaller or less expensive vehicle? Instead of a magazine, what about a newsletter or tabloid? Rather than a newsletter, what about a one-page "infogram" or a flier?

pr reporter also noted that publication evaluation methods need to become as sophisticated as the marketing objectives PR staff people are trying to achieve. This means avoiding the outdated readership questionnaires bound into the publication that ask "How much of every issue do you read?" This method fails the test of valid research because it's a self-selected sample of people who tend to be the most avid readers. People who hate or don't read the publication don't return the questionnaire, and those who do return it tend to answer ideally, with what they think they ought to do rather than what they actually do. A better evaluation method is to use personal or phone interviews of a randomly selected sample, asking content questions to determine what they actually read and remember.

If the periodical's main objective is to serve as one channel to convey messages that are being communicated through a multifaceted campaign, then evaluative research should measure the awareness levels of people who receive the periodical and people who don't, to see if there's any difference. Conversely, some messages can be sent only through the periodical channel; in this case, measuring awareness of that message among periodical recipients can help evaluate the effectiveness of the periodical. A third ongoing, monitoring evaluation method is to keep track of calls or requests received in answer to direct-response mechanisms included in the periodical.

It seems unlikely that the periodical, in one format or another, will vanish as a communications method in the near future. But concerns over effectiveness require that targeting and evaluation be as precise as possible. It is equally important for the PR manager to clarify what role the periodical is to play in achieving overall marketing and communications objectives.

☐ Special-Purpose Publications

As with periodicals, the key question that must be answered when developing a special-purpose publication is: Why are we doing this publication? What do we want to have happen as a result of someone reading it? Special-purpose, external audience publications in health care fall into two basic categories: patient publications and promotional publications. (Special-purpose publications for internal audiences are addressed in chapter 15 for employees and chapter 16 for physicians.)

Patient Publications

Patient publications are usually developed to educate or inform patients about their care or treatment.

- Patient handbooks, which attempt to answer every question the person hospitalized for inpatient care may have (a nearly impossible task unless you publish a 48-page manual, which some hospitals actually do)
- Explanatory types of brochures ("All about your mammography exam")
- Educational publications to help patients learn how to live in a healthier way or to cope with health problems

There are several factors to be considered when developing patient publications:

1. These publications will be read (if they are read) by people who are sick, stressed, or anxious. The more difficult the materials are to comprehend or use ("How do you find the cafeteria hours in this handbook?"), the less likely they are to be read.
2. These publications will be given to a very, very diverse audience, many of whom do not read easily. Pictures, graphics, and diagrams are essential.
3. Many of the people who are given these publications will be elderly, with failing eyesight. The use of 12-point or larger type is mandatory.

4. Some of these publications will have to be used and reused for many weeks (publications that help the patient learn about how to deal with ongoing health problems, like menu selection and meal planning for diabetics). These may need to be extra sturdy.

In short, these are publications that need to be functional. And that function needs to be analyzed while the publication is being considered. Perhaps there are other methods — personal teaching or a video on a VCR or the in-house TV system, for instance — that might work better. If a publication appears to be the best communications method, or is needed to support or enhance the other methods, then the usage and functionality of the publication must be carefully studied. Patient care staff members can help identify the "most commonly asked questions," which can be included in the brochure's content, as can focus groups with former patients. Focus groups can also be used to pretest content and design.

Promotional Publications

Promotional publications can be of the following types (but the list is really endless):

- Publications that educate and "sell" a product to the public
- General capabilities or "viewbooks" that provide a general introduction to the health care organization and set the positioning tone for other communications
- Recruitment publications, for employees (especially nurses), physicians, nursing or medical students, and so forth
- Calendars
- Direct-mail publications used for fund-raising or other specific purposes
- Annual reports, which in the corporate world are issued to provide required financial information but in the nonprofit sector are used to create awareness and support for the institution
- And many others, ranging from invitations to special events to coloring books

The two key factors that must be considered when designing a special-purpose publication are:

- What is the audience and objective — why are we spending the time and money to produce this publication?
- What techniques can be used to make this publication as readable and attention grabbing as possible?

The publication's execution — writing, design, graphics and photos, format, and printing — can often make the difference between the publication being at least looked at versus being tossed out or put aside.

☐ Principles of Effective Writing and Design

A publication's effectiveness is determined in some part by who produces it. There are a number of options used by health care organizations, as illustrated in table 12-1. These models occur in decreasing frequency; the first and second options are used by more health care organizations than the last.

Whether the publication is written or designed internally or externally, the PR manager must be aware of the essentials and quality standards that contribute to effectiveness. Following is a list of how-tos and tips compiled from the personal experiences of health care and higher education publications people (colleges do more brochures than health care organizations). Although the list is not all-inclusive, it does identify some of the essentials.

1. A consistent graphic identity is critical. All publications should be easily identified as the health care organization's, with consistent use of name and logo.
2. Every publication should carry the health care organization's complete mailing address and phone number.
3. Although there can be exceptions, publication sizes, type styles, and colors should be kept somewhat consistent while still offering variety (three or four standard sizes, three or four standard typefaces, two or three basic colors or a variety of shades that are all within the same color family).
4. Format — size, number of pages, sturdiness — should be related to function.

Table 12-1. Options for Publication Production

Option	Writing	Design
1	In-house staff member(s)	Writers (using basic design or desktop publishing following standardized formats)
2	In-house staff member(s)	Free-lance designer
3	In-house staff member(s)	In-house designer
4	Free-lancer	Any of the above
5	Agency	Agency

5. Size, paper stock, inks, and use of special effects (such as foil-stamping and die-cutting) send a message whether or not the recipient reads the publication. Before decisions are made about these components, the publication's "tone" should be established—ritzy, businesslike, high tech, and so forth.

6. Even though the factors listed in point 4 and the design/graphics of a publication are critical in terms of impact, the writing is equally important. If the words weren't important, you wouldn't be doing a publication.
   - Copy should be as simple as possible, avoiding health care and medical jargon.
   - When possible, use the audience's language.
   - Copy should be tightly written, especially in patient publications.
   - Headlines, subheads, and graphic captions (cutlines) may be the only items a reader looks at. The headline should pull the reader into the story or publication, while subheads and cutlines should tell the key points of the copy.

7. Effective typography can make it either easier or more difficult to read the copy. In general:
   - The minimum type size is 10 point, and 12-point type is better (even larger for senior citizens).
   - Serif typefaces are easier to read than sans serif.
   - A medium weight should be used for body copy (light or bold type is too hard to read when there's more than a headline or a cutline of it).
   - All capital letters are hard to read, even in headlines. Capitalize the first word and proper nouns only.
   - One to four points of leading between lines is preferred.
   - Lines should generally be no shorter than 18 picas wide and no longer than 24 picas wide. Anything else makes it hard for the eye to quickly move across the line and back to the beginning of the next line.
   - Right margins can either be justified—every line ends at the same place and extra space is added to make all the lines end up equal—or ragged—ending wherever the word ends without adding spaces or extra hyphenation. Justified is more traditional and formal (and because it's more commonly used, the eye is more familiar with it), although ragged right is easier to read.

8. Layout should be open and airy, with white space that helps the eye move across the page, unless there is a specific objective to be achieved by using a format with tightly filled pages (textbooks, for instance).

9. Black ink on white paper is the most common combination because it's the most easily read. Black, navy, or a dark-color ink on a lighter paper are also readable. Light type on a dark background is extremely difficult to read. A second or more colors add excitement and emphasis.
10. Photos and graphics (charts, graphs, and so on) tell the story and, with many readers, have to stand alone when the readers bypass the story copy.
11. One strong, large photo is more effective than a layout of mediocre, smaller photos.
12. Whether or not to use a total production facility—typesetting, printing, and mailing—or specialists depends on the designer's preference, the budget, and the expertise of the vendors. Generally, the firm that specializes in typesetting only, or one that specializes in printing or mailing, may have more expertise than the firm that tries to do everything.
13. Generic publications—purchased from a publisher who imprints the health care organization's name on the cover—may be better than nothing, but these publications make the assumption that the audiences of all health care organizations are alike.

Finally, some tips on cost cutting are presented. The following list of 32 ways to cut publications costs while maintaining effectiveness is adapted from an article by Eleanor Crandall (University of Colorado, Boulder), which was adapted from an article by Robert S. Topor originally published in the June 1983 issue of *CASE Currents*. It is reprinted here with permission from the Council for Advancement and Support of Education:[3]

1. Edit. Edit. Edit. Tight copy saves space and has more impact.
2. Get clearances before you set type. Do anything you can to avoid changes after copy is set.
3. Proofread copy before it's set. If you're the author, ask someone else to check your copy.

Typesetting

4. Typesetting, compared with reproducing typed copy, can save money. You'll need less paper and fewer negatives and proofs, and you will reduce printing, folding, collating, and mailing costs.
5. Submit all copy at the same time. Typesetters often charge extra for minimum amounts of copy. (It takes the same amount of office work to log in, track, account, and bill a small job as a large one.)
6. Avoid author's alterations (AAs), which are often charged for by the line.

7. Provide your copy on a disk that the typesetter can cover. Most type-setting costs are for labor (keystroking). Doing the keystroking yourself reduces costs dramatically. You'll improve accuracy, too.
8. Standardize design of several publications. Use grid systems. Standardization imposes continuity and creates a "family" image.
9. Use standard sizes. Avoid odd-size publications that cannot be produced from standard press sheets without expensive trim loss.
10. Avoid bleeds. They cost more to print.
11. Avoid oversize art. The printer's camera has limited reduction capability. Make sure the art can be reduced to printing size in one shot.
12. Avoid silhouetting and other special effects, such as mezzotints, in photo conversion. They are costly.
13. Gang photos for reduction—that is, have several photos with the same reduction percentage shot at the same time.

Paper

14. Use lightweight stock, but check printed samples for printability and opacity.
15. Take advantage of quantity discounts by using the same stock for several publications.
16. Get bids from the printer on equivalent paper stock (house sheet).
17. Plan distribution carefully. Order the correct quantity to avoid unneeded copies or a shortage that requires reprinting.
18. Don't skimp on printer's proofs. Mistakes are more costly than proofs.
19. When printing reports, manuals, and handout material, use both sides of the sheet.
20. Ask about quick printing, especially if the quantity is small, the design simple, and photographic quality is not important.
21. Don't assume that photocopying is less expensive than offset printing. When the quantity reaches 2,000, printing starts to become more cost-effective.
22. Print color mastheads for newsletters in quantity, then print individual issues in black for an inexpensive two-color effect.
23. Avoid large areas of solid ink coverage. These are much more difficult to print successfully.
24. Save art boards and negatives for future use.

Binding

25. Use self-covers rather than separate covers. This saves money on paper and in production.
26. Avoid blind embossing, die-cutting, hot foil stamping, special scoring, fancy folds, and four-color unless your marketing plan justifies expensive publications.

27. Hire students to do expensive hand operations such as collating, assembling, and inserting.
28. Use bulk-rate permits. Avoid first-class mailings if you can.
29. Use self-mailers to cut envelope and insertion costs.
30. Cull mailing lists. Review them frequently.
31. Use standard-size envelopes. The Postal Service charges extra for odd sizes.
32. Plan! Plan! Plan! Nothing saves you money like careful planning.

☐ Summary

Publications trends come and go—four-color is in, four-color is out; coated stock is dramatic, uncoated stock is elegant. The PR manager or publications editor must keep audience, objective, and relationship of the publication to a total communications or marketing campaign in mind and then study competitors' publications to strive for differentiation and the creation of the desired image.

References

1. Publications now: how to develop effective publications in an over-communicated world. *pr reporter* 32(23):1, June 5, 1989.
2. Publications now.
3. Topor, R. S. *CASE Currents*, June 1987. [Quoted in Crandall, E.]

Suggested Readings

Hudson, H. *Publishing Newsletter.* New York City: Scribner's, 1988.

Kopec, J. A. The communications audit. *Public Relations Journal*, May 1982.

Newsom, D., and Siegfried, T. *Writing in Public Relations Practice: Form and Style.* Belmont, CA: Wadsworth Publishing Company, 1989, appendix A, pp. 334–37.

Severin, W. J. *Communication Theories.* New York City: Longman, 1987, chapter 6, pp. 69–87.

Thieblot, B. Rating your readability. *Currents* 14(2):38–40, Feb. 1988.

Marketing Communications and Advertising

Marketing communications — developing communications programs that are part of the promotion phase of marketing — is a somewhat new term for health care organizations. Health care public relations professionals have been creating programs to send specific messages to specific audiences for decades. Today, when these programs have a designated marketing objective, they are called marketing communications, and they represent a growing segment of the health care PR manager's responsibilities.

□ Establishing Marketing and Public Relations Responsibilities

The models of accountability and responsibility for planning and implementing marketing communications plans vary from institution to institution. If the PR function is also responsible for marketing, then public relations will have sole responsibility for the promotional communications. If there is a separate marketing function, PR and marketing staff members may collaborate on planning the campaign, with public relations responsible for execution. Or marketing may simply provide research and strategies, with public relations planning and implementing the campaign. Alternatively, in some health care organizations, the marketing department handles all product and service marketing communications (including execution), while public relations is responsible for image and general-audience communications.

As discussed in chapter 3, there is obviously some overlap between marketing and PR skills and activities, which can lead to confusion or debates about which function should be responsible for marketing communications. Ideally, the process should be collaborative, because each discipline brings a different viewpoint and different expertise to the process. In the campaign strategy and planning phase, marketing can bring the product planning and research expertise and public relations can bring the creative and communications skills, as well as a sensitivity to the concerns all of the health care organization's audiences (even and especially those who are not targets of the campaign but may nevertheless receive the message). In the execution of the campaign phase, either marketing or public relations can take the lead, with the other department having approval rights, although PR professionals generally have more experience and training in communications and are often better prepared to handle execution of the plan.

Because the two key commandments of successful marketing communications are "know your audience" and "know your product," it is important that PR staff members are also involved in the initial phases of marketing—especially product development and place-of-delivery decisions. Because of the PR manager's responsibility for knowing the health care organization's audiences—and the audiences' characteristics, concerns, needs, and wants—and for being informed about the external environment, including competitors, the PR manager can offer valuable insights into what services and programs are needed or perceived as being needed by various audiences. The PR manager can also offer input on delivery system and place alternatives based on knowledge of the audiences and competitors. Conversely, the PR manager, by being part of the product development process, can gain a better understanding of all facets of the product and its strengths and weaknesses, which will enhance the development of an effective promotion campaign.

☐ Identifying Audiences and Objectives

The first decisions made when developing a marketing communications campaign are among the most critical: identifying which audiences and which marketing objectives are to be accomplished by the communications campaign. These first steps, and the succeeding steps in developing and implementing the campaign, are usually the responsibility of a team comprising a PR staff member, the product manager, and marketing staff members (if the health care organization has a separate marketing function). Creating this team and beginning the planning process are described in chapter 6, which notes that establishing specific objectives is an essential part of the plan.

The objectives of the marketing communications campaign should be derived from the total marketing plan, but it's very important to identify those specific objectives that the communications efforts are to achieve. For instance, a marketing campaign for a maternity center could have a goal of increasing births by 15 percent, and the marketing objectives would include recruiting two new obstetricians; increasing admissions from splitters (physicians who deliver at more than one hospital); negotiating an exclusive referral arrangement, via discount pricing, with two HMOs; and increasing consumer awareness, preference, and direct inquiries about the program. The responsibilities for these objectives would be designated to the following functional areas within the health care organization:

- Recruiting physicians—physician relations
- Increasing splitter admissions—physician relations (via direct contact) and marketing communications (via communications and promotion)
- Negotiating HMO contracts—finance and marketing
- Increasing consumer awareness, preference, and response—marketing communications

Thus, the marketing communications campaign would be targeted at splitter physicians and segments of the consumer population, with specific objectives developed for each audience. The marketing communications campaign would not be aimed at objectives related to HMOs or physician recruitment, and the PR staff would not be held responsible for achieving these objectives (although the PR staff might develop or assist with materials to be used by the physician recruiters or the finance staff). When there is a joint responsibility—such as the efforts related to the splitter physicians—it is even more important to identify the desired outcomes and which staff members are responsible for achieving those outcomes. With the splitters, for instance, the marketing communications efforts could be expected to increase these physicians' awareness of the maternity unit and its capabilities, while the physician relations staff would be responsible for working internally to eliminate any negatives preventing the splitters from bringing more patients to the health care organization.

This process of identifying the specific objectives of the communications campaign is essential to prevent any misunderstandings or confusion about what the PR department's marketing communications efforts can and can't accomplish. Holding public relations responsible for the outcome of the total marketing campaign is clearly unrealistic because, as in the maternity program example, there are going to be objectives, like discount pricing for HMOs, that cannot be achieved by a communications campaign.

It's also important to have clear agreement among all team members about what the communications campaign is to achieve, as discussed in chapter 6. If the heart center manager, for instance, thinks that a print ad campaign will result in calls from 250 people asking to schedule EKGs, but the marketing communications campaign is aimed at increasing awareness, obviously the heart center manager is not going to be satisfied with a 20 percent increase in unaided awareness on the next consumer survey. Being clear about expected objectives also helps the PR manager design an effective campaign. Achieving an awareness goal would involve a totally different approach than would be used for a direct consumer response goal. The PR person responsible for the marketing communications campaign must make sure that he or she and the product manager (and the marketing staff, if appropriate) are in agreement on the desired outcomes of the campaign.

An integral part of this process of setting objectives is, of course, identifying all appropriate audiences. In the maternity marketing example, for instance, focusing the entire program on consumers would be ineffective if there were only a few physicians delivering at the hospital and their practices were all full. Changing consumer awareness and preference would have no impact because the consumers would not be able to choose hospital-affiliated physicians and thus have access to the maternity program. Conversely, increasing admissions by recruiting physicians and changing splitters' behavior would be difficult to achieve if the members of the consumer audience were not aware of the program or had a negative impression of the hospital and refused to be admitted there.

Thus, when creating a marketing communications program, it is important to identify every audience that can have an impact on the achievement of the overall objectives and to develop specific strategies to reach each audience. These audiences will almost always include physicians, will often include consumers, and may also include other audiences. For an alcoholism treatment program, for instance, those other audiences could include corporate employee assistance programs, social service agencies, high school counselors, and so forth.

Generally, the two most common audiences are physicians and potential patients (consumers). Strategies for reaching the physician audience are discussed in more detail in chapter 16. The present chapter will focus primarily on communicating to the nonphysician, consumer audience. While the discussion will center around reaching the consumer/potential patient audience, the techniques can be used with other nonphysician audiences.

☐ Understanding the Consumer or Potential Patient Audience

"Patients now expect to take part in the hospital choice," wrote St. Louis University Medical Center researchers Frederic Wolinsky and Richard

Kurz in 1984.[1] Theirs was some of the earliest reported research on the issue of consumer choice. Consultant Pat Mages also heralded the new consumerism, noting, "There is ample evidence that physician influence in the purchase decision is declining, and the consumer customer is making independent health care purchase decisions more and more."[2]

Public relations and marketing staff members in health care organizations had been monitoring the role that consumers were playing in the health care selection process for many years, and the increasing involvement of these consumers was the primary factor that led to the increase in marketing communications campaigns aimed directly at consumers. These communications efforts provided the consumer with more information about health care services, which, in turn, led to increasing independence on the part of the consumers. "Members of the public are being told as never before that when they need medical treatment they have choices, they have a right to expect the best; that, in short, they are much more than the 'breathing bricks' they used to be treated as. They are becoming sophisticated and demanding purchasers of health care," wrote marketing consultant Richard Ireland.[3]

By 1987, according to *Hospitals* magazine, 75 percent of consumers surveyed in a national poll indicated that they would ask their physicians to reconsider hospital recommendations if those recommendations conflicted with the consumers' choices. And one-third of the respondents said they would go so far as to change physicians in order to go to their preferred hospitals.[4]

Health care organizations got the message clearly: consumers believed that they had at least some degree of choice about where they received health care. And marketers began studying that choice process, to attempt to identify the factors that influenced the consumer's choice. Traditional models of consumer behavior—Lavidge and Steiner's "Knowledge–Awareness–Preference–Conviction–Purchase" model[5] or Tosdal's classic AIDA model (attention–interest–desire–action)[6]—relate well to the purchase of goods or services that are desired or needed by the consumer. These models also define a two-party interaction (buyer/seller) and are more appropriate when the consumer is the person who needs, decides to buy, and pays for the purchase.

There are two differences between these classic consumer purchase decision models and the consumer involvement in health care decisions:

- *The patient does not have absolute freedom of choice.* There are at least four parties involved in the health care buying interaction: the recipient (patient); the orderer (generally the physician, although when payers contract with managed care plans, they become orderers); the payer (insurer or employer); and the provider (health care organization and, to a degree, physician). Thus, rather than a simple two-party relationship, in health care there are often four parties involved, and several of the parties may play dual roles. The implication for consumer marketing campaigns is clear: the consumer is not the only decision maker. Physicians and payers can guide, direct, or limit the patient's choices, although the increasingly educated and decisive consumer can exercise the option of choosing a different physician or health insurance plan. However, even the most self-directed patient will encounter some instances in which there is no choice. A patient who needs treatment that is only offered at one hospital in the region has no choice, nor can he or she choose a hospital if the only physician specializing in the necessary type of care has an exclusive contract with one hospital. Finally, the patient usually has little opportunity to make a choice when he or she is being transported by a life squad in an emergency situation.

- *The product is generally not something the consumer is actively seeking; in fact, the product is something most people hope they never have to use.* Consumers do not choose to get sick so that they can purchase health care services, nor can health care organizations create a demand for most of their services (programs like weight control or exercise are exceptions). Thus, unlike general consumer promotion, where the objective is to persuade consumers who want the product to buy your brand, in health care the goal is to create enough ongoing top-of-mind *awareness* "so that when they have to choose, you're the first one they think of." A related objective is to get potential patients to think about which brand of health care (what health care organization) they have a *preference* for before they need it, so that they don't make hasty or uninformed decisions.

These two factors suggested a *new model* of the consumer purchase decision:

Awareness–Preference–Opportunity to Choose–Choice

With this type of model in mind, health care marketers studied the factors that played a role in developing consumer preference for a hospital or for specific health care services. Initial research identified "good medical care," convenience/location, past history with the hospital, and physician recommendations as reasons why consumers had chosen the hospital for their most recent stay. Consumers also indicated that new technology, staff courtesy, and the availability of medical specialists were important factors, although they weren't sure they had enough information about these factors.[7] By 1986, "reputation" was also identified as a key choice factor in a Louis Harris poll of Americans.[8]

Marketers and PR professionals knew that direct communications to consumers could have an impact on several of these choice factors, by giving the consumers information and persuasive messages about health care organizations. Advertising—more controlled and targeted than traditional PR channels—was seized upon as a new way to communicate with consumers. A major advertising agency executive noted that: "Health care, like *Tide* detergent, is a product which responds to consumer advertising. Increasingly we are seeing in the health care marketplace the same factors which govern the detergent marketplace and have driven that category to rely on advertising—factors which are important to the consumers, such as quality of overall brand image, the role of convenience for the consumer, and the new and increasing introduction of price as a factor in health care decisions."[9] Consumers and even physicians seemed to agree; 70 percent of consumers said hospitals should advertise to get their message out,[10] and half of the physicians contacted in a 1987 survey said that advertising was an effective means of informing the public about hospital services.[11] "Hospitals learn the hard sell" noted a *Time* magazine story in 1987.[12]

Although consumers generally were aware of hospital advertising (nearly half of the respondents in a 1987 national survey recalled seeing hospital ads and nearly 90 percent of them could identify the sponsor[13]), hospitals eventually discovered that consumer advertising alone could deliver only limited results. Deemed more effective were total marketing communications campaigns, including PR techniques. And as noted earlier, communications and promotion efforts aimed at other audiences (physicians, payers, referrers) were also needed.

☐ Developing the Consumer Marketing Communications Plan

Most of the material in this section on how to develop marketing communications plans is excerpted from "TV: When and How," a chapter of *Hospital Marketing: Step by Step*, and is used with the permission of the publisher, St. Anthony Hospital Publications, Washington, DC.

Prerequisites of an Effective Consumer Marketing Communications Plan

Before a creative or media strategy can be developed, there are a number of prerequisites that should be met:

1. *A good product.* That means good in terms of clinical quality indicators, and also in terms of efficient and courteous delivery. The

latter factors are often more important to the consumer than clinical quality, because the consumer can't measure quality but can evaluate the way in which the service is delivered. For instance, it's ineffective to promote a sleep center when there's already a 12-week wait for appointments or to promote an outpatient pharmacy if the prices aren't competitive and the staff are known to be overworked and rude to customers.

2. *An "O" service.* Consumers must have the *opportunity* to make or have an impact on the decision about what health care organizations they will go to for the service. The consumer can make or have an impact on this decision in a number of ways:
    * Choosing the health care facility from among a number of facilities that his or her physician mentions
    * If the physician does not mention the health care facility the consumer prefers, asking the physician to admit the patient to that facility
    * Changing physicians or selecting a physician who admits to the preferred health care facility
    * Self-referring to programs such as substance abuse, sleep disorders, and a growing number of services for which the health care organization will refer the patient to a staff or affiliated physician

3. *A product that is either profitable or has referral/linkage possibilities for establishing relationships with consumers and encouraging them to use other services of the health care organization.* Maternity services often fall into the latter category.

4. *Comprehensive market research before, during, and after the campaign.* Focus groups and consumer surveys can identify existing consumer awareness, perceptions, needs, and concerns. Pretesting of communications strategies, concepts, and copy or storyboards of actual communications pieces can help identify the messages consumers are receiving, pinpoint any negatives, and identify which concept is most appealing. Research during the campaign can identify any problems that may be occurring while there's still time to make changes, and a commitment to doing research after the campaign is essential in terms of measurement and evaluation.

5. *A response system in place so that consumers can respond to the campaign's "call to action" or seek more information.* This system can include direct channels (a special phone number or mailing address) or indirect channels (making sure physicians are educated and ready to respond to patients who ask about the service being promoted).

6. *An effective strategic position for the service.* As one PR veteran put it, "Is our position unique, very unique or totally unique?" What's different/better/special about the product? Is it newer? Cheaper? In a more attractive setting? Highest perceived quality (by

consumers)? Conveniently located to a specific target audience? Designed for a specific group or audience (such as working women, senior citizens, and so on)? Designed for an unmet community need? Does it provide superior service (and you have to be able to demonstrate that it's consistently superior—for example, a 10-minute maximum wait for lab tests, all the time). Joan Aho Ryan, A.P.R., and George W. Lemmond, educating PR professionals on how to "think like brand managers," identified the five important rules of good positioning:[14]

- *Be specific.* "A good positioning should be so tight it makes you sweat." Don't try to be comprehensive and all things to all people. For a heart program, that may be, "we care for more heart attack patients than anyone else." For maternity, "every mother and baby have a private suite."
- *Convey an important benefit.* "Tell people why your product is important to them. Look for major benefits. Find out what they want and give them more of it. Find out what they don't want and give them less of it."
- *Lead from strength.* Don't excuse shortcomings—focus only on strengths of your product. Develop positioning programs that are so in sync with the product's unique attributes that the competitors don't want to try to copy them.
- *Be real.* "You can't wish for any position you want and get it." If a hospital delivers thousands of babies every year, it can't bill itself as "small and personal."
- *Keep it simple.* Make "one point that is easy to understand."

In addition, product positioning must match or be congruent with the health care organization's institutional positioning. If the organization's ongoing image campaign emphasizes high-tech and specialized care, promoting a product with a "warm and personal" position will confuse the audience and undercut both efforts.

The main reason a strong product position is important is that it's a waste of money to promote a product that seems, to the consumer, to be just like several other products. The communications campaign can give the audience no real reason to prefer the product over its competitors.

In today's health care organizations, where many if not most of the services are also provided by competing organizations, there may be cases in which the organization's product doesn't appear to have a differentiated position. If this is the case, there are several alternatives:

- *Restructure the product.* Develop a strength that makes it different— location, amenities or delivery, convenience, new technology, more of something, and so on.

- *Don't promote the product directly to consumers.* Rely on distribution channels (physicians, managed care plans, referrers, and so on).
- *Use communications messages and methods to create a perception of difference.* Developing a creative theme that's very different from the messages of other health care organizations is one method. Using different channels—in-home "Tupperware" parties (see chapter 9) when the competition is using TV advertising, for instance—is also effective.

If these prerequisites are not in place, the PR manager must consider whether it's appropriate to launch a marketing communications campaign. If the product is not sound, a promotional effort may hasten its demise (more people use the service and discover how bad it is). If there is no research available, the PR manager is in the position of jumping out of the plane without a parachute—expedient, but risky. If there are no response or measurement systems in place, the product and PR managers can't determine if the campaign has achieved its objectives. And if there is no effective strategic position available for the product, then the marketing communications campaign will have to create a perception of difference—much more difficult to do than to promote a differentiated product. When faced with any of these situations, the PR manager needs to negotiate with the marketing and product managers to determine whether or not to go forward with a consumer promotion campaign, cognizant of the fact that chances of success are reduced when any of these prerequisites are absent. However, if the prerequisites are present, then the PR manager and staff can begin to develop the communications campaign.

The Key to a Successful Consumer Communications Campaign: The M⁴ Rule

The "M to the fourth power" rule is a good guideline for any marketing communications campaign. That rule states, "Receiving a message from multiple media maximizes the recall and credibility of the message."

This saturation approach, using a number of advertising and nonadvertising promotional methods to send the same message to the same target audience, can have a significantly greater impact than relying on a single medium, and is particularly effective in the early stages of a persuasive communications campaign. Putting this rule into practice would mean that a comprehensive campaign for a health care product or service could include:

- Print, broadcast, outdoor, and/or direct-mail advertising
- Media coverage

- Special events
- Brochures and collateral materials
- Speakers and tours
- Promotion via existing general-audience channels (the health care organization's magazine, newsletters, and so on)
- Other PR techniques described in chapters 8 through 16

In addition, the hospital's "internal sales force" (employees, volunteers, auxilians, medical staff and spouses, board members, and so forth) are informed, educated, and persuaded, so that they can serve as "expert references" in the community by reinforcing the advertising and PR messages.

With this "multiple media" rule in mind, the PR manager can evaluate advertising and nonadvertising promotional methods to select those that are most effective with the campaign's target audience, message strategy, and, of course, budget.

Uses of Advertising in a Marketing Communications Campaign

Advertising offers a number of advantages in terms of sending a specific marketing message to a target audience:

- In a competitive environment, *advertising can create awareness*, letting consumers know that the health care organization offers specific services and providing details about those services. Although many health care administrators assume that all consumers are very aware of what the organization offers, in fact once consumers have seen promotional campaigns for a specific service at a hospital X, they can make the assumption that if they haven't heard about that service at other hospitals, hospital X is the only hospital with that service.
- *Advertising offers control of message content.* Unlike media coverage, which can often omit parts of the message, or worse, send incorrect information or cast the information in a negative light ("Hospital Opens Birthing Center, Adds to Overbedded Conditions"), advertising allows the communicator to select every word and control the emphasis and tone in ways that would be impossible via media, word-of-mouth, or other nonadvertising techniques. For instance, a news release about a women's health center could hardly include the fact that the program is targeted to upscale women. In a print ad or a TV spot, however, the selection of models, wardrobe, set and decor, and so forth can convey the upscale image subtly but unmistakably.

- *Advertising also offers more control of message delivery.* A news story runs when the editor wants it to run. A release to radio stations may be used by only three or four stations with audiences that don't fit the campaign's target audiences. Using physicians as a message distribution channel means relying on them to agree to and remember to send the message. With advertising, the PR manager selects the audience as well as the dates, times, and frequency the message is delivered. Although mass media cannot guarantee pinpoint accuracy (they can describe their audience in general terms, but cannot identify exactly which viewers will be watching or listening to the program or which readers will look at the page your ad is on), they do offer much more control than some nonadvertising methods. And use of more segmented, small-audience outlets (such as specialized magazines or highly targeted TV programs) allows for even greater pinpointing.
- Because of the control of message and creative strategies, *advertising can create an image for the product or institution.*
- *Advertising can appeal to the consumer's emotions,* which is a very important factor in terms of consumer choice. Consumers generally make decisions based on facts—what they know—and emotions—what they feel. Persuasive advertising—especially using strong visuals (video or photos)—can create an emotional response that is doubly effective when the consumer is already aware of the facts he or she needs to satisfy his or her intellectual concerns. For instance, through advertising and other methods, a consumer may learn that a hospital's alcoholism program is experienced, has a number of treatment options, and is accredited. Those facts give him or her logical reasons for and create awareness of the program's assets if someone in his or her family needs treatment. But a print ad or a TV commercial that has a powerful emotional appeal (either positively, with a teenager and his dad talking about being together again, or fearfully, with a teen contemplating suicide) can provide the jolt of overriding emotion that can turn awareness into top-of-mind preference.
- As mentioned earlier, *a distinctive advertising approach can create a perception of difference, even if the product is very similar to competing services.* If five hospitals have women's health services, a memorable (strong creative) or a massive (heavy reach and frequency) advertising campaign may position one service as the preferred choice.

Advertising can also be more expensive than nonadvertising promotion methods, depending on the market and the nonadvertising promotion methods used. In some markets, a print or radio campaign can cost little more than 200,000 copies of a 28-page, glossy, four-color, foil-stamped, and die-cut annual report. But generally, consumer advertising is more costly than PR methods.

Advertising is not a panacea, nor is it the perfect vehicle for all communications campaigns. There are a number of things advertising cannot do, including:

- Save a bad product (in fact, exposure may kill it more quickly)
- Eliminate the need for guest relations, employee communications, physician relations, or PR programs
- Be effective if it's of poor quality, short-term, wrong medium, and so on (detailed later in this chapter)
- Sell every product, because there are some services that are either so technical (carotid endarterectomies) or so sensitive (although even impotency programs are now advertising, with mixed results) that they don't lend themselves to effective ads
- Accomplish multiple objectives (educate and persuade simultaneously) or send multiple messages to different audiences (the ad becomes so detail-laden and/or unfocused that it's worthless)
- Sell a service for which there's no need (among consumers or physicians)
- Sell a service that consumers can't access directly or for which they can't have an impact on the selection process
- Affect a target audience in an individual market if the entire campaign has been borrowed or purchased from a hospital in a very different market ("If it worked for hospital X, it will work for us.")

When considering advertising for use as part of a marketing communications campaign, it is important to remember that advertising is merely a technique—not a miracle—and that it will always work better as part of an M^4 campaign using PR or nonadvertising promotion (NAP) techniques along with advertising.

Uses of Nonadvertising Promotion Techniques in a Marketing Communications Campaign

Nonadvertising promotion is another way to describe the many traditional PR methods that have been part of communications campaigns for decades. Public relations techniques, called NAP techniques when they are used for marketing communications, include community relations (speakers, tours, special events), media coverage, brochures and other publications, external periodicals, and so on. They can almost always be used with advertising (as part of the M^4 rule) but can also be used instead of advertising when:

- The budget isn't large enough to buy advertising space or time, or to pay for high-quality creative and production services—a very common situation for many health care organizations, and even big-budget organizations rarely can afford high-quality advertising campaigns for all their products
- Using advertising is creating a backlash in the community (from payers, civic officials, and so on)
- Medical staff members are strongly opposed to advertising
- So many competing health care organizations are advertising that the channels are crowded and research shows that consumers can't differentiate the messages
- The health care organization has been advertising for several years and research shows that the consumers are no longer paying attention to the messages
- The advertising channels available reach audiences that are broader than the communications campaign has targeted

Veteran PR counselor Daniel J. Edelman noted that "in the right circumstances, public relations can outperform advertising" or can boost the impact of advertising.[15] Those circumstances include when a health care organization is:

1. Introducing a breakthrough new product by providing the intense media coverage that heightens consumer awareness and creates more credibility.
2. Generating new consumer excitement for an old product. Swift's "Turkey Talk Line" is the brand's primary marketing vehicle today.
3. Working with a small budget and giant competition.
4. Marketing a very complicated product or service.
5. Using a campaign objective that includes spotlighting the reputational dimensions of the product—goodwill, quality, community contributions, and so forth.
6. Trying to ensure very fast impact—a press conference or series of media interviews can get the word out more quickly than an effective ad can be developed.

Even with the increase in advertising by health care organizations, the majority of all health care product and image marketing communications campaigns rely on NAP techniques, with advertising utilized for the profit-making products that consumers can access directly or independently. Developing effective NAP techniques is covered in earlier chapters of this book, and creating effective advertising programs is detailed in the following section of this chapter.

☐ Developing Effective Advertising Campaigns

There are literally dozens of textbooks on advertising, some of which are referenced at the end of this chapter and others of which can be located through the library, the advertising departments of local universities, or professional associations. In this chapter, general techniques and methods will be identified.

Developing Ads That Work

What factors make ad campaigns effective? The list is as endless as the 30-second spots that march across the TV screen during prime time. Some of the most important factors include:

- *Strong and differentiated creative factors.* Hospital ads that don't look like hospital ads. Ads that break through the clutter and compete not only with other hospital ads, but with every other ad the consumer sees.
- *Research that pinpoints exactly how the consumers in the health care organization's market area and target audience feel.* This generally precludes relying totally on syndicated, "generic" ad campaigns. Although they have a lot of appeal (less money, less hassle, and less time than doing it yourself), syndicated ads must be so generic (in order to be sold to health care organizations across the country) that they can end up being ineffective. There is no such thing as a generic consumer or a generic audience, unless there's also a generic health care organization. Syndicated ads, if they are to be used, work best with services that are very similar from institution to institution (such as physician referral services), although as noted earlier in this chapter, health care organizations are advised to develop ways to make their services unique and differentiated (or to use ads to create differentiation). If generic ads are used for a generic service, the result may also be generic—the lack of response that characterizes the majority of ad campaigns.
- *Language that's aimed at consumers, not physicians.* No "intraocular." Delete "tertiary." Omit "multiphasic." Talk like real people.
- *Quality production.* Eye-catching design. Arresting headlines. Visually striking photos and video. Audio that's music to the ear. If you can't afford to do it right, don't do it.
- *Appeals to more than one sense.* People most effectively process information and learn through their sense of sight, followed by hearing.
- *A medium that works in the health care organization's market, based on what the target consumers say they read, watch, or listen to.* And

based on the type of message that's being sent (factual, emotional, and so on).

- *Long-term thinking.* Think months and years — not days and weeks. Any advertising takes time to have an impact greater than a short-term response blip.

To learn about other factors that can affect the effectiveness of ad campaigns, there are a number of "learning activities" for PR managers and staff members who are new to advertising, whether or not an agency is going to be used to actually execute the campaign. These learning activities include the following:

1. Read *Ogilvy on Advertising.*
2. Read *Advertising Age* and other industry publications.
3. Watch a lot of television and try to figure out what works, why you like the spots you like and remember. (Tape hours of programming, especially at times when you don't normally see television or TV spots, and then zap through the programs to watch the spots.)
4. Listen to local radio while driving and jot down which products you remember after you get home.
5. Read a lot about consumer advertising—not just health care advertising.
6. Really look at billboards—and read all your direct mail.
7. Make your world an informal focus group. Ask friends, neighbors, coworkers, and so on, what ads they have seen this week. Ask them why they remember those ads.
8. Take advantage of professional association seminars and publications on advertising.

Once the PR manager feels somewhat familiar with advertising and how it can fit into a total marketing communications campaign, the next steps are to determine what media will be used and to consider selecting an agency. These decisions may be made simultaneously, or one may precede the other. Because the media that are going to be used can play a role in what kind of agency is going to be selected, this chapter will discuss media selection first, followed by working with an agency.

Selecting Media

Although it's easy to find articles or speakers who advise that "TV is the best medium," or "print always works better," in fact, such broad generalities cannot be drawn for several reasons. Media penetration and costs vary from city to city, market to market. The cost of television, for instance, may be enormous in a major city like Dallas or Los Angeles, while in a more rural area, it may be more cost-effective to use regional television than to buy space in 20 or 30 weekly newspapers. Media effectiveness also varies from one demographic group to another. Older adults rely more on newspapers than television, while commuting workers can be reached with drive-time radio, among other methods. Media effectiveness also varies from market to market, especially for hospital advertising. Whereas television may work very well in Toledo, Ohio, for instance, print may deliver more impact in Columbus, only two hours away.

It is essential that the PR manager rely on consumer research in his or her service area—research that asks about current media usage, where hospital ads have been seen or heard, and so on. Relying on national experts or national research is useless, and even relying solely on a local agency's recommendations can be dangerous. Some agencies base their recommendations on which media they can make the largest commissions from or on long-standing "relationships" they have established with local media. Each medium has positives and negatives that should be considered.

Print is generally less expensive than television and can be less expensive than radio (but not always). Print can convey details and facts, but is less effective in creating emotion. Print has some degree of "shelf life" (in that the ad can be clipped or saved), but in newspapers especially, high-quality reproduction is difficult to achieve. Daily newspapers tend to reach very broad audiences—good for image advertising—but may reach customers you don't need for specific products. Print only utilizes one sense—visual—and is also a problem for the growing number of illiterate consumers or consumers who just don't like to read. Print does reach a more upscale, educated consumer in most markets.

Radio is less expensive than television and can even be more affordable than print in terms of reach (how many people hear the ad) and frequency (how many times they hear the ad). Radio can be easier to produce—but this belief often leads advertisers to think they can get by very cheaply, which leads to poor-quality production. Radio stations allow more targeted placement (audiences vary from station to station and program to program). Because radio reaches only one sense—hearing rather than sight—it is more difficult for the listener to process and assimilate the message, so the message points have to be very simple and repeated several times (especially when people are listening while also doing something else like driving or working).

Outdoor advertising (billboards) can have very dramatic impact, but because of their limited nature (7–10 words are the limits on effectiveness) billboards are generally used in conjunction with other media. Billboards can increase the impact of other media and boost awareness.

Direct mail is proliferating at an exponential rate and can be effective if done well (see the production section of this chapter). Costs depend on the size and quality of the piece being mailed and the scope of the mailing. A letter to 10,000 households can work with a limited budget, but a color brochure mailed first class to an entire community can rival print advertising in cost.

Television is probably the most controversial medium. Its assets:

- Almost everyone watches some television, and with the illiterate, semiliterate, and too-busy-to-be-literate ranks growing daily, television is becoming the preferred source of information for many people.
- Television is an efficient and, overall, cost-effective way of reaching a broad or large audience.
- Generally (again, check your own market), television works for the best customers of health care organizations—women ages 18–49, the family health care decision makers.
- Television appeals to both senses—hearing and sight—and can provide a strong emotional appeal that other mediums can't. (Remember "I'd like to teach the world to sing" or the "Hey kid" Mean Joe Greene Coke commercials?)

Television also has a number of drawbacks, primarily costs (production is expensive, as is media time in many markets, and with today's clutter, it takes greater frequency over a longer period of time to make an impact), wasted coverage owing to reaching broader audiences than are needed, and a limit on the ability to convey specifics.

No medium should be included or excluded automatically. Media selection should be a careful decision, based on a number of criteria, including:

- What media work in your market?
- What media do your target audience use?
- Where is your competition advertising? Your research can tell you whether you need to avoid the competition's media (so you can have more impact in another medium) or whether you need to engage them directly (because their message is being so well received).
- What can you afford to do well? Do you have the capability for high-quality production under a large enough time and space budget to achieve the reach and frequency needed for the message to be remembered?

Finally, despite the fact that short-term, quick-results communications campaigns are generally ill-advised, if quick results are a goal, the medium selected has to be one that can achieve fast responses. By making at least preliminary decisions about which media may be used, the PR manager can use this information in assessing advertising agencies.

Working with an Advertising Agency

The preliminary decisions about whether to use an agency and what kind of agency to use (advertising, marketing, or PR; local, regional, or national; consumer or health care focused) are detailed in chapter 5. Generally—and this can certainly vary from market to market and institution to institution—the more sophisticated the medium that's going to be used, the greater the need for an agency. Producing a TV spot is complex and costly, and if it doesn't work, thousands of dollars are wasted.

Few PR departments in health care organizations have staff members skilled in TV production. Although radio is less costly to produce and is thus presumed "easy to do"—just some copy, a good announcer, and some background music—that's the reason so many radio spots are so pedestrian. Print, direct-mail, and outdoor advertising are often viewed as the easiest to do in-house because most PR professionals can write and have access to design services. What needs to be considered is whether the staff can write good ad or direct-mail copy (very different from employee magazine copy) and whether the designer is skilled in these very different media.

With the right kind of in-house staff members, the PR department can:

- Develop ad concepts (although it is an art)
- Write copy (print, television, radio)
- Contract directly with a production house or designer
- Even handle media buying (saving the 15 percent commission less the costs of the computer software and staff training)

In most PR departments in health care organizations, the staff members who are performing these functions are relatively inexperienced in advertising and are also handling other responsibilities. An agency, on the other hand, provides specialists whose sole focus and business is advertising. The agency offers that important "outsider's" viewpoint, whereas even the best in-house staff members may end up focusing on the message "we" want to send rather than the message that will move the consumer.

An agency can handle the entire process of developing an ad campaign—from research through media buying and evaluation—or can provide only specific services requested by the client. The agency can save a lot of the PR staff's time by dealing with all of the assorted vendors and suppliers that are needed for a campaign, can handle the hassle of media buying, and can come up with great creative approaches. All of these services cost money—but the creative services alone are generally well worth the money if the campaign's design is successful.

Table 13-1 shows the alternative sources that can be used to develop parts of an advertising campaign. Once the decision has been made to consider using an agency, the primary criteria should be to get an agency that does an excellent job of what the health care organization

Table 13-1. What Do You Need for a Good Advertising Campaign?

| Task | Who Can Perform the Task? | | |
	Public Relations (in-house)	Agency	Other Sources
Research	Rarely	Most agencies broker research (hire outside firm to actually do the research)	Research firm
Positioning strategies	Should be intimately involved	If capable	Consultant; marketing firm
Advertising plan	Partially or completely	Yes	Consultant
Ad concepts	Depending on staff, PR staff can conceive ideas or work closely with agency	Yes	Production house or staff members, depending on capabilities
Creative—print	If department has great designers and writers	Yes (or can just do design or writing)	Designer; free-lance writer
Creative—broad-casting	Can possibly do copy, but few hospitals can do production	Most broker production	Production company
Media buying—print, outdoor	Depends on size of market, but generally can be done by staff members	Yes	
Media buying—radio and television	Requires 0.5 to 1.0 full-time employees on staff	Yes (but they get the 15% commission)	

needs done; if a TV campaign is needed, hire an agency that does excellent TV work. If the creative concept and execution is the key service that an agency can provide, then demonstrated creative excellence should be the main determining factor.

There are three things that should be remembered when working with an agency:

- The PR manager's job is the one at stake if the campaign fails. Therefore, the manager should stay in control. (See figure 13-1 for some typical areas of PR manager's involvement in the development of a TV spot.)

Figure 13-1. Typical Involvement Level for Television Campaign for In-House Medical Center Client Product or Service

1. Research—set objectives, approve general design, approve final draft of questionnaire, approve methodology, observe focus groups if held, meet with the client and research staff members to analyze results.
2. Meet with the client and ad agency staff members to begin preliminary discussions.
3. Select production company.
4. Meet with director/producer from production company to explore preliminary ideas.
5. Review at least four or five proposals per spot from agency; recommend best to client (or reject all and start again).
6. Meet with production company to review choices, get their input. (Can we actually implement this concept?)
7. Make final decisions on concepts jointly with agency and production staff.
8. Approve plan for and observe focus groups to pretest concepts.
9. Approve, change, tinker with, collaborate on agency's copy—usually 5-6 versions before everyone is happy (and then the director hates it).
10. Approve visual concept via storyboard.
11. Approve production site (studio location).
12. Approve budget.
13. Attend casting session or review and make choices from casting tape.
14. Meet with the production staff and the agency staff the week before shoot to review everything possible.
15. Attend shoot. Walk through every scene with director, provide input on talent's interpretation, make final wardrobe decisions, watch video, ask questions, help move props, whatever (rewrite script on the spot, go out for coffee . . .).
16. Participate in off-line edit, concur on final selections of specific takes.
17. Participate in on-line edit and audio production.
18. Provide specific decision on audience demographics and advertising objectives for media buyer.
19. Approve final media buyer.
20. Carefully check and approve bills.
21. Measure ad campaign results.
22. Monitor postcampaign buy analysis to make sure stations delivered the ratings they promised (so you can demand "make goods").

- The process, to be successful, has to be collaborative. Five or six fertile minds can come up with more good ideas than one or two, and the PR staff shouldn't try to "one up" the agency staff. Everyone is working for the same objective and the same client.
- Although the agency staff members know advertising, the PR manager knows the health care organization and what the internal audiences (board members, medical staff members, employees, and so forth) will accept.

The following are suggestions on how to find the right agency for your organization.

1. Decide what you can do in-house and what services you can contract directly for (research, media buying, production) without the use of the agency.
2. Find out who does the work you've seen that is exceptionally memorable (locally and throughout the industry).
3. Ask around—consult colleagues and peers.
4. Ask for preliminary information (client lists, success stories, history and information on agency, references, and so on) from all potential agencies.
5. Narrow down the list and ask for proposals. It's a nice idea at this point to provide some up-front creative money ($500 to cover costs of developing the presentation). Make sure you share research data with and meet with all bidders. Give the agencies the benefit of all possible information and insights.
6. Evaluate the proposals:
   - Is the creative approach exciting, memorable, fresh?
   - How much experience have they had with the media in which you'll be working? If none, eliminate this agency unless you want them to "learn by doing" at your expense.
   - How much work did they put into their proposal?
   - Do you feel comfortable with the people at the agency?
   - What does their other work look like?
   - To whom do they broker research, production, and so on?
   - Are they flexible? (Pitch them a couple of curve balls and see how quickly they respond.)

Once you've selected the agency, establish a clear definition of the expectations you have of them and the expectations they should have of the PR department. The following is a list of the steps in the process about which you should have a clear and mutual understanding.

- Decide in advance what things they will do (and charge for), what things you will do, and what things will be brokered out (and marked up 15–22 percent).

- Set up a final approval process on the creative concept.
- Learn, in detail, how they charge, how they bill, what's negotiable, and when the clock starts running.
- Establish to whom you are to talk about what. Can you cut red tape? Who's who?
- Review billing/charge options: retainer, hourly, commission, per project, and so on.
- Ask whether you can have cost estimates in advance.
- Assess how close the agency's estimates are to reality.
- Review what will happen if you make lots of changes.
- Determine the stages at which you can or should sign off.
- Determine what happens if you reject the entire concept.
- Meet regularly, in person (or by phone if the agency is out of town). Weekly scheduled meetings, especially during a campaign, are often in order.
- Expect, and ask for, written monthly summaries of activities.
- Expedite the approval process, and limit those with the power to approve ads to the smallest practical number. Advertising-by-committee seldom produces high-quality, effective ads.
- Expect the agency to conduct or commission research before developing ads (and expect to pay for that research).
- Expect the agency to develop — or to help develop — a support infrastructure (telemarketing to follow up on inquiries, for instance) for the ad campaign before it is launched.
- Expect the agency to develop an evaluation mechanism that can monitor the ongoing campaign and quickly evaluate it upon completion.

Finding the Best Creative Approach

In advertising, the adage "creative is everything" is old, but still true. Even the biggest budget and the heaviest media schedule can't save a spot or an ad that simply doesn't get the audience's attention or deliver the message. Literally thousands of ads are created each year that fail to achieve any degree of consumer recall or attention — or at worst, become the objects of consumer ridicule (remember Burger King's "Herb"?).

In evaluating creative approaches, there are a number of factors that can be considered:

- *Emotion sells.* Health care organizations often get hung up on presenting facts, which are important but are not the only focus. And health care organizations are inherently dramatic.
- *Using celebrity spokespeople can be a problem.* People remember them but may forget the product.

- *Humor can also be dangerous.* Generally, consumers don't find health care a very funny subject, although there have been exceptions to this for health-related products. When in doubt, pretest the concept with focus groups.
- *Show and talk about the product, not the process.* If the client is a physician referral service, the product is actually a physician, not a phone number or an operator.
- *For television, send the message via both senses, sight and hearing.* For instance, have the name and phone number superimposed on the screen, but also have the announcer say it (some people use television like radio—to listen to).
- *Emphasize the service*—the benefit to the consumer, not the source (the health care organization and its assets).
- *A great opening or headline is essential to get the audience's attention.* They may not listen to the entire spot, or read all the copy.
- *Print, outdoor, direct-mail, and TV ads have to be visually arresting.*

Be cautious with "educational" and "scare tactic" ads. Advertising by its nature is designed to persuade, convince, and sell. One hospital spent thousands of dollars producing and airing a year-long campaign of physicians discussing medical specialities and health conditions, in very educational terms. The spots did not ever try to push the hospital's services, which were not even discussed by the physicians. The only mention of the hospital was the tag line at the beginning and end of the spots. The physicians loved the campaign. Consumers not only didn't recall it, but actually exhibited greater awareness of and preference for other hospitals that were advertising less, but using their ads to sell and promote. "Scare tactic" ads are also increasingly being used by health care organizations and other industries (insurance, auto parts, and so on), but there is conflicting research on whether or not the ads achieve their final objective. They may create awareness and have high recall, but there is some concern among advertising experts that fear can actually turn off the audience and create a negative impression of the advertiser.

In summary, finding the right creative approach to break through the clutter and make an impact will generate results. Hospital ads have a tendency to look alike because the products (hospital services) tend to be fairly similar. Most OB programs, for instance, have Lamaze classes, rooming in, sibling/grandparent visitation, labor–delivery–recovery rooms, and so forth. All can come up with a photo of a smiling mom and dad with the obligatory newborn, and a headline about "we make having your baby a special occasion." Finding the creative approach that looks different—and that emphasizes the product's differences—is essential. The best guideline for accepting or rejecting a creative approach is that, if it looks like what other hospitals or other advertisers in the market are already doing, reject it.

Some Basics on Advertising Production

Print Ads

The major issue involving what works in print advertising is the ongoing debate about copy length. There are proponents of short copy ("people won't read long copy"), but there are also numerous examples of ads with very heavy copy that have achieved great results ("long copy makes it look like you've got something to say"). Copy length should depend on the message, the audience, the layout — and if it's well written, well displayed, and meaningful to the audience, they'll read it. "The issue isn't long or short — it's whether it's good," said one copywriter. Boldface type and subheads with extra leading (space) between lines of type help make copy more readable.

Headlines are critical to the success of a print ad, because the headline is often the only thing many of the readers take time to read. The head should tell the story, preferably identify the product (although there are successful exceptions to that rule), and if the ad is aimed at a very specific audience, the headline can send up a flag to alert that audience ("For parents of asthmatic kids . . .").

Photos and illustrations bring drama and excitement to the ad, but should be carefully considered in newspaper ads, because some newspapers cannot reproduce photos well. Generally, although designs can vary, one large photo will have more impact than several smaller photos.

It's important to note that print ad copywriting and design are specialized "art forms," and that journalists or publications writers may not necessarily be good at writing print ads. Finding the right "hook" for a headline isn't easy, and coming up with an eye-catching design for an ad to fit an 8½ × 11-inch space is different than laying out a newsletter.

Radio

Because of the speed of production and the relatively inexpensive costs of producing radio spots, there's a mistaken belief that they're easy to make. It may be easy to make spots — anyone can read copy into a microphone — but it is not easy to make *good* spots.

Among the key factors that differentiate the good from the bad in radio are the following:

- *A message or "promise" that can be conveyed in a 30-second spot—* simple, direct, clear. Yes, the announcer can talk very fast and read a long list of product details—but listeners will not understand half of what's said, nor will they remember the key point of the spot.
- *An effective radio voice.* Not every actor or good speaker can sound natural reading radio copy. Use an experienced radio spot talent (radio newspeople may sound too forced).
- *Very well-written copy.* Radio copy has to be tightly written and easy to hear and understand (avoid words that run together in an awkward way, like half-fast). The message has to be repeated several times so the casual listener can get it—without sounding like "Call now—operators are standing by."
- *Natural-sounding, professionally done sound effects and music.* The wrong music actually detracts from the message of the spot, and phony-sounding effects take the listener's attention away from the copy.

With radio, the brand and the promise need to be identified early and often, and the beginning of the spot needs to be dramatic enough to pull the listener's attention.

Direct Mail

Although many health care organizations mail publications to audiences, there is an art to designing a direct-mail campaign that draws specific responses (such as donations or calls to register for a service). Thomas Noakes, in "How to Mount an Effective Direct Mail Campaign" in *Bankers Digest*, identified a number of components to a successful direct-mail campaign, including:[16]

1. Select the right list (lists compiled from other sources, subscribers, buyer/inquiry lists), and don't ignore internally generated lists.
2. Make the offer clear, simple, and unique—something that the customers perceive to fit their needs that isn't duplicated by the competition.
3. Make envelopes stand out—different sizes, colors, closed face (not window). Don't give away the product in envelope copy.
4. In the letter, state the offer immediately and simply—then define it, summarize, restate, and explain the response mechanism. (Two-page letters outperform single pagers.)
5. Make the response device clean and easy to fill out. *Pay for return postage.*
6. Consider supportive materials—a brochure or a "lift note" from someone other than the letter signer.

As with all types of advertising, writing and designing direct-mail campaigns requires specialized expertise. If this expertise isn't available in-house, using outside sources (agencies, free-lancers, and so on) can be a sound investment.

Television Commercials

Because TV advertising is relatively new to many PR managers, there's a greater learning curve involved. Developing a successful spot involves three phases — preproduction decisions, shooting the spot, and editing and finalizing the spot (postproduction). Although most PR managers will be working with agencies to develop spots, the manager will probably want to be heavily involved in the process, given the costs and accountability that go with doing television.

1. *Preproduction decisions.* There are five categories of decisions that must be made before any production can begin:
   - *Talent — national actor, local/regional actor, real person?* There's no right answer, but generally, the more important a role the actor plays in the spot, the more you need an actor with experience doing TV spots (it's nothing like stage or movie acting). If the actor is an extra or has a nonspeaking part, less experience is needed. A lousy actor can ruin even the best script — and voice, physical presence, and the ability work with the camera are critical. Using "real people" can lend a touch of authenticity to a spot, but *very few* amateurs can handle the demands of saying it right in 6.5 seconds. If it's important that the copy be read as written, a professional actor is almost a necessity. Many clients (in this case, the PR manager) take an active role in selecting the talent — either viewing a tape of auditions or actually attending the casting session — rather than letting a director or the agency pick the talent.
   - *Studio or location?* Again, no right answer. Location looks more realistic for "slice of life" spots, but it's much more difficult to control lighting, background noise, and so on, and location shoots can be more expensive than studio shoots. However, there are some hospital scenes that just cannot be replicated with a set.
   - *Film or videotape?* Videotape is cheaper and easier to do; film generally looks better (less harsh lighting, richer color, a better-quality appearance). Consider the budget and the "look" desired, and make the best choice, but if the cheaper choice can't produce a high-quality look, don't do TV spots. Pick a medium that can be afforded.
   - *Production company and director — Hollywood or Pittsburgh?* There's a lot of hype about how a Los Angeles director or a New

York director is critical, but there are dozens of extremely competent, creative directors working with highly professional production companies in cities between the two coasts. Consider budget ("big-time" directors charge more per day and may have to travel a day to get to your city), and look at the reels (sample tapes of spots the director has done). You want creativity and a solid track record of satisfied clients.

- *"Little details" that can ruin a spot—wardrobe, set, and props.* What the actors wear conveys an image—right down to earrings ("those look like rich lady earrings"). Don't count on the talent or the production company to come up with the right wardrobe—it's pretty expensive to stand around on a set while a production assistant goes out to find a different sweater. The same caution applies to props and set decor—the more specific you can be, the fewer the problems that will occur on the day of the shoot.

2. *The shoot.* The following are four principles PR staff members should observe:
   - *Be there.* Although many national clients are content to let the agency represent them when the commercials are being shot, they usually have budgets that allow them to reshoot spots if there's a problem. Unless your agency has been with your health care organization for years, someone from the health care organization should be present at the shoot (to point out that the talent is mispronouncing a medical term, for instance).
   - *Be patient.* Shooting a 30-second spot can take 8 to 10 hours—or more. All of those little details—camera angles, lights, special effects, prop placement, and so on—can make the difference between a spot that looks professional and one that looks amateurish.
   - *Ask a lot of questions, so you learn and understand what's going on, but follow protocol on that set.* Some directors are happy to talk with you during the shoot; others want to stay focused on the talent and the camera and would rather have you talk with the producer or someone from the agency or crew.
   - *Be assertive.* If you see or hear something that bothers you—the way the talent reads a line, lights that cast ugly shadows, whatever—speak up. Listen to the explanations (there may be a good reason), but if it really bothers you, make sure the director understands why and is willing to discuss a compromise or alternative.

3. *Postproduction.* How a spot is edited—each scene selected and sequenced together—and finally produced (music, logos, special effects added) can have as much impact on the finished product as the talent does. Again, it's advisable to be present and have input into these decisions. The more costly alternative is to look at the completed spot and discover something that has to be changed.

The Science of Media Buying

If developing the creative concept is the art of advertising, media buying is the science, although the skill involved varies with the medium. Placing an ad can be as simple as calling the newspaper ad sales rep to come and pick up the Velox of a print ad or as difficult as developing a year-long TV schedule on six stations and aimed at several divergent audiences. Placing magazine, radio, and outdoor ads generally falls somewhere in between, although (it can't be repeated often enough) every market differs.

The three key decisions in media placement are the following:

1. *Who is the target audience?* Whom do we want to see the ad? The more specific we can be, the easier it is to select a medium and a media schedule to reach that audience. "Women over age 18," for instance, is a fairly broad group that would require multiple media and, if television or radio were involved, programs that reach a broad audience (and may be more expensive). A more defined target — professional women ages 25–40 — allows the media buyer to select magazines aimed at working women, TV programs that have a more upscale audience, and so forth.
2. *How many people in this audience do we want to see this ad (reach)?* Are we satisfied if only half the audience sees it, or are we trying for 90 percent? The broader the reach we want, the more media we may need if there isn't one medium that will give us 90 percent.
3. *How many times do we want them to see the ad (frequency)?* With TV or radio ads, research has shown that the consumer must see or hear the ad several times before it has an impact, because the ad is ephemeral — it catches their attention and then it's gone. With a print ad, the reader can read and reread, and even keep the ad, although some repetition is needed to reach people who don't read that issue of the paper or magazine.

The overriding objective with any advertising campaign, whatever the target audience, is sending the message often enough (frequency) to get the audience's attention and help them understand the message, and sending the message to a proportion of the audience (reach) that's large enough to generate desired responses.

In general, long-term approaches are the key to a successful campaign. With a long-term campaign, reach and frequency can be achieved more cost-effectively. Short-term campaigns may produce a blip of responses (calls to the physician referral service increase during the four-week TV campaign but drop off as soon as the ad schedule is completed). But building the ongoing top-of-mind awareness discussed earlier in this chapter and changing or developing preference require time and repeated exposures of the audience to the message.

To save money, many health care organizations handle their own print media placement and may also do outdoor, magazine, and radio placements, rather than using an agency. This can be cost-effective if the health care organization has a staff person who can handle this function, although it's often easier (in terms of details and hassle) to let the agency do it. If the PR staff members are doing the production, they will generally do placement. There are a few examples of health care organizations that have actually created in-house agencies that handle even TV buying — developing an entire media schedule and placing specific spots on specific programs at specific times — but it's rarely cost-effective to purchase the software and train a staff member to do TV buying unless the health care organization is consistently placing heavy TV schedules. For instance, if the hospital is doing $500,000 in TV advertising, the commission paid to the agency for media buying would be $75,000. In this case, training a PR staff member to buy media, dedicating part of his or her salary to that function, and buying the software needed would probably represent a cost savings.

□ Summary

Because marketing communications campaigns are expected to contribute to the measurable success of a service or program of the health care organization, they require careful planning, strategy, and execution. The PR manager must ensure that the campaigns have carefully targeted audiences, clearly stated objectives, research-based strategies, effective creative execution, and a combination of communications methods to achieve the needed reach and frequency.

References

1. Wolinsky, F. D., and Kurz, R. How the public chooses and views hospitals. *Hospital & Health Services Administration* 29(6):59, Nov.–Dec. 1984.
2. Mages, P. Why customer relations programs fail. *Health Marketing* 7(2):1, Mar. 1983.
3. Ireland, R. C. The rise of the externally focused hospital. *Entelechy,* Fall 1985, p. 2.
4. Powills, S. MD influence on consumers waning slightly. *Hospitals* 61(9):44, May 4, 1987.
5. Lavidge, R. A., and Steiner, G. A. A model for predictive measurement of advertising effectiveness. *Journal of Marketing,* Oct. 1961, p. 59.
6. Tosdal, H. *Principles of Personal Selling.* Chicago: Shaw, 1925, p. 61.
7. Inguanzo, J. M., and Harju, M. What makes consumers select a hospital? *Hospitals* 59(6):90, Mar. 16, 1985.

8. Graham, J. Providers not picked by price. *Modern Healthcare*, Nov. 7, 1986, p. 16.
9. Capturing the health care consumer: hearts vs. hamburgers. *Healthcare Marketing Report*, Mar. 1986, p. 16.
10. Powills, S. Central region hungry for info. *Hospitals* 60(13):68, July 5, 1986.
11. Powills, S. Half of physicians say ads are effective. *Hospitals* 61(14):40, July 20, 1987.
12. Koepp, S. Hospitals learn the hard sell. *Time*, Jan. 12, 1987, p. 56.
13. Powills, S. Health care ad exposure picks up. *Hospitals* 61(1):30, Jan. 5, 1987.
14. Ryan, J. A., and Lemmond, G. W. Thinking like a brand manager. *Public Relations Journal* 45(8):26, Aug. 1989.
15. Marketing PR can outperform advertising. *pr reporter* 32(44):3, Oct. 30, 1989.
16. Noakes, C. T. How to mount an effective direct mail campaign. *The Bankers Magazine* 172(1):24–27, Jan.–Feb. 1989.

Suggested Readings

Cooper, P. *Health Care Marketing: Issues/Trends.* Rockville, MD: Aspen Publishers, 1985.

Goldman, J. *Public Relations in the Marketing Mix.* Chicago: Crain Books, 1984.

Health Care Marketing and Public Relations. 16(4), July–Aug., 1990.

Jefkins, F. *Public Relations for Marketing Management.* London: Macmillan, 1984.

Kotler, P., and Clarke, R. *Marketing for Health Care Organizations.* Englewood Cliffs, NJ: Prentice-Hall, 1987.

Ray, M. *Advertising and Communication Management.* Englewood Cliffs, NJ: Prentice-Hall, 1982.

Other Public Relations Methods

The preceding chapters have covered the methods that are most often used in public relations programs. This very brief chapter identifies a variety of other methods that are either more specialized or newly emerging. The list is not exhaustive—PR techniques are evolving so rapidly and so creatively that there is new ground being broken continually. But the list does provide the PR manager with ideas beyond the traditional, ideas that can also inspire creation of hybrids and other new techniques. The best source for more ideas is your peers!

☐ Audiovisual Methods

Audiovisual communication provides the double impact of sight and sound—and with video and films, the added impact of motion. Various types of audiovisual productions—from simple one-projector slide shows with a narrator reading a script to the professionally produced video or film—can be used for:

- Broadcast news releases, either providing a slide or video bite for use by a local station or developing a fully produced video news release that can be released to national media
- Employee orientation, communications, training
- Marketing, as a tool for use by the sales staff or sent as a marketing piece directly to customers including physicians and consumers
- Community relations, as aids to be used by speakers or tour programs or sponsored films or videos to be given to schools and libraries

Audiovisual communications work for audiences with all levels of education and reading capability, and although they may not be used as a primary communications medium, they can be ideal as supplementary vehicles, particularly for employee communications.

The downside of audiovisual is the cost involved in high-quality production and the time commitment involved in developing the vehicles. Doing high-quality production is essential, because audiences raised on television and movies have very sophisticated tastes. Although producing a simple slide show can be handled primarily in-house (public relations doing concepts and scripts, audiovisual or photography shooting the photos, with outside help on reading and recording the audio track and mixing it with music), few health care organizations have in-house capabilities for producing videos. However, a cost-value analysis can show that developing a slide or video show that can be used repeatedly and can free up staff time from repetitive presentations may actually be very cost-effective.

☐ The Telephone as a Public Relations Tool

Communicators are rediscovering the most basic of communications tools: the phone. As a call-in medium, the phone is personalized, as long as the hot line is answered by a person. (Consumers even appear willing to tolerate talking to machines, as long as they can have access to the information they need.) And it allows the health care organization to communicate with those consumers who are genuinely interested in the service or program (persons who are "prequalified" because they've responded to this service in the past) rather than sending the message via advertising or other mass methods to a broad audience of people who are relatively uninterested. Health information lines, physician referral services, "heart lines," and parent help lines are only a few examples of the ways health care PR staff members have embraced the phone as an ideal way to create a link with consumers who are already interested. And staffed or prerecorded message hot lines are ideal employee communications techniques to receive questions or feedback (and a machine can even take the questions) or to quickly dispel rumors and spread truth.

As a call-out medium, the phone again provides for a personal approach, although the proliferation of human and prerecorded marketing calls being received in the average household is beginning to cause consumer irritation. Calls to audiences targeted as potential users of the health care organization's services (newcomers for physician referral lines, upscale women for a women's health center, and so on) allow operators to quickly identify solid prospects. And call-out services can also be used to communicate with discharged and past patients.

With today's harried and stressed consumers, developing programs that require travel—even three blocks—to participate is increasingly difficult. The telephone may fill the personal interaction gap.

☐ Electronic Methods

Although the use of highly specialized electronic communications methods by health care PR departments is extremely limited at this time, the use of computers (both on-line and interactive) and satellite teleconferencing may have some applications for health care organizations. In-house computer mail can be a timely method for employee communications, although often there are departments without access to an on-line computer and employees who are unable to work with the computer. And although the method is ideal for sending "news flash" items throughout the house quickly, it is more appropriate for basic announcements and information rather than for major announcements of change, which should be communicated in person. Satellite teleconferencing can be used by major medical centers announcing medical developments or can be used for interactive continuing education programming linking a number of cities.

☐ Emerging Methods

Wherever there are two or more PR professionals together, there's the possibility of new techniques being created. An intriguing new idea that surfaced in the May–June 1989 issue of *Hospital Marketing and Public Relations*[1] is "cooperative promotional opportunities," working with area firms "that are already capturing significant numbers of the target audience," and developing ways to work with one or more of them to deliver the message. For example, the health care organization could cohost a high-profile event, cosponsor a direct-response program, or piggyback its message onto existing distribution channels. An ophthalmology campaign, for instance, could include a tie-in with a local chain of optical stores for discounts on eyeglasses.

Public relations managers should subscribe to publications that cover "what's news/what's good" in public relations, especially in the world outside health care. These publications can be a never-ending source of ideas and methods that can be adopted and adapted by the health care organization's PR department to add variety and impact to the traditional PR campaigns. Two good publications to start with are: *pr reporter*, P.O. Box 600, Exeter, NH 03833; and *Public Relations Journal*, 33 Irving Place, New York, NY 10003.

Reference

1. Andrews, S. Nontraditional services demand nontraditional marketing. *Hospital Marketing and Public Relations*, May–June 1989, p. 4.

Suggested Readings

Co-op marketing. *Strategic Health Care Marketing* 7(3), Mar. 1990.

Dogen, C. *Understanding and Using Video.* San Francisco: Knowledge Industry, 1985.

Health Care Marketing and Public Relations 16(4), July–Aug., 1990.

Talley, L. Getting high quality video. *Strategic Health Care Marketing* 7(5):8, May 1990.

Employee Communications

After years of too often being taken for granted, employees are emerging as a major—perhaps the most critical—audience for U.S. companies. And health care organizations, which have focused renewed attention on physicians, then on patients, and then on payers (insurers, employers, legislators) are following the trend toward placing as much emphasis on the internal public as on the external publics.

Some of the reasons for this increasing emphasis on employee communications are described by Richard G. Charlton, A.P.R., A.B.C., vice-president for corporate communications at the Parker Hannifin Corporation, in a January 1990 *Public Relations Journal* article aptly titled "The Decade of the Employee."[1] Charlton noted the following factors:

- Companies cannot sustain a good image with external publics if the image hasn't been earned internally. A dissatisfied employee, talking with friends or neighbors, can undercut even the most well-orchestrated external image campaign.
- With the advent of new technology in the workplace, and concurrent economically motivated work-force reductions, fewer employees are producing more work. "Therefore, each employee is proportionately more important to the employer."
- As layers of management have been removed and participative management techniques emphasized, greater responsibility is being placed on the worker, who must have information.
- High turnover can lead to increased overhead, pool product or service quality, and resulting market share and legal problems.

There is one other factor imparting a sense of urgency to the employee relations and communications efforts—the growing shortage of workers. In the 1970s, three million people entered the labor force every year; by the 1990s, that number will drop to 1.3 million a year. The general work force is shrinking, in sheer numbers, and the pool of educated and trained professionals required by the health care industry is also declining. Additionally, the work force is growing increasingly diverse — in the 1990s, 80 percent of the new workers will be women and minorities, adding another challenge for institutions built around white, male value systems. Health care CEOs, like their counterparts in other industries, are focusing even greater attention on employee communications, and health care PR managers are accepting this challenge, beginning by trying to identify the characteristics and concerns of the "new" work force.

☐ Understanding the "New" Work Force

"What do these employees want from me?" paraphrases the refrain of CEOs in health care and other industries. The answer to that question is usually easily available — via national studies, as well as employee attitude and opinion surveys that are routinely conducted by most health care organizations, or through the even easier method of simply talking to employees.

Whatever the source of the information, the answers seem clear and consistent. First of all, it's a different work force — better educated, aspiring to the success symbols seen daily via the mass media, and, for the present, dominated by the baby boom generation, which is 60 percent larger than the preceding generation. This mass of workers in the same age range means that a lesser proportion of them will be able to reach the limited number of top management positions.

A benchmark survey conducted by Sirota, Alper, and Pfau in 1989 asked employees the "what's important to you about your job?" question, with the following responses:[2]

- *Most important*
  1. Safe environment
  2. Good benefits
  3. Open and honest communication
  4. Respect
- *Moderately important*
  1. Performance recognition
  2. Opinions are sought by management
  3. Advancement opportunities
  4. Compensation
- *Least important*
  1. Day-care assistance
  2. Equal employment opportunity program
  3. Challenging work
  4. Decision-making opportunity

These results may be surprising to many managers for several reasons. First, pay doesn't rank in the top category, nor do some of the trendier employee relations programs like day care or getting employees involved in making decisions. Second, three of the most important factors — respect, open and honest communication, and recognition — cost relatively nothing to provide, unlike day-care centers, big pay raises, and heavily funded employee suggestion programs.

Another surprise — 66 percent of the employees surveyed are moderately well satisfied with their pay. Not surprising to most PR people, half of the employees rated management poorly on communications.

In E. Zoe McCathrin's excellent overview of the "new employee communications" field in the July 1989 *Public Relations Journal*,[3] experts interviewed by McCathrin made the following observations about the new work force:

- Employees are concerned about a lack of information about where their companies are going, and why, and how.
- Employees define an effective manager as one who is "willing to listen, and not just talk down."
- Seventy-five percent say free exchange of information — from employees to management, management to employees, and department to department — is very important to them, but only 35 percent say this is happening in their companies.
- Numerous studies in different industries, including the massive 32,000-employee survey conducted by International Association of Business Communications and Towers Perrin, reveal that the majority of employees don't believe that company communication is candid and accurate — two-thirds say it's incomplete and more than half say it's top-down only.

Finally, *Time* magazine's 1989 special report, "Working Scared,"[4] identified concerns about declining loyalty, massive employee discontent, and fear and anxiety on the job that dwarf complaints about communication in terms of critical impact on the survival of U.S. companies. Writer Janice Castro noted, "the dominant mood in a lot of American companies is one of fear and anxiety. . . . In industry after industry U.S. companies have carried out drastic cost-cutting programs and massive layoffs . . . discarded traditional notions about job security, compensation and seniority."

Although these actions have left companies more profitable, or at least able to continue to exist, according to Castro, "businesses may have sown the seeds of a more enduring and costly problem: company loyalty is dying. Even as American business seeks to inculcate a new corporate credo of worker participation and involvement, it is confronting a shell-shocked, apathetic and risk-averse labor force."

Castro noted that in addition to layoffs and downsizing, workers are troubled by the growing practice of "rightsizing," ongoing work-force alterations involving use of more part-time, informal, contract, and contingent workers, and in some industries, week-to-week or even day-to-day adjustments based on demand, which result in employees being called and told "don't come in today." These practices obviously cause anxiety and also destroy work unity morale ("I'm working alongside people I don't even know—every day the group can change"). The end result, described by one laid-off manager: "People see a company slowly disintegrating. They keep their heads down and become part of the furniture."

Predicts Castro, "Companies will have to find ways to inspire new levels of commitment and productivity . . . to restore the tie that binds. Companies must figure out how to make their workers feel like part of the team. If they do not, productivity is likely to fall—or another company will find the way."

Health care organizations encounter other special work force-related problems. Because health care workers tend to be much better educated (as a group) than the average corporate work force, they have much higher expectations and aspirations. "You can't tell a Ph.D. laboratory chemist to just do his job and not ask any questions," observed a hospital operating officer.

Additionally, it's generally agreed that there are much higher stress levels in health care organizations than in other types of companies. The factor making the biggest contribution to that stress level is, of course, the fact that rather than worrying about making a flawed product or insulting a customer, health care workers understand that their work can affect people's health and lives. This stress is particularly acute for the direct patient care employees and is often exacerbated by the personal needs and demands of patients and their families and interactions with demanding physicians. Even the behind-the-scenes workers have been well taught that their work "has an impact on patient care," and when these employees take that message to heart, it can add to their stress level. The pressure of working for a round-the-clock operation, particularly for employees who are forced to work alternate shifts and some weekends, and to be on call when demand rises, heightens an already stressful environment.

Health care employees are also grappling with the shock of finding that their jobs are no longer assured. In the past, health care organizations had done a very good job of communicating a job security, we're-all-part-of-the-family message to employees for decades—and that resulted in shock, outrage, and growing skepticism and cynicism when the first hospital layoffs began. Even nurses, rarely subject to losing their jobs and certainly able to find other work immediately, have had to adjust to a world where "their" unit may be closed because of low census. In such cases, the nursing staff may be assured of jobs — but in other units or on other shifts. And the development of census and acuity-based staffing models means that the full-time nurse can no longer even count on working every day. Other health care employees fear that this demand-based fluctuating staffing will soon be extended to other departments. "If you don't have a full house and they're telling nurses not to come in, pretty soon they're going to realize that they can get along on low-census days without all of my department workers, too," said a hospital housekeeper. In this atmosphere of unmet worker expectations and aspirations, increasing anxiety and decreasing loyalty, the role of employee communications has taken on an increasing importance for the very survival of American companies.

☐ The Role of Public Relations in Employee Communications

Chief executive officers and PR and human resources managers can sum up the role of employee communications in a simple phrase: contribute to increased worker satisfaction. This satisfaction is expected to contribute to increased productivity; decreased absenteeism, turnover, and on-the-job behavioral problems; improved customer service; and fewer employee lawsuits. A 1987 IABC survey of CEOs found that 71 percent of them said that employee communications, by influencing job satisfaction, employee commitment, and productivity, can directly affect the bottom line.[5]

In a 1988 study, corporate communicators identified the following priorities that had been established by the top management of their companies for employee communications:[6]

- *High priority*
  - Improving morale and fostering goodwill between employees and management
  - Informing employees about internal changes
  - Explaining compensation and benefit plans
  - Changing employee behavior toward becoming (1) more quality oriented, (2) more productive, (3) more entrepreneurial
- *Moderate priority*
  - Increasing employee understanding of the company and its (1) products and organization, (2) changing corporate culture, (3) external business environment, including codes and policies regarding corporate ethics

— Encouraging employee participation in community activities
— Increasing employee understanding of major health/social issues or trends affecting them (such as child or elder care, drug abuse, and AIDS)

Who is responsible for achieving these priorities? The PR department? The human resources department? Both? No one? In health care organizations, the responsibility for developing employee communications programs to achieve these priorities is not uniformly assigned. There are a number of models:

1. In some health care organizations, the function is part of the human resources division, which has full-time communicators who handle all employee communications. This responsibility is sometimes part of an organizational development department or function.
2. In other health care organizations, the human resources department may assign responsibility for developing employee communications efforts to a human resources staff member, who works with a PR staff member who actually develops the communications vehicles.
3. Another model assigns primary responsibility to the PR staff, whose members consult and work cooperatively with human resources staff members.
4. And in some other health care organizations, there's uncertainty about who has final responsibility for employee communications, with human resources handling benefits and policy compensation, public relations handling employee publications and events, and operating managers told to "make sure you're communicating with your people."

Clearly, with the importance that employee communications must play in the survival of health care organizations in the 1990s, it's essential that the function be carefully managed. Charlton, in his overview of the changing employee communications field, noted that the trend is toward recognizing employee communications as "an important management responsibility."[7] "Employee communication has ceased to be an illegitimate child," he noted, adding that the function is increasingly being positioned in the PR or corporate communications department.

This positioning came about "when management realized the good sense of having all of the communication oars — external and internal — rowing in the same direction, to achieve maximum synergy and productivity." Splintering the function among several departments, or maintaining a separate function, is no longer effective or affordable, Charlton added. And communications experts almost uniformly recommend that the primary responsibility for developing communications programs should rest with the staff members who are most skilled and expert—the company's PR staff members. Obviously, there must be ongoing and intensive interaction with the human resources staff in terms of message and program development. And creation of an employee communications team that also includes operating administrators and managers who are responsible for the majority of the health care organization's employees helps to broaden the input, the creativity, and the base of support for the program. If the operating administrators don't feel any inclusion in nor ownership of the employee communications effort, they may simply ignore the program or refuse to accept their role in the system.

Because of the importance of the employee communications function, it is ideal for it to be assigned as a full-time responsibility, although in smaller hospitals this may not be possible. An alternative is to create an internal communications function that also includes physician communications. If a staff member cannot be dedicated to employee communications, then the PR manager needs to make it a top priority for his or her personal involvement and supervision.

If the employee communications function is not assigned to the PR department, it is vital that the PR manager urge that it be assigned as a primary responsibility to human resources or another department, rather than simply letting it be handled piecemeal or worse, be ignored. If the function is not part of public relations, the PR manager should make every effort to be involved in the role of communications expert, ensuring that effective message content and methods are selected.

☐ Developing the Effective Employee Communications Program

An effective employee communications program must be comprehensive, well organized, and multifaceted, using a number of methods to send and receive information.

Developing a Comprehensive System

The overriding goal of any employee communications program should be to create a comprehensive, consistent, multifaceted system, rather than a program that's little more than a collection of publications. This system must include a variety of methods, which can include written communications (newsletters, bulletins, letters, manuals, handbooks, fliers, posters), audiovisual communications, special events, and person-to-person communications. These methods must be used in various combinations to send a consistent message to employees *and* to receive input from employees and channel that input back into the management system. Any employee communications program that is one-dimensional—merely sending information to employees—cannot be effective. It is equally as important for the health care organization to listen, to hear the concerns and ideas from employees, as it is to provide information to them.

Development of this employee communications system begins with research—both employee attitude and opinion surveys (usually conducted by the human resources department) and a communications audit designed to identify every single communications channel that exists in the health care organization and to assess how well those channels are working. This audit provides the PR manager with a look at how employees actually receive information, which can often be in ways that are very different from the formally organized communications function. "After we did our research and our audit," said one hospital PR vice-president, "I found that the staff in the housekeeping department were the most active and credible communicators in the hospital. They seemed to know everything that was going on, and passed it along to all other departments as they went through the house on their cleaning rounds. I thought about dumping our employee newsletter and just briefing the housekeepers daily."

The research process should identify: (1) what employees know (to be compared with what information has been sent), (2) how employees are now getting information, and (3) how they would prefer to get information. The research should attempt to gather data from individual work units (departments, patient care units, and so on) to determine if there are variations in awareness and satisfaction levels that need to be addressed specifically.

Once the research is completed, the PR manager can develop method alternatives for review and discussion by the human resources staff, the employee communications team, and the CEO—and it's also highly valuable to seek employee feedback on proposed methods.

Selecting the Best Methods to Send and Receive the Message

There is a vast array of methods available to communicate with employees. Each method has its strengths and liabilities, and the most effective systems use a combination of methods.

Traditional Print Vehicles

Print is still the dominant method, despite increasing illiteracy and research that shows employees prefer other methods. This is due, in part, to tradition—"it's what we've always done"—and in part because written communication is something tangible that employees can hold in their hands (a symbol that the health care organization cares enough to spend money on them) and also something that they can refer to for follow-up. Print vehicles for employee communications include:

- Lengthy magazines or tabloids, including news and feature stories and photos, issued quarterly, semimonthly, or monthly
- Smaller tabloids or newsletters, primarily aimed at conveying news (may include photos), issued more frequently—from monthly to weekly
- Quick news updates, either one-page or smaller format, distributed daily to provide fast-breaking information
- Employee annual reports, lengthier publications that provide a yearly overview and a look ahead
- Paycheck stuffers, often used for compensation and benefit information
- Fliers or posters ("Please post in your department") for timely news or messages that need to be considered on an ongoing basis (safety and customer service messages, for instance)
- Handbooks or manuals that include large amounts of detailed, relatively constant information to which employees may need to refer back

Emerging Audiovisual and Electronic Methods

Although audiovisual and electronic methods are being increasingly used, they are still considered complementary to print. The costs involved and the general lack of in-house capabilities to produce these vehicles in a high-quality way have contributed to the slower-than-predicted use of audiovisual methods for employee communications. Audiovisual and electronic methods used in employee communications include:

- Slide shows—ranging from multiprojector, synchronized-sound shows to simply setting up a projector in the cafeteria to show slides from the employee picnic
- Videos, which can sometimes be produced by in-house staff members
- Films, a method that is used less often owing to costs
- Electronic messaging—using in-house computer networks to send breaking news or daily briefings

Personal and Direct Communications Methods

Employees, via opinion and attitude surveys, have repeatedly expressed their preference for getting information personally (from their supervisors or managers, senior executives, and in small group meetings, in that order), not only because the situation is more personal and the information easier to understand, but also because face-to-face communication provides a chance to ask questions and obtain feedback, compared with print and video, which are basically one-way, outbound communications. Personal communications methods include:

- Large group presentations to announce major changes or to serve an annual report function.
- Small group meetings involving employees and the CEO (often part of an ongoing breakfast or lunch series that is either by invitation, or open to any employee who wants to attend).
- Routine department meetings, when managers or supervisors update employees and receive feedback; meetings that should be part of a controlled chain of information sharing beginning with the CEO and top administrators, moving on to administrators, managers, and supervisors, and finally reaching employees, with employee feedback sent back up the chain. To be successful, this information distribution chain must move quickly—preferably within a day or two, to prevent news from being spread via the grapevine or being stale by the time employees hear it. The CEO's participation in and support of this system is essential. If information is not passed down from that level, the system will be perceived as being ineffective. ("All our department head tells us is stuff about policies and minor changes—if it's important, we won't hear about it until it's in the newspaper.")
- Direct employee question or response programs, including hot lines employees can call to leave questions that are answered via existing channels, or write-in programs in which employees can send comments directly to the CEO or receive personal responses (these are screened by a coordinator, who removes the employee's name before submitting the question to an administrator for a response).

Despite the employee preference for face-to-face communication, these methods are not yet widely nor routinely used and are used far less than print methods. Mike Emanuel, president of Myron Emanuel/ Communications, Inc., a firm specializing in internal communications, says that there's obviously a gap between what employees prefer and what they're getting. "We've substantiated the need for interaction between managers and employees over and over, but it just isn't happening."[8]

One reason why it isn't happening may be that many CEOs, administrators, managers, and supervisors do not feel comfortable or expert at public speaking, or at conducting small group meetings, especially if they are afraid of receiving negative feedback from employees.

The employee communications manager should be responsible for providing training and resources for supervisors and department heads to help them learn how to handle small group meetings. This can be coordinated with in-house organizational development or training staff members, or outside experts can be hired to assist. Providing support materials — outlines, key-point lists, facts and statistics, graphs, and so on — can also help the meeting conveners. If this kind of training to help all "message carriers" in the system communicate effectively is not done, the fabled message entropy will begin to occur. (The CEO understands 100 percent of the message, but as it passes through the vice-presidents, managers, and supervisors, it becomes increasingly garbled, so that by the time it reaches the employees, they're getting only 20 percent of the content.)

The employee communications manager should also monitor the system, doing spot checks to make sure that meetings are being held, and doing periodic research to determine if key messages being sent through the system are being received and retained. This can be done as simply as announcing in an administrative meeting that there's a specific piece of information that needs to be shared with all employees and then checking with a sample of department heads, supervisors, and hourly employees a week later to see if they've heard the message and where they heard it. (If they heard it through the grapevine, the system isn't working.)

The M⁴ Rule

The effective employee communications program is never limited to one method only. The M^4 rule of marketing communications (see chapter 13) also applies to the employee communications program, which will be more effective if it combines a number of methods. Using multiple media maximizes the impact of the message, and each method provides a different way to send the message. Print allows for more details, whereas video adds excitement and the ability to demonstrate. Hearing the message personally from a supervisor or the CEO adds credibility and lets the employees ask questions. In addition, using several different methods maximizes the reach of the communications program. Employees who can't or don't read can watch a video or attend a meeting. Employees who don't want to or can't attend the meetings can take a newsletter home to read. Again, relying on only one channel to communicate with employees automatically lessens the impact of the message.

For example, when a health care organization is making changes in its benefits program or taking another significant action, the following campaign model, using already existing communications channels, would ensure the maximum message reception and retention:

- *Day 1.* The CEO and human resources vice-president brief administrators and solicit feedback to help clarify and refine message content (assuming that the concepts and alternatives have been discussed previously with this group and the group has had input into or participated in the final decisions). The employee communications manager finalizes a draft of a written communications piece — an issue of the regular newsletter, a briefing sheet, or a special communication.
- *Day 2.* Managers and supervisors are backgrounded at a meeting with the CEO and human resources vice-president. Administrators should also attend so they hear the presentation and the questions and answers. All receive copies of the written communications piece.

  Employee meetings are conducted by the CEO and/or human resources vice-president and held several times on all shifts. (A tight timing schedule is needed to prevent message lag and/or "leaks" preceding the CEO's meetings, as occurs when one or two supervisors discuss the changes with their employees who in turn leak word through the grapevine. Additionally, if it's a major announcement, once it has been shared with managers, the press may soon hear about it, and employees must be notified before they read it in the paper.)

  Employees receive copies of the written communications piece.

  One of the presentations is videotaped for use in department meetings for employees who couldn't attend the presentation and for individual viewing by other employees.

  Details of the message are available through on-line electronic mail (if available).
- *Days 3–4.* Managers and supervisors have small group meetings with their employees to repeat the message, answer questions, clarify, and ask for feedback.
- *Day 5.* Feedback flows back to human resources and/or public relations. "Answers to commonly asked questions" sheet is prepared and available on day 6.
- *Week 2.* Managers and supervisors discuss events in regularly scheduled departmental meetings.
- *Week 3.* Spot research is conducted to assess awareness and retention of the message and to identify any misinformation or problems that may be arising. Results are shared with administrators verbally and/or in writing, depending on how extensive the information is, and they share it with supervisors and department heads.
- *Week 4.* Employee periodical carries follow-up story clarifying, adding any new information, and so forth.
- Follow up in regularly scheduled department meetings.

This type of multifaceted approach should not be used only when there's a major change to announce. The system of print, video/electronic, and personal communications methods must be in place and functioning smoothly so that it can be used for major announcements, but the system's primary function should be to communicate the kind of day-to-day news that keeps employees feeling informed.

Defining the Messages

Health care employees today may enjoy reading profiles of fellow employees or hearing reports about grants that the health care organization has received, but they are more interested in hard news that concerns them, such as:

- How the health care organization is responding to competitors' activities
- Details about the health care organization's strategic plan
- Expectations about their performance
- Ways they can be involved in making the health care organization successful
- Advice on productivity and safety
- Census, utilization, and budget reports—good or bad
- Details about progress and failures
- Information about the external environment and how it affects the health care organization
- Interpretations of how the health care organization's actions, changes, and so on will affect their working environment, their work, and their opportunities for personal growth
- Details on all kinds of internal changes (moving a department from one floor to another may seem like a minor issue, but the people who work in, visit, and utilize that department want to know what's happening as well as when and how)
- Insights into the "whys" of the health care organization's actions and administrative decisions

The last category of message information is among the most important in terms of gaining employee support and cooperation. The *why* is equally as important as the *what*. For example, if the health care organization has to move employee parking to a site several blocks away from the health care facility, that move will probably irritate or even anger employees no matter how far in advance it is announced or how many details (such as maps and shuttle bus information) are included.

If, on the other hand, the announcement includes the items in the following list, then the decision will probably still generate irritation, but employees will be less angry, more understanding, and more willing to be cooperative, rather than reacting with an attitude of "those administrators don't care about us at all."

- Information on the reasons behind the move (for example, construction of new surgery will close patient parking lot; choice was either to make sick and/or elderly patients park far away or to ask employees to make the sacrifice)
- Details on all of the alternatives that were considered and why they were rejected (costs to build closer temporary lot would mean reducing budget in some other area; inconveniencing patients could mean loss of market share and is inconsistent with mission of concern for patients)
- Frank comments from the administrators who made the decision about the difficulty of the decision, factors that had to be weighed, and empathy for employees (plus facts that tardiness rules will be relaxed, that administrators will be parking in same lot, and so forth)

Employees also like to receive practical information that they can use in their personal lives—such as wellness, financial planning, and child-rearing tips—but this information can't be the sole focus nor can it take the place of substantive information about what the health care organization is doing, and why.

In addition to substantive content, the process of message development should be sensitive to the diversity of today's work force. This diversity means that employees bring very different values and expectations to their jobs, values and expectations that will affect the way they understand and respond to messages—and this diversity of response can be very confusing and/or frustrating to managers. "I told my employees they were getting a 4 percent raise, and all they wanted to do was complain about not being treated with respect by the doctors," said a veteran head nurse. With her "you work hard to get rewarded with an annual raise" value system, she had a hard time understanding 25-year-old B.S.N.s to whom a 4 percent raise is not a lot of money, and whose education has led them to expect to be part of a physician–nurse care team. This divergence of values is often most pronounced when CEOs, who believe that employees are most concerned with money and benefits, are surprised when employees take money and benefits for granted and want to talk about participation and involvement.

Employee communications managers must take this diversity into account when framing the "why" messages to employees and must rely on personal, survey, and focus group research to gain insights into the employees' values and expectations. These insights can be used in developing communications messages and in helping managers and supervisors gain a better understanding of their employees so that they can handle personal communications more effectively.

One other key consideration in message content and development is reality. If the employee communications program overpromises candor, teamwork, involvement, participation, openness, and "family," when the CEO and/or administrators are not ready to deliver, the result will be worse than it would have been without such statements of commitment. Some health care human resources and PR managers have forged ahead of their CEOs and management teams, communicating a philosophy of change and involvement that is clearly what employees want and expect, and then have had to cope with employee disillusionment, which can turn into renewed skepticism and cynicism.

Conversely, the PR manager may also need to counsel the CEO who likes to deliver speeches about participation and open communication but then refuses to share planning or budget information with employees. Employees continually observe administrative behavior, testing to see if actions match words. Once they discover inconsistencies, they become skeptical and eventually refuse to believe anything they're told by the CEO or through the communications system. If the PR manager knows that the CEO is uncomfortable or unwilling to operate in an open, forthcoming way, the PR manager can counsel and advise and encourage the CEO to change this style, but the PR manager must also ensure that inaccurate messages and overpromises are not included in the communications messages.

□ Special Employee Communications Challenges

In addition to managing the comprehensive, ongoing employee communications program, the PR staff may also be involved in areas of emerging significance, such as training, recruitment, and employee relations activities. Because these functions are viewed as very important to the health care organization's success, the involvement of the PR staff can be a plus for the department in terms of its strategic positioning as an essential part of the health care organization's management team.

Training

The PR manager can be an invaluable resource in helping the human resources or education staff develop training programs, systems, and materials. Although the person responsible for training must develop the content, the PR staff members have the communications expertise that can save time and money, contribute to the effectiveness of the programs, and add a level of quality and professionalism that enhances the image of the in-house training programs.

Recruitment

Recruiting employees is becoming a major challenge for the health care human resources staffs and the PR staff members can support the process in a number of ways, including:

- Conducting audience research with prospective employees
- Developing positioning and creative strategies that appeal to prospective employees
- Creating materials—brochures, displays, audiovisual shows, giveaway items, ads—for use by recruiters
- Developing or working with the human resources staff to develop special events aimed at prospective employees
- Personally participating in the recruitment process by attending events, meeting with prospects, and so forth, when the human resources department is short-handed

In many health care organizations, the recruitment function may be fragmented (someone in human resources has it as one of six responsibilities, whereas nursing has its own recruiter, and department heads try to do their own hunting), or it may be conducted using methods from the 1950s or 1960s (the standard help-wanted ads and a basic brochure). The analytic, strategic, and creative skills of the PR staff members can make a significant difference in how effective the health care organization's recruitment efforts can be.

Employee Relations Activities

Employee relations efforts today may include the traditional—summer picnic, Christmas party, service awards dinner—but human resources staff members are trying to re-create these events and develop new ways to recognize and reward employees via special activities. Even though many PR managers have traditionally tried to stay away from taking on responsibility for these programs (they're hard-to-do, time-consuming, and thankless tasks), the PR staff members can be invaluable resources in terms of creative ideas and approaches. As with recruitment, the development of effective employee relations programs is seen as an emerging priority for today's health care organizations, and if the PR staff participates in this effort, it not only benefits the health care organization but also enhances the PR department's image as contributing to the bottom line.

☐ Summary

Employee communications is going to be a major concern of all employers in the 1990s and a particular concern to health care organizations. Health care organizations are facing a shortage of skilled, trained employees in a number of fields as well as a need to motivate existing employees to help contain costs while maintaining quality of care. Although many experts predict that there will be a "PR versus HR war" over who controls the employee communications function, the savvy PR manager will work in partnership with the human resources staff to develop comprehensive communications systems that go beyond the employee newsletter and the annual picnic. An experienced PR staff can bring research, analytical, and communications skills to the process of developing an effective program to help employees understand and support the institution's goals.

References

1. Charlton, R. G. The decade of the employee. *Public Relations Journal* 45(1):26, Jan. 1990.
2. What do employees want most today? *pr reporter* 32(24):3, June 12, 1989.
3. McCathrin, E. Z. Beyond employee publications: making the personal connection. *Public Relations Journal* 45(7):14, July 1989.
4. Castro, J. Where did the gung-ho go? *Time* 134(11):52, Sept. 11, 1989.
5. McCathrin.
6. Restructuring: good and bad news for employee communications. *Public Relations Journal* 45(4):6, Apr. 1989.
7. Charlton.
8. McCathrin, p. 16.

Suggested Readings

D'Aprix, R. D. *Communication for Productivity.* New York City: Harper and Row, 1982.

Lewis, P. *Organizational Communication: The Essence of Effective Management.* Columbus, OH: Grid, 1980.

Reuss, C., and Silvis, D., editors. *Inside Organizational Communication.* New York City: Longman, 1985.

Relationships with Special Audiences: Physicians, Payers, and Legislators

Although health care organizations have numerous stakeholders, there are three audiences that have special significance and should be addressed in every public relations program: physicians, payers, and legislators. This chapter will describe these audiences and discuss ways in which the PR staff can direct the health care organization's efforts to develop relationships with those audiences.

□ The Physician Audience

For decades, health care organizations took physicians pretty much for granted. The role of the physician in bringing patients to the institution was clear, but because there were plenty of patients and abundant revenues, the health care administrator didn't spend much time thinking about what was an ideal situation. As the situation changed, and health care organizations were forced to compete for patients and revenues, many organizations heeded the siren song of consumer marketing.

"Since 1965, the physician as primary distribution channel for the hospital has begun to erode significantly," noted an article in *Health Care Strategic Management* in 1986.[1] "The dominant influence of doctors over patients has eroded," stated *Cost Containment Newsletter*, a message that was echoed in numerous articles in trade journals and health care publications.[2] Research studies showed that patients were "controlling" their health care decisions to a greater and greater degree.[3] That message was taken so literally, and was so well heeded, that by the early 1980s, numerous health care organizations were spending thousands of dollars a year on consumer marketing activities, whereas medical staff relations efforts were limited to a monthly newsletter and an annual dinner with an open bar. By the mid-1980s, however, more sophisticated and detailed research showed that although consumers stated they were playing a greater role (and perceived that they were being more involved *than they used to be*), in fact, physicians were still controlling anywhere from 50–80 percent of the admission decisions.[4]

Health care administrators began to realize that they had over-reacted to the "consumer dominant" market theories, especially when they analyzed the role of the physician in the consumer health care purchase decision model discussed in chapter 13. That model, APOC (awareness, preference, opportunity to make a choice, choice), can be affected by physicians at every step.

- *Awareness.* The physician is the primary source of information for many people and serves as a secondary/reinforcing or verifying source for others.
- *Preference.* The physician is a key authority figure for many people and can provide the "seal of approval" they want before they develop a preference.
- *Opportunity to make a choice.* The physician can deter consumers from seeking a health care organization's program, by refusing to admit to that program or by literally requiring consumers to use a particular hospital's service.
- *Choice.* Consumers now have greater opportunity to interact with their physicians and make their wishes known, but the majority will not insist on their choice of health care facility if it means changing physicians.

Health care administrators, who for years had paid scant attention to selling to customers and to distribution channels and then had bypassed the existing distribution channels (physicians) to try to directly attract users, now moved with a vengeance to develop programs to attract, satisfy, and retain medical staff members. Those programs ranged from the simple to the sublime. Robert Rubright of Washington University described the cutting-edge physician relations program as including a complete physician data base, a physician referral program, a director of medical affairs with physician practice support staff, practice enhancement services, a young physicians' section, a guest relations program aimed at physicians' needs, and physician inclusion in all major programs, services, and events.[5]

John Horns, nationally recognized for developing an extraordinarily comprehensive medical staff development program, and his co-worker Chris Schaefer described the components of that program during a presentation at a 1987 seminar: computer networks, practice management services, physician service liaisons, group buying, banking services, temporary staffing services, office staff recruitment and training, biomedical engineering support, printing, physician referral service, advanced admissions program—in addition to the communications and social events programs that most hospitals have.[6] Between a program with that kind of scope and the 1970s newsletter/annual dinner model, there are many variations—but all have the same focus: building relationships with current and potential medical staff members and referring physicians.

The PR manager should take a lead role in developing and supporting these programs. Although in some health care organizations PR managers have responsibility for marketing, and thus direct supervision for total physician relations programs, in other organizations a separate physician relations department handles all physician communications, with input from public relations. The more common model seems to be a discrete physician relations function (which may be part of marketing or an existing medical staff affairs office), with public relations responsible for handling routine hospital communications to physicians, marketing communications programs to promote referrals to medical staff members, communications projects for medical staff recruitment and marketing programs, and counseling programs for physicians on PR issues (as described in chapter 2).

Communicating with Medical Staff Members

Consultant J. Daniel Beckham identified two primary reasons health care organizations should pay attention to communicating with physicians:[7]

- "Familiarity with a hospital and an established 'sense of belonging' are big roadblocks to shifting physician loyalties." Ongoing medical staff communications programs can heighten that sense of belonging and familiarity.
- "Poor communication is a primary source of physician dissatisfaction." Physicians are interested in two types of communication—clinical and organizational—the second of which recognizes the physicians' role as stakeholders.

Beckham also notes that the physician communications program must be "actively managed," not just allowed to happen or divided up among numerous staff members. Clearly the PR manager is the person to manage this function.

A prerequisite to creating a physician communications program is research to develop a solid understanding of the values, motivations, concerns, and needs of the health care organization's medical staff members. This is an audience that has changed tremendously—to the point of being covered in a *Time* magazine cover story titled "Sick and Tired."[8] As described in chapter 2, today's physicians are hardly a homogenous group, and the communicator must understand the characteristics of the subgroups that are part of that larger audience. Because physician attitudes and opinions vary from community to community and even from institution to institution, it is essential that sophisticated survey and focus group research be conducted with the health care organization's medical staff, and that for this research a diverse group of staff members be studied, including heavy admitters, splitters, and rare users.

In addition to this formal research, the PR manager is advised to spend some time informally with physicians, to get an idea of how they feel—about being physicians, about their patients, about their lives, and secondarily, about the health care institution. Once this research is completed and the PR manager has a good understanding of the physician audiences, messages can be developed that address the general concerns of the medical staff and, through segmented communications channels, the needs and concerns of specific subgroups.

A wide range of methods can be used to reach the physician audience: publications, newsletters, personal visits, meetings and special events, videos, audiotapes, and so on. The keys to selecting effective communications methods are actually fairly simple:

- "Physicians are dyslexic," said John Horns,[9] noting that messages have to be repeated, and repeated, and repeated, literally year after year. This is largely a result of the physicians' incredibly busy schedules, the huge amount of information they must process, and the kind of stress levels that block reception of messages. The PR manager should have a list of key messages that the health care organization wants to send to physicians, which should be repeated in nearly every communications vehicle, albeit in a different style.
- There is no single best method for communicating with physicians. You have to use multiple media (just like the M^4 rule in marketing communications described in chapter 13), not only to maximize the impact of the message, but also to simply reach the majority of the staff. Some physicians don't read any of the health care organization's newsletters but do check the bulletin boards. Others don't read anything but are intrigued with listening to tapes in their cars. Some routinely attend staff and department meetings. And the only way you're going to reach some is by personally visiting them in their offices. A one-method communications program is doomed to failure.
- The physician's office staff members play a significant role in communicating with him or her. They can actually be the *communicator,*

screening and selecting information to be presented to the physician; an *influencer*, adding their support to a message the health care organization is sending; or a *barrier*, either by not sending the message or by passing it along with a negative endorsement. Although office staff members enjoy gifts and being wined and dined, they're also pretty quick to spot patronization or manipulation. The special treatment needs to be accompanied by an ongoing program of visits and communications aimed directly at the office staff.

If the health care organization's messages are framed to touch the multiple and different needs and concerns of the medical staff, are repeated consistently and sent through a variety of channels, and are supported and enhanced by the physician's office staff, the communications program is positioned to be successful.

Marketing for and to Physicians

Another key function for the PR manager is developing physician marketing communications programs, both those the health care organization uses to promote the medical staff to potential patients and those that are used by the physician relations staff to recruit physicians. Many physicians—and the majority of consumers, according to national research—are still skeptical, nervous, or concerned about physicians directly promoting themselves to consumers via advertising. They are much more comfortable with the idea of the health care organization doing the promotion, generating the consumer interest, and then funneling the referrals to the medical staff members.

Today, physician referral services are in existence at the majority of hospitals, and promoting those services is a major task for the PR department. Finding a niche for a service that is very much like every other hospital's service can be difficult. Some hospitals try to differentiate their referral services—staffing the service with registered nurses, providing all kinds of health information, catering to a specific type of referral—and others rely on different creative approaches to catch consumer attention. Among the approaches: slogans, jingles with catchy music, cute names or phone numbers that spell out words like DOCS, and humorous ads or ads that target specific audience segments (older consumers whose physicians are retiring, newcomers, young adults who don't have a physician, people who want second opinions, new HMO members, and so on).

Whatever the promotional approach, the key to a successful physician referral program is customer service—both to consumers and medical staff members. Consumers want a range of physicians so their specific needs can be met. Physicians want to be treated fairly in terms of referrals.

In addition to promoting physicians through referral services, health care PR managers may also be involved in assisting physicians in marketing themselves via patient satisfaction programs, new patient acquisition efforts, and promotion and PR efforts. A 1988 survey of physicians by National Research Corporation showed that marketing and advertising were being provided to physicians by 44 percent of the hospitals surveyed and that those services were the number-one new service being requested by physicians.[10]

The PR manager needs to be cautious in terms of becoming committed to these efforts. Although they are very valuable in terms of building physician loyalty, they can quickly eat up hours of PR staff time. If the physician relations program manager feels it is essential to provide these services free to medical staff members, then that program may have to provide budget support for an additional staff member or a portion of a PR staff member's time. Alternatives are for the physician to pay the health care organization for the services or for the PR manager to assist and advise the physician in hiring a free-lancer or an agency.

Finally, the PR manager may also be responsible for developing communications programs to help recruit new medical staff members and/or attract referrals from regional physicians. These programs range from glossy recruitment brochures and regional physician newsletters to slide shows and videos, from special weekend extravaganzas (all expenses paid) that combine continuing medical education with social events for physicians and their spouses to a vast array of "stuff"—clocks and flashlights and key rings and mugs and pens with the physician's birthday on them, and on and on and on. The PR staff can provide the communications expertise to make these programs successful and sustaining.

Beyond Communications: Advising the Top Management

A communications program by itself cannot build positive physician relations. Even if the PR manager is not responsible for the total physician relations effort, it is incumbent on the PR manager, in the senior management counseling role, to advise the CEO to develop what Dan Beckham calls "the physician-focused hospital." Beckham advises hospitals to do the following:[11]

- Implement physicians' needs assessment
- Regard the physician as a customer—demonstrate your personal commitment to meeting physicians' needs
- Systemize communication
- Concentrate expertise to expand physician practices

- Be committed to physician convenience
- Be prepared to commit human and financial resources
- Develop a well-integrated marketing plan

William R. Fifer, M.D., clinical professor of medicine and public health at the University of Minnesota, said that physicians must be fully involved in the decision-making process—in strategic planning, marketing, and resource allocation.[12] The PR manager must help the CEO achieve this full physician involvement, which forms the basis of successful relationships with medical staff members. And these relationships are increasingly likely to include working together to approach another key audience—payers.

☐ The Payer Audience

As described in the introductory chapter of this book, payers—employers and governmental bodies that pay for the health care provided to employees and Medicare and Medicaid recipients—have become the newest audience to demand the attention of health care executives, a demand reflected in payers' active steps to have an impact on and to control some aspects of the health care system. "Employers are now becoming managers of risk, cost and quality," according to Robert E. Patricelli, former deputy undersecretary of the Department of Health and Human Services.[13] Employers are using a broad range of methods to try to keep their health care costs from rising as rapidly as they have in the past—methods that have a direct impact on hospitals' admissions and revenues. Those methods range from pushing employees toward outpatient care to limiting lengths of stay, from increasing copayments and deductibles to offering health maintenance organizations (HMOs) and preferred provider organizations (PPOs) that only involve selected hospitals and to directly contracting with hospitals for discounted rates in return for delivering volume.

Health care organizations have responded to these employer initiatives in a number of ways: creating their own HMOs or PPOs, trying to control inappropriate utilization by working with the medical staff, developing single hospital–physician entities to contract with buyers, and actively pursuing direct contracts with volume buyers. In a landmark program in Dallas, seven major hospitals, a medical school, and business leaders banded together to form a system with the aim of direct contracting for business from employers across the United States.[14]

Although the primary health care provider selection factor for employers is based on costs, the experiences of health care organizations that have negotiated with employers indicate that the organization's reputation, image, and perceived "standing" in the community can have an impact on buying decisions, especially when prices are fairly comparable. Thus, it's important that health care organizations ensure that the corporate leaders to whom they may be selling are very familiar with and have a favorable image of the organization.

Because business leaders receive their information in very different ways than does the general public, assuming that a general public awareness and preference campaign will reach and affect business leaders is risky. One hospital discovered this when executives were asked to make presentations to the CEOs of the community's major employers who were making decisions about what hospitals to contract with. The major tertiary care competitor was the "carriage trade" hospital, which had always attracted the upper-class segment of the patient market. After the PR vice-president presented the hospital's capabilities and noted that the hospital was the only one in the area to provide a full-service heart program with all board-certified physicians, the CEOs' questions revealed that they had been almost totally unaware of the hospital's capabilities, despite an extensive consumer advertising and PR program that had achieved wide awareness and preference among the general community. In addition, the competing hospital's reputation with this corporate audience was so strongly positive that they refused to believe that this hospital's heart program was not equal to, or better than, the presenting hospital's. "Your facts are wrong," the PR vice-president was told. The CEOs also ascribed to the competing hospital several services that were actually provided at the presenting hospital. When the decision was made, the presenting hospital was not chosen; the competing hospital was. Costs were a factor, but clearly the competing hospital had created such overwhelmingly positive awareness and preference levels with these corporate executives that they simply couldn't imagine not including that hospital.

Just as consumer research has shown, image can have an impact on buying decisions, even if those decisions are primarily price-driven. And health care organizations are increasingly going to be competing for employer support—through direct contracts or inclusion in HMOs and PPOs. For that reason, the PR manager must ensure that corporate and insurance company executives and decision makers are very well informed about the hospital's capabilities, areas of excellence, and unique services that should be available to the corporations' employees.

The first step in this process is, of course, research—compiling a detailed data base of information on corporate and insurance executives, benefits managers, and other key decision makers. Informal "what's this guy like" research should be conducted to determine the values and management style of the CEOs (who tend to involve their benefits managers in the contracting decisions, but may also be very involved themselves and often actually control the process).

The PR manager should then develop a multifaceted communications campaign designed to build awareness of the health care organization's strengths, capabilities, unique programs, and ongoing efforts and successes in cost containment. The health care organization needs to position itself as a medical leader or provider that meets a unique market need and as a health care organization that's fiscally responsible.

Among the methods to send this message and create this image are:

- Briefings and small (very small) group meetings with corporate leaders — conveniently scheduled and located, with a specific focus that goes beyond "getting to know each other"
- Periodic newsletters that are concise (very concise), focused on a specific item of interest to the corporate executives
- Strategically placed ads — in business publications or on pages of the daily newspaper — touting the health care organization's cost-containment message
- Personal interactions between the CEO and corporate leaders, through attending country club activities, participating in upscale civic activities (the major donor to the museum or symphony, for example), and ensuring that the health care organization's executives are serving on the same civic boards as the corporate leaders (the objective here is to develop the first-name relationships with the CEOs that create a sense of trust and familiarity)

Additionally, the PR manager should work with the financial staff to ensure that the health care organization's proposals and presentations are effective and that the financial staff members are comfortable and expert in both presenting and negotiating (and if they aren't, make sure they get help). A CFO who is perceived as abrasive, who mumbles or can't seem to find the data that are requested, or who can only talk numbers when the CEOs want to talk capabilities and quality, is a problem.

☐ The Legislative Audience

In addition to concentrating communications efforts on corporate payers, the PR manager may also need to take the lead in developing effective communications with the people who write the laws and regulations and who make decisions about the Medicare and Medicaid funding that is so vital to the health care organization's survival. To cite sources or lists of how government can affect health care organizations is needless; everyone who works in health care is painfully aware of the regulatory and financial impact of city, state, and federal governments on every facet of health care operations.

What's surprising is how few health care organizations have ongoing, effective legislative relations programs. While legislators haven't exactly been the forgotten audience, most health care organizations' relationships with them are limited to contact when there is a specific piece of legislation that threatens the health care organizations. Most corporations have active and highly sophisticated legislative relations/ public affairs programs that involve employees, retirees, suppliers, wholesalers and distributors, and even customers as allies, according to *Purview.* [15] Many of these programs use computer software to identify and reach constituent groups that are asked to support the corporation's legislative efforts. Few health care organizations have anything remotely approaching what is a fairly routine function for large companies—despite the fact that legislative actions often have a far greater impact on health care organizations than they do on businesses.

Health care organizations have tended to assume that the American Hospital Association or the state hospital association lobbyists can do it alone—a mistaken assumption. Although these expert lobbyists do an effective job making sure that the health care industry's positions (when the health care organizations as a group can agree on a position) are communicated to legislators, individual health care organizations and their constituencies must demonstrate the kind of grassroots power that legislators respect.

As described in chapter 3, many health care organizations' legislative relations efforts fall to planners (because legislators pass regulations and planners have to deal with regulators) or are simply ignored unless there's a critical issue. This is hardly the way to develop relationships with people who can shape the health care organization's future.

The PR manager needs to take the lead in establishing a formal legislative relations program, whether it reports directly to or is part of the institutional PR program or whether it reports to another staff function. Legislative relations are too important to be an afterthought or a function that is only sporadically executed. Legislators are far less inclined to respond to constituent organizations that they only hear from every other year and only when there's a major problem.

The basic steps in setting up a formal legislative relations program and building legislative relationships include the following:

1. Know who the health care organization's legislators are—federal, state, and local. A remarkably large number of heath care managers

can't even identify all of their district's state representatives and senators. A detailed data bank needs to be compiled, including the legislators' committee assignments, voting record, background, and biographical information. This kind of homework is essential.

2. Set up meetings with the CEO and the health care organization's legislators and city officials. Face-to-face contact is crucial, and this should not wait until there is a critical issue. The PR manager can be up front about the meetings —"we want to get to know you and to have you know about us."

3. Get to know the legislators' staff members — field reps at their local offices and administrative assistants in the statehouse and federal offices. These staff members, especially at the federal level, can exert a great amount of control over the representative's or senator's schedule and position on an issue. Often you have to sell the administrative assistant or chief aid first, because they have to be protective of the legislator's time.

   One way to develop good relationships with the staff is to be helpful. Offer to provide background information for their constituent newsletters (and make sure it's accurate). Offer the legislator the chance to address the health care organization's employees, medical staff members, board members, or other large, influential gatherings. This gives the health care organization's audiences a chance to ask questions and get to know the legislator and gives the legislator a chance for exposure.

4. Make sure your state hospital association keeps you updated on the key issues and positions of your state and federal representatives.

5. Consider establishing key contact programs, modeled after those used by corporations, in which line or staff managers are given part-time public affairs responsibilities, are extensively trained, and are assigned to develop relationships with specific legislators.

6. When meeting with a legislator about a specific bill or issue, ensure that everyone participating in the meeting is prepared. Legislators spend a lot of time listening to proficient, skilled lobbyists who can effectively and persuasively present a case. The health care organization's representatives need to know the details of the bill — number, sponsors, provisions, progress through the committee system — so that the legislator or assistant doesn't have to spend time finding that information. Know what the opposition is saying and present counterarguments. Present specific examples of how the bill will hurt *people* — not hurt health care organizations, which many legislators perceive as inefficient, overfunded, whiny organizations. Position the health care organization as a representative of the people — the legislator's constituents. Personal examples, with names

of real people, are effective. Make sure you bring written summaries and background information to leave behind.

7. Don't rely on massive letter-writing campaigns — they've been done
to the point of being ineffective. Members of congress receive more
than 300 million pieces of mail a year — even boxes of letters don't
get much attention anymore, because legislators are quite aware
of the machinations of letter-writing campaigns. Mailgrams or
phone calls are better, although if there's an equal level of communication from those on the other side of the issue, the campaign's impact can be negated.

8. Conduct briefings for legislators at the health care organization
at least yearly — and make your schedule fit theirs. Update them
on changes and achievements, and share your position on any pending or potential issues.

9. Involve political leaders in your health care organization's board.
Few legislators have time to accept a board assignment, and some
feel it is a conflict of interest, but political leaders (chairmen of
the major parties' county political organizations, for instance)
generally have lines of influence to elected officials.

10. Take the lead in getting health care organizations to work together
on key issues. One health care organization can have only limited
impact — and legislators are quick to ask, "What are the other health
care organizations in the city (region/state) doing about the issue?"
In the aggregate, health care organizations are the major employer
in many cities. Make sure legislators understand that clout.

11. Focus the health care organization's message on people. David M.
Kinzer, former CEO of the Massachusetts Hospital Association,
points out that recent hospital efforts to secure more equitable
funding have convinced many legislators "that all hospitals care
about is money. This problem is now much worse than it was
before. Our messages aren't transmitting much compassion. Our
credibility is down. Many politicians simply don't believe hospitals."[16] For instance, instead of the national "Elect to Protect Medicare" campaign, which translated into "protect hospital funds" to
many legislators, perhaps the theme should have been a creative
version of "Protect Sick and Old People."

There are a number of excellent publications that the PR manager
can use to become more familiar with public affairs activities, two of
which are cited in the suggested readings at the end of this chapter.
Although there may not be strong pressure from within the health care
organization to develop a legislative relations program, the PR manager
needs to create an understanding of the value such a program can have
for the organization.

☐ **Summary**

As with employee communications, building relationships with special audiences is an area of emerging importance to U.S. health care organizations. The PR manager who can step forward to provide leadership in developing relationships with physicians, the corporate community, and legislators has the opportunity to solidify his or her role and value to the institution. Whether or not the health care organization has an organized physician relations program, the PR manager should be involved in creating focused communications programs designed to reach the highly diverse physician audience. Similarly, effective PR techniques should be focused on building awareness and preference among corporate leaders who will increasingly be involved in making decisions about what health care organizations their companies will use as providers. Finally, PR managers should take the lead in developing consistent, ongoing communications programs aimed at the legislators whose decisions can affect the health care organization's very survival.

References

1. Nich, D. L., and Meyers, V. W. Why the traditional hospital won't survive. *Health Care Strategic Management* 4(9):24, Sept. 1986.
2. Advertising: is it integral to hospital marketing? *Cost Containment Newsletter*, Sept. 11, 1984, p. 5.
3. Kurz, R. S., and Wolinsky, F. D. Who picks the hospital: practitioner or patient? *Hospitals & Health Services Administration* 30(2):99, Mar.–Apr. 1985.
4. Physicians continue to play key role in health care decisions. *Health Care Competition Week*, May 12, 1986, p. 3.
5. Rubright, R. Hospitals focus on physician relations. *Health Progress* 68(7):69, Sept. 1987.
6. Horns, J., and Schaefer, C. A. Presentation before Society for Hospital Planning and Marketing, Third National Forum on Medical Staff Marketing, Oct. 26, 1987.
7. Beckham, J. D. The dynamics of physician utilization. *Healthcare Executive*, Sept.–Oct. 1988, p. 17.
8. Gibbs, N. Sick and tired. *Time*, July 31, 1989.
9. Horns and Schaefer.
10. Jensen, J. Physician liaison programs: what's working. *Healthcare Executive* 3(5):39, Sept.–Oct. 1988.
11. Beckham.
12. Fifer, W. R. The hospital medical staff of 1997. *Quality Review Bulletin* 13(6):196–97, June 1987.
13. Patricelli, R. E. Employers as managers of risk, cost and quality. *Health Affairs* 6(3):75, Fall 1987.

14. Simnacher, J. Good medicine. *Dallas Morning News,* July 5, 1989, p. D-1.
15. Winning at the grassroots. *Purview* [supplement to *pr reporter* 32(9):1, Feb. 27, 1989].
16. Kinzer, D. M. The future of the hospital association mission. *Hospitals* 63(10):26, May 20, 1989.

Suggested Readings

Coan, G., editor. *Sierra Club Political Handbook.* San Francisco: Sierra Club, 1979.

Dominiquez, G. *Government Relations: A Handbook for Developing and Conducting a Company Program.* New York City: John Wiley and Sons, 1982.

Gibbs, N. Sick and tired. *Time,* July 31, 1989.

Goldstein, D. E., and McKell, D. C. *Medical Staff Alliances: How to Build Successful Partnerships with Your Physicians.* Chicago: American Hospital Publishing, 1990.

Wagelschmidt, J. S. *The Public Affairs Handbook.* New York City: Amacom, 1982.

Special Challenges: Ethical and Legal Issues

Every organization must operate within acceptable ethical and legal standards, but in health care, that responsibility takes on even greater importance because the health care organization's "product," as it were, directly affects people's lives and health. Additionally, as organizations that are perceived as community service operations (regardless of ownership or tax status), health care institutions are subject to even more public scrutiny and higher expectations than are manufacturers and other kinds of service corporations. Health care public relations professionals must be concerned with their own ethical behavior, as well as the ethical standards of the health care organization, and must be aware of the legalities related to the practice of public relations, which are more complex than commonly perceived.

☐ Ethics in Health Care Public Relations

There are two facets of ethics that are of concern to the health care PR manager: the personal and professional ethics involved in the practice of public relations and the ethical behavior of the health care organization. These two facets are inextricably intertwined: a PR manager cannot be contented that he or she personally behaves ethically while working for an organization that is engaged in unethical activities, nor can an organization that is operated in an ethical manner tolerate unethical PR practices.

Personal Integrity: Ethics and the Public Relations Manager

The PR manager in any industry has a unique role in that the manager's behavior must satisfy:

- Personal ethical standards
- The needs and concerns of the employer (which may or may not be ethical)
- The ethical standards of the PR profession, as expressed in the Codes of Ethics of the Public Relations Society of America and other professional associations
- The public interest

Although all managers must contend with their own ethical beliefs and must reconcile those beliefs with their obligation to their employers, PR practitioners must also live up to the ethical expectations of their profession and, as their organization's spokespersons and public representatives, must be accountable to the publics in the communities in which their organizations operate. It is this latter responsibility that distinguishes public relations from other management functions and places an additional burden of ethical behavior on the PR manager. And because the public has unusually high expectations of ethical behavior from health care organizations, the health care PR manager must operate in an unusually scrutinized environment.

Robert L. Dilenschneider, president and CEO of Hill and Knowlton, one of the world's largest and most respected PR firms, said:[1]

Where the exercise of ethics becomes operative in public relations is in making hard choices:

- Do you do the questionable thing when the boss demands it?
- Do you sacrifice your sense of honesty as a means of saving face when dealing with a political or financial hot potato?
- Do you duck truth-telling when you know your employer would rather hear something else?
- Are you tempted to twist the facts a little when dealing with the media to avoid having the truth revealed?
- Do you condone corporate actions that you know in your bones would be condemned if they became public?

We all know what is right. If such questions become troublesome in the course of a career, it is not because we do not recognize the ethical answer, it is because following the ethical course may cost us something — sometimes even our jobs. It is more difficult to realize that not following the ethical course can cost something too — our honesty, our self-respect and possibly our reputations.

Don Bates, executive director of the Institute of Public Relations Research and Education, puts it simply in *Tips and Tactics*, a supplement of *pr reporter* (Exeter, NH):[2]

Ethical behavior for the PR practitioner boils down to his or her personal response to questions large and small that arise almost daily in the conduct of the programs and communications s/he is charged with. Here are just a few:

- Will I lie to my boss or staff?
- Will I cover up a difficult or dangerous situation?
- Will I steal or engage in bribery?
- Will I take advantage of privileged information?
- Will I hide or destroy evidence?
- Will I break a trust or confidence?
- Will I deliberately mislead or misinform?

In other words, will I compromise my personal beliefs, the codes of professional standards of my field and the law to avoid unpleasant complications, or save my skin or the skin of my employer?

The health care PR manager should be sensitive to these ethical concerns, and to three basic guidelines that have particular impact on the practice of public relations in the hospital setting—honesty, openness, and protection of individuals' privacy rights.

Honesty

As the chief spokesperson for the health care organization (personally or through supervision of communications programs) to the media, to external audiences, to current and potential patients and their families, and to internal audiences, the PR manager must be personally committed and organizationally authorized to be unfailingly honest in providing information. This means honesty in:

- *Media relations.* The PR manager must provide truthful answers to questions, or if there are overriding reasons for not providing answers (patient privacy, CEO concern about sharing strategic information, liability involved in certain situations), the PR manager must refuse to answer the question, indicating the reason the question is not being answered. Misleading or lying is unthinkable, for ethical and practical reasons. First, there are always people who know the truth—very often, employees or physicians—so that the PR manager will not only lose credibility but will also face the risk that those who know the truth will share it with internal and external audiences. The health care PR manager who denies employee layoffs when employees know that their colleagues are being let go will forever be perceived as what he or she is—a liar. The other peril of dishonesty is that the media will eventually find the truth by digging and digging until they find it.

- *Promotion.* Any PR professional must be careful to avoid distortions, misrepresentations, or "hype," but health care PR managers must be even more circumspect. Claims about painlessness, lifesaving techniques, revolutionary methods, and the like are inexcusable unless they can be proven to be true 100 percent of the time, for all patients. New medical developments—from laser surgery to drugs like streptokinase—are exciting and interesting to the public and the media. But implying that these developments are appropriate for all patients, or seeming to guarantee results, is not only an ethical but also a legal risk. Great care must be taken in news releases, media stories, and promotional materials and ads to balance the exciting information about the new technique or technology with information about its appropriateness and any limitations. If the PR manager errs, it is better to err on the side of discretion and underplaying, rather than overplaying, because any short-term market advantage that might be gained by "miracle" claims can quickly be offset by physician outrage, competitor criticism, or, later on, consumer lawsuits because the service didn't live up to its hype.

Openness

Whether a health care organization is publicly owned, privately owned, nonprofit, or part of a profit-making corporation, it will be perceived by the public as a "public" institution because of its role in serving the community and its general accessibility to the public. George Adams, editor of *Health Care Weekly Review*, noted that, "however annoying it may be, clearly health care has come within the public's vision."[3]

Noting that "hospitals in the United States operate at least in part as a public service," Adams said that the vast majority of hospitals "are blessed with the status of charitable enterprises, exempt from taxes and funded to a large extent through public finance. In this sense, they are debtors to society, and they fully repay that debt by providing health care."

Because of hospitals' "special place" in society, Adams and other observers emphasize that hospitals must expect and be willing to be open to public scrutiny. "There is an ethical imperative that demands both accessibility and accountability from our hospital administrations. . . . [S]ociety allows hospitals to exist and operate . . . and that relationship with the community would seem to forbid the existence of barriers between the community—either directly or through the press—and hospital administration."

This commitment to openness goes beyond simply being accessible to the news media, and beyond just providing answers to questions. It requires a proactive sharing of information about the health care organization's plans and services not only with the media but also directly with stakeholders—audiences who are influenced by and/or can influence the health care organization. Health care organizations ask their communities for support, understanding, and trust. In return for this trust, communities expect that the health care organization will be open and honest with them.

Protection of Individuals' Privacy Rights

The commitment to openness, combined with the public and media's natural interest in health care and health care organizations, can often conflict with the organization's ethical and legal responsibility to protect the privacy of patients and their families. This responsibility, as discussed in chapter 10 on the release of patient information to the media, is sacrosanct, and hospital PR staff members must go to any extreme to safeguard the privacy rights of their patients, no matter how notorious the patient or how great the public interest. In some states, health care organizations may release limited information about patients involved in certain situations—"public record" situations where the coroner or law enforcement officials are involved; in other states, the health care organization may release no information without the patient's permission. (Refer to appendix B for some guidelines, but be sure to discuss your state law with your own legal counsel.)

Today, there's an increasing number of situations, like organ harvesting and transplants, for instance, which elicit great public interest. The health care PR manager has to balance the public's interest, often expressed through the news media's "right to know" requests, with the patient and family's rights and wishes about privacy. If there is a problem, the patient's rights take precedence. Just as health care PR managers should err on the side of discretion in situations involving promotion and "hype" of medical breakthroughs, they should err on the side of protecting the patient in patient privacy/media inquiry situations. When patients come to a health care facility, either voluntarily or even under emergency situations, they place their trust in the health care organization to care for them as completely and expertly as possible. Guarding their privacy is part of that caring and transcends any obligations to media or the broader general public.

Although protecting patient privacy may lead to conflicts with media—and through the media, with other public audiences—the health care organization's primary responsibility is to its patients and their families. The PR manager must continually educate the media about this responsibility and must convey to the members of the public that it is in their best interest for health care organizations to protect patient privacy, because someday they might be the patient.

The PR manager must also protect the privacy rights of physicians and employees, rights discussed in the legal section of this chapter.

Institutional Integrity: The Role of the
Public Relations Manager in Interpreting Ethical Issues

The list of ethical issues affecting health care organizations grows longer every year:

- Right to be born, right to live, right to die
- Access to/rationing of health care
- Animal rights
- Human experimentation
- Prospective payment systems and patient "dumping"
- "Brain death"
- Physician ventures and "kickback" schemes
- Informed consent
- Religious beliefs that conflict with medical treatment
- Human and animal organ transplantation
- Who shall pay?
- Care for AIDS patients (and protecting staff members who care for those patients)

These are just some of the issues that health care organizations are grappling with that have ethical implications for health care institutions, physicians, patients, and society as a whole. They are complex issues—not easily understood, even by health care professionals, and certainly issues with no right or wrong answers or approaches.

Initially, some health care PR managers might believe that because these issues don't all have a direct and immediate impact on their health care organization, the managers don't need to be concerned about them. In fact, most of these issues can affect nearly every health care organization at some point. Although a health care facility may not handle organ transplants, any health care organization may find itself involved in an organ harvest. Right to die, living will, and brain death cases can occur at any facility that provides inpatient care. And access, indigent care, and patient dumping are issues that every health care organization is grappling with. Whereas the more specialized situations, like animal rights or human experimentation controversies, may not occur at every health care institution, the public nevertheless looks to its local health care institutions for information and insights into the implications of these issues.

Techniques for handling media and public communication in these ethical situations are described in chapters 10 and 11. But whether or not the PR manager actually has to cope with these situations as they are happening—handling animal rights activists or dealing with media inquiries about the family of an accident victim that wants to disconnect the patient's respirator—the PR manager may be asked for comment on any of these ethical issues, even if they do not affect the manager's organization. When possible, these requests should be honored, for several reasons. Refusing to comment sends a message that the health care organization either doesn't care or is uninformed about what the public may view as an important issue. It also implies that the health care organization will never have to cope with that type of case, which is a risky assumption to make. More important, all health care organizations benefit when the media and the public have more accurate information about ethical issues. A small community hospital, for instance, may not be involved in performing animal research, but patients benefit daily from treatments and technology developed by using animal subjects. If the hospital says "We have no comment because that issue doesn't involve our hospital," it ignores the fact that the issue does, indeed, eventually affect the hospital and its patients (a link that the public can certainly understand). This answer does not contribute to creating an informed, educated public able to participate in the kind of public discussion and policy shaping that must take place if these ethical dilemmas are to be solved.

If the health care organization has no physician or staff member willing to be interviewed, then obviously the media request will have to be refused, but it's preferable to avoid this by deciding in advance that one or more members of the organization's ethics committee will attempt to handle specific topics. A substantive interview is preferred over having the PR or media relations manager issue a prepared statement, because these issues do not lend themselves to cursory consideration. And in order to have staff members and physicians who are able to address these ethical issues with the media, contemplation and discussion of the issues must continually be occurring within the health care organization. The PR manager can help create an internal forum—whether formal or informal—to encourage discussion of these ethical situations.

In addition, the PR manager should play a role in developing communications programs that help interpret the implications of these issues to the general public in the health care organization's community. A number of health care organizations have sponsored lecture series, community forums, or opinion leader briefings to explore ethical issues—educational efforts that take place not during the midst of an ethical crisis, but in a calmer, quiet atmosphere of reflection and dialogue.

The existence of an institutional ethics committee or, at the very least, the involvement of a medical ethicist is helpful to the PR manager and staff both in responding to media inquiries and in developing proactive educational programs. If such a committee or individual is not available in the health care organization, the PR manager should encourage the CEO to develop this function. Legal counsel should also be involved, inasmuch as ethical and legal issues often overlap. No health care organization will be able to avoid confronting ethical issues in the coming decades, and the organization's actions and comments can help the community understand and address these issues.

Institutional Integrity: The Role of the Public Relations Manager in Ethical Institutional Decision Making and Operation

In addition to acting in an ethical manner, and helping the health care organization and the community address medical ethical issues, the PR manager also has a critical responsibility in ensuring that the health care organization operates in an ethical manner. Health care organizations, like other organizations, must make ethical decisions routinely. Some are specifically related to health care, others are situations that any company could face.

- If we suspect employees are selling drugs, should we try to keep it secret or go to the authorities and risk bad publicity?
- Do we admit indigent maternity patients, who may have offensive personal hygiene or habits, to semiprivate rooms with "paying patients"?
- Do we scrupulously protect the privacy of AIDS patients, or do we warn employees and thus "brand" the patient?
- Do we give employees two weeks' notice if they are being laid off, and risk them upsetting the other employees before they leave, or do we show them the door immediately?
- Do we tell the uninsured parents of a preemie with a life-threatening heart problem that there is specialized (and very expensive) surgery that has a remote chance of helping?

Often decisions such as these are made primarily on the basis of financial and legal impact, with cursory consideration of how internal audiences may react, and even less consideration of how the public will react if news of the action or decision becomes known to it.

John Budd, vice-chairman of the PR firm of Carl Byoir, notes that many CEOs spend their lives dealing with hard facts — what will it cost, can we get sued — and are not comfortable with abstracts, with gray areas. Budd warns PR professionals to help CEOs avoid the following pitfalls:[4]

- Inability to grasp the significance of perception. A CEO may rationalize decisions on the basis of legal acceptability, but if the public thinks it's wrong, then it's wrong.
- Reliance on bad or intimidating counsel — lawyers, bankers, finance officers — who insist on bottom-line concerns or advise against candor because "straight talk can lead to lawsuits."
- Choosing to deny the public a simple explanation of their actions when there's a problem or crisis. Contrast the stonewalling and dissembling of the top brass at Exxon during the Alaskan oil spill scandal against Lee Iacocca's "We did a bad thing; we apologize and we'll make up for it" response to the Chrysler odometer tinkering incident.

Budd advises PR professionals to be concerned with the ultimate court after the bottom line has been served and the lawsuits avoided or won: the court of public opinion.

Because ethical issues come in shades of gray — with no black or white, absolutely right or absolutely wrong answers — many decisions are "no win." One group may be pleased with the action, another group will be upset. When decisions of this type are being considered, the PR manager must counsel the CEO and top management team to "do the right thing" according to the health care organization's mission, values, and ethical standards, rather than respond to pressure or financial or legal concerns. In the real-life example of a group of hospital employees selling drugs, one administrator pointed out that the employees were not selling drugs to hospital employees or patients and there was no evidence of drug use on hospital property. Another administrator noted that the resulting publicity could damage the hospital's reputation (and market share and bottom line) and that eventually the police would probably catch the sellers anyway, without a tip from the hospital. The human resources officer was concerned about how employees would react if the hospital was seen as "turning in" employees.

The PR manager framed the ethical issue succinctly: If we know or have very good reason to suspect that anyone is selling drugs, and we do nothing about it and they continue to sell drugs, have we done the right thing for society and our community? Even if people think badly of the hospital for employing people who sold drugs, and decide to go elsewhere for care, will they not at least respect the administration for helping to bring the dealers to justice? She also posed the counter-issue: If we do nothing, and eventually the public learns that we knew there was a problem, won't we risk the same market share and image problems — compounded by the fact that we deliberately chose not to address the problem?

The best counsel that the PR manager can offer the CEO and top management when confronting issues such as these is quite simple: do the right thing and weather any negative consequences. Making an unethical choice, and then defending it on the basis of financial impact, is simply disastrous for health care organizations, which the public perceives as philanthropic service organizations. Making an unethical choice, even if it is technically legal, wins no points in the court of public opinion.

The responsibility for raising these points and guiding the institution toward a decision that can be publicly defended (even if there are audiences who decry the decision) falls to the PR manager, in his special role of representing the public's concerns and needs. In this role, the PR manager can pose questions that can help managers pinpoint the "right thing." The following first questions can be used when the health care organization is considering making a decision and then trying to keep it quiet: "What if our actions end up being described in a page-one story in the local paper? How would we look? What would people think?" The following questions should be posed when a potentially unethical decision is being considered strictly for financial or risk-avoidance reasons: "How are we going to explain the reasons for this? What will we tell the employees? How will it sound when we tell the press, 'We're doing this to avoid a lawsuit,' or, 'We're doing this to make more money'?"

It generally falls to the PR manager to subject institutional decisions to the same kind of scrutiny that they will receive from the public, and to function as what is often called "the corporate conscience." Because of the special status health care organizations enjoy in our society, that conscience role is especially important for health care PR managers.

In addition to serving as the corporate conscience, and subjecting decisions to ethical scrutiny, the PR manager must also serve as an "early warning system" to help identify situations that have ethical implications — from different treatment for patients who can and can't pay for care, to sexual harassment of employees by a physician. The earlier these situations can be identified and addressed, the less chance there is of the situation becoming an issue with internal or external audiences.

This role of corporate conscience can be challenging, but is ultimately one of the most critical senior management functions in any institution. At its most practical, guiding the institution toward ethical decisions is preventive public relations—helping the PR manager avoid having to cope with scandals, crises, and media exposés. At its highest levels, serving as the champion of ethical behavior is one of the greatest contributions the PR manager can make to the health care organization, to the people it employs and serves, and to the community.

□ The Legal Dimensions of Public Relations

There are a number of legal concepts that the health care PR manager must be cognizant of in the development and implementation of communications programs. The actions of PR staff members can break laws or subject the health care organization to legal action, from copyright violations to unsubstantiated claims in advertisements, from unauthorized use of patient photos to failure to safeguard against unsafe conditions at an open house at the health care facility. The PR manager must be aware of the potential for risk and legal action in terms of patient privacy (covered in detail in chapter 10) and in the areas described in general terms in the following pages and adapted from *Public Relations: Strategies and Tactics:*[5]

- Conspiracy
- Defamation
- Rights of employees
- Photo releases
- Events
- Ownership of ideas
- Copyright and trademarks
- Advertising claims

If the PR manager is involved in any of the activities mentioned or has concerns about the legality of any PR work, the manager should consult the health care organization's staff counsel or legal firm.

Conspiracy

If the health care organization is found guilty of any type of illegal act, the PR manager is at risk if he or she is found to have provided advice or even tacitly supported that activity. This can include participating in the decision, covering up information, issuing false statements, counseling on development of policies that relate to the illegal act, or cooperating in any way with the illegal act, which could range from race, sex, or age discrimination, to collusion with another health care organization or organizations to restrain trade or fix prices.

Defamation

Making statements that damage a person's reputation is called slander if it's spoken and libel if it's written (if such statements are made on broadcast news, even though they are spoken, it's still considered libel). Public relations people have been found guilty of libel in news releases or slander in press conferences, in discussing union leaders or competitors, for instance.

Defamation against corporate entities is harder to prove, because damage to a corporation's reputation is difficult to assess. The company must prove that what was said or written is absolutely not true, and that it has been actually damaged. Judges generally apply the "fair comment and criticism" standard, which says that the company, by choosing to be in the marketplace, is subject to fair comment, whether good or bad. So a critical letter to the editor, or a negative commentary by a TV personality, is probably not actionable.

Public relations professionals should also be familiar with the public figure concept as it pertains to the health care organization's CEO, senior administrators, or prominent medical staff members. If the person who has possibly been defamed is ruled to be a public figure by the courts, he or she must not only prove that he or she has been defamed but also that the media acted irresponsibly and with malice — and malice is very difficult to prove. In addition, persons defined as public figures are not generally held to have a right to privacy. Chief executive officers need to be warned that if they voluntarily step into the limelight to take part in a public debate, they are more likely to be deemed public figures, and that the corporate leader who has simply done his or her job and stayed out of public scrutiny is more likely to be able to win a defamation or privacy suit. Additionally, if the health care organization is involved in a major news event, it is harder for the CEO to claim to be a private citizen.

Rights of Employees

Employees have rights to privacy that apply in terms of internal publications, media coverage, and use of employees to promote the hospital. Employee publications, to avoid invasion of privacy, should focus on work topics — no items about employees' personal lives, jokes or slams, and so forth. Even printing birthdays has been found to raise privacy issues.

If employees' names or photos are used in any promotional materials, the PR manager can be charged with "misappropriation of personality." To avoid this, the manager should get signed releases from the employees. Some organizations believe that they have an implied consent (if the employee agrees to work here, that implies that we can use his or her name or photo) or ask employees to sign blanket consents. It is safer, although more time-consuming, to have specific consent forms each and every time a particular name or likeness is used for promotion. Some organizations even pay a small fee to further indicate that the employee has given permission. The alternative is to use models to portray employees, although this can cause negative reactions from employees.

Release of information about employees to the media is another area with legal restrictions. Generally, the only information the health care organization should release without permission, unless required by law, is confirmation that the person works at the institution, as well as title, job description, and dates of employment. Salary, address, or other information should not be released. The reporter can either be referred directly to the employee (who has been advised about his or her rights of privacy by the PR staff), or the PR staff can routinely solicit biographical information and permission to release it to the media in advance of receiving media requests.

Employees also have legal rights, under federal and state law, to receive benefits information that is clearly written and understandable, and to have easy access to information about health and safety regulations, worker's compensation guidelines, and so forth. (*Special note:* The requirement to provide understandable written pension information may soon be challenged because a growing number of employees can't read. The rulings in these cases should set precedents that will have far-reaching implications for health care PR managers.) Finally, employees do have the right of free speech, and a substantial body of case law is being developed that protects employees from being fired or disciplined for whistle-blowing or internally or externally criticizing the company.

Photo Releases

Whenever a photo or video is shot involving employees (as described earlier), patients, physicians, or others, the PR manager should obtain written permission to shoot and use the photo. The release form should indicate how the photo will be used (in a publication, for an ad or promotional brochure, for research or teaching, and so on) and should be signed by the individual (or parent/guardian), witnessed, and dated. A carefully organized central photo release file should be maintained and generally cross-referenced by name of the person signing the release and title or subject of the publication or audiovisual use.

Making photo release forms as small as possible and printing them in pads makes them more portable and easier for photographers and PR staff members to use. A three-part carbonless form allows the photographer to have a copy for the file, the PR staffer to have a copy for writing cutlines, and the person photographed to have a copy.

Events

Some risk is involved when the health care organization sponsors events on-site or off-campus. The PR staff should take all possible precautions to avoid dangerous conditions (for example, a pool of melted snow at the entrance during an open house or taking a group of elderly people on a tour that involves lots of walking up and down stairs) and should ensure that the owners/operators of any off-campus sites that are used take similar precautions.

The PR manager should check with the health care organization's risk manager and/or legal counsel to make sure they are aware of the event and that the health care organization has the appropriate insurance to cover any problems. Guests should be required to sign "hold harmless" forms to protect the health care organization in the event of accidents beyond its control.

Ownership of Ideas

Ideas submitted by employees or by the general public are important ways of improving the quality of health care services and delivery systems. But once those ideas are submitted, who owns them?

With employee suggestion programs, the health care organization should clearly state the organization's policy (most often, it's that the health care organization owns all ideas submitted and that the employee gives up rights to the idea by submitting it) in all communications about the program. This includes making the policy clear in promotion and internal publication stories, and on the forms and supporting materials that are used as part of the program.

When the public submits ideas, even if voluntarily, the health care organization can choose either not to accept the ideas (and thus avoid any future liability) or to ask for a signed release, often in return for a token payment. Regardless of the source of the idea, it is essential that the PR manager ensure that, before any submitted idea is used, the submitter understands that he or she is giving up any rights to the idea and actually gives the health care organization permission to use the idea.

Copyright and Trademarks

The PR manager deals with copyright and trademarks in two different ways: to protect the health care organization's materials and to avoid improperly using materials that are protected by another organization. Public relations managers should familiarize themselves with the fine points of copyright law in consultation with legal counsel, to protect their work and avoid illegally using other people's work. (The U.S. Copyright Office, Library of Congress, also publishes a series of pamphlets explaining various aspects of copyright law.)

Copyright protects original works of authorship. It protects the expression of those ideas, not the ideas themselves. A concept, discussed or theorized, cannot be protected by copyright. Public relations managers should copyright all important materials (annual reports, publications, ads, and so on) to prevent unauthorized use by competitors. Legal counsel can advise on the process of copyrighting. In addition, use of copyrighted material is subject to limitations (permission must be granted if the material is used as part of an effort to promote sales or gain profit; material should not be used out of context; and if copies of copyrighted material are going to be widely distributed, quantity reprints should be secured from the publisher).

A trademark is a "name, symbol or other device identifying a product, officially registered and legally restricted to the use of the owner or manufacturer."[6] While most health care organizations do not have trademarks for numerous programs or services, they do need to protect their organization's logos and any service names that identify unique programs. Although this is a fairly detailed procedure that should involve legal counsel, there are some general guidelines of which the PR manager should be aware:

1. *Before adopting a logo or a product name, request that legal counsel conduct a computerized search to ensure that the name or symbol isn't already trademarked by another organization.* If the preferred name or logo is already owned, the health care organization can either come up with another choice or purchase rights to use that name or logo (more easily granted if the owner is not doing business in or near the health care organization's service area). Using a trademarked name without buying rights to it is risking not only a lawsuit, but also the costs of having to change all signs, letterhead, materials, and so forth.
2. *Once a name has been selected, move immediately to register it (indicated by a small capital "R" in a circle).* This can be a lengthy process—months or years—but is essential to protect the name or logo. Putting "TM" in small capital letters indicates a company's

common-law claim to right of a trademark, or that registration is pending, but does not provide the same rights as an officially registered trademark.

3. *To continue to protect the trademark, use it as registered at all times.* The name must be capitalized and the "R" or "TM" symbol used—at all times. If the PR department slips and omits the symbol or routinely fails to capitalize the name, competitors or others who want or are claiming rights to the trademark can begin using it because it is not being protected.

Advertising Claims

The Federal Trade Commission (FTC) monitors ads and publicity efforts, looking for examples of the following:

- Unsubstantiated claims
- Misleading claims
- Exaggerated claims
- Fraudulent testimonials
- Deceptive demonstrations or prices
- Defamation of the competition
- Fraudulent contests
- Misuse of the word *free*
- Bait-and-switch tactics

Although many of these do not apply to health care organizations ("I know you came in for an appendectomy, but we're having a special price on face-lifts"), and although the FTC is kept busy scrutinizing national advertising, health care PR managers do need to be aware of the regulations concerning claims made in ads. Untrue statements (for example, "first angioplasty," "largest heart program," and so on) can be grounds for regulatory review, or, on a local level, an investigation by the Better Business Bureau or public criticism from other health care organizations or physicians. Misleading statements, as discussed earlier in this chapter, can be unethical—they can also be actionable by the FTC. The PR manager must be careful to check and double-check facts (sometimes physicians or product managers can get carried away, or may truly believe that theirs is a biggest, best, first) and to avoid seeming to guarantee that any technique, technology, or program can achieve the same positive results for all patients. Violating FTC regulations can result in monetary fines, signing a consent decree, or even being required to do "corrective publicity," not to mention the embarrassment and lack of credibility the health care organization will incur.

☐ The Public Relations Manager– Legal Counsel Relationship

Although lawyers and PR professionals may often end up on opposite sides of an argument over an action taken by the health care organization, they both have a common goal: to protect the health care organization. The lawyer is concerned about the court of law; the PR manager is concerned about the court of public opinion.

Conflicts may arise when the legal counsel is recommending an action that will help the health care organization avoid a potential (not actual) liability, but which may cause negative public or media response. The PR manager must argue that risking a loss of public esteem and support is not worth avoiding "potential liability" or even that risking legal action can be preferred over doing something that will damage the health care organization's reputation.

There are also many cases when the PR manager and legal counsel can work together. For example, if the contemplated action is clearly illegal, the PR manager can point out that doing something illegal is definitely bad public relations. Conversely, when the PR manager is making a strong case against an action that would cause a negative public reaction, if the corporate counsel is an ally he or she can support the PR manager's case by noting that the action "might also be illegal," giving the CEO another reason to reconsider the action. As key senior staff members, the PR officer and legal counsel should work cooperatively to protect the health care organization from risk of legal or public opinion problems and to identify ways in which the health care organization can act legally and with the support and understanding of the public.

☐ Summary

The ethical and legal dimensions of the practice of public relations are too often relegated to a once-a-year discussion at the local PR society meeting. But, particularly in the health care setting, an understanding of the legalities of the practice of PR is critical. Confidentiality and privacy issues can cause serious problems in a health care setting, and the PR manager must make a serious effort to ensure that the health care organization is aware of and in compliance with all applicable laws.

Health care PR managers also come face-to-face with ethical issues and concerns on a routine basis. Although these situations rarely involve the ethics of the PR practitioner, he or she is often called upon to help explain and interpret the issues to the media and the public. Taking the time to read about and discuss ethical issues that can arise in a health care setting before confronting those issues in reality is a valuable exercise for the PR manager.

References

1. Dilenschneider, R. L. Ethics in public relations. *Perspectives* (Ball State University) 9:5, 1988.
2. Bates, D. The public relations practitioner's role in ethical organizational behavior. *Tips and Tactics* [supplement to *pr reporter* 32(11):1, Mar. 13, 1989].
3. Adams, G. Communications as an ethical imperative. *Michigan Hospitals* 24(12):34, Dec. 1988.
4. Opportunity and critical area for public relations guidance. *pr reporter* 30(20):11, May 15, 1989.
5. Wilcox, D. L., Ault, P. H., and Agee, W. K. *Public Relations: Strategies and Tactics*. 2nd ed. Cambridge, MA: Harper and Row, 1989.
6. Wilcox and others.

Suggested Readings

Hamilton, S. PR ethics. *Public Relations Quarterly*, Fall 1986.

Nelson, H. L., and Teeter, D. L., Jr. *Law of Mass Communication*. Mineola, NY: The Foundation Press, 1981.

Public Relations Society of America. *Code of Ethics of the Public Relations Society of America*. New York City: PRSA, 1983.

Simon, M. J. *Public Relations Law*. New York City: Appleton-Century-Crofts, 1969.

Turning lawyers into allies. *Public Relations Journal* 46(1):24, Jan. 1989.

Wright, D. K., and Burger, C. Ethics and public relations. *Public Relations Journal* 39(12):12–17, Dec. 1982.

Evaluation

"What do we get out of all this PR stuff, anyway?" has been a question that public relations professionals have encountered for decades. Today, the science of evaluation, although not yet perfected, has progressed to the point at which many PR managers can answer that question by citing specific results elicited by PR programs. Routine evaluation of all PR activities is certainly not universal — Ketchum's national survey on research and evaluation found that 43 percent of senior PR practitioners feel it is not even possible to measure PR outcomes[1] — but the remaining 57 percent of the PR managers in health care and other industries say they can evaluate their programs (although only 16 percent routinely use research to measure effectiveness and outcomes). Because a number of evaluation methods have been outlined in the planning and methods chapters of this book, this chapter will provide an overview of the whys, whats, whens, and hows of evaluation.

☐ Why Evaluate?

In a PR utopia, the PR manager would want to evaluate every program so that he or she personally would know how well the program worked, even if no one else in the organization cared. And in fact, many PR professionals have long been quietly evaluating the success of some of their efforts, albeit in informal or nonscientific ways.

Today, there is another overriding reason for evaluating the results of PR programs. In today's health care environment of tight budgets and competition for resources, every department must demonstrate its contribution to the health care organization's survival. Nonoperating, support departments are under even more pressure, although staff functions like human resources and finance are generally assumed to be essential. Because of that pressure, even the most traditional "we've always done this" PR activities are expected to justify their existence by achieving certain objectives. It is increasingly difficult for PR managers to receive funds for programs that are done because: (1) "we've always done it," (2) "every other health care organization does it," or (3) "we ought to do it."

Instead, PR activities—either as individual projects or as total programs—are expected to contribute to the achievement of institutional goals. Through formal evaluation programs, the PR manager determines if the objectives were achieved and to what degree. The results of the evaluation process can be used to:

- Demonstrate the value of the programs to the CEO and senior management (plus board members, employees, physicians, and any other groups who ask why the PR programs exist)
- Make decisions about what methods or programs will be continued in the future
- Make changes in ongoing programs that do not appear to be achieving their objectives
- Identify success stories that can be used to boost staff morale
- Identify existing public image problems and areas of opportunity

☐ What and When to Evaluate

Ideally, each and every PR activity should be formally evaluated. In reality, there are limitations on the extent of evaluation efforts, including:

- The amount of staff time involved in evaluation procedures
- The cost of formal research and other evaluation methods
- The lack of effective methods to measure the precise impact of media relations, speakers, tours, and other "soft" PR activities that contribute to the public's awareness and preference

Because of these limitations, one of the first evaluation decisions the PR director makes is to decide—and negotiate with the CEO—what programs will be evaluated, how often, and to what extent.

There are some general guidelines about what programs should be priorities for formal evaluation:

- Programs that are intended to have the most direct impact on the bottom line—generally, marketing communications programs for specific products and services
- Programs that are very expensive to implement (publications, audiovisual productions, advertising, and so on)
- Programs that are either new or "experimental"

If the choice is between evaluating the four-color magazine that's mailed quarterly to 25,000 people at a cost of $145,000 or the visitors' brochure that costs $6,000, clearly the magazine is the investment that ought to be measured first, using formal research methods as described in chapter 7. That doesn't mean that the visitors' brochure should be produced year after year without some evaluation—staff members can ascertain whether the brochure is accurate, what percentage of visitors are picking it up, whether staff members report more or fewer incidences of visitors getting lost or asking basic questions, and so on. Informally organized focus groups of visitors or people who have never visited the health care facility (friends of PR staff members) can be asked for input on the brochure's readability, clarity, and format.

One might consider that programs tied to general image, awareness, and preference goals are already being evaluated as part of what should be routine community/general-audience surveys. However, more precise research should be focused on specific marketing communications methods ("How did you hear about the heart center? Did you ever see heart center advertising?").

The PR manager must use a combination of common sense and sensitivity to CEO/organizational concerns when conducting evaluation efforts. At a minimum, a yearly measure of awareness, preference, and message content/medium reception should be conducted as an evaluation of the institution's total PR program. Then high-ticket and direct bottom-line impact programs should be added to the "must evaluate" list. Finally, any programs that the PR manager is concerned about (is this worth the money, is this a program that could be eliminated if budgets get tighter or if we need money to create some new programs) should be evaluated, as well as any programs that the CEO or other administrators have specifically singled out for questioning or criticism. If the CEO consistently questions the need for a speakers' bureau, for instance, even though the PR manager knows that these programs serve to reinforce impersonal methods and can cite national studies supporting that belief, the PR manager had better come up with some hard numbers for the CEO using some of the methods described in this chapter.

One veteran PR vice-president summed up his approach to evaluation as follows: "I make sure I've got hard data about changes in general-audience awareness—the major community survey research—because that's really the broad purpose of the PR program. And the advertising and marketing communications stuff for the big revenue programs have to be evaluated. Then I pick two or three specific programs—magazine readership/recall one year; in the second year, differences in opinions between people who've participated in some of our special events versus people who haven't; and the third year, the satisfaction of people who come to our screenings. Once you've gotten some kind of a measure for a specific kind of program, you can justify its existence for several years based on that data. But anything that's either really expensive or really controversial—like advertising—I evaluate every year, because every year I have to fight for the budget to continue it."

☐ How to Evaluate

Although evaluation may seem like a tedious process, especially in the midst of a hectic work schedule, once it is systematically organized, it can become just another step in the management of an effective PR program.

Establishing Objectives

Establishing objectives for programs is discussed in detail in chapter 6. To summarize, objectives must:

- *Be measurable.* "Improve the hospital's image" is not measurable. "Increase awareness of hospital services among elderly consumers by 25 percent" is measurable, as is "Have the hospital ranked as number one for alcoholism treatment by employee assistance program directors and social service workers." To determine if an objective is measurable, ask the question "How will we know if we achieved it?"
- *Be something on which a communications activity can actually have an impact.* A consumer advertising campaign as part of a program with the overall goal of increasing admissions to the pediatric unit cannot be expected to achieve that objective if the only pediatricians admitting to the unit are not accepting any new patients and are already referring all their patients to the unit. A legislative relations campaign can be targeted to generate a specific number of constituent letters to a congressman, but cannot be held responsible for the congressman's vote.
- *Be realistic.* "Having the hospital become the most preferred hospital for heart care" when the hospital is the fourth preferred out of five hospitals (and 70 percent of the audience doesn't even know the hospital has a heart program) is unrealistic.
- *Be behaviorally oriented.* The objective may actually be a behavior (asking the public to do something, not do something, or let the organization do something) or may relate to a behavior (consumer behavior research has proven that awareness, and usually preference, must precede any consumer action, so increasing awareness or preference is

an appropriate communications campaign objective). Activity objectives—generate 2,000 media coverages, publish a magazine every quarter, place speakers with 150 groups—are not acceptable, since there is no way to prove that the activity had any impact on the target audience's behavior.

When objectives are established, the "what do we want to have happen as a result of this activity" question is answered, and this answer will help determine how to evaluate the outcome of the activity.

Evaluation Methods

In 1988, PR research expert Walter Lindenmann, A.P.R., noted that "the majority of PR programs still go unmeasured, with practitioners relying on gut feeling and blind faith as to whether or not they've hit the mark." Lindenmann added that many PR evaluation efforts measured outputs (activity) rather than outcomes (changes in attitudes or behaviors). Lindenmann's research showed that clip analysis remained one of the most widespread evaluation techniques, albeit being "souped up" to appear to be more scientific.[2]

Clip analysis—number of media placements × potential audience for each placement × cost of that amount of space at advertising rates = value of activity—not only is limited by being an activity measure rather than outcome measure (what did the people who saw the media coverage do or believe as a result of seeing it?), but also measures only one facet of a total PR program. Going beyond the clip analysis, PR researchers and practitioners have identified a number of methods that can be used to measure the impact of PR activity, although no single method has been universally adopted. Among the most commonly used evaluation methods are:

1. *Precampaign and postcampaign surveys.* These are used to measure changes in awareness and preference among general and/or target audiences. There are two types of awareness/preference research:
   * Survey of a random sample of the target audience, as a predictor of the entire audience, to measure changes in awareness and preference. Relying on this method means that it must be assumed that any changes in awareness and preference are a result of the communications campaign—an assumption that is sometimes challenged. There are more sophisticated statistical analysis techniques that can be used to identify the impact of a specific campaign component—isolating the subgroup of individuals who recall one or more of the campaign components and measuring whether their awareness/preference levels are significantly different from the individuals who do not recall the campaign.

- Survey of those persons known to have been exposed to the message (people who heard speakers, received direct mailings, participated in opinion leader briefings) to measure any changes that have occurred. Changes in this group can be compared to changes in a group of people who were not exposed to the message to accurately assess the impact of the communications program.
2. *Consumer behavior measures.* It is important to go beyond mere awareness measures to preference measures, which are far greater predictors of behavior than mere knowledge of a program or service. Counting direct responses (such as phone calls to an 800 number, number of people who show up for a special event, coupons returned, and so on) can measure how well the PR technique used can elicit the desired response, but does not measure whether or not the respondents' attitudes or preferences changed as a result of their interaction with the health care organization.

   On the other hand, direct responses are the best method for evaluating the effectiveness of communications programs that are intended to make direct sales — mammography appointments, new patients at a clinic or private practice office, self-admissions to an alcoholism treatment program. A secondary evaluation of those direct sales communications efforts is to measure changes in awareness/preference of consumers who saw the communications vehicles but did not purchase the product.
3. *Specialized methods.* There are a number of other formal research methods that can and probably should be part of a PR evaluation program — for example, readership studies, participant satisfaction studies, and media gatekeeper awareness/comprehension studies. In addition, the PR staff can develop informal methods to get at least a basic evaluation of the value of "small" PR activities — department managers and employees can anecdotally describe patient response to and use of brochures, nurse educators can assess how well patients comprehend and comply with information presented in educational materials, and so forth.

The frequency of evaluation, as discussed earlier in this chapter, should relate to the significance of the program to the bottom line, the cost of the program, and organizational concerns about the value of the program.

☐ Barriers and Motivators to Evaluation

The Barriers

Public relations managers who don't routinely evaluate any of their programs cite the following barriers:

- If I spend money on research and evaluation, I have less money for the communications programs.
- I don't have the time or staff to worry about evaluation.
- I/we don't have the expertise in research and evaluation.
- What will I do if I find out the program isn't working?

The last concern is natural, but shortsighted. There's a strong probability that at least some of the programs are working, because the techniques are ones that are known to be effective. If the evaluation identifies programs that aren't working, then the PR manager can alter or abandon those programs. The alternative is to do nothing, wait until the CEO insists that the program justify its existence, and *then* have to share the evaluation with the CEO and answer the more critical question "Why are you still doing these programs if they don't work?"

The other concerns are realistic. Lack of funding, time, staff members, and expertise are factors that PR staff members must grapple with. However, it's probably advisable to dedicate a portion of the PR budget to evaluation in order to have results that can be used to justify the budget to continue the programs.

One way to address the time and expertise issues is to use outside expertise. This doesn't mean spending thousands to hire one of the major national research firms—in most areas, there are small, local firms that can handle simple survey research, or colleges or universities with faculty who can assist in the process. In-house help—both in developing survey research programs and in measuring direct responses—is also available through the manager of the product or service department that's being promoted.

Although there are obviously going to be barriers to evaluation, none of them can justify continuing to spend money on PR programs that may not be achieving their objectives. If the PR manager or product managers aren't interested in identifying results, the CEO is—or soon will be.

The Motivators

The primary motivators for evaluation activities are:

- The concern of the CEO and/or those who make decisions about budgets
- The product manager's need to demonstrate a contribution to the bottom line
- The PR manager and staff's real desire to find out what's working—so that things that aren't working can be fixed or abandoned and things that are working can be continued

- The sense of fun and accomplishment that occurs when the readership studies, participant evaluation forms, and community surveys are completed and the PR staff members can say "We did it!"

The last factor can be the best motivation to evaluate PR programs, so that the evaluation becomes a reward in itself. However, the first item is the overriding reason why it is imperative that PR managers begin to routinely evaluate at least the most significant of the health care organization's PR activities.

Without measurable, demonstrable results, the merit and value of the PR program can and will be questioned by those who believe that the money could be better spent elsewhere. When an evaluation program is initiated and the first results are shared with the administrative team, if those results are generally positive, the PR manager will be able to spend less time debating the value of the PR program and more time implementing it.

☐ Summary

Although the need for effective PR programs in U.S. health care organizations has never been greater, there is also an increasing concern among health care administrators about the "real value" of these programs. Ideally, health care PR managers—and all PR professionals—should want to continuously evaluate their efforts. Practically, such evaluation is becoming a necessity in terms of competing for increasingly scarce resources available for staff functions in health care organizations.

The critical decisions for the PR manager are to determine which programs must be evaluated and which evaluation methods are the most affordable and functional. This requires that PR programs have specific objectives with measurable results and that there be careful assessment of some of the traditional PR programs "that we've always done." The benefits of evaluation efforts are multiple—helping the PR manager determine what methods work, forcing client departments to focus on what their communications programs should actually achieve, and giving the PR staff (and senior management) the satisfaction of knowing the results of the health care organization's PR efforts.

References

1. *Ketchum Nationwide Survey on Public Relations Research, Measurement, and Evaluation.* New York City: Ketchum Public Relations, 1989.
2. Lindenmann, W. K. Beyond the clipbook. *Public Relations Journal* 45(12):22, Dec. 1988.

Suggested Readings

Jacobsen, H. K. Guidelines for evaluating public relations programs. *Public Relations Quarterly,* Summer 1980.

Larson, M. A., and Massetti-Miller, K. L. Measuring change after a public education campaign. *Public Relations Review,* Winter 1984.

Lesly, P. Multiple measurements of public relations. *Public Relations Review,* Summer 1986.

Public Relations Society of America. *Code of Ethics of the Public Relations Society of America.* New York City: PRSA, 1983.

Swinehart, J. W. Evaluating public relations. *Public Relations Journal* 36(6):13–16, July 1979.

Wright, D. K. Some ways to measure public relations. *Public Relations Journal* 36(6):17–18, July 1979.

Looking Ahead

What are the societal, industrial, and public relations practice issues facing the health care PR managers in the coming decades?

The social issues are numerous, but among the most critical are the following:

- Changing demographics. The population is getting older — and having more senior citizens, fewer babies, and fewer children will have a major impact on the health care industry. The work force will become more diverse, as women, members of minority groups, and people with disabilities move into the work force in unprecedented numbers.
- "The ugly side of race relations predicted to be the issue of the 90s," said *pr reporter.* "Impact on organizations ranges from blockbuster to subtle but even white supremacist David Duke calls it an economic problem." Public relations professionals will need to "put every organizational move under intense scrutiny for any possible backlash." (The report noted that the FBI has termed civil unrest—"a conflict between the haves and have nots"— as a serious domestic threat for the 1990s.)[1]
- Continuing fragmentation and segmentation of what used to be thought of as "discrete" audiences (such as working women, retired men, and so on) into even more specific subgroups with distinct values and needs.

The issues facing the health care organization are graphically illustrated by reading the table of contents in the fourth quarter, 1989, issue of *Health Management Quarterly,* which asked leaders from inside and outside the health care system to talk about U.S. health care in the 1990s. The topics:[2]

- Re-visioning health care: technology has new benefits to bring
- Healing connections: the patients' role may change medicine

- Looking to the East: the Japanese might try running U.S. hospitals
- Completing unfinished business: significant policy issues are unresolved
- Calling for reform: public sentiment is demanding change
- Dealing with the black health crisis: equity and access for all must be guaranteed
- Fulfilling obligations: affordable access means prioritizing benefits
- Taking charge of change: prescribing a proper future for health care
- Solving the nursing problem: improving quality, reducing costs, meeting needs
- Instituting the four proposals: moving toward an improved American system (by Ralph Nader)
- Ensuring that consumers are well informed: more information leads to better medicine
- Expanding the federal role: is a federal system feasible, beneficial
- Ensuring strategic choices for all: freedoms and obligations go hand in hand
- Establishing affirmative politics: principles must guide bold initiatives.

Clearly health care organizations face a challenging future—and PR managers will need to take a lead role in helping their organizations not just survive, but thrive.

Bob Clay, veteran communicator and principal of Clay Communications, told *pr reporter* that we are moving into an era of "noncommunication," with nonthinkers, nontalkers, nonlisteners, and nonreaders. To reach them, he advised:[3]

- "Spoon feed your audience info in easily digested bites." For health care communicators, that means demystifying and dejargoning our industry.
- "Personalize everything"—even news releases—and use handwritten notes when possible.
- "Go beyond creativity. You can't build relationships through creativity. Any relationship that begins because of your creative approach will probably end up not being a relationship at all . . . creativity can capture initial attention, but simple, human relationship building on a down-to-earth level must complete the cycle."
- "Substitute personalized, participative vehicles for mass communications. There is no more mass audience. Open houses, advisory committees, meetings and conferences actually reach—through networking—more people today than the old mass vehicles. And they are many times more persuasive and believable."

Other challenges for the health care PR manager are the following:

- Ensuring that management's approach to key audiences is balanced—no more going overboard on just consumers, just physicians, and so on—and long-term, not just a quick-results emphasis
- Communicating "quality" in a way consumers and payers can understand
- Developing more sophisticated evaluation and measurement systems that recognize the different factors that influence patient behavior and can better pinpoint the contribution PR programs make to that behavior
- Achieving a consistent, industrywide understanding of the fact that public relations is a senior management function for the contemporary health care organization

The senior PR professionals interviewed for the *Public Relations Journal* story and quoted in the introductory chapter of this book also offered advice on how health care PR managers can survive and thrive during the "whitewater revolution in the industry":[4]

- Lead the efforts to forge industrywide initiatives and cooperation. Health care PR managers should take the lead in focusing on the common concerns and needs of all facets of the health care industry: acute care and rehabilitation hospitals, the American Medical Association (AMA) and physician organizations, insurers and HMOs, medical schools, organizations like the American Cancer Society, health care-related foundations, nursing homes, and PR agencies and consultants who serve the health care field. These initiatives should unite PR professionals from all areas of health care to address issues that affect not only all of our organizations but also the American public, and to create strategies to help the health care industry communicate to and build relationships with key publics.
- "Broaden your skills, knowledge and perspective," advised a health care foundation CEO. "See your job as more than PR—you are a communicator, demographer, behavioralist, sociologist, problem solver, and the voice of the consumer."

  Broadening skills and roles also prepares practitioners to move into newly developing areas in the health care industry, or be targeted for new responsibilities in their own organizations. One example is Frank Weaver's move from the senior public affairs position in one organization—The Cleveland Clinic Foundation—to the top executive slot in a unique multihospital consortium in Dallas. And when the AMA decided to launch two major long-term initiatives—to take the lead in defending and protecting the U.S. health care system and to reposition the AMA with its major audiences by developing a new corporate identity effort—the association turned to Steve

Seekins, then vice-president for public and professional communications. Seekins was reassigned to report directly to the AMA's COO and made part of the senior management team of the organization's multitiered administrative structure. Seekins reassigned some of his day-to-day communications division responsibilities to free up his time to head a matrix-organization working group with a single charge from the COO: "Tell us what the AMA should be doing on these two projects, which are the most important efforts the AMA will undertake during the next five years." It's a major move into the organizational decision-making arena of what is described as the most powerful health care organization in the United States, and the choice of a PR professional to head up these efforts is indicative of the opportunities that exist for the experienced, broad-based practitioner in today's complex and changing health care industry.

- "Get involved in fund-raising," offered another veteran. "You don't join a corporation and say you don't care about the bottom line or where the income comes from. You don't go into a nonprofit organization and say you don't care about fund-raising. Fund-raising and PR cannot be separated."

- "Be flexible," advised an insurance company PR director. "PR practitioners have got to know how the issues are changing and be open to the changes they will have to make in their thinking. Holding on to past ways, no matter how successful they have been, or assuming that the issues will remain the same, is guaranteed failure."

One "old way" that is beginning to fall is the notion that "once a competitor, always a competitor." Joint ventures, consortiums, and cooperative efforts are proliferating and often require even more PR skills than handling communications during an outright merger or acquisition. In Toledo, Ohio, the area's two largest hospitals created a joint venture to sponsor an HMO and other cost-containment efforts. Senior PR staff members were called on to develop ongoing communications plans for the joint ventures, while simultaneously continuing to compete actively for hospital service market share. In Winston-Salem, NC, necessity was the motivation behind a highly successful program to promote health care careers, which was jointly sponsored by two competing hospitals. The immediate beneficiaries were local educational institutions, who reported maximum class enrollments and waiting lists; the long-term beneficiaries will be Forsyth Memorial and North Carolina Baptist hospitals, who developed this creative approach.

- Develop and implement systems to measure and evaluate PR efforts. "We have to be able to measure and demonstrate results in hard terms." "More sophisticated and effective tracking of efforts must continue to grow." "Don't wait for the top management to tell you to

prove what you do works. Do it as part of an integrated PR/marketing program."
- Don't just talk about being part of top management—function like part of institutional management. Kenneth E. Trester, director of planning and marketing at the University of Michigan Medical Center, noted that PR practitioners in the health care arena need to be relevant to their institution's agenda, rather than trying to adapt that agenda to the needs of public relations. "We have to bring added value to the Board and CEO's highest objectives."
- Stress the counseling role as another facet of functioning as part of top management. Steve Seekins noted that the counseling role may mean "being bold and willing to give the organization tough advice that is not always easily received." To Frank Karel, vice-president of communications at the Rockefeller Foundation, the counseling/advocacy function is "the ability to play a substantial role in shifting organizational work force and personal gears toward a service orientation that recognizes the primacy of the customer/patient over the 'business as usual' attitudes and practices of organizations."
- Bring an end to any lingering PR-marketing squabbles. The concept of total institutional advancement is the trendsetter. "Integrating functions related to organizational advancement, including PR, marketing, strategic planning and fund development is the key way to achieve greater efficiency and effectiveness," noted Frank Weaver.

And Gary Buerstatte, vice-president of corporate development at Waukesha (Wisconsin) Hospital System, made a powerful case in his article in the July–August 1989 issue of Hospital Marketing and Public Relations. "In a time of enormous pressures on the hospital industry, when budgets are getting harder and harder to shape and meet, when each day brings a new or stronger challenge, we have to recognize and act constructively on the notion that fundamentally different functions like marketing and PR have overlapping, common interests and a shared goal. That goal—to advance our hospitals—is one that must be pursued together. We must find new and creative ways to advance our organizations by defining and acting on the synergies between our disparate functions."[5]

Moving beyond the turf wars benefits not only institutions, but also practitioners. According to one senior health care PR professional who now consults with hospital CEOs on structuring their PR and marketing functions, "The CEOs are getting very, very tired of listening to whines about who's in charge, who has the power, who gets a bigger budget. All those 'that's my responsibility' complaints sound pretty childish to CEOs, who are desperately in need of leadership from their senior-level PR people."

This rapprochement, "I'll take the high road" approach is seen by some observers as part of what's been described as a "renaissance of public relations" within the health care industry. Supporters of the rebirth motif point to the expanding role of PR practitioners in many health care organizations and to the clear need for their skills and talents in this turbulent, "whitewater" environment:

- "Accountability is being demanded by the public, and public relations can help organizations respond to those demands."
- "As the profession becomes more proficient, CEOs are realizing that public relations goes beyond publicity and promotion."
- "With stakeholder groups becoming more significant in number and in education and sophistication, reaching out to them more effectively and comprehensively is critical to the success of any health care institution."
- "Development of a strong corporate identity is becoming an essential in this era of proliferating organizations and causes. Public relations is the keeper of that identity and image, which makes it a very powerful function."
- Finally, as one PR vice-president summarized, "Perceived quality is becoming the single most important differentiating factor for health care organizations. Those perceptions of quality are often dependent on establishing positive relationships—and that's where PR professionals can take the lead."

Frank Karel looks to the future. "This renaissance will prove brief and hollow unless practitioners can influence and help guide their organizations in adapting to the rapidly changing environment, in addition to the more traditional 'getting the message across' tasks."

Seekins and Weaver summarized the critical challenge that health care PR practitioners face. Said Seekins: "We must be in the business of offering the best, most objective advice possible. We must develop the most competitive programs and plan strategically for the future with our senior management teams. To do that, we need to stay up to date, tuned in and creative."

Concluded Weaver, "Our task is to position the function of public relations at the highest level to assure our ability to counsel top management based on a thorough and scientific understanding of our constituents, and an accurate vision of the future."

References

1. Ugly side of race relations predicted to be the issue of 90s. *pr reporter* 32(36):1, Sept. 4, 1989.

2. *Health Management Quarterly,* fourth quarter, 1989, p. 1.
3. Is the information age turning into the non-communication era? *pr reporter* 32(13):1, Mar. 27, 1989.
4. Comments made during interviews conducted by the author in preparing "Health Care: Critical Conditions," which appeared in the December 1989 issue and are reprinted with the permission of *Public Relations Journal.*
5. Buerstatte, G. End the debate with the total advancement concept. *Hospital Marketing and Public Relations,* July–Aug. 1989, p. 2.

Suggested Reading

Big changes ahead for healthcare. *pr reporter* 32(36), Oct. 30, 1989.

1988 Membership Profile of the American Society for Health Care Marketing and Public Relations

The following material is reprinted with permission from a handout prepared for the Tenth Annual Educational Conference, American Society for Hospital Marketing and Public Relations (now the American Society for Health Care Marketing and Public Relations), August 1988. A total of 1,294 ASHMPR members responded to the survey described in the handout. Percentages cited in the document should be interpreted as roughly a percentage of that total inasmuch as not all respondents answered every question.

The 1988 ASHMPR Membership Profile was conducted to give members an idea of the composition of the Society and an opportunity to examine how their jobs compare with those of their colleagues. The Membership Profile was designed by the 1988 Research and Development Committee. Results were presented at ASHMPR's Tenth Annual Educational Conference in August, 1988. ASHMPR is grateful to Bob Hiett, president of KCA Research, Alexandria, VA, for coordinating and compiling the results of the survey.

The Membership Profile illustrates the broad spectrum of professionals that make up the Society. Although there is much we have in common, there is also a wide range of differences in everything from job titles and responsibilities to education and salaries. It seems logical that these differences reflect the diversity of marketing and PR needs in health care organizations across the country.

☐ Areas of Responsibility

A large majority (80 percent) of ASHMPR members have management responsibility for advertising, community relations, media relations, PR planning, and publications. This represents a slight decline in PR responsibilities, which nearly 90 percent reported during the 1986 membership survey.

As PR functions decline somewhat, ASHMPR members' level of responsibility for marketing functions is increasing. In a 1986 membership survey, 44 percent of respondents reported being responsible for internal marketing. The 1988 survey shows that 66 percent of respondents now have that responsibility. Marketing plans are the responsibility of 59 percent of members, while 47 percent are taking care of market research in their organizations.

Another increasingly important area of responsibility for ASHMPR members is physician relations/recruitment. One third of members report having management responsibility for medical staff marketing functions. In 1986, only 26 percent of members reported being involved with physician relations/recruitment.

☐Level of Responsibility and Reporting Relationship

The levels of responsibility reported by members illustrates that ASHMPR is an organization for those who are leaders in their organizations. The majority (63 percent) of members responding to the survey are department directors, with 17 percent of members at the vice-president/assistant administrator level. The remainder of respondents are assistant department director (7 percent); consultant (5 percent); department staff member (4 percent); and chief executive officer (3 percent).

Half of ASHMPR members report directly to the CEOs of their organizations, and 27 percent report to someone at the vice-president/assistant administrator level. A small number of members report to their department director, chief operating officer, or chairman of the hospital board of trustees.

☐ Employers

An overwhelming majority (75 percent) of respondents are currently working in hospitals. Of these, 75 percent are in nonprofit, nongovernment hospitals, while 8 percent are in for-profit organizations, and 9 percent are in nonfederal government facilities. Twelve percent of respondents work in the corporate office of a health care system, and 4 percent indicate they serve as consultants.

☐ Staffing

In general, marketing and PR staffs are remaining relatively small. Nearly half (45 percent) of members report they have 1–2 full-time PR professionals in their organizations. A quarter of respondents have 3–5 full-time PR professionals, and 8 percent have 6–10. Nineteen percent of respondents report their organizations have no full-time PR professionals.

In the area of marketing, 45 percent of respondents report there are 1–2 full-time professionals in their organizations. Fifteen percent report having 3–5, and 5 percent have 6–10. Fully 32 percent of members have no full-time marketing professionals.

More than half (57 percent) of respondents report to have no full-time planning professionals on staff. Whereas 34 percent of respondents report 1–2 professionals, 8 percent report a staff of 3–5 full-time planning professionals.

In total, the largest number of respondents (31 percent) report to have 3–5 full-time professionals covering marketing, public relations, and planning for their organizations. While 23 percent of respondents report 1–2 staff professionals, 22 percent have 6–10. Ten percent of respondents have 11–20 staff members, and 12 percent of respondents report there are no full-time marketing, PR, or planning professionals in their organizations.

☐ Total Annual Hospital Budget

The total annual hospital budgets reported by members were relatively evenly spread over a broad range. The biggest percentage (15 percent) reported a hospital budget of less than $10 million. Eleven percent reported an annual budget of $10–$20 million; 11 percent reported $21–$30 million; 14 percent reported $31–$50 million; 12 percent reported $51–$75 million; 8 percent reported $76–$100 million; and 9 percent reported $101–$150 million. The numbers became much smaller at the $151–$200 million mark, with 4 percent at that level; 3 percent at $201–$300 million; and 4 percent with over $300 million.

☐ Marketing and Public Relations Budget

In terms of marketing and PR budgets (with salaries excluded), the numbers are also evenly spread across the board. In both areas, the largest percentage of respondents (17 percent in response to the marketing question, 18 percent in response to the PR question) reported they did not have separate budgets for the two functions.

The largest percentage (17 percent) of respondents reported a $51–$100 thousand annual budget for public relations. Closely following was a $101–$200 thousand budget, reported by 16 percent of respondents. Seven percent reported a $0–$25 thousand budget; 11 percent have $26–$50 thousand; 11 percent have $201–$350 thousand; 5 percent have $351–$500 thousand; and 5 percent have a budget [between $501 thousand and] up to $1 million. Two percent of respondents reported a PR budget over $1 million.

Organizations are spending more on marketing than public relations, but because of different organizations' definitions of the two functions, it's difficult to determine exactly what activities are covered under which heading. The largest percentage (15 percent) of respondents report having a $101–$200 thousand budget for marketing, followed closely by 14 percent with $51–$100 thousand. Twelve percent of respondents report budgets of $201–$350 thousand; 9 percent have $351–$500 thousand; 8 percent have $501–$999 thousand; and 5 percent of respondents have a marketing budget of over $1 million. Eleven percent of respondents report having a budget of $50 thousand or less.

☐ Advertising Budget

Nearly half (48 percent) of respondents report their organizations' advertising budget will increase in the next year. But the fact that 36 percent of respondents report their ad budgets will remain the same and 15 percent report their ad budgets will decrease seems to point to a disenchantment with advertising. Because marketing and PR budgets continue to increase, this suggests that health care organizations are looking to alternative methods for marketing and PR efforts.

☐ ASHMPR Members' Personal and Professional Characteristics

It's virtually impossible to come up with a composite of a typical member, as responses are scattered across a wide range of ages, educational backgrounds, and levels of experience.

Of the 1,279 members who responded to the survey [item on sex], 876 (68.5 percent) are women, and 403 (31.5 percent) are men. These numbers seem to substantiate the idea that public relations, and to a lesser extent, marketing, is an industry dominated by women.

Because the health care marketing and PR industry has undergone tremendous growth quite recently, the majority of professionals are young. While less than 2 percent of members are under 24, 15 percent of respondents are 25–29 years old, and 44 percent of respondents are between the ages of 30 and 39. Eighteen percent of respondents are between 40 and 44, 15 percent are between 45 and 54, and 6 percent are between 55 and 64.

The majority (41 percent) of members have an academic major in communications or journalism. A large number (40 percent) of members report to have an academic major other than journalism, [while others cited degrees in] public relations (5 percent), advertising (1 percent), marketing (4 percent), business (6 percent), or clinical science (4 percent).

In terms of education, the largest percentage (35 percent) of respondents have a B.A. degree. Fewer (22 percent) have a B.S., followed by 13 percent with an M.A. Interestingly, with 8 percent of respondents holding an M.B.A., 7 percent of respondents report they have less than a college degree. Seven percent have an M.S., 2 percent have an M.H.A., and 1 percent each have a Ph.D. or an M.P.H. Four percent list their highest academic degree as "other."

The responses to the question of "length of time in current position" served to illustrate the transient nature of professionals in health care marketing/public relations. Slightly more than half (51 percent) of respondents report they have been in their current positions less than three years. Fully 28 percent of respondents have stayed in the same position 3–5 years, with 14 percent at 6–10 years and 4 percent at 11–15 years. Only 2 percent of respondents report to have been in the same position for more than 15 years.

☐ Professional Experience and Expectations

The largest percentage (33 percent) of respondents report they have 6–10 years' experience in marketing/public relations. Twenty-four percent report 3–5 years of experience, with 17 percent reporting 11–15 years' experience and 16 percent with more than 15 years of experience. Fully 11 percent report less than 3 years' experience in marketing/public relations.

When asked about experience specifically in health care marketing/public relations, the numbers vary slightly. The largest percentage (31 percent) is still at the 6–10-year mark, but the number of professionals with 3–5 years' experience in health care increases to 29 percent. Fully 21 percent report less than 3 years' experience in health care, and 12 percent have 11–15 years in the field. Although the number of respondents reporting over 15 years in marketing/public relations is 15 percent, the number who have had that experience specifically in health care is only 7 percent.

Remembering that 63 percent of respondents are currently at the department director level, it is interesting that in five years only 15 percent expect to be at that level (4 percent as director of marketing, 11 percent as director of public relations). This again underscores the mobility of members.

The largest percentage (16 percent) see themselves as vice-president/director of public relations and marketing in five years. Twelve percent hope to be vice-president/assistant administrator of marketing; 7 percent see themselves as vice-president/assistant administrator of public relations; and 8 percent envision themselves as vice-president/director of communications. Vice-president/director of corporate development is the position expected in five years by 3 percent of respondents, and 6 percent feel they will be consultants by that time. Fully 13 percent didn't venture a guess as to what their positions will be in five years, and 5 percent believe they will be out of the health care field by that time.

☐ Salary

The peak percentage (18 percent) in respondents' salary is still $31,000–$35,999, exactly the same as found in the 1986 survey. However, the lower end of the salary range has dropped off considerably, and the higher end of the range has grown appreciably.

In 1986, 9 percent of respondents were making less than $20,999. In 1988, only 5 percent are at that salary level. Eleven percent of respondents are making $21,000–$25,999, compared with 15 percent at that level in 1986; 15 percent of respondents make $26,000–$30,999, compared with 20 percent at that level in 1986. As members' salaries go past the $35,000 mark, 14 percent are making $36,000–$40,999 (compared with 12 percent in 1986); 11 percent are making $41,000–$45,999 (8 percent in 1986); and 7 percent are making $46,000–$50,999 (5 percent in 1986).

Whereas in 1986 only 7 percent of respondents were making $51,000–$60,999, today slightly more than 9 percent are at that salary level. In this survey, 5 percent of respondents report to be making $62,000–$75,999, compared with 3 percent in 1986. Two years ago, there were no respondents making $76,000 or above: today fully 4 percent are above that level, with 1 percent making over $100,000 a year.

General Guide for the Release of Patient Information by the Hospital

The following guide was adapted from the "Release of Information" section of Hospitals and the News Media: A Guide to Good Media Relations, *by Mary Laing Babich, copyright 1985 by American Hospital Publishing, Inc. (out of print). The guide is now available under the title* General Guide for the Release of Patient Information, *catalog number 166851, from the American Hospital Association, P.O. Box 99376, Chicago, Illinois 60693.*

The following information may be released by the hospital for any inpatient or emergency department patient [depending on state statutes]:

- Name
- Address
- Occupation
- Sex
- Age
- Marital status

However, the restrictions described should be observed whenever possible or practical before any information is released.

Author's Note: This guide is general. It is important to be aware that laws regarding patient privacy, confidentiality, and "public record cases" vary from state to state. The PR manager should consult with the organization's legal counsel before finalizing any policies on release of patient information.

□ Condition of Patient

Except for the following one-word conditions, no information about the patient may be released without the patient's permission. Only a physician may discuss the patient's diagnosis and/or prognosis, if the patient has given permission for the physician to do so. The following terms can be used to describe the patient's condition:

- *Good.* Vital signs are stable and within normal limits. Patient is conscious and comfortable. Indicators are excellent.
- *Fair.* Vital signs are stable and within normal limits. Patient is conscious but may be uncomfortable. Indicators are favorable.
- *Serious.* Vital signs may be unstable and not within normal limits. Patient is acutely ill. Indicators are questionable.
- *Critical.* Vital signs are unstable and not within normal limits. Patient may be unconscious. Indicators are unfavorable. [Note: By definition, a critical patient cannot be stable.]
- *Unconscious.* The hospital may release information that the patient was unconscious when brought to the hospital.
- *Dead.* The death of a patient is presumed to be a matter of public record and may be reported by the hospital after the next of kin has been notified or after a reasonable time has passed. Information regarding the cause of death must come from the patient's physician, and its release must be approved by a member of the immediate family (when available).

[Note: Although often used, the terms *stable* and *guarded* do not have universally accepted definitions and, therefore, should not be used.]

□ Nature of Accident or Injury

The hospital spokesman may give out only limited information about the various kinds of accidents or injuries in order to protect the privacy of the patient.

- *Battered children.* The spokesman may not discuss possible child abuse. However, the injuries sustained by the child may be described as indicated below.
- *Burns.* The spokesman may state that the patient is burned, but the severity and degree of burns may be released only after a physician's diagnosis.
- *Fractures.* The spokesman may provide information on the location of the fracture only if a limb is involved and may say whether the fracture is simple or compound.

- *Head injuries.* The spokesman may state that the injuries are of the head. It may not be stated that the skull is fractured until diagnosed by a physician.
- *Internal injuries.* The spokesman may state that there are internal injuries, but no information may be given as to the location of the injuries until a physician has made a diagnosis.
- *Intoxication or drug abuse.* The spokesman may not provide information that the patient was intoxicated or had abused drugs, or characterize the patient as an abuser. The spokesman should be wary of indicating a diagnosis that might imply substance abuse; for example, saying that a patient had cirrhosis could indicate alcohol abuse.
- *Poisoning.* The spokesman may state only that the patient is being treated for suspected poisoning. No statement may be made concerning either motivation or circumstances surrounding a patient's poisoning. The suspected poisonous compound may be identified only by the patient's physician.
- *Sexual assault.* The spokesman may not say that the patient has been sexually assaulted nor provide information regarding the nature of the sexual assault or injuries. Only the condition of the patient may be given.
- *Sexually transmitted and communicable diseases.* The spokesman may not provide information that the patient has a sexually transmitted or communicable disease. The spokesman should be careful not to indicate a diagnosis that might imply a communicable disease. For example, saying that a patient has Kaposi's sarcoma could indicate the patient has AIDS.
- *Shooting or stabbing.* The spokesman may provide the number of wounds and their location if these facts have been definitely determined by a physician. No statement may be made as to how the shooting or stabbing occurred.
- *Suicide or attempted suicide.* The spokesman may not provide any statement that there was a suicide or attempted suicide.
- *Transplant recipients and organ donors.* The spokesman may release information regarding the nature of the transplant and the condition, age, and sex of the recipient. However, the release of the names of the recipient and/or donor requires prior consent. If the donor is deceased, the name may not be given out without the consent of the legal next of kin.

☐ Matters of Public Record

Matters of public record refer to those situations that are by law reportable to public authorities, such as the police, coroner, or public health officer. Examples of matters of public record are the following:

- Persons under arrest or held under police surveillance
- Persons brought to the hospital by the fire department or by any law enforcement agency
- Persons who have been shot, stabbed, poisoned, injured in automobile accidents, or bitten by dogs or other animals
- Persons with any other injuries that are usually reported to governmental agencies regardless of the mode of transportation to the hospital

☐ Coroner's Cases

Generally, in accordance with state law, the hospital must provide the coroner with information in any of the following circumstances:

- When the body is unidentified or unclaimed
- When a sudden death is not caused by a readily recognized disease or when the cause of death cannot be properly certified by a physician on the basis of prior (recent) medical attendance
- When the death occurred under suspicious circumstances, including those deaths in which alcohol, drugs, or other toxic substances may have a direct bearing on the outcome
- When the death occurred as a result of violence or trauma, whether apparently homicidal, suicidal, or accidental (including those resulting from mechanical, thermal, chemical, electrical, or radiational injuries or from drownings or cave-ins) and regardless of the time elapsed between the time of injury and the time of death
- When there is a fetal death, stillbirth, or death of any baby within 24 hours after its birth and the mother has not been under the care of a physician
- When the death has resulted from an abortion, whether therapeutic or criminal, self-induced, or otherwise
- When operative and perioperative deaths are not readily explainable on the basis of prior disease

The hospital should check with its attorney to find out what other types of situations are required by state law to be reported to the coroner.

[Note: When the media ask questions about such cases, the hospital spokesman should not attempt to answer them (beyond the basic information described in this guide) and should refer reporters to the coroner.]

☐ Accidents and Police Investigations

The spokesman may release the name, address, age, nature of injury, condition (if determined), and the disposition of such patients, that is, whether they have been hospitalized. No attempt should be made to describe the event that caused the injury, and no statement about any of the following should be made:

- Whether a person was intoxicated
- Whether the injuries were the result of an assault, attempted suicide, or accident
- Whether a patient was poisoned (accidentally or deliberately)
- Whether a patient is suspected of being a drug addict
- The circumstances that resulted in a patient's being shot or stabbed
- The circumstances related to an automobile or industrial accident